LEADERSHIP, POWER, AND POLITICS

LEADERSHIP, POWER, AND POLITICS

First Edition

Edited by Sigalit Ronen

California State University, Northridge

cognella®

SAN DIEGO

Bassim Hamadeh, CEO and Publisher
Mieka Portier, Acquisitions Editor
Tony Paese, Project Editor
Berenice Quirino, Associate Production Editor
Jackie Bignotti, CoverDesigner
Michael Skinner, Licensing Associate
Natalie Piccotti, Director of Marketing
Kassie Graves, Vice President of Editorial
Jamie Giganti, Director of Academic Publishing

CONTENTS

INTRODUCTION

Leadership is and always has been one of the most interesting and important social phenomenon in the history of mankind. Many great leaders have led humanity toward major accomplishments and have shaped history by making contributions to the prosperity, progress, and well-being of millions of people around the world. The world has witnessed a great variety of leadership styles, some of which can be characterized as bringing positive change to humanity, and some that can be described as destructive and responsible for a great deal of misery and suffering in the lives of many people. Your prosperity, well-being, and freedom in the present have their roots in the acts of leaders who came before you and those who were able to make decisions that affect your life today. Leadership in your country, state, city, community, and the organizations you are part of can contribute to your ability to thrive and actualize your potential, or otherwise be detrimental to your future.

As you acknowledge the impact leadership has on you and on the people around you, you should remember that you can make a difference in people's lives as well. The more you know how to use your power and influence others, and the more people are willing to accept your leadership, the more you will be able to assert yourself and affect the lives of those around you.

This textbook, *Leadership, Power, and Politics*, gathers articles written by renowned leadership scholars and is designed to help you learn about theories and research in these areas. My main goal as a scholar and an educator is to help you gain thorough knowledge and understanding that you can put to practical use as you develop your personal leadership practice.

Leadership is ubiquitous—it exists everywhere—at work, with your peers, subordinates, customers, and managers; in your family, love life, and social life; and in your community. It affects every aspect of your behavior, from the way you carry yourself and deal with daily hassles to your ability to make a difference in people's lives and make this world a better place for all humanity. Most important, behavioral research and studies in neuroplasticity indicate that people can become leaders through the process of observing, learning, training, practicing, and adopting positive habits. This textbook presents knowledge on best leadership practices, and it can be used as a guide for self-development. It includes five parts and ten chapters. It is recommended that you follow the recommendations in the syllabus and read the chapters prior to attending class on the respective topics.

Part 1 introduces the topic of leadership effectiveness, and it attempts to clarify what effective leaders do that others do not. Peter Drucker, a renowned leadership authority, once suggested that leaders do the right things and managers do the things right. After reading Part 1 you will be able to address such questions as: How can a leader know that he or she is doing the right things? What are the right things, anyway? How can a leader come across as a positive and effective leader?

Part 2 focuses on characteristics of leaders. For many years researchers have attempted find those characteristics that are shared by all great leaders. Most have come to realize that effective leadership can have many different faces and appearances, and that there is no one profile that applies to all leaders. This part of the book deals with a group of variables such as emotional intelligence, intelligence, and extraversion that have been found to be associated with leadership effectiveness. This part will provide you with some insights as to how to assess your leadership characteristics and improve your leadership practice and how to manage the impression you make on others.

Part 3 presents main leadership theories and research. Today, there are approximately eighty different leadership theories. This part presents well-known and researched theories that focus on different aspects of the leadership concept. It will help you get familiarized with many different conceptualizations of leadership and will invite you to think more critically about leadership-related concepts and ideas.

Part 4 deals with destructive leadership. It is estimated that two out of ten leaders suffer from a severe psychological disorder that can render them unfit to lead other people. These individuals are lacking empathy, among other things, and as a result cause a lot of harm to the people they interact with, including their subordinates. Despite the high prevalence of this phenomenon and the well-documented destructive nature of these characteristics, organizations keep hiring and promoting these individuals and assigning them to key leadership positions. This part of the book brings awareness to this important problem and provides some insight on ways to deal with destructive leaders in the organization.

Part 5 focuses on power and politics in organizations. Although the connotation of power tends to be negative, it is important to acknowledge that many of the greatest contributions to humanity have been made by powerful people who have used their influence in a manner that has helped sustain and improve the lives of the less fortunate. This part describes the concepts of power, politics, and influence and can help you learn how to develop and use power and influence to achieve your goals and make positive contributions to those around you.

I hope that you will find this textbook enriching and helpful as you develop your leadership practice.

Sincerely,
Dr. Sigalit Ronen

PART I

INTRODUCTION TO LEADERSHIP

CHAPTER 1

What Does Effective Leadership Mean?

A Critical Assessment of Research on Effective Leadership Behavior

Gary Yukl and John W. Michel

Abstract

Much of the research on effective leadership over the past half century has involved studies of leader behavior. Progress in learning about effective leadership has been limited by a narrow focus on one or two broadly-defined behaviors or styles of leadership, by confounding observable behaviors with leader traits and values, by a lack of attention to situational variables, and by the frequent use of weak research methods. The weaknesses in much of the research on charismatic and transformational leadership, and in the earlier research on task-oriented and relations-oriented behavior, are also limiting progress in the recent research on ethical, servant, and authentic leadership. The research on effects of leader behavior is briefly reviewed, the limitations are explained, and ways to improve future research are suggested.

Introduction

For decades, scholars have sought to understand what it takes to be an effective organizational leader. Much of the theory and research on effective leadership involves the effects of leadership behavior on outcomes such as subordinate attitudes and performance. It has been common practice to define and measure leadership behavior in terms of broadly defined constructs or "metacategories." The focus on one or two metacategories in most studies on leadership behavior has weakened results and made them more difficult to interpret. Other limitations in much of the behavior research include confounding of behavior with leader traits and values, reliance on weak research methods, and insufficient attention to situational variables and explanatory processes. In this chapter, we will briefly review what was found in decades of research on prominent behavior metacategories. Then, the weaknesses that have limited progress in the behavior research are described, and suggestions are presented for improving future research on effective leadership.

Research on Behavior Metacategories

In the early period of leadership theory and research from 1955 to 1980, the dominant metacategories were task-oriented behavior and relations-oriented behavior. From the early 1980s to the current time, much attention was devoted to research on charismatic and transformational leadership. In the past decade, there has been growing interest in ethical leadership, servant leadership, and authentic leadership. Each type of leadership behavior is described, along with findings in the research on it.

Task-Oriented and Relations-Oriented Behavior

The relations-oriented metacategory includes behaviors that are primarily intended to improve interpersonal relations between the leader and a subordinate or among subordinates in a group. The task-oriented metacategory includes behaviors that are primarily intended to improve task performance by an individual or group. The labels used for the two metacategories varied for different scholars; examples include Consideration and Initiating Structure (Fleishman, 1953; Halpin & Winter, 1957), Supportive and Instrumental Leadership (House, 1971), Employee-centered and Production-centered leadership (Likert, 1961), and Task-oriented and Relations-oriented leadership (Yukl, 1971). The specific component behaviors for each metacategory also vary somewhat for different scholars and measures.

Examples of component behaviors for the relations-oriented metacategory include doing personal favors for a subordinate, listening to a subordinate's problems, defending a subordinate, and treating a subordinate as an equal. Later research also identified other component behaviors such as providing praise and recognition for subordinate achievements and contributions, and facilitating the development of skills relevant for a subordinate's career success. Some versions of the relations-oriented metacategory include giving subordinates influence over leader decisions that affect them.

Examples of component behaviors for the task-oriented metacategory include assigning tasks to subordinates, clarifying role requirements, setting goals for individual or group performance, monitoring performance, and resolving problems that disrupt the work. In research on leadership in teams, additional task behaviors include planning, organizing, and coordinating team activities. Task-oriented and relations-oriented behavior can also occur in interactions with people outside of a leader's work unit, but these behaviors were seldom examined closely in the early research, and they are also part of a different metacategory called external behavior (Yukl, 2012).

Many studies were conducted to determine how the two metacategories are related to leadership effectiveness (Bass, 2008). A meta-analysis of the results from the survey research using behavior description questionnaires found that both types of behavior are related to follower satisfaction, motivation, and job performance (Judge, Piccolo, & Ilies, 2004). The strongest and most consistent finding is a positive correlation between relations-oriented behavior and subordinate satisfaction with the leader or leader-member relations. Results were weakest for studies with independent measures of subordinate or work-unit performance.

Unmeasured situational differences within and between studies are one reason for lack of stronger, more consistent results in research on task and relations metacategories. After the importance of the leadership situation was recognized, several contingency theories were proposed to explain how situational variables can enhance or limit the effects of a leader's task-oriented and relations-oriented behaviors. The contingency theories based on behavior metacategories include Path-goal Theory (House, 1971), Leadership Substitutes Theory (Kerr & Jermier, 1978), and Situational Leadership Theory (Hersey & Blanchard, 1977). Many studies were conducted to test these contingency theories, but little support was found for them (Podsakoff, MacKenzie, Ahearne, & Bommer, 1995; Thompson & Vecchio, 2009; Wofford & Liska, 1993).

Charismatic and Transformational Leadership

The lack of progress in research on effects of task-oriented and relations-oriented behaviors encouraged leadership scholars to examine other types of leadership behavior, and much of the subsequent research involved testing theories of charismatic and transformational leadership. Charismatic leadership theories attempt to explain how leaders influence followers on an emotional and ideological level (Conger, 1989; Conger & Kanungo, 1998; House, 1977; Shamir, House, & Arthur, 1993). Conger and Kanungo (1998) proposed that charismatic behavior includes articulating an innovative strategic vision, taking personal risks and making self sacrifices to attain the vision, and identifying threats and opportunities in the external environment. The behaviors emphasized by House (1977) and Shamir et al. (1993) include articulating an appealing vision, emphasizing ideological aspects of work, communicating high performance expectations, expressing confidence in subordinates, showing self-confidence, modeling exemplary behavior, and doing things to increase identification with the team or organization. Some versions of the theory emphasize the importance of situational variables for attributions of charisma to a leader, but few empirical studies were designed to assess the effects of situational variables.

Transformational leadership theories describe how some leaders influence subordinate task motivation (Bass, 1985). The component behaviors vary somewhat for different scholars and even for the same scholars at different points in time. A majority of the studies on transformational leadership have defined it in terms of four component behaviors identified by Bass and Avolio (1990). Idealized influence involves setting an example of task commitment and making self-sacrifices that benefit followers or the work unit. Intellectual stimulation involves encouraging others to view problems in a new way and find creative solutions. Individualized consideration involves providing support, encouragement, and coaching. Inspirational motivation involves articulating an appealing vision and attempting to inspire commitment to the mission of the team or organization. Another measure of transformational leadership (Podsakoff, Mackenzie, Moorman, & Fetter, 1990) included six component behaviors: articulating an appealing vision, modeling appropriate behavior, providing individualized support, providing intellectual stimulation, fostering acceptance of group goals, and communicating high performance expectations. These behaviors were assumed to be relevant for all leaders, and few studies on transformational leadership have included situational variables.

Many leadership scholars regard charismatic and transformational leadership as equivalent constructs and use similar measures for them. Meta-analyses of this research find positive correlations with outcomes such as subordinate satisfaction, organizational commitment, job performance, and work-unit performance (DeGroot, Kiker, & Cross, 2000; Judge & Piccolo, 2004; Lowe, Kroeck, & Sivasubramaniam, 1996; Wang, Oh, Courtright, & Colbert, 2011). However, the results in studies with independent measures of leadership effectiveness were much weaker than studies with same-source measures, and some studies failed to support the theories (van Knipenberg & Sitkin, 2013). For example, research using case studies of chief executives found that charismatic leadership was not required for effective organizational performance (e.g., Bennis & Nanus, 1985), and sometimes it resulted in weaker performance or a failed organization (e.g., Finkelstein, 2003; O'Connor, Mumford, Clifton, Gessner, & Connelly, 1995). In a longitudinal study of CEOs, ratings of charismatic leadership were correlated significantly with a company's past financial performance but did not predict future performance (Angle, Nagarajan, Sonnenfeld, & Srinivasan, 2006).

Studies on transformational leadership sometimes include another behavior metacategory called transactional leadership, which includes using reward contingencies to motivate subordinates, monitoring their performance, and taking corrective action when poor performance is found. Some measures of transactional leadership include examples of relations-oriented behavior (providing praise and recognition) and task-oriented behavior (active monitoring). Research on the effects of transactional behavior suggests that it can have a positive effect on subordinate performance in some situations, but negative effects can also occur (Lowe et al., 1996). Bass (1985) proposed that effective leaders use a combination of transformational and transactional leadership, but few studies have examined how the two metacategories jointly influence independent measures of work-unit performance.

Ethical Leadership

Ethical leadership has been defined in many different ways, and the construct usually includes a combination of values and behaviors (Brown & Treviño, 2006; Brown, Treviño, & Harrison, 2005). One key attribute of ethical leadership behavior involves acting in a way that is as consistent with widely accepted ethical standards. Behaviors commonly regarded as morally correct include treating people fairly, providing accurate information and honest answers to questions, keeping promises and commitments, observing the same rules and standards applied to others, and acknowledging responsibility for mistakes while also seeking to correct them.

Another type of ethical leadership behavior involves attempts to influence the ethical behavior of others (Treviño, Brown, & Hartman, 2003). Examples include leader statements about the importance of ethics; dissemination of ethical guidelines for members of the organization; modeling ethical behavior to set an example for others, including ethical behavior in the assessment of performance; and criticizing or punishing unethical behavior. A limitation of this aspect of ethical leadership involves questions about the extent to which it is appropriate for leaders to set moral standards for others in the organization or to make subjective judgments about the morality of subordinates.

Research on the consequences of ethical leadership is still limited, but several studies have found more employee satisfaction, task commitment, organizational citizenship behaviors, willingness to report problems, and ethical behavior (e.g., Kacmar, Bachrach, Harris, & Zivnuska, 2011; Mayer, Aquino, Greenbaum, & Kuenzi, 2012; Mayer, Kuenzi, Greenbaum, Bardes, & Salvador, 2009; Piccolo, Greenbaum, Den Hartog, & Folger, 2010; Walumbwa, Morrison, & Christensen, 2012; Yukl, Mahsud, Hassan, & Prussia, 2013). However, most measures of ethical leadership include a diverse set of leader traits, values, and behaviors, and most studies only examined how the composite score on the measure was related to subordinate attitudes and behavior. How ethical leadership is related to objective measures of performance has not been closely examined, and some case studies found evidence that short-term company profits were increased by unethical practices (e.g., Sims & Brinkman, 2003).

Servant Leadership

Servant leadership includes nurturing, defending, and empowering followers (Greenleaf, 1977), which are examples of relations-oriented behavior. Servant leadership also includes aspects of ethical leadership. Servant leaders must listen to followers, learn about their needs and aspirations, and be willing to share in their pain and frustration. Service includes nurturing, defending, and empowering followers. Trust is established by being completely honest and open, keeping actions consistent with values, and demonstrating trust in followers. The servant leader must stand for what is good and right, even when it is not in the financial interest of the organization. Social injustice and inequality should be opposed whenever possible. Different questionnaires have been developed to measure servant leadership (Barbuto & Wheeler, 2006; Dennis & Bocarnea, 2005; Liden, Wayne, Zhao, & Henderson, 2008; van Dierendonck & Nuijten, 2011), but the best way to define and measure this construct has not been resolved. Most measures require respondents to make difficult judgments about a leader's integrity, authenticity, and stewardship.

Research on the consequences of servant leadership is still limited, but several studies found positive outcomes such as more subordinate commitment, self-efficacy, and organizational citizenship behavior (e.g., Ehrhart, 2004; Liden et al., 2008; Mayer, Bardes, & Piccolo, 2008; Neubert, Kacmar, Carlson, Chonko, & Roberts, 2008; van Dierendonck, 2011; Walumbwa, Hartnell, & Oke, 2010). However, the research seldom included independent measures of work-unit performance, and the objective of serving followers is sometimes inconsistent with the objective of improving performance. How leaders can resolve tradeoffs in benefits for different stakeholders remains an unresolved question.

Authentic Leadership

Authentic leadership theories have been proposed by several scholars (Avolio, Gardner, Walumbwa, Luthans, & May, 2004; George, 2003; Ilies, Morgeson, & Nahrgang, 2005). The definition varies somewhat across different versions, but they all emphasize the importance of leader integrity. Authentic leaders have positive core values (e.g., honesty, kindness, fairness, accountability, and optimism) that motivate them to do what is right and fair for followers. These leaders create a special type of relationship that includes high mutual trust, transparency, shared objectives, and emphasis on follower welfare and development. Core component behaviors include keeping leader actions consistent with espoused and actual values, articulating an appealing vision, modeling appropriate behaviors, and expressing optimism and encouragement when there are problems in accomplishing task objectives. With regard to other leadership behaviors, there is less agreement among the different versions of the theory. The measures of authentic leadership include leader traits and values such as self-awareness and an internalized moral perspective in addition to observable behaviors. As with ethical and servant leadership, it is not clear to what extent each attribute is necessary for effective leadership or is only an ideal that any leader should strive to attain (Caza & Jackson, 2011).

The amount of research on authentic leadership is still limited, but a recent review by Gardner, Cogliser, Davis, and Dickens (2011) showed that it was related to follower job satisfaction and organizational commitment. However, few studies included objective measures of performance or identified the independent effects and relative importance of the values and behaviors that define authentic leadership.

Limitations of the Behavior Research

Several conceptual and methodological limitations in much of the behavior research have made it more difficult to find strong, consistent results that explain how leaders influence individual, group, or organizational performance. The limitations include varying content for a metacategory, overlap among metacategories, unique and joint effects of component behaviors, confounding of behavior with traits and values, weak survey studies, failure to examine curvilinear relationships, failure to examine lagged effects, lack of attention to explanatory processes, lack of multiple independent criteria, and lack of attention to situational variables.

Varying Content for a Behavior Metacategory

Most of the behavior metacategories used in the leadership research lack a clear definition and adequate criteria for identification of relevant component behaviors. One basis for grouping specific behaviors into a metacategory is that they have the same objective. The task-oriented and relations-oriented metacategories are examples of a taxonomy based on leadership objectives. A limitation of this approach is that some specific types of leader behavior can be used to achieve more than one objective, and attempts to create measures of mutually exclusive metacategories may result in the deletion of these effective behaviors. Another limitation is ambiguity about what objectives should be considered when developing a behavior taxonomy. Behavior metacategories with important objectives such as facilitating change and influencing outsiders were not included in the early behavior research. The problems created by behaviors with multiple objectives and exclusion of relevant behaviors can be minimized by using accurate measures of specific behaviors likely to influence all important outcomes for the type of leader studied and by focusing attention on these relationships rather than on results for the metacategories. Unfortunately, this type of leadership study is very rare.

The component behaviors for a metacategory are not the same for different versions of a leadership theory, when the measures are developed by different researchers, or when the definition of the metacategory changes over time as more is learned about it. For example, the early definition of relations-oriented behavior did not explicitly include some of the component behaviors found in more recent measures of this metacategory (e.g., providing praise and recognition, increasing member confidence, encouraging cooperation among subordinates, empowering subordinates). It is more difficult to compare results from different studies or to interpret results from a meta-analysis of many studies when the same component behaviors are not used in each study and only the composite score for a metacategory is used in the data analyses.

Overlap Among Metacategories

Conceptual overlap among supposedly different metacategories is a related problem in leader behavior research (DeRue, Nahrgang, Wellman, & Humphrey, 2011). Sometimes the same component behavior is included in different metacategories. For example, providing praise and recognition has been included in some measures of relations-oriented behavior, transformational leadership, and transactional leadership. When the metacategories included in a study have some of the same content and only composite scores for the metacategories are used in the analyses, it is more difficult to interpret the results. A related problem occurs when the metacategory in a study includes some component behaviors from unmeasured metacategories. For example, measures of transformational leadership include some relations-oriented behaviors (e.g., supporting and developing subordinates) and some change-oriented behaviors (e.g., articulating an appealing vision, encouraging innovative thinking). Research that examined results for a broad range of specific behaviors found that the effects attributed to transformational leadership can be accounted for primarily by relations-oriented and change-oriented behaviors (Michel, Lyons, & Cho, 2011).

Unique and Joint Effects of Component Behaviors

Most leader behavior studies use only the composite score on a metacategory to assess the effects on outcomes rather than examining the unique effects of specific component behaviors.

Broadly defined categories of leader behavior have limited utility for understanding how leaders can influence work-unit performance. The component behaviors are not equally relevant for influencing performance; they have different relationships with mediating variables, and they may be affected in different ways by the context. For example, clarifying goals and problem solving are both task-oriented behaviors. However, clarifying goals helps to ensure that subordinates know what to do, how to do it, and the expected results; whereas, problem solving is used to deal with disruptions of normal operations and member behavior that is unsafe or illegal. Supporting and developing are both relations-oriented behaviors. However, supporting is used to show positive regard, build cooperative relationships, and help people deal with stressful situations; whereas developing is used to increase subordinate skills and confidence. Sometimes effective leadership involves using a combination of complementary behaviors from the same metacategory or from different metacategories (Piccolo et al., 2012). The relatively small number of studies that examine the unique and joint effects of specific behaviors is one likely reason for the lack of stronger results in the behavior research.

Confounding Behavior With Values and Traits

Many leadership studies are attempts to test a theoretical conception of an ideal leader (e.g., authentic, ethical, and servant leadership), or a theory about universally effective forms of leader influence (e.g., transformational leadership). The theories and measures used to test them usually include personality traits and values as well as a mix of diverse behaviors. Behaviors are different from values or personality traits. Most leader behaviors can be directly observed, but values and traits are usually inferred from behavior or measured with some type of personality test or self-report questionnaire. Traits and values are relatively stable characteristics for adults, whereas behaviors can be changed with training and development interventions. Leader traits influence leader behaviors, but there is not a simple, direct causal relationship. When these different types of constructs are included in the same scale and results are analyzed for a composite score, their effects will be confounded and the results difficult to interpret (Yukl, 2012). A better research strategy is to treat other types of leader attributes as a separate set of variables that can influence behavior or moderate its effects (DeRue et al., 2011).

Weak Survey Studies

The dominant method in the research on effects of leader behavior has been a survey study with a leader behavior questionnaire used by subordinates to retrospectively rate how much or how often a leader has used each type of behavior (Gardner, Lowe. Moss, Mahoney, & Cogliser, 2010). The high correlations commonly found among supposedly different behaviors in these studies suggest that the ratings of leader behavior are influenced by common response biases, implicit theories about effective leadership, and general satisfaction with the leader. When the same respondents (usually subordinates of each leader) provide the data for both the leader behavior and the outcomes, the correlations are likely to be inflated by respondent biases and attributions.

These problems are not adequately assessed by the statistical analyses many researchers use to claim that common method variance is not a problem.

Other research methods can be used to measure leadership behavior, including coding of behaviors in audio or video recordings, diaries, interviews, critical incidents, case studies, biographies, and documents for prominent leaders (e.g., presidential speeches). Leader behavior can be manipulated in scenario studies, laboratory simulations, and field experiments. All research methods have limitations, and the best strategy is to use multiple methods that are relevant and feasible for the research question. Consistent findings from different methods enhance confidence in the findings (Bryman, 2004).

Curvilinear Relationships

Another limitation in most of the behavior research is to focus on linear relationships between leader behavior and outcomes when curvilinear relationships are more plausible. In some cases, the effects of a behavior are best described by an inverted U-shaped curve in which benefits increase up to an optimal point, after which they decline. In some other cases, the benefits from a behavior will increase until reaching an optimal point, after which more use of the behavior will not result in any additional increases in benefits. Even when doing more of a behavior does not reduce the benefits or have negative side effects, spending more time than necessary on a behavior means that the leader is losing the opportunity to use more beneficial types of behavior (Yukl, 2012). Several studies have found curvilinear relationships between leader behavior and outcomes (Fleishman & Harris, 1962; Kaplan & Kaiser, 2006; Pierce & Aguinis, in press; Stouten, van Dijke, Mayer, De Cremer, & Euwema, 2013). However, merely testing for curvilinear relationships is not enough, because it is difficult to detect them unless there are accurate measures of leader behavior and effectiveness.

Lagged Effects

Most leader behavior studies examine events that occur during a time interval that is too short for the independent variables to have an effect on the mediator or dependent variables. Cross-sectional research is unable to determine how leaders develop relationships with subordinates, improve motivation and optimism, build effective teams, and lead change initiatives over weeks, months, or years. The effects for mediators, such as subordinate skill and task commitment, usually occur sooner than effects on performance outcomes that depend on the mediators. The lagged effect is longer for some types of leader behaviors than for others, and some effects are negative before they become positive. For example, introducing a major change often results in a temporary decline in performance before it results in significant improvements. Sometimes the beneficial effects of a leader's action or decision are only temporary and will eventually vanish unless the leader continues to use appropriate behaviors. Reciprocal causality may also occur, as when leader behavior is adjusted after receiving feedback about the initial effects of the behavior. A longitudinal study with repeated measures of behavior and outcomes is necessary to detect these complex relationships. Relatively few longitudinal studies have been conducted on the effects of leadership behavior, and some did not include accurate measures and an appropriate time interval.

Explanatory Processes

A major limitation in most of the leader behavior research is insufficient attention to mediating variables and causal processes that can explain leader influence on the type of outcomes of primary interest to the researcher (e.g., the performance of an individual subordinate, team, or organization). Prior research on organizational behavior has already identified common performance determinants for an individual, group, or organization, and they can be used to identify specific leadership behaviors likely to be effective in a given situation. Unfortunately, most leader behavior studies do not measure any mediating variables, and they are seldom used to select relevant, specific behaviors to include in a study. In studies that include only one or two of the relevant mediators, confounding with unmeasured mediators makes it difficult to interpret the results. Studies that examine mediators only for metacategories fail to identify differential mediating effects for the specific component behaviors and are less likely to find strong, clear results.

Multiple Criteria and Tradeoffs

Independent measures of leadership effectiveness are more useful for identifying the effects of leader behavior than ratings provided by the same persons who describe the behavior, but same-source measures are much more common in the leader behavior research. Relatively few studies examine the effects of leader behaviors on a wide range of relevant performance outcomes (Gardner et al., 2010; Kaiser, Hogan, & Craig, 2008). Studies that measure only one or two outcomes are unable to detect unintended negative consequences for outcomes that are important but not measured. Examining a wide range of outcomes is especially important for ethical and servant leadership, because decisions or actions carried out to benefit subordinates in some way may harm them in other ways or at a later time. Moreover, when the primary objective is to enhance or protect subordinate welfare, a leader's decisions and actions are more likely to have adverse consequences for other stakeholders and may reduce organizational performance.

Situational Variables

Many situational variables can enhance or limit the effects of leader behavior on outcomes such as subordinate commitment and group performance (Howell, Dorfman, & Kerr, 1986; James & Brett, 1984; Yukl, 2012). Examples of situational variables include the nature of the work performed by the leader's group (e.g., task complexity, structure and novelty, skill requirements, quality requirements); dependence on others for resources, information, approvals, and assistance; frequency and seriousness of disruptions in work-unit operations (e.g., equipment failures, supply shortages, natural disasters, terrorist attacks, strikes or sabotage); leader authority, position power, and autonomy; and the amount of change and uncertainty in the external environment for the organization (e.g., new technology, intense competition, social-economic change).

Deficiencies in any of the performance determinants for an individual, group, or organization represent another type of situational variable, because a leader can improve performance by eliminating these deficiencies (Yukl, 2013). For example, if subordinates lack essential skills and experience to perform an important new task, the leader can provide coaching, arrange for them to get more training, provide personal coaching, hire more talented employees, or hire consultants to help with the work.

An important determinant of effectiveness for many leaders is the ability to adapt their behavior to fit changing conditions in their current position or different conditions in a new position (Yukl & Mahsud, 2010). Leaders with behavioral flexibility are able to use a wide range of specific behaviors, and they use behaviors that are relevant for the situation (Hart & Quinn, 1993; Hooijberg, 1996; Yukl & Mahsud, 2010).

The effects of situational variables are not the same for all the specific component behaviors in a metacategory, and the differential effects will not be found by examining only results for composite scores on behavior metacategories. To understand how the situation can enhance or constrain the effects of specific leader behaviors, it is necessary to have accurate measures and adequate variance for the situational variables and analyses that examine how they jointly moderate the effects of specific leader behaviors. This type of research is difficult, and it is seldom conducted.

Suggested Improvements in Future Behavior Research

To make faster progress in learning about effective leadership, it is desirable to improve the way behavior constructs are defined and methods used to study leader behavior. Both subjects are discussed in this section of the chapter.

Behavior Constructs and Taxonomies

Despite the limitations of metacategories, they have benefits that justify using them for theory development and research. Organizing specific behaviors with a common purpose into meta-categories can facilitate the development of general theories of effective leadership and make them more parsimonious and easier to understand. The metacategories should be meaningful in terms of important leadership roles, functions, and objectives. Each metacategory should include distinct and observable component behaviors. A wide range of behaviors should be examined, including some that are not adequately represented in any of the popular metacategories. Specific behaviors that have multiple objectives should not be excluded. An example of a hierarchical taxonomy was recently proposed by Yukl (2012) to integrate much of the previous behavior research. The taxonomy has four behavior metacategories: task-oriented, relations-oriented, change-oriented, and external behavior. Some of the change-oriented and external behaviors have been overlooked in much of the research on effective leadership.

The objective for change-oriented behavior is to encourage and facilitate collective learning, innovation, and changes that will improve the effectiveness of the leader's work unit (Ekvall & Arvonen, 1991; Yukl, 1999; Yukl, Gordon, & Taber, 2002). Examples of specific change behaviors include advocating why change is necessary, communicating a clear and compelling vision of the benefits to be gained, proposing major changes or new initiatives, taking personal risks to get proposed changes approved, planning how to implement changes, encouraging innovation and flexibility, and encouraging collective learning (Yukl, 2012). The change-oriented behaviors did not get much attention in the early leadership research, and only a few of the component behaviors are represented in measures of charismatic and transformational leadership. Research on change-oriented behavior as a distinct metacategory is still limited, but a positive relationship has been found with outcomes such as job attitudes, managerial effectiveness, and independent ratings of leader performance (Barling, Weber, & Kelloway, 1996; Gil, Rico, Alcover, & Barrasa, 2005; Kim & Yukl, 1995; Michel et al., 2011).

The objective for external (or "boundary spanning") behavior is to represent the work unit, promote and defend work-unit interests, and get important information, resources, and political support for it. Examples of specific external behaviors include networking to build and maintain favorable relationships, scanning the external environment to identify threats and opportunities, negotiating agreements with other units or outsiders, and lobbying for resources and assistance from bosses or peers (Yukl, 2012). Only a small number of leadership studies have included external behavior, and one reason may be that subordinates—who are often the source of information about leader behavior—are seldom able to directly observe a leader's external behavior. Several studies have found a positive relationship between external behaviors and indicators of leadership effectiveness (e.g., Ancona & Caldwell, 1992; Druskat & Wheeler, 2003; Grinyer, Mayes, & McKiernan, 1990; Kim & Yukl, 1995; Kotter, 1982).

Ethical aspects of leader behavior also deserve more attention in future research on effective leadership. The research should determine if it is useful to treat ethical leader behavior as a distinct metacategory with unique component behaviors. In research on ethical, servant, and authentic leadership, it is essential to identify any specific behaviors not already represented in other metacategories and to differentiate these behaviors from other types of constructs such as leader values and personality traits. Future research should examine the separate and joint effects of these unique behaviors and other specific relations-oriented behaviors that are used to benefit subordinates (Yukl et al., 2013). Studies should be conducted to examine how leader traits and values influence a leader's choice of behavior and moderate its effects. Finally, more attention should be paid to leader intentions and interpretation of the situation when studying the determinants and consequences of leader behavior.

Research Methods

Survey studies with convenience samples and same-source measures should not continue to be the primary method for studying the effects of leadership behavior. Whenever possible, leadership researchers should use stronger methods like field experiments and lab experiments with simulated groups to assess the effects of leadership behavior. Because each type of research method has limitations, it is desirable to use more than one method whenever possible.

When survey studies are conducted, the accuracy of behavior description questionnaires should be improved. Behavior ratings should be provided by respondents who are trained to recognize the behaviors and have ample opportunity to observe them. Whenever possible, descriptions of actual incidents involving the behaviors should also be obtained and used to verify the accuracy of the behavior ratings and to help understand the behaviors. Instead of convenience samples, researchers should find samples that are appropriate for the research objectives.

In future research on effective leadership, multiple outcomes should be measured independently at appropriate times, and the outcomes should include some objective measures of performance for the leader's work unit. Relevant mediating processes should be assessed as well as situational variables likely to enhance or limit the effects of leader behavior. Longitudinal research designs should be used to assess lagged and temporary effects, and the timing of measures should be consistent with the underlying causal processes in the model being tested.

Credible rival hypotheses and alternative explanations should be identified and investigated whenever feasible. Analyses should be conducted for specific behaviors as well as for metacategories, and competing models should be compared to determine the relative benefits of the two types of constructs for predicting indicators of effective leadership. When alternative methods of data analysis are feasible but they do not provide consistent results, the discrepancies should be reported rather than selecting the one with the most favorable results. Any serious limitations in the sample, measures, or analyses should be clearly identified in the research report and suggestions made for avoiding them in future research.

Conclusions

The purpose of this review was to provide an overview of research on leadership behavior during the past half century and evaluate progress in learning about effective leadership in organizations. The conclusion is that despite some important findings, several limitations have made progress much slower than it should have been. Progress was limited by a focus on a one or two vague metacategories, confounding of observable behavior with other constructs, a lack of attention to the situation and explanatory processes, and infrequent use of strong research methods.

A hierarchical taxonomy of behavior metacategories can be useful for integrating the complex results found for the effects of specific, observable behaviors into a comprehensive and parsimonious model of causal relationships. However, it is important to remember that behavior constructs are conceptual tools to facilitate theory development and research, and there is no magic answer to the question of how to describe effective leadership behavior. As more is learned about effective leadership, taxonomies for describing leadership behavior will continue to evolve and improve. It is likely that some unique component behaviors will be necessary to describe how leaders influence an individual subordinate, a team, or an organization. It may also be necessary to identify some unique behaviors for different types of leaders than the managers and administrators studied in most of the leadership literature (e.g., elected political leaders, leaders of social groups, religious leaders, coaches of sports teams), and for leadership in specific contexts such as conducting meetings, making decisions, or leading a multicultural team.

Faster progress in future research will also require the use of stronger research methods, including experiments in which leaders are trained how to use effective behaviors. Survey studies can be useful, but only if appropriate samples are obtained, behavior is measured accurately, and relevant outcomes are measured independently. More longitudinal studies should be conducted to assess lagged effects, temporary effects, and reciprocal causality. Whenever possible, leader behavior studies should also include measures of relevant situational variables and mediating processes.

It will not be possible to make faster progress in efforts to understand effective leadership until limitations in much of the behavior research during the past half century are acknowledged and better studies are conducted. Improvements in leadership research will provide many benefits, including the development of better theories and more useful practical applications. A good understanding of effective leadership is an important way to improve the performance of groups and organizations, and it is a subject that deserves more intensive and systematic investigation by leadership scholars.

References

Ancona, D. G., & Caldwell, D. F. (1992). Bridging the boundary: External activity and performance in organizational teams. *Administrative Science Quarterly, 37,* 634–665.

Angle, B. R., Nagarajan, J. N., Sonnenfeld, J. A., & Srinivasan, D. (2006). Does CEO charisma matter? An empirical analysis of the relationships among organizational performance, environmental uncertainty, and top management team perceptions of CEO charisma. *Academy of Management Journal, 49*(1), 161–174.

Avolio, B. J., Gardner, W. L., Walumbwa, F. O., Luthans, F., & May, D. R. (2004). Unlocking the mask: A look at the process by which authentic leaders impact follower attitudes and behaviors. *Leadership Quarterly, 15,* 801–823.

Barbuto, J. E., & Wheeler, D. W. (2006). Scale development and construct clarification of servant leadership. *Group & Organization Management</emphasis>, 31*(3), 300–326.

Barling, J., Weber, T., & Kelloway, E. K. (1996). Effects of transformational leadership training on attitudinal and financial outcomes: A field experiment. *Journal of Applied Psychology, 81,* 827–832.

Bass, B. M. (1985). *Leadership and performance beyond expectations.* New York, NY: Free Press.

Bass, B. M. (2008). *Handbook of leadership: A survey of theory and research.* New York, NY: Free Press.

Bass, B. M., & Avolio, B. J. (1990). The implications of transactional and transformational leadership for individual, team, and organizational development. In W. Pasmore & R. W. Woodman (Eds.), *Research in organizational change and development* (Vol. 4, pp. 231–272). Greenwich, CT: JAI.

Bennis, W. G., & Nanus, B. (1985). *Leaders: The strategies for taking charge.* New York, NY: Harper & Row.

Brown, M. E., & Treviño, L. K. (2006). Ethical leadership: A review and future directions. *Leadership Quarterly, 17,* 595–616.

Brown, M. E., Treviño, L. K., & Harrison, D. A. (2005). Ethical leadership: A social learning perspective for construct development and testing. *Organizational Behavior and Human Decision Processes, 97,* 117–134.

Bryman, A. (2004). Qualitative research on leadership: A critical but appreciative view. *Leadership Quarterly, 15,* 729–769.

Caza, A., & Jackson, B. (2011). Authentic leadership. In A. Bryman, D. Collinson, K. Grint, B. Jackson, & M. Uhl-Bien (Eds.), *The Sage handbook of leadership* (pp. 352–364). London, UK: Sage.

Conger, J. A. (1989). *The charismatic leader: Behind the mystique of exceptional leadership.* San Francisco, CA: Jossey-Bass.

Conger, J. A., & Kanungo, R. (1998). *Charismatic leadership in organizations.* Thousand Oaks, CA: Sage.

DeGroot, T., Kiker, D. S., & Cross, T. C. (2000). A meta-analysis to review organizational outcomes related to charismatic leadership. *Canadian Journal of Administrative Science, 17,* 356–371.

Dennis, R. S., & Bocarnea, M. (2005). Development of the servant leadership assessment instrument. *Leadership and Organization Development Journal, 26(*8), 600–615.

DeRue, D. S., Nahrgang, J. D., Wellman, N., & Humphrey, S. E. (2011). Trait and behavioral theories of leadership: An integration and meta-analytic test of their relative validity. *Personnel Psychology, 64,* 7–52.

Druskat, V. U., & Wheeler, J. V. (2003). Managing from the boundary: The effective leadership of self-managed work teams. *Academy of Management Journal, 27,* 435–457.

Ehrhart, M. G. (2004). Leadership and procedural justice climate as antecedents of unit-level organizational citizenship behavior. *Personnel Psychology, 57,* 61–94.

Ekvall, G., & Arvonen, J. (1991). Change-centered leadership: An extension of the two-dimensional model. *Scandinavian Journal of Management, 7,* 17–26.

Finkelstein, S. (2003). *Why smart executives fail.* New York, NY: Portfolio.

Fleishman, E. A. (1953). The description of supervisory behavior. *Personnel Psychology, 37,* 1–6.

Fleishman, E. A., & Harris, E. F. (1962). Patterns of leadership behavior related to employee grievances and turnover. *Personnel Psychology, 15,* 43–56.

Gardner, W. L., Cogliser, C. C., Davis, K. M., & Dickens, M. P. (2011). Authentic leadership: A review of the literature and research agenda. *Leadership Quarterly, 22,* 1120–1145.

Gardner, W. L., Lowe. K. B., Moss, T. W., Mahoney, K. T., & Cogliser, C. C. (2010). Scholarly leadership of the study of leadership: A review of *The Leadership Quarterly's* second decade, 2000–2009. *Leadership Quarterly, 21,* 922–958.

George, B. (2003). *Authentic leadership: Rediscovering the secrets to creating lasting value.* San Francisco, CA: Addison-Wesley.

Gil, R., Rico, R., Alcover, C., & Barrasa, A. (2005). Change-oriented leadership, satisfaction, and performance in work groups. *Journal of Managerial Psychology, 20,* 312–328.

Greenleaf, R. K. (1977). *Servant leadership.* New York, NY: Paulist.

Grinyer, P. H., Mayes, D., & McKiernan, P. (1990). The sharpbenders: Achieving a sustained improvement in performance. *Long Range Planning, 23,* 116–125.

Halpin, A. W., & Winter, B. J. (1957). A factorial study of the leader behavior descriptions. In R. M. Stogdill & A. E. Coons (Eds.), *Leader behavior: Its description and measurement.* Columbus: Bureau of Business Research, Ohio State University.

Hart, L. S., & Quinn, E. R. (1993). Roles executives play: CEOs, behavioral complexity, and firm performance. *Human Relations, 46*(5), 543–575.

Hersey, P., & Blanchard, K. H. (1977). *The management of organizational behavior* (3rd ed.). Englewood Cliffs, NJ: Prentice-Hall.

Hooijberg, R. (1996). A multidimensional approach toward leadership: An extension of the concept of behavioral complexity. *Human Relations, 49*(7), 917–947.

House, R. J. (1971). A path-goal theory of leader effectiveness. *Administrative Science Quarterly, 16,* 321–339.

House, R. J. (1977). A 1976 theory of charismatic leadership. In J. G. Hung & L. L. Larson (Eds.), *Leadership: The cutting edge* (pp. 189–207). Carbondale: Southern Illinois University Press.

Howell, J. P., Dorfman, P. W., & Kerr, S. (1986). Moderator variables in leadership research. *Academy of Management Review, 11,* 82–102.

Ilies, R., Morgeson, F. P., & Nahrgang, J. D. (2005). Authentic leadership and eudaemonic well-being: Understanding leader-follower outcomes. *Leadership Quarterly, 16*(3), 373–394.

James, L. R., & Brett, J. M. (1984). Mediators, moderators, and tests for mediation. *Journal of Applied Psychology, 69,* 307–321.

Judge, T. A., & Piccolo, R. F. (2004). Transformational and transactional leadership: A meta-analytic test of their relative validity. *Journal of Applied Psychology, 89,* 36–51.

Judge, T. A., Piccolo, R. F., & Ilies, R. (2004). The forgotten ones? The validity of consideration and initiating structure in leadership research. *Journal of Applied Psychology, 89,* 36–51.

Kacmar, K. M., Bachrach, D. G., Harris, K. J., & Zivnuska, S. (2011). Fostering good citizenship through ethical leadership: Exploring the moderating role of gender and organizational politics. *Journal of Applied Psychology, 96*(3), 633–642.

Kaiser, R. B., Hogan, R., & Craig, S. B. (2008). Leadership and the fate of organizations. *American Psychologist, 63*(2), 96–110.

Kaplan, R. E., & Kaiser, R. B. (2006). *The versatile leader: Make the most of your strengths without overdoing it.* San Francisco, CA: Pfeiffer.

Kerr, S., & Jermier, J. M. (1978). Substitutes for leadership: Their meaning and measurement. *Organizational Behavior and Human Performance, 22,* 375–403.

Kim, H., & Yukl, G. (1995). Relationships of self-reported and subordinate-reported leadership behaviors to managerial effectiveness and advancement. *Leadership Quarterly, 6,* 361–377.

Kotter, J. P. (1982). *The general manager.* New York, NY: Free Press.

Liden, R. C., Wayne, S. J., Zhao, H., & Henderson, D. (2008). Servant leadership: Development of a multidimensional measure and multi-level assessment. *Leadership Quarterly, 19,* 161–177.

Likert, R. (1961). *New patterns of management.* New York, NY: McGraw-Hill.

Lowe, K. B., Kroeck, K. G., & Sivasubramaniam, N. (1996). Effectiveness of correlates of transformational and transactional leadership: A meta-analytic review of the MLQ literature. *Leadership Quarterly, 7,* 385–442.

Mayer, D. M., Aquino, K., Greenbaum, R. L., & Kuenzi, M. (2012). Who displays ethical leadership, and why does it matter? An examination of antecedents and consequences of ethical leadership. *Academy of Management Journal, 55*(1), 151–171.

Mayer, D. M., Bardes, M., & Piccolo, R. F. (2008). Do servant-leaders help satisfy follower needs? An organizational justice perspective. *European Journal of Work and Organizational Psychology, 17,* 180–197.

Mayer, D. M., Kuenzi, M., Greenbaum, R., Bardes, M., & Salvador, R. (2009). How low does ethical leadership flow? Test of a trickle-down model. *Organizational Behavior and Human Decision Processes, 108*, 1–13.

Michel, J. W., Lyons, B. D., & Cho, J. (2011). Is the full-range model of leadership really a full-range model of effective leader behavior? *Journal of Leadership and Organizational Studies, 18*, 493–507.

Neubert, M. J., Kacmar, K. M., Carlson, D. S., Chonko, L. B., & Roberts, J. A. (2008). Regulatory focus as a mediator of the influence of initiating structure and servant leadership on employee behavior. *Journal of Applied Psychology, 93*, 1220–1233.

O'Connor, J., Mumford, M. D., Clifton, T. C., Gessner, T. L., & Connelly, M. S. (1995). Charismatic leaders and destructiveness: A historiometric study. *Leadership Quarterly, 6*, 529–555.

Piccolo, R. F., Bono, J. E., Heinitz, K., Rowold, J., Duehr, E., & Judge, T. A. (2012). The relative impact of complementary leader behaviors: Which matter most? *Leadership Quarterly, 23*, 567–581.

Piccolo, R. F., Greenbaum, R., Den Hartog, D. N., & Folger, R. (2010). The relationship between ethical leadership and core job characteristics. *Journal of Organizational Behavior, 31*, 259–278.

Pierce, J. R., & Aguinis, H. (in press). The too-much-of-a-good-thing effect in management. *Journal of Management*.

Podsakoff, P. M., MacKenzie, S. B., Ahearn, M., & Bommer, W. H. (1995). Searching for a needle in a haystack: Trying to identify the illusive moderators of leadership behaviors. *Journal of Management, 21*, 423–470.

Podsakoff, P. M., Mackenzie, S. B., Moorman, R. H., & Fetter, R. (1990). Transformational leader behaviors and their effects on followers' trust in leader, satisfaction, and organizational citizenship behaviors. *Leadership Quarterly, 1*, 107–142.

Shamir, B., House, R. J., & Arthur, M. B. (1993). The motivational effects of charismatic leadership: A self-concept based theory. *Organization Science, 4*, 1–17.

Sims, R. R., & Brinkman, J. (2003). Enron ethics (or culture matters more than codes). *Journal of Business Ethics, 45*, 243–256.

Stouten, J., van Dijke, M., Mayer, D. M., De Cremer, D., & Euwema, M. C. (2013). Can a leader be seen as too ethical? The curvilinear effects of ethical leadership. *Leadership Quarterly, 24*, 680–695.

Thompson, G., & Vecchio, R. P. (2009). Situational leadership theory: A test of three versions. *Leadership Quarterly, 20*, 837–848.

Treviño, L. T., Brown, M., & Hartman, L. P. (2003). A qualitative investigation of perceived ethical leadership: Perceptions from inside and outside the executive suite. *Human Relations, 55*, 5–37.

van Dierendonck, D. (2011). Servant leadership: A review and synthesis. *Journal of Management, 37*, 1228–1261.

van Dierendonck, D., & Nuijten, I. (2011). The servant leadership survey: Development and validation of a multidimensional measure. *Journal of Business & Psychology, 26*, 249–267.

van Knipenberg, D., & Sitkin, S. B. (2013). A critical assessment of charismatic-transformational leadership research: Back to the drawing board? *Academy of Management Annals, 7*, 1–60.

Walumbwa, F. O., Hartnell, C. A., & Oke, A. (2010). Servant leadership, procedural justice climate, service climate, employee attitudes, and organizational citizenship behavior: A cross-level investigation. *Journal of Applied Psychology, 95*, 517–529.

Walumbwa, F. O., Morrison, E. W., & Christensen, A. L. (2012). Ethical leadership and group in-role performance: The mediating roles of group conscientiousness and group voice. *Leadership Quarterly, 23*, 953–964.

Wang, G., Oh, I. S., Courtright, S. H., & Colbert, A. E. (2011). Transformational leadership and performance across criteria and levels: A meta-analytic review of 25 years of research. *Group & Organization Management, 36,* 223–270.

Wofford, J. C., & Liska, L. Z. (1993). Path-goal theories of leadership: A meta-analysis. *Journal of Management, 19,* 858–876.

Yukl, G. (1971). Toward a behavioral theory of leadership. *Organizational Behavior and Human Performance, 6,* 414–440.

Yukl, G. (1999). An evaluative essay on current conceptions of effective leadership. *European Journal of Work and Organizational Psychology, 8,* 33–48.

Yukl, G. (2012, November). Effective leadership behaviors: What we know and what questions need more attention? *Academy of Management Perspectives,* 66–85.

Yukl, G. (2013). *Leadership in organizations* (8th ed.). Englewood Cliffs, NJ: Pearson.

Yukl, G., Gordon, A., & Taber, T. (2002). A hierarchical taxonomy of leader behavior: Integrating a half century of behavior research. *Journal of Leadership and Organizational Studies, 9,* 15–32.

Yukl, G., & Mahsud, R. (2010). Why flexible, adaptive leadership is important. *Consulting Psychology Journal, 62*(2), 81–93.

Yukl, G., Mahsud, R., Hassan, S., & Prussia, G. E. (2013). An improved measure of ethical leadership. *Journal of Leadership & Organizational Studies, 23,* 38–48.

Discussion Questions

Theory and research on effective leadership practices describe the effects of positive leadership behavior on outcomes such as subordinate attitudes and performance. Answer the following questions and use examples from the chapter to support your opinion.

1 What constitutes a positive leadership behavior?

2 What behaviors reflect poor leadership?

3 How does leadership affect subordinate attitudes and performance? What outcomes are associated with effective leadership?

4 Describe the limitations of behavioral research on leadership, and discuss ways to overcome these limitations.

PART II

LEADERS' CHARACTERISTICS

CHAPTER 2

Traits Associated with Leadership Effectiveness

Individual Differences, Mental Ability, and Personality

Andrew J. DuBrin

In early 2014, Satya Nadella, a 22-year company veteran, became the third CEO in the history of Microsoft Corporation, following Bill Gates and Steve Ballmer. Forty-six years old when he was appointed CEO, Nadella had been responsible for some of Microsoft's most complex and technology-intensive businesses. These included software for server systems, cloud-computing services, and research and development.

In addition to Nadella's intensive knowledge of technology, he has also demonstrated considerable insight into organizational structure. When he was placed in charge of the division for producing computer-server and cloud technologies, he merged groups dedicated to separate products, and thinned out layers of management. Furthermore, he made software developers more responsible for their products. The changes in structure facilitated teamwork and blurred lines between products, which resulted in more idea sharing and better use of engineers.

Nadella sees the mission of Microsoft broadly as developing technology to help people live better lives and business firms to run more efficiently. His vision of Microsoft entails ubiquitous computing and ambient intelligence. The former refers to computers surrounding us, often referred to as the *Internet of things*, such as connecting a microwave oven to a smartphone. Ambient intelligence moves almost into the realm of science fiction—electronic environments that are sensitive and responsive to the presence of people. Two examples are turning up the heat in a vehicle when skin temperature drops, or turning on a favorite TV channel when walking into the family room.

Many past and present colleagues of Nadella say that his greatest asset is an affable and agreeable collaborative style in a company that is known for big egos and interpersonal conflict. It has been observed that Nadella's positive personality and extensive technical background will help retain key engineers and programmers who have plenty of job opportunities. The former head of Microsoft's India operations said, "It's hard to find a single person who doesn't have a nice thing to say about him. He's humble, incredibly humble."

Nadella studied electronics and communication engineering at Manipel Institute of Technology in India, and earned a bachelor's degree in electrical engineering at Mangalore University, a master's degree in computer science from the University of Wisconsin, Milwaukee, and an MBA from the University of Chicago.[1]

The story about the Microsoft CEO just presented illustrates how the combination of high intelligence and positive personality traits contributes to individual success and organizational effectiveness. The purpose of this chapter is to explain how individual differences affect performance. In addition, we describe key sources of individual differences: demographic diversity, mental ability, and personality. In Chapters 3 and 4, we will consider other sources of individual differences that influence behavior in organizations: learning, perception, values, attitudes, and ethics. Although our focus in this chapter is on individual differences, we also describe principles of human behavior that apply to everyone. For example, everyone has different components to his or her intelligence. We all have some capacity to deal with numbers, words, and abstract reasoning.

---

1   Original story created from facts and observations in the following sources: Shira Ovide, "Nadella Pushes for a Leaner Microsoft," *The Wall Street Journal*, July 11, 2014, pp. B1, B5; Don Clark, Monica Langley, and Shira Ovide, "Microsoft's CEO Pick: From India to Insider," *The Wall Street Journal*, February 1 2, 2014, pp. A1, A2; Adam Bryant, "Satya Nadella, Chief of Microsoft, on His New Role," *The New York Times* (www.nytimes.com), February 20, 2014, pp. 1–4; Simon Blisson, "Decoding Satya Nadella's Microsoft," *CITEWorld* (www.citeworld.com), June 11, 2014, pp. 1–4; Shira Ovide, "Microsoft Pick: Change Agent?" *The Wall Street Journal*, February 3, 2014, pp. B1, B6.

Individual Differences

People show substantial **individual differences**, or variations, in how they respond to the same situation based on personal characteristics. An extraverted production planner might attempt to influence a plant superintendent by taking him to lunch and making an oral presentation of her ideas. In the same situation, an introverted planner might attempt to influence the superintendent by sending him an elaborate report. Understanding individual differences helps to explain human behavior, but environmental influences are also important.

The importance of understanding individual differences for managing people is highlighted by the research of Marcus Buckingman, who studied over 80,000 managers, using both survey questionnaires and interviews. He concluded that exceptional managers come to value the particular quirks and abilities of their employees. Exceptional managers analyze how to capitalize on the strengths of workers and tweak the environment to adapt to employee strengths. For example, the manager might modify a job description so the worker can do more work that fits his or her talents, such as giving a very bright employee more opportunity to troubleshoot.[2]

LEARNING OBJECTIVE 1

Explain how individual differences influence the behavior of people in organizations.

individual differences Variations in how people respond to the same situation based on personal characteristics.

Rawpixel/Shutterstock.com

Individual differences are a key aspect of organizational behavior.

---

2 Marcus Buckingham, "What Great Managers Do," *Harvard Business Review*, March 2005, pp. 70–79.

A basic proposition of psychology states that behavior is a function of a person interacting with his or her environment.[3] The equation reads $B = f(P \times E)$, where B stands for behavior, P for the person, and E the environment. A key implication of this equation is that the effects of the individual and the environment on each other determine a person's behavior. For example, working for a firm that requires many levels of approval for a decision might trigger a person's tendencies toward impatience. The same person working in a flatter organization (one that requires fewer layers of approval) might be more patient. Have you ever noticed that some environments, and some people, bring out your best traits? Or your worst traits?

Another way of understanding the impact of individual differences in the workplace is to say that these differences *moderate* how people respond to situations. Assume that a new organizational structure results in most professional-level workers having two bosses. (Each worker has a manager in his or her own discipline, plus a project leader.) Workers who have a difficult time tolerating ambiguity (a personality trait) will find the new structure to be frustrating. In contrast, workers who tolerate ambiguity well will enjoy the challenge and excitement of having two bosses.

Here we identify seven consequences of individual differences that have a major impact on managing people:

1 *People differ in productivity.* A comprehensive analysis of individual differences illustrates the magnitude of human variation in job performance.[4] Researchers synthesized studies involving over 10,000 workers. They found that as jobs become more complex, individual differences have a bigger impact on work output. An outstanding industrial sales representative might produce 100 times as much sales revenue as a mediocre one. In contrast, an outstanding store cashier might produce only twice as much as a mediocre one. (An industrial sales position is more complex than the job of a cashier. Industrial selling involves a variety of activities, including persuading others, analyzing problems, and accessing relevant data.)

2 *Quality of work varies because people vary in their propensity for achieving high-quality results.* Some people take naturally to striving for high quality because they are conscientious, have a good capacity for precision, and take pride in their work. Workers who are less conscientious, less precise, and have little pride in their work will have more difficulty achieving quality targets.

3 *Empowerment is effective with some workers, but not with all.* People differ in how much they want to be empowered and involved. A major thrust of the modern workplace is to grant workers more authority to make decisions by themselves and to involve them in suggesting improvements. Many workers welcome such empowerment and

3   Kurt Lewin, *A Dynamic Theory of Personality* (New York: McGraw-Hill, 1935).
4   John E. Hunter, Frank L. Schmidt, and Michael E. Judiesch, "Individual Differences in Output Variability as a Function of Job Complexity," *Journal of Applied Psychology*, February 1990, pp. 28–42.

enrichment because they seek self-fulfillment on the job. However, many other workers are not looking for more responsibility and job involvement. They prefer jobs that require a minimum of mental involvement and responsibility.

4   *A given leadership style does not work with all people.* People differ in the style of leadership they prefer and need. Many individuals prefer as much freedom as possible on the job and can function well under such leadership. Other individuals want to be supervised closely by their manager. People also vary with respect to the amount of supervision they require. In general, less competent, less motivated, and less experienced workers need more supervision. One of the biggest headaches facing a manager is to supervise people who need close supervision yet resent it when it is administered.

5   *People differ in their need for contact with other people.* As a by-product of their personality traits and occupational interests, people vary widely in how much human contact they need to keep them satisfied. Some people can work alone all day and remain highly productive. Others become restless unless they are engaged in business or social conversation with another employee. Some workers will often drop by the work area of other workers just to chat. Sometimes a business luncheon is scheduled more out of a manager's need for social contact than a need for discussing job problems.

6   *Company management will find that commitment to the firm varies considerably.* Some employees are so committed (or engaged) to their employers that they act as if they are part-owners of the firm. As a consequence, committed and loyal employees are highly concerned about producing high-quality goods and services. They also maintain excellent records of attendance and punctuality, which helps reduce the cost of doing business. At the other extreme, some employees feel little commitment or loyalty toward their employer, and therefore are not work engaged. They feel no pangs of guilt when they produce scrap or when they miss work for trivial reasons.

7   *Workers vary in their level of self-esteem, which, in turn, influences their productivity and capacity to take on additional responsibilities.* People with high self-esteem believe that they can cope with the basic challenges of life (self-efficacy) and also that they are worthy of happiness (self-respect). A group of economists found that self-esteem, as measured by a personality test, had a big impact on the wages of young workers. The researchers found that human capital—schooling, basic skills, and work experience—predictably had a significant impact on wages. Yet 10 percent of this effect was really attributable to self-esteem, which highly correlated with human capital. It was also found that differences in productivity, as measured by comparative wages, related more to differences in self-esteem than to differences in human capital.[5]

---

5   "The Vital Role of Self-Esteem: It Boosts Productivity and Earnings," *Business Week*, February 2, 1998, p. 26.

The sampling of individual differences creating the consequences cited is usually attributed to a combination of genetic makeup and environmental influences. Some workers are more productive because they have inherited better problem-solving abilities and have lived since childhood in environments that encourage the acquisition of knowledge and skills. Many other personality traits, such as introversion, also are partially inherited.

Despite the importance of heredity, a person's environment—including the workplace—still plays a significant role in influencing job behavior. The manager must therefore strive to create a positive environment in which workers are able to perform at their best.

Demographic Diversity

Workers vary widely with respect to background, or demographic characteristics, and these differences sometimes affect job performance and behavior. **Demographic diversity** refers to the differences in background factors relating to the workforce that help shape workers' attitudes and behavior. Key sources of demographic diversity include gender, generational differences, and age. As is well known, the U.S. workforce is becoming increasingly diverse. We will mention cultural diversity at various places in this book, including it as the subject of the final chapter. Understanding demographic differences among workers can help a manager both capitalize on diversity and avoid negative stereotyping. For example, some managers still hold the stereotype that single people are less conscientious than married people.

Sex and Gender Differences

A topic of intense debate is whether men and women differ in aspects of behavior related to job performance. (*Sex* differences refer to actual biological differences, such as the average height of men versus that of women. *Gender* differences refer to differences in the perception of male and female roles.) A series of studies suggests that gender differences in personality exist. These findings include the following:

- Women are better able to understand nonverbal communication.
- Women are more expressive of emotion.

- The average woman is more trusting and more nurturing than the average man.[6]
- To a slight degree, women feel more actively engaged in their work than do men.[7]

More closely related to job behavior, much has been written about the different styles and communication patterns of men and women. Chapter 8 presents more details about male–female differences in communication patterns. A major finding is that men more typically communicate to convey information or establish status. Women are more likely to communicate to establish rapport and solve problems.

Men are generally more aggressive than women and therefore less sensitive to the feelings of others. Women generally tend to be more courteous and polite.

Despite the existence of these gender differences, the overall evidence suggests that there are few differences between men and women in factors such as ability and motivation that will affect job performance. A meta-analysis of the evidence about gender differences suggests that the similarities between men and women far outweigh the differences. According to the gender-similarities hypothesis, as advanced by Janet Shibley Hyde, males and females are alike on most, but not all, behavioral variables. An example of a slight difference is that males tend to be slightly more aggressive than females. Hyde observes that overinflated claims of gender differences can do harm in the workplace.[8] Two examples would be denying a woman a job as a bill collector because women are thought to be less aggressive than men, or denying a man a job as a home healthcare aide because men are thought to be less nurturing than women.

Generational and Age-Based Differences

The generation to which a person belongs may have a strong influence on his or her work behavior and attitudes. Greg Hammill observes that this is the first time in American history that we have had *four* different generations interacting in the workplace.[9] In Chapter 4, we will explore these generational differences more specifically from the standpoint of values. The general point is that people may behave differently on the job based somewhat on the behaviors and attitudes typical of many members of their generation. We emphasize that we are dealing in stereotypes that represent tendencies of the typical worker in a generational category. An extreme negative stereotype is that younger workers are disloyal and older workers are very loyal. In reality, some younger workers are quite loyal to their employer and some older workers are disloyal.

6   A brief review of the literature is presented in Leonard Sax, "Maybe Men and Women Are Different," *American Psychologist*, June/July 2002, p. 444.

7   Gallup Organization survey results reported in Nanette Fondas, "Women Are More Likely to Be Engaged in Their Jobs," *The Atlantic* (www.theatlantic.com), June 6, 2013, p. 2.

8   Janet Shibley Hyde, "The Gender Similarities Hypothesis," *American Psychologist*, September 2005, pp. 581–592.

9   Greg Hammill, "Mixing and Managing Four Generations of Employees," *FDUMagazine Online*, Winter/Spring 2005 (www.fdu.edu/newspubs/magazine/05ws/generations.htm).

According to Constance Patterson, every generation is influenced by the major economic, political, and social events of its era, such as the Great Depression, the women's movement, and advances in information technology.[10] Emerging standards of etiquette also influence work-related behavior. A middle-aged recruiter was aghast when a young job candidate put her on hold twice to respond to call-waiting during a telephone job interview. The candidate, in turn, thought it was natural to interrupt one person to accept a phone call from another. As this example illustrates, generational differences can lead to communication problems. Patterson encourages members of mixed-generation groups to seek a balance between building on traditional procedures and supporting flexibility and imaginative thinking to effectively blend the work ethics of the several generations.[11]

Age is related to generational differences with a subtle difference—age differences include a focus on mental and physical capabilities. Age and experience are not synonymous. For example, a person age 35 might have 14 years' experience as a restaurant manager, whereas a person age 65 might have 5 years' experience in such a position. Nevertheless, age and experience are usually related.

The research evidence about job-related consequences of age is mixed. One study of 24,000 federal workers found that age was barely related to performance. Not surprisingly, both age and experience predicted performance better for high-complexity jobs than for other, less complicated jobs.[12] A review of articles spanning 22 years studying the relationship between age and performance (involving almost 40,000 workers) found that age and job performance were generally unrelated. Advances in technology are now helping workers compensate for mental losses, such as less acute memory, associated with age. Two examples are memory-enhancing drugs, and the use of Internet search engines to quickly retrieve information that the worker may have forgotten.

Even if being older and more experienced does not always contribute to job performance, older workers do have notable attributes. In contrast to younger workers, they have lower absenteeism, illness, and accident rates; higher job satisfaction; and more positive work values.[13] For top-level executive positions, age is often valued because the older executive may have more wisdom based on experience. The discussion of practical intelligence later in this chapter reintroduces the topic of wisdom based on experience.

---

10   Cited in Melissa Dittman, "Generational Differences at Work," *Monitor on Psychology*, June 2005, pp. 54–55.

11   Dittman, "Generational Differences at Work," p. 55.

12   Bruce J. Avolio, David A. Waldman, and Michael A. McDaniel, "Age and Work Performance in Nonmanagerial Jobs: The Effects of Experience and Occupational Type," *Academy of Management Journal*, June 1990, pp. 407 422.

13   Susan R. Rhodes, "Age-Related Differences in Work Attitudes and Behavior: A Review and Conceptual Analysis," *Psychological Bulletin*, March 1983, pp. 328–367; Milt Freudenheim, "More Help Wanted: Older Workers Please Apply," *The New York Times* (www.nytimes.com), March 23, 2005, p. 1.

Mental Ability (Cognitive Intelligence)

Mental ability, or **cognitive intelligence** (the capacity to acquire and apply knowledge, including solving problems) is a major source of individual differences that affect job performance and behavior. Intelligent workers can best solve abstract problems. More than 100 years of research findings consistently indicate that intelligence, as measured by mental ability tests, is positively related to job performance.[14]

General mental ability is also a good predictor of job performance and success in training for a wide variety of occupations in the European community.[15] An example of the widespread use of mental ability tests to predict job performance is that most National Football League (NFL) teams use the Wonderlic Personnel Test, a standardized measure of cognitive ability, as part of the selection process. In general, quarterbacks—the position calling for the most analytical skills—tend to have the highest mental ability test scores.[16]

bokan/Shutterstock.com

Intelligence is a real asset in business.

LEARNING OBJECTIVE 3

Explain how mental ability relates to job performance.

cognitive intelligence The capacity to acquire and apply knowledge, including solving problems.

14   Orlando Behling, "Employee Selection: Will Intelligence and Conscientiousness Do the Job?" *Academy of Management Executive*, February 1998, p. 78.
15   Jesús F. Salgado, et al., "A Meta-Analytic Study of General Mental Ability Validity for Different Occupations in the European Community," *Journal of Applied Psychology*, December 2003, pp. 1068–1081.
16   Sam Walker, "The NFL's Smartest Team," *The Wall Street Journal*, September 30, 2005, pp. W1, W10.

Few people seriously doubt that mental ability is related to job performance. Controversy does abound, however, about two aspects of intelligence. One is how accurately and fairly intelligence can be measured. It is argued, for example, that intelligence tests discriminate against environmentally disadvantaged people. The second controversial aspect is the relative influence of heredity and environment on intelligence. Some people believe that intelligence is mostly the product of genes, while others believe that upbringing is the key factor.

The argument that environment is the major contributor to intelligence centers on evidence that many people, if placed in an enriched environment, are able to elevate their intelligence test scores. People with genes favoring high intelligence will gravitate toward mentally enriching experiences, thereby relying on the environment to boost their natural cognitive advantage.[17] Related to this argument is the fact that IQs have been steadily rising worldwide, with the average IQ of each successive generation higher than that of the previous generation. Possible explanations for gains in mental ability (as measured by IQ tests) include better nutrition, more training in mental tasks, and more sophistication in taking tests. All of these reasons indicate that environment heavily influences intelligence.[18] (If it is true that mental ability can be improved by a stimulating environment, giving employees ample opportunity to stretch themselves mentally will help them improve their intellectual skills.)

Based on hundreds of studies, it appears that heredity and environment contribute about equally to intelligence. This finding does not mean that a person with extremely limited mental capacity can be made super-intelligent through specialized training. Nor does it mean that a naturally brilliant person does not need a mentally stimulating environment.

A current synthesis of the evidence suggests that, among members of higher socioeconomic groups, heredity has a bigger impact on intelligence than among people from lower socioeconomic groups. Among members of higher socioeconomic groups, the shared environment accounted for very little difference in cognitive intelligence. It could be that members of higher-class groups have more consistent environments that support learning.[19]

Here we describe two aspects of mental ability that have implications for organizational behavior: the components of intelligence and practical intelligence. Emotional intelligence is described under the category of personality.

Components of Intelligence

Intelligence consists of multiple components. A component of intelligence is much like a separate mental aptitude. A standard theory of intelligence explains that intelligence consists of a

---

17 Research cited in Sharon Begley, "Good Genes Count, but Many Factors Make Up High IQ," *The Wall Street Journal*, June 20, 2003, p. B1.

18 James R. Flynn, "The Discovery of IQ Gains over Time," *American Psychologist*, January 1999, pp. 5–20; Richard E. Nisbett et al., "Intelligence: New Findings and Theoretical Developments," *American Psychologist*, February/March 2012, pp. 130–159.

19 Nisbett et al., "Intelligence," p. 140.

g **(general) factor** along with *s* **(special) factors** that contribute to problem-solving ability. Another way of describing *g* is that it represents a general cognitive factor that pervades almost all kinds of mental ability. Scores on tests of almost any type (e.g., math or creative ability) are influenced by *g*. High scores on *g* are associated with good scholastic performance. In the workplace, *g* is the best predictor of success in job training, job performance, occupational prestige, and accomplishment within occupations. Also, *g* is related to many social outcomes, including early death due to vehicular accidents.[20] The *g* factor helps explain why some people perform so well in many different mental tasks—they have the *right stuff*.

Various researchers have identified different *s* factors contributing to overall mental aptitude. Figure 2-1 lists and defines seven factors that have been consistently noted. Being strong in any mental aptitude often leads to

g **(general) factor** A major component of intelligence that contributes to problem-solving ability.

s **(special) factors** Components of intelligence that contribute to problem-solving ability.

- *Verbal comprehension:* The ability to understand the meanings of words and their relationship to one another, and to comprehend written and spoken information.

- *Word fluency:* The ability to use words quickly and easily, without an emphasis on verbal comprehension.

- *Numerical:* The ability to handle numbers, engage in mathematical analysis, and do arithmetic calculations.

- *Spatial:* The ability to visualize forms in space and manipulate objects mentally, particularly in three dimensions.

- *Memory:* Having a good rote recall for symbols, words, and lists of numbers, along with other associations.

- *Perceptual speed:* The ability to perceive visual details, to pick out similarities and differences, and to perform tasks requiring visual perception.

- *Inductive reasoning:* The ability to discover a rule or principle and apply it in solving a problem, and to make judgments and decisions that are logically sound.

Figure 2.1   Special Factors Contributing to Overall Mental Aptitude

Source: These seven factors stem from the pioneering work of L. L. Thurstone, "Primary Mental Abilities," *Psychometric Monographs*, 1 (1938).

---

20   Arthur R. Jensen, *The g Factor: The Science of Mental Ability* (Westport, CT: Praeger, 1998).

practical intelligence The type of intelligence required for adapting to an environment to suit an individual's needs.

enjoyment of work associated with that aptitude. Conversely, enjoyment of an activity might lead to the development of an aptitude for that activity.

Practical Intelligence

Many people, including specialists in organizational behavior, are concerned that the traditional way of understanding intelligence inadequately describes mental ability. An unfortunate implication of intelligence testing is that intelligence as traditionally calculated consists largely of the ability to perform tasks related to scholastic work. Thus, a person who scored high on an intelligence test could follow a complicated instruction manual but not have good common sense and judgment, which would be needed for an endeavor such as operating a successful small business. To overcome the limited idea that intelligence involves mostly the ability to solve abstract problems, the concept of **practical intelligence** has been proposed. This type of intelligence is required for adapting to an environment to suit an individual's needs.[21]

Practical intelligence helps explain why a person who has a difficult time getting through school can still be a successful businessperson, politician, or visual artist. It incorporates the ideas of common sense, wisdom, and street smarts. One reservation about practical intelligence derives from the implication that people who are highly intelligent in the analytical sense are not practical thinkers. In truth, most executives and other high-level workers score quite well on tests of mental ability. Also, leaders at many levels in business who receive higher performance and actual productivity evaluations tend to score slightly higher on mental ability tests. These tests usually measure analytical intelligence.[22]

The relevance of practical intelligence was demonstrated in a study about entrepreneurs. The study was conducted by interviewing 22 printing industry CEOs and reviewing survey responses from 283 founders of early-stage printing and graphics businesses. Practical intelligence was measured by looking at responses to three scenarios directly relating to the printing industry, such as dealing with declining sales. The task requiring practical intelligence was to rank 10 different possible actions to deal with a specific problem. "Preferred action sequences" were ranked in terms of their effectiveness by industry experts. Two findings particularly relevant to the understanding of practical intelligence were as follows:

---

21 Timothy A. Judge, Amy E. Colbert, and Remus Ilies, "Intelligence and Leadership: A Quantitative Review and Test of Theoretical Propositions," *Journal of Applied Psychology*, June 2004, pp. 542–552.

22 Robert J. Sternberg, *Beyond IQ: A Triarchic Theory of Human Intelligence* (New York: Cambridge University Press, 1995).

- Industrial experience and practical intelligence are the most positively related when the entrepreneurs are strongly oriented to learn through concrete experience. Venture experience was also more closely related to practical intelligence when the entrepreneurs had a strong orientation to learn through concrete experience.

- The positive relation between entrepreneurs' practical intelligence and new venture growth is stronger when the growth goals are high.[23]

LEARNING OBJECTIVE 4

Identify major personality variables that influence job performance.

A useful takeaway for the individual from this study is that experience helps develop practical intelligence. "Experience" in the study included both longevity and creating new ventures.

For organizations, an important implication about practical intelligence centers on problem-solving ability and age. Analytical intelligence may decline from early to late adulthood. Ability of this type is referred to as *fluid intelligence*, and is needed for on-the-spot reasoning, abstraction, and problem solving. However, the ability to solve problems of a practical nature is maintained or increased through late adulthood. Such ability is referred to as *crystallized intelligence* and centers on accumulated knowledge such as vocabulary, arithmetic, and general information.[24] As people become older, they compensate well for declining raw mental energy by focusing on things they do well. In job situations calling for wisdom, such as resolving conflicts, age and experience may be an advantage.

Personality Differences

Personality characteristics contribute to success in many jobs. Most job failures are not attributed to a person's intelligence or technical competence but to personality characteristics. The subject of personality is therefore important in organizational behavior. However, some controversy still centers on the concept of personality, despite hundreds of studies linking personality to job performance (several are referred to later). There is disagreement as to whether personality can be accurately measured and whether it is influenced more by heredity or environment.

---

23   J. Robert Baum, Barbara Jean Bird, and Sheetal Singh, "The Practical Intelligence of Entrepreneurs: Antecedents and a Link with New Venture Growth," *Personnel Psychology*, No. 2, 2011, pp. 397–425.

24   Tomoe Kanaya, Matthew H. Sculin, and Stephen J. Ceci, "The Flynn Effect and U.S. Policies," *American Psychologist*, October 2003, p. 779.

personality The persistent and enduring behavior patterns of an individual that are expressed in a wide variety of situations.

Personality refers to the persistent and enduring behavior patterns of an individual that are expressed in a wide variety of situations. Your personality is the combination of attributes, traits, and characteristics that make you unique. Your walk, talk, appearance, speech, and creativity all contribute to your personality. Personality can therefore be regarded as the core of who you are.[25]

We approach the topic of personality by first describing nine key personality traits related to job performance and behavior, including a sampling of relevant research. Two experiential activities related to personality will also be presented.

Rawpixel/Shutterstock.com

Our personality influences our interactions with coworkers.

Nine Major Personality Factors and Traits

According to the Five Factor Model (also known as the *Big Five*) of personality, the basic structure of human personality is represented by five broad factors: neuroticism, extraversion, openness to experience, agreeableness, and conscientiousness. Each factor has more narrow traits that make up the factors. Although the Five Factor Model of personality is well documented, other aspects of personality still have merit. We therefore present

---

25   "From 'Character' to 'Personality,'" *APA Monitor*, December 1999, p. 22.

four other traits of particular significance to job behavior: self-monitoring, risk taking and thrill seeking, optimism versus pessimism, and narcissism.

People develop all traits to different degrees, partially from growing up in a particular environment. For example, a person might have a natural tendency to be agreeable. An environment in which agreeableness was encouraged would help him or her become even more agreeable.

All nine traits have a substantial impact on job behavior and performance. The interpretation and meaning of these traits provide useful information because they help to pinpoint areas for personal development. Although these traits are partially inherited, most people can improve their development of them.

1. *Neuroticism (low emotional stability).* This trait reflects neuroticism versus emotional stability. People with high neuroticism are prone to psychological distress and coping with problems in unproductive ways. Traits associated with this personality factor include being anxious, insecure, angry, embarrassed, and worried. A person of low neuroticism — or high emotional stability — is calm and confident, and usually in control.

2. *Extraversion.* Traits associated with extraversion include being social, gregarious, assertive, talkative, and active. An outgoing person is often described as extraverted, whereas a shy person is described as introverted. Many successful leaders are extraverted, yet some effective leaders are introverted because they rely on other factors such as giving feedback and encouraging others. (Note that *extraversion* in everyday language is spelled *extroversion*.) Introversion is associated with work activities requiring critical and analytical thinking such as computer programming and engineering.

3. *Openness to experience.* People who score high with openness have well-developed intellects. Traits associated with this factor include being imaginative, cultured, curious, original, broadminded, intelligent, and artistically sensitive. Many successful managers and professionals search printed information and the Internet for useful ideas. Also, many top-level executives support the arts.

4. *Agreeableness.* This factor reflects the quality of a person's interpersonal orientation. An agreeable person is friendly and cooperative. Traits associated with the agreeableness factor include being courteous, flexible, trusting, good natured, cooperative, forgiving, softhearted, and tolerant. Agreeableness is a plus for customer service positions, such as a hotel receptionist.

Introversion can be an asset for performing analytical work.

Blend Images/Shutterstock.com

Conscientiousness is a key personality characteristic for helping others.

5 *Conscientiousness.* A variety of meanings have been attached to the conscientious factor, but it generally implies dependability. Studies of conscientiousness suggest it consists of six sub-factors: industriousness, order, self-control, responsibility, traditionalism, and virtue.[26] Other related traits include being hardworking, achievement oriented, and persevering. Being conscientious to the extreme, however, can lead to workaholism and perfectionism. Take the "Self-Assessment 2-1" quiz to think about your tendencies toward being conscientious.

6 *Self-monitoring behavior.* The self-monitoring trait refers to the process of observing and controlling how we appear to others. High self-monitors are pragmatic and are even chameleon-like actors in social groups. They often say what others want to hear. Low self-monitors avoid situations that require them to adopt different outer images. In this way, their outer behavior adheres to their inner values. Low self-monitoring can often lead to inflexibility. People who are skilled at office politics usually score high on the self-monitoring factor.

7 *Risk taking and thrill seeking.* Some people crave constant excitement on the job and are willing to risk their lives to achieve thrills. The willingness to take risks and pursue thrills is a personality trait that has grown in importance in the high-technology era. Many people work for employers, start businesses, and purchase stocks with uncertain futures. Both the search for giant payoffs and daily thrills motivate these individuals.

A strong craving for thrills may have some positive consequences for the organization, including the willingness to perform dangerous feats such as setting explosives, capping an oil well, controlling a radiation leak, or introducing a product in a highly competitive environment. However, extreme risk takers and thrill seekers can create problems such as involvement in a disproportionate number of vehicular accidents and imprudent investments. Take the "Self-Assessment 2-2" quiz to measure your tendency toward risk taking.

8 *Optimism* refers to a tendency to experience positive emotional states, and to typically believe that positive outcomes will be forthcoming from most activities. The other end

26 Brent W. Roberts, Oleksandr S. Chernyshenko, Stephen Stark, and Lewis R. Goldberg, "The Structure of Conscientiousness: An Empirical Investigation Based on Seven Major Personality Questionnaires," *Personnel Psychology*, Spring 2005, pp. 103–139.

of the scale is *pessimism*—a tendency to experience negative emotional states, and to typically believe that negative outcomes will be forthcoming from most activities. Optimism versus pessimism is also referred to in more technical terms as *positive*

Self-Assessment 2-1

The Conscientiousness Quiz

Indicate the extent to which each of the following statements describes your behavior or attitude by circling one number. The numbers refer to Very Inaccurate (VI), Moderately Inaccurate (MI), Neither accurate nor inaccurate (N), Moderately Accurate (MA), and Very Accurate (VA). Consider enlisting the help of someone who knows your behavior and attitudes well to help you respond accurately to the statements.

STATEMENT RELATED TO CONSCIENTIOUSNESS	VI	MI	N	MA	VA
1. I follow almost all rules on the job.	1	2	3	4	5
2. People who know me consider me to be quite dependable.	1	2	3	4	5
3. I frequently cut corners.	5	4	3	2	1
4. I am very involved in my work.	1	2	3	4	5
5. I go about my work methodically.	1	2	3	4	5
6. If somebody doesn't like the work I perform, it's that person's problem, not mine.	5	4	3	2	1
7. I typically plan my workday.	1	2	3	4	5
8. I attempt to avoid working too hard, so I have energy left over for life outside of work.	5	4	3	2	1
9. I go about my work with a sense of urgency.	1	2	3	4	5
10. I would strive for excellent performance only if I thought it would lead to a salary increase or bonus.	5	4	3	2	1
11. While at work, I regularly check personal e-mails, text messages, or my favorite websites.	5	4	3	2	1
12. I think I am much better organized than most of my coworkers.	1	2	3	4	5
13. I strive hard to reach the goals my supervisor has established for me.	1	2	3	4	5
14. I strive hard to reach the goals I have established for myself.	1	2	3	4	5
15. I lose patience easily when I am attempting to solve a difficult problem.	5	4	3	2	1

Scoring and Interpretation: Calculate your score by adding up the numbers circled:

60–75: You are a highly conscientious person who is probably also self-disciplined.

45–59: You have an average degree of conscientiousness, including dependability.

15–44: You are below average in conscientiousness, dependability, and self-discipline. Solicit feedback from others to see if this low score is warranted. If the score is accurate, strive to become more conscientious in order to do well in your career.

Self-Assessment 2-2

The Risk-Taking Scale

Answer true or false to the following questions to obtain an approximate idea of your tendency to take risks, or your desire to do so:

	TRUE	FALSE
1. I send and receive text messages while driving.	☐	☐
2. I think that amusement park roller coasters should be abolished.	☐	☐
3. I don't like trying foods from other cultures.	☐	☐
4. I would choose bonds over growth stocks.	☐	☐
5. I like to challenge people in positions of power.	☐	☐
6. I will eat fruit from a store or street vendor without first washing it.	☐	☐
7. I sometimes talk on my cell phone while driving at highway speeds.	☐	☐
8. I would love to be an entrepreneur (or I love being one).	☐	☐
9. I would like helping out in a crisis such as a product recall.	☐	☐
10. I would like to go cave exploring (or already have done so).	☐	☐
11. I would be willing to have at least 1/3 of my compensation based on a bonus for good performance.	☐	☐
12. I would be willing to visit a maximum-security prison on a job assignment.	☐	☐

Key: 1. T; 2. F; 3. F; 4. F; 5. T; 6. T; 7. T; 8. T; 9. T; 10. T; 11. T; 12. T.

Give yourself one point each time your answer agrees with the key. If you score 10–12, you are probably a high risk taker; 6–9: you're a moderate risk taker; 3–5: you are cautious; 0–2: you're a very low risk taker.

Source: The idea of a test about risk-taking comfort, as well as several of the statements on the quiz, come from psychologist Frank Farley.

affectivity versus *negative affectivity*, and is considered a major personality trait. A person's tendency toward having positive affectivity (optimism) versus negative affectivity (pessimism) also influences job satisfaction. Being optimistic, as you would suspect, tends to enhance job satisfaction.[27] An appropriate degree of pessimism is helpful in many job situations, including being willing to point out a flaw in a group decision.[28]

27 Remus Ilies and Timothy A. Judge, "On the Heritability of Job Satisfaction: The Mediating Role of Personality," *Journal of Applied Psychology*, August 2003, pp. 750–759.

28 Research reported in Sumathi Reddy, "A Perfect Dose of Pessimism": Is the Glass Half Full? Or Empty?" *The Wall Street Journal*, August 5, 2014, p. D1.

9   *Narcissism* refers to an extremely positive and inflated view of the self, combined with limited empathy for others. The narcissist is self-absorbed, self-adoring, and self-centered, and has a grandiose preoccupation with his or her importance. In recent years, narcissism in the workplace has been researched because of its relationship with job performance for a wide variety of people whose work involves considerable interaction with others, including leaders. With a reasonable dose of narcissism, a person can be productive in a high-level position, such as a charismatic leader being self-confident, self-promoting, and flamboyant.[29]

Although personality is relatively stable, current research suggests that, as measured by the Five-Factor Model, some aspects of personality improve with age. Based on a sample of 132,000 subjects who took the personality tests on the Internet, it appears that people generally become more responsible, organized, and focused with age. The study examined traits over time. Conscientiousness tended to increase in adulthood, particularly in a person's 20s. Both men and women scored higher on agreeableness and openness as they reached age 30. Later research on the subject found that between the ages of 20 and 65, people perceive themselves to be stronger on positive traits, such as conscientiousness, and also to improve on negative traits, particularly in becoming less neurotic.[30] Personality theorists call this improvement in personality the *Maturity Principle*.[31] Readers interested in testing themselves on the Five Factor Model of personality can visit www.outofservice.com.

Research Evidence about Personality and Job Behavior Performance

Depending on the job, any one of the nine personality factors mentioned previously can be important for good job performance. The most consistent finding is that conscientiousness is positively related to job performance for a variety of occupations. Furthermore, the combination of intelligence ("can do") with conscientiousness ("will do") is especially important for job performance. In a study of 91 sales representatives for an appliance manufacturer, the combination of intelligence and conscientiousness made accurate predictions of job success. Representatives who scored high on intelligence and conscientiousness tended to sell more appliances and receive better performance ratings from their supervisors. In a related study with the same sales representatives, extraversion was a good predictor of job performance.[32]

You may recall that moderator variables are important in understanding many aspects of organizational behavior, and this proves to be true with conscientiousness. A series of four

---

29   Emily Grijalva and P. D. Harms, "Narcissism: An Integrative Synthesis and Dominance Complementarity Model," *Academy of Management Perspectives*, May 2014, pp. 108–127; Andrew J. DuBrin, *Narcissism in the Workplace: Research, Opinion, and Practice* (Cheltenham, UK: Edward Elgar, 2012), pp. 1, 77.

30   Research reported in Rosemarie Ward, "Ripening with Age: Key Traits Seem to Improve as We Grow Older," *Psychology Today*, July/August 2003, p. 12.

31   Elizabeth Bernstein, "We Actually Get Nicer With Age," *The Wall Street Journal*, April 22, 2014, p. D1.

32   These studies and similar ones are reviewed in Leonard D. Goodstein and Richard I. Lanyon, "Applications of Personality Assessment to the Workplace: A Review," *Journal of Business and Psychology*, Spring 1999, pp. 293–298.

studies of several different occupations found that workers needed good social skills for conscientiousness to be related to aspects of job performance and to interpersonal effectiveness.[33] For example, a conscientious sales rep still needs good social skill to close deals.

A meta-analysis of 73 studies demonstrated a relationship between the Five Factor Model and the two criteria of leadership effectiveness and stepping forth as a leader. Extraversion was the factor most frequently associated with the two leadership criteria.[34]

Self-monitoring is another personality factor whose relationship to job behavior has been supported by extensive research. Meta-analyses were conducted for 136 samples and over 23,000 employees to understand the relationship between work-related behaviors and self-monitoring. It was found that high self-monitors tend to receive better performance ratings and more promotions than low self-monitors. High self-monitors were also more likely to emerge as leaders.[35] In short, it pays to tell people what they want to hear if you want to succeed in business.

The "Organizational Behavior in Action" box illustrates how some companies rely on personality measures for key work assignments.

A major consideration about the relationship between personality and job performance is that most traits have a *curvilinear relationship* with job performance. A curvilinear relationship means that an optimum amount of trait helps job performance, whereas being too low or too high with that trait might impair job performance. The optimum level is seen as having the ideal amount of a personality trait that enhances job performance, such as a manager having the right amount of extraversion to be warm toward people, yet still be a good listener and a careful thinker.[36]

Imagine a truck driver who is very low on conscientiousness. He or she will often be late with deliveries based on a lack of concern for timeliness. A driver with the right degree of conscientiousness will strive to be on time and overcome minor hurdles, such as a traffic jam. A superconscientious driver might get into trouble in an effort to deliver the truckload of goods on time, such as attempting to drive through a blinding snowstorm and having an accident as a result.

A group of researchers conducted two studies in several work settings that generally supported the idea that both conscientiousness and emotional stability (low neuroticism) had a curvilinear relationship with job performance. One interpretation of their results was that workers who are too high on conscientiousness are rigid and inflexible. It is also conceivable that persons with very high emotional stability might become a little anxious when needed, such as worrying about achieving a sales quota. Another finding of the study was that the curvilinear relationship was less likely to

33   L. A. Witt and Gerald R. Ferris, "Social Skill as Moderator of the Conscientiousness-Performance Relationship: Convergent Results across Four Studies," *Journal of Applied Psychology*, October 2003, pp. 809–820.

34   Timothy A. Judge, Joyce E. Bono, Remus Ilies, and Megan W. Gerhardt, "Personality and Leadership: A Quantitative and Qualitative Review," *Journal of Applied Psychology*, August 2002, pp. 765–780.

35   David B. Day, Deidra J. Schleicher, Amy L. Unckless, and Nathan J. Hiller, "Self-Monitoring Personality at Work: A Meta-Analytic Investigation of Construct Validity," *Journal of Applied Psychology*, April 2002, pp. 390–401.

36   Nathan T. Carter et al., "Uncovering Curvilinear Relationships between Conscientiousness and Job Performance: How Theoretically Appropriate Measurement Makes a Difference," *Journal of Applied Psychology*, July 2014, pp. 564–586.

Organizational Behavior in Action

Wealth Management Group Places More Emphasis on Introversion for Financial Consultants

The Wealth Management Group of a major national bank is responsible for managing the investment portfolios of bank clients with financial assets of a minimum of $1 million, not including the value of the client's residence. The financial consultants almost all have degrees in business or finance and usually have a minimum of ten years' experience in banking and finance before working in the wealth-management group.

Applicants for wealth-management specialist positions (the financial consultants) are chosen also on the basis of their personalities. Using both interview impressions and personality test results, extraversion is considered to be an important criterion for success as a financial consultant. The reasoning offered by bank executives and the HR department is that a wealth manager has to be friendly toward clients, and also be assertive enough to sell them investments.

Bank management began to observe that the wealth-management group did not appear to be attaining higher sales than comparable groups in other banks or at brokerage firms. Some data even suggested that the wealth-management financial consultants were performing at a below-average level. Top-level executives working with the HR group decided to hire an outside talent selection specialist to examine their selection criteria for financial consultants.

The outside specialist concluded that the bank was basing its selection decisions somewhat on inaccurate stereotypes of a financial consultant's role. She noted that a financial consultant in a wealth-management group should be extraverted enough to be warm and supportive toward clients. Yet, at the same time, the wealth managers should have a few qualities of the introvert, such as carefully listening to clients, and being quite reflective and deliberate when making recommendations about investments.

Working with HR, the director of the wealth-management group made two key changes. One would be that any new financial consultants to be hired for the group should be a mix of extraversion and introversion. The other initiative was to conduct interpersonal skill training for all wealth-management specialists in the art of carefully listening to clients, and appearing to be more reflective and somber when making recommendations.

A review of results 18 months after modifying the selection criteria for financial consultants and offering training about being more introverted, suggested that the approach was providing good financial results. Revenue to the bank improved 12 percent, and loss of clients was reduced by 9 percent.

LEARNING OBJECTIVE 5

Explain how emotional intelligence is an important part of organizational behavior.

Questions

1 In what type of selling do you think a high degree of extraversion would be a strong asset?

2 Visualize yourself as a wealth-management client. Explain whether you think that it would benefit you if your financial consultant was a balanced blend of extraversion and introversion.

Source: Original story with a couple of facts derived from the following sources: Deb Koen, "Introverts Can Leverage Skills to Succeed," *Democrat and Chronicle,* March 20, 2013. p. 5B; Sumhathi Reddy, "How an Introvert Can Be Happier: Act Like an Extrovert," *The Wall Street Journal,* July 28, 2013, pp. D1, D2.

appear for jobs of high complexity.[37] So don't worry if your computer security specialist or brain surgeon is highly conscientious and emotionally stable.

In general, favorable results when using personality measures to predict job performance are more likely to occur when the job requirements are carefully analyzed. For example, agreeableness is more important for an airline reservations assistant than a Web designer. Another essential requirement for the use of personality testing for job selection and the development of employees is that the test be scientifically constructed by experts in human behavior. Robert Hogan, a leader in the field of personality assessment in industry, contends that only a handful of personality tests are legitimate in terms of being substantiated by research.[38]

The role-plays in the "Skill-Development Exercise" give you an opportunity to practice managing for individual differences in personality. Remember that a role player is an extemporaneous actor. Put yourself in the shoes of the character you play and visualize how he or she would act. Because you are given only the general idea of a script, use your imagination to fill in the details.

Emotional Intelligence

Research into the functioning of the human brain has combined personality factors with practical intelligence, indicating that people's effective use

---

37 Huy Le et al., "Too Much of a Good Thing: Curvilinear Relationships between Personality Traits and Job Performance," *Journal of Applied Psychology,* January 2011, pp. 113–133.

38 Cited in Arielle Emmett, "Snake Oil or Science? That's the Raging Debate on Personality Testing," *Workforce Management,* October 2004, p. 90.

of their emotions has a major impact on their success. The topmost layers of the brain govern componential intelligence functions, such as analytical problem solving. The innermost areas of the brain govern emotional functions, such as dealing with anger when being criticized by a customer.

Emotional intelligence refers to qualities such as understanding one's own feelings, empathy for others, and the regulation of emotion to enhance living. As the concept of emotional intelligence has gained in popularity, many definitions have been proposed and more and more behavior has

emotional intelligence Qualities such as understanding one's own feelings, empathy for others, and the regulation of emotion to enhance living.

Skill-Development Exercise

Personality Role-Plays

Run each role-play for about 7 minutes. The people not involved in the role-play will observe and then provide feedback when the role-play is completed.

1. *Narcissism.* One student plays the role of a worker whose creative ideas for saving the company about $1 million annually on shipping costs have resulted in a cash bonus and a letter of appreciation from the CEO. He decides to share this good news with a coworker who is a total narcissist, interested in talking about only his or her personal accomplishments. Another student plays the role of the narcissist.

2. *Openness.* One student plays the role of an experienced worker in the department who is told to spend some time showing around a new coop student. It appears that this worker is open to experience. Another student plays the role of the co-op student, who is also open to experience and eager to be successful in this new position.

3. *Conscientiousness.* One student plays the role of a team member who is dependent on another team member for his or her contribution to a team project for which the entire team will receive the same grade. The second student was to have collected extensive data about how energy companies establish wholesale and retail prices for gasoline, but is not ready with the input. The first team member has observed from the start of the group project that the second team member is the opposite of a conscientious person. The report is due in 5 days, and the professor is known for not accepting excuses for late papers.

been incorporated into the concept. Emotional intelligence has to do with the ability to connect with people and understand their emotions. A worker with high emotional intelligence can engage in behaviors such as sizing up, pleasing, and influencing people.

Tests of emotional intelligence typically ask you to respond to questions on a 1 to 5 scale (never, rarely, sometimes, often, consistently). For example, indicate how frequently you demonstrate the following behaviors:

I can laugh at myself.	1	2	3	4	5
I help others grow and develop.	1	2	3	4	5
I watch carefully the nonverbal communication of others.	1	2	3	4	5

Emotional intelligence is regarded by some researchers as an ability that focuses on the recognition and control of personal emotion. The person who insults the boss during a group meeting would be deficient in this regard. Researchers also view emotional intelligence as a combination of intellect and various personal traits and emotion.[39] Among the traits included in this approach would be insensitivity, such as making a derogatory comment about a coworker's hairstyle. Reflecting the broader view of emotional intelligence, Daniel Goleman and his associates regard this type of intelligence to include four key factors:[40]

1   *Self-awareness.* The ability to understand one's own emotions is the most essential of the four emotional intelligence competencies. Having high self-awareness allows people to know their strengths and limitations and have high self-esteem. Effective individual contributors use self-awareness to accurately measure their own moods, and to intuitively understand how their moods affect others. Effective managers seek feedback to see how well their actions are received by others. A manager with good self-awareness would recognize factors such as whether he or she was liked, or was exerting the right amount of pressure on people.

Rawpixel/Shutterstock.com

Emotional intelligence helps us interact smoothly with others.

2   *Self-management.* The ability to control one's emotions and act with honesty and integrity in a consistent and adaptable manner is important. The right

39   Dana L. Joseph and Daniel A. Newman, "Emotional Intelligence: An Integrative Meta-Analysis and Cascading Model," *Journal of Applied Psychology*, January 2010, pp. 54–78.
40   Daniel Goleman, Richard Boyatzis, and Annie McKee, "Primal Leadership: The Hidden Driver of Great Performance," *Harvard Business Review*, December 2001, pp. 42–51.

degree of self-management helps prevent a person from throwing temper tantrums when activities do not go as planned. Effective workers do not let their occasional bad moods ruin their day. If they cannot overcome the bad mood, they let work associates know of the problem and how long it might last. A manager with high self-management would not suddenly decide to fire a group member because of one difference of opinion.

3   *Social awareness.* Having empathy for others and having intuition about organizational problems are key aspects of this dimension of emotional intelligence. Socially aware leaders go beyond sensing the emotions of others by showing that they care. In addition, they accurately size up political forces in the office. A team leader with social awareness, or empathy, would be able to assess whether a team member has enough enthusiasm for a project to assign him or her to that project. A CEO who has empathy for a labor union's demands might be able to negotiate successfully with the head of the labor union to avoid a costly strike.

4   *Relationship management.* This includes the interpersonal skills of being able to communicate clearly and convincingly, disarm conflicts, and build strong personal bonds. Effective leaders use relationship management skills to spread their enthusiasm and solve disagreements, often with kindness and humor. A corporate professional with good relationship management skills would not burn bridges and would continue to enlarge his or her network of people to win support when support is needed.

Among the many practical outcomes of having high emotional intelligence is the ability to cope better with setbacks. A review of many studies concluded that low emotional intelligence employees are more likely than their high emotional intelligence counterparts to experience negative emotional reactions to job insecurity, such as high tension. Furthermore, workers with low emotional intelligence are more likely to engage in negative coping behaviors, such as expressing anger and verbally abusing an immediate supervisor for the organization failing to provide job security.[41]

A concern about the validity of the concept of emotional intelligence is that a person with good cognitive intelligence would also engage in many of the behaviors of an emotionally intelligent person. Another concern is that the popularized concept of emotional intelligence has become so broad it encompasses almost the entire study of personality. Some approaches to presenting emotional intelligence appear to present a long list of desirable qualities, such as resiliency and vision.[42]

Emotional intelligence underscores the importance of being practical minded and having effective interpersonal skills to succeed in organizational life. Many topics included in the study of organizational behavior, such as communication, conflict resolution, and power and politics,

---

41   Peter J. Jordan, Neal M. Ashkanasy, and Charmine E. J. Hartel, "Emotional Intelligence as a Moderator of Emotional and Behavioral Reactions to Job Insecurity," *Academy of Management Review,* July 2002, pp. 361–372.
42   Gerald Matthews, Moshe Zeidner, and Richard Roberts, *Emotional Intelligence: Science and Myth* (Cambridge, MA: The MIT Press, 2003), p. 531.

are components of emotional intelligence. The message is an old one: Both cognitive and non-cognitive skills are required for success!

Implications for Managerial Practice

A major implication of individual differences in cognitive ability and personality is that these factors have a major impact on the selection, placement, job assignment, training, and development of employees. When faced with such decisions, the manager should seek answers to such questions as the following:

- Is this employee intelligent enough to handle the job and deal with out-of-the-ordinary problems?

- Is this employee too intelligent for the assignment? Will he or she become bored quickly?

- Is this employee's personality suited to the assignment? For instance, is the employee conscientious enough? Is the employee open to new learning?

How to Become a Better Leader

Ginka Toegel and Jean-Louis Barsoux

Good leaders make their work look easy. But the reality is that most have had to work hard on themselves — by managing or compensating for potentially career-limiting traits. To grow as an executive, you need to recognize and manage your strongest tendencies.

By Ginka Toegel and Jean-Louis Barsoux

When executives identify a leader they admire, they often underestimate how much that individual may have struggled to curb certain patterns of behavior or certain dominant facets of his or her personality. Great leaders make it look easy. But in truth, the majority of effective leaders that we have observed — even so-called naturals like Virgin Group's Richard Branson — have worked hard on themselves.

The traits that serve an executive well in one leadership position often do not work well in another. Moving up the hierarchy into new roles or environments, executives may find they need to play up or rein in different facets of their personality. What were strengths can become weaknesses.

Fortunately, advances in personality research can provide executives with a much richer picture of their personality. Psychologists have identified countless traits that distinguish individuals from one another. Research in recent decades has converged toward five broad dimensions, each comprising a cluster of traits. These dimensions appear so robust that they have been dubbed the Big Five. Now widely accepted, the

THE LEADING QUESTION

How can leaders recognize and manage their psychological preferences?

FINDINGS

- Executives need to understand their natural inclinations in order to modify them or compensate for them.
- Most successful executives have had to work hard on themselves.
- Leaders need to recognize their outlier tendencies and learn how others perceive those tendencies.

same five factors are found consistently with different research methods, as well as across time, contexts and cultures. (See "The Making of the Big Five," p. 53.)

In contrast with other models of personality, the Big Five were derived from the everyday language that people use to describe one another. Starting with a master list of nearly 18,000 personality descriptors, the list was eventually boiled down to five fundamental factors: need for stability,[1] extraversion, openness, agreeableness and conscientiousness.

Of course, personality scores are not performance scores; no personality traits lead directly to positive or negative performance. However, those scores can alert executives to areas that require attention. A trait that is effective in one context may become redundant or counterproductive when the situation changes.[2] (See "The Curse of Your Qualities," p. 54.)

Common Leadership Pitfalls

Leaders at all levels are under intense pressure to push harder and go faster. Under these conditions, executives sometimes have difficulty controlling their inherent psychological preferences. And the higher they go in an organization, the more their behaviors come under scrutiny and influence others.

Drawing on our extensive coaching work with senior executives, we identify some of the most common leadership pitfalls associated with high and low scores on each of the Big Five personality dimensions. (See "About the Research.") We offer a mix of testimony from high-profile executives and anonymous quotes from executives we have coached to illustrate those potential hazards and how to deal with them. (See "Risks and Remedies, p. 55.")

1. Need for Stability

How Much Stress is Too Much?

Emotional stability can be a valuable quality for executives, helping them cope with stress, setbacks and uncertainty. But it has its drawbacks, too.

---

1 Labels for the Big Five have varied, particularly the "N" dimension, which is also known as "negative emotionality" or "neuroticism." We prefer the more neutral term "need for stability."
2 T.A. Judge, R.F. Piccolo and T. Kosalka, "The Bright and Dark Sides of Leader Traits: A Review and Theoretical Extension of the Leader Trait Paradigm," Leadership Quarterly 20, no. 6 (December 2009): 855–875.

About The Research

The research for this article is based on findings from more than 2,000 in-depth conversations with international executives regarding their personality scores. These interviews were conducted by us separately, while the executives were attending leadership programs at Duke University, London Business School and IMD.

We used the NEO PI-R five-factor instrument, which has become the dominant framework for researching personality and a staple ingredient in many leadership development programs. (Executives who have not been exposed to it can assess themselves free on a noncommercial version of the test, IPIP, available at http:// www. personalitytest.net/ipip/ipipneo1.htm.)

The personality inventory comprises 30 facets, but not all of these are equally relevant to the work environment. Based on our experience, particularly Ginka Toegel's previous work as a practicing psychotherapist, we spent 80% of the time in our one-to-one sessions talking about 15 of those dimensions, which we believe represent the top challenges for most executives.

The confidential nature of these sessions prevent us from naming the executives, so we cite them anonymously. We also draw on publicly available interviews with high-profile business figures. Although we did not conduct Big Five personality inventories with these leaders, their comments reflect key insights about personality traits that they learned to manage as they moved into positions of leadership.

You can be too composed. Poise under pressure helps executives project a reassuring image when others may be inclined to panic. Many executives we coach pride themselves on their ability to remain calm. The risk of this trait is that they can appear uninspiring or lacking in urgency. They may have difficulty understanding why others are worried.

Moreover, such executives may come across as unduly confident. One strategy to counter over-optimism is to create mental lists. Alongside three hopeful reasons for why something will work out, an executive prone to overoptimism should come up with three gloomy reasons why it may not.

Or you can be too impatient—and overreact. Sometimes successful executives have a pronounced tendency to be impatient. Robert Iger, CEO of Walt Disney, has acknowledged in an article in the *New York Times* that this is an area he's worked on: "I've learned, in general, to be more patient. ... I've learned to listen better and manage reaction time better. What I mean by that is not overreacting to things that are said to me, because sometimes it's easy to do that."[3]

Certain executives we coach are less resilient to stress and struggle to stay calm, reflecting a high need for stability. Too often, they deal with their anger by suppressing it. The problem is

---

3   A. Bryant, "He Was Promotable, After All," New York Times, May 2, 2009, 2.

The Making of the Big Five

Psychologists have identified countless personality traits and dimensions that distinguish us from one another. But research in recent years has converged toward five broad dimensions, each comprising a cluster of traits that account for the majority of the differences among individual personalities. These dimensions have been dubbed the Big Five.

Although researchers did not set out to find five dimensions, that is what emerged from their analyses of the data. The line of research began with Gordon Allport and Harold Odbert, who scoured dictionaries to identify 17,953 words in everyday language that people use to describe one another and published their results in 1936. That master list was reduced, in several stages, until it was eventually boiled down to just five dimensions in 1961 by two U.S. Air Force researchers, who had rare access to mainframe computers. Unfortunately, their findings failed to reach an academic audience until the 1980s. At that point, the introduction of the personal computer and the availability of specialized software enabled other research teams to factor analyze the data and confirm the existence of five overarching domains. The first inventory based on the Big Five factors was launched by Paul T. Costa, Jr. and Robert R. McCrae in 1985.[i] These five factors have since proved a rich conceptual framework for integrating diverse research findings and theory in personality psychology.

The stronger the trait, the more likely it is that the person in question will display trait-related behaviors in terms of how he or she relates to people, solves problems, plans work and expresses himself or herself. Investigations into where those traits actually come from suggest that around half of the variance is inherited and the other half is acquired through experience, especially in early childhood.[ii] Though major life crises occasionally produce shifts on some personality dimensions, most changes in adulthood tend to be gradual and limited.[iii]

---

i.   P.T. Costa and R.R. McCrae, "The NEO Personality Inventory Manual" (Odessa, Florida: Psychological Assessment Resources, 1985).

ii.   T.J. Bouchard Jr. and M. McGue, "Genetic and Environmental Influences on Human Psychological Differences," Journal of Neurobiology 54, no. 1 (January 2003): 4–45.

iii.   J. Specht, B. Egloff and S.C. Schmukle, "Stability and Change of Personality Across the Life Course: The Impact of Age and Major Life Events on Mean-Level and Rank-Order Stability of the Big Five," Journal of Personality and Social Psychology 101, no. 4 (October 2011): 862–882.

that the anger can accumulate unseen and unexpressed until it spills over on an unsuspecting victim. To avoid overreacting, executives need to find ways of emptying their anger container before it reaches the brim. The simplest method is to verbalize those negative emotions: "I feel disappointed/frustrated/upset/irritated because … ." Research in brain imaging suggests that putting our feelings into words dampens those feelings.

Whether stating an emotion or writing it in a journal, the simple act of expressing it activates a region of the brain involved in forms of self-control and self-regulation.[4] It is a bit like drilling a hole in the side of the anger container. Executives sometimes worry that verbalizing emotion will make them look weak. In fact, it conveys confidence. It expels negative energy while providing others with a better understanding of how the executive ticks.

2. Extraversion

How Much Company is Too Much?

Extraversion reflects our desire to be with other people and to draw energy from them. Leadership is about influencing people, so it can be an advantage to be outgoing, assertive and energetic. There is strong evidence that these characteristics help executives to be perceived as leaderlike.[5] The association with effective leadership is much weaker.[6]

You can be too assertive—or too energetic. High scores on the extraversion dimension can trigger perceptions that the executive is too talkative or domineering—with the added implication that he or she tends not to listen. Many executives face this challenge, including the country manager of a global foods giant we coached. Discussing his proposed action plan, he conceded: "I've realized that I have a habit of taking over in meetings. I want to get better at listening and to give less assertive people more space to express their opinions. So I need to listen more, but I also need to show I have processed what they've said. The personality scores just confirm feedback I've received in the past but not paid much attention to."

A simple remedy for executives with a tendency to dominate proceedings is the "four sentence" rule: Whatever you have to say, limit yourself to four sentences. Then ask: "Do you want me to carry on?"

Another facet of extraversion is higher activity levels. This would seem to be an advantage in terms of inspiring others, but it can prove wearing. This was a key learning point for a senior executive from the retail sector, who told us: "There's a fine dividing line between energetic and frenetic—and I probably overstep that boundary on occasion. In the process, you end up

---

4   M.D. Lieberman and N.I. Eisenberger, "Neuroscience: Pain and Pleasures of Social Life," Science 323, no. 5916 (Feb. 13, 2009): 890–891.

5   R. Hogan, G.J. Curphy and J. Hogan, "What We Know About Leadership: Effectiveness and Personality," American Psychologist 49, no. 6 (June 1994): 493–504.

6   T. A. Judge, J.E. Bono, R. Ilies and M.W. Gerhardt, "Personality and Leadership," Journal of Applied Psychology 87, no. 4 (August 2002): 765–780.

creating chaos and unsettling people, rather than invigorating them." Fast-paced people need to recognize others' needs and adapt their energy levels accordingly.

In particular, leaders with high energy levels need to be aware that this disposition can create tension with slower-paced people, especially those whom the leaders regard as slow-minded or uncommitted. Worse, these slower-paced individuals may then underperform, living down to the executive's diminished expectations.[7] As a senior executive from the finance sector told us: "Whenever I had to meet with [one unhurried colleague], he would absolutely suck the life out of me. I just tried to avoid dealing with him. But then we were mandated to work on the same cross-functional team and I realized that beneath that leisurely exterior was a very sharp mind. I've become much more accepting of his ways because of what he can bring to the table."

Or you can be too introspective. Executives who are more internally focused often need to learn to behave like extraverts—to adopt behaviors that are more communicative, to give presentations and to socialize.

Constant communication can be draining for those who have some introverted tendencies. Take the example of Carol Bartz, the former CEO of Yahoo. She described herself as "kind of a borderline extrovert-introvert" in an interview with the *San Francisco Chronicle* in 2004. As Bartz told the *Chronicle*, "I recharge my batteries by getting a little alone time and gardening. ... Introverts refresh by having some time to themselves."[8]

Executives who are both reserved and serious often wear solemn facial expressions. They may be given to frowning or pursing their lips. One remedy for solemn-looking executives is to find an object that prompts them to think about their facial expression.

We suggest they buy a mug, perhaps with a humorous motto on it, to carry around with them. And this mug is a reminder: "What is your expression right now?" The idea is not to smile if you don't feel like it—just to remember to relax your facial muscles. Relaxing (and smiling) has been shown to have a physiological impact, not only on the executive but also on colleagues, who tend to mirror the emotion.[9]

3. Openness

How Much Newness is Too Much?

Openness includes people's tendency to show intellectual curiosity, independence of judgment and big-picture orientation. Higher scores on these dimensions have value for leadership roles.[10] But they don't necessarily help the leader connect with others.

---

7   J.-F. Manzoni and J.-L. Barsoux, "The Set-Up-to-Fail Syndrome" (Boston: Harvard Business School Press, 2007).

8   K. Howe, "On the Record: Carol Bartz," San Francisco Chronicle, Feb. 15, 2004, sec. I, p. 1.

9   A. Erez, V.F. Misangyi, D. E. Johnson, M.A. LePine and K. C. Halverson, "Stirring the Hearts of Followers: Charismatic Leadership as the Transferal of Affect," Journal of Applied Psychology 93, no. 3 (May 2008): 602–616.

10   Judge et al., "Personality and Leadership."

You can be too innovative or too complex. Speculating on alternative viewpoints and seeking additional perspectives can be frustrating for colleagues who are looking for clarity, consistency and direction. If the leader is easily drawn into "what if" discussions, it can be very unsettling. In the *Harvard Business Review*, Kevin Sharer, CEO and now chairman of Amgen, noted: "I'm fascinated with long-term strategic alternatives. ... I like to reflect on and talk about those options." But Sharer has realized that when a CEO often discusses possible change, "it can be destabilizing to the organization."

Leaders with this experimental orientation may need someone alongside them to keep them grounded. Sharer has learned to impose his own discipline: "I've decided that I need to look at these big-picture options two or three times a year and then put them away."[11]

Executives who possess a great deal of intellectual curiosity or creativity can also overwhelm others with the complexity or abstraction of what they are trying to communicate. They can end up confusing others rather than enlightening them. They must force themselves to simplify the message and to translate their thoughts into terms that others relate to.

Someone who struggled with overelaborate thinking is Cristóbal Conde, former CEO of Sun-Gard Data Systems. In a *New York Times* article, he recalled a piece of advice he received: "A boss once told me: 'Cris, you're a smart guy, but that doesn't mean that people can absorb a list of 18 things to do. Focus on a handful of things.' Very constructive criticism, and the way I've translated that is, when I do reviews, everything is threes ... three positives and three things they should do differently."[12]

In addition to highlighting the critical objectives, executives inclined to overcomplicate should adopt a coaching-oriented approach, whereby they check that others follow their meaning and have a chance to contribute.

Or you can be too conventional. Leaders at the more conformist end of the spectrum risk coming across as resistant to new ideas. In the words of a chief technology officer we worked with: "I came up through the manufacturing operations. And that suited my temperament. I'm a data guy. I insist on seeing the facts. But now I'm at a [senior] level where people are very willing to share their opinion and expect an opinion. So I've had to teach myself to get out of that conservative zone—and in part, I've done that by volunteering for task forces that give me more of an opportunity to see the big picture."

The challenge for executives uncomfortable with ambiguity is to move when not all the information is available. Leaders understanding this tendency in themselves can work to push themselves out of their comfort zone and build up their openness to new experiences.

---

11 All quotes from P. Hemp, "A Time for Growth," Harvard Business Review 82, no. 7/8 (July/August 2004): 66–74.

12 A. Bryant, "Structure? The Flatter, the Better," New York Times, Jan. 16, 2010, 2.

The Curse of Your Qualities

Each of the Big Five personality dimensions consists of a cluster of traits—and those traits can be perceived as both positive and negative.

BIG FIVE DIMENSION		PERSONALITY TRAITS	CAN BE PERCEIVED AS
Need for Stability	High	Resilient, calm	Unconcerned, uninspiring
	Low	Reactive, excitable	Unstable, insecure
Extraversion	High	Sociable, assertive	Attention-seeking, domineering
	Low	Reserved, reflective	Aloof, self-absorbed
Openness	High	Creative, receptive	Unpredictable, unfocused
	Low	Pragmatic, data-driven	Closed-minded, dogmatic
Agreeableness	High	Compassionate, cooperative	Naïve, submissive
	Low	Competitive, challenging	Argumentative, untrustworthy
Conscientiousness	High	Persistent, driven	Stubborn, obsessive
	Low	Flexible, spontaneous	Sloppy, unreliable
No Strong Preferences (on all five dimensions)		Adaptable, moderate, reasonable	Unprincipled, inscrutable, calculating

4. Agreeableness

How Much Confrontation is Too Much?

Agreeableness is a measure of the importance people place on getting along with others. On the other four dimensions of the Big Five, effective executives typically cluster more on one side of the continuum than the other. With agreeableness, there is no such pattern.[13] The location of the majority varies sharply by national culture, by industry, by company culture and even by function.

To give an extreme example, our coaching work with investment bankers revealed a very low average score on agreeableness. And that is an advantage in an ultracompetitive environment. Executives who score low on agreeableness provide edge and a results focus that is invaluable in business. They are also precious team members, as they are comfortable voicing criticism and disrupting groupthink.

You can be too rational, competitive and watchful. Executives who are tough-minded and direct tend to be unflinching in facing conflict and tough issues. As a senior executive from the luxury goods sector told us: "I'm a straight talker. I have no problem telling people that they messed up—and I'm always puzzled why people make such a big deal out of it. I mean, we're all adults and we're all trying to improve." She has a point, but her failure to comprehend the discomfort felt by others could lead them to see her as blunt or aggressive.

For executives like this, coaching advice often revolves around the issue of how the comments are packaged. The goal is to make it clear that the critique relates to the idea, not the individual submitting it. There are various ways of softening criticism. Executives can take the edge off their remarks by drawing attention to the feedback-providing role they are playing.

---

13   Judge et al., "Personality and Leadership."

Risks and Remedies

Moving up the hierarchy into new roles or environments, executives may find they need to play up or rein in different facets of their personality. What were strengths can become weaknesses.

BIG FIVE DIMENSION	KILLER QUALITY	RISKS OF THAT QUALITY	TIPS FOR SELF-DEVELOPMENT
Need for Stability	High: Too Fiery	• Liable to overreact; short-tempered	• Verbalize emotions. • Drain the "anger container."
	Low: Too Composed	• Seem too laid back; overoptimistic	• Create a mental spreadsheet to highlight the negatives as well as the positives.
Extraversion	High: Too Assertive	• Wearing for those who try to keep up; harsh view of those with low energy	• Create a mental spreadsheet to highlight the negatives as well as the positives.
	High: Too Energetic	• Wearing for those who try to keep up; harsh view of those with low energy	• Reassure others that you don't expect them to keep your pace. • Don't assume people who are slow are also slow-minded.
	Low: Too Introspective	• Socializing is painful. • Serious facial expression can deflate people.	• Create time-outs to recharge. • Find an object that reminds you to relax your face.
Openness	High: Too Innovative	• Unsettling for followers who crave consistency; easily bored	• Find someone to keep you grounded. • Regulate your bouts of creativity.
	High: Too Complex	• Lose people with abstraction or multiple priorities	• Highlight the critical few objectives. • Start from the problem and move to the context, not vice versa.
	Low: Too Conventional	• Uncertainty-avoidant; unwilling to experiment without conclusive data	• Challenge yourself. • Do one thing each day that scares you.
Agreeableness	High: Too Considerate	• Perceived as naïve, easy to manipulatxe, spineless	• Change your mind-set from "I want to be liked" to "I want to be perceived as fair."
	Low: Too Competitive	• Perceived as ruthless, uncaring, self-promoting	• Remember to articulate what's in it for others.
	Low: Too Watchful	• Perceived as political, calculating, untrustworthy	• Tell people about yourself to bond. • Use self-deprecation, including humor.
	Low: Too Rational	• Perceived as blunt, aggressive	• Stress the role you are playing. • Remember the packaging of the message.
Conscientiousness	High: Too Thorough	• Micromanagement inhibits subordinates and delays problem recognition. • Lose sight of the big picture	• Switch to coaching mode and ask questions, rather than making suggestions. • Invite subordinates to challenge your involvement in low-value-adding areas.
	High: Too Committed	• Burnout, work-life balance issues	• Start cutting off 15 minutes from the working day. • Break the "my time is expandable" mentality.
	Low: Too Decisive	• Hasty or seat-of-the pants decisions; too trusting of intuition	• Check the analytics. • Sleep on it. • Appoint a devil's advocate on the team.

Using phrases such as "Let me play devil's advocate for a moment" or "If I put on my critic's hat" is one way to accomplish this. If it is hard to find a diplomatic way of saying what needs saying, executives can preface their comments with an acknowledgment that what follows "may seem harsh."

Similarly, executives with a strong competitive streak can come across as ruthless, uncooperative or lacking in larger perspective. They may get results, but colleagues and subordinates are less likely to trust them. They hence have difficulty building up a strong network; that absence of peer support becomes critical as they reach senior levels. A plant manager in the high-tech sector told us: "When I started as a manager, I was pretty aggressive. I could really intimidate people. But that approach will only take you so far. I think I've gone from making my way by trying to be the smartest guy in the room—constantly picking faults in the arguments of others—to trying more to build on the input of others."

Once he realized the discomfort he was creating for those on the receiving end, that executive changed the way he framed his feedback. Rather than laying into the person's flawed logic, he developed a softer touch, explaining that the proposal was perhaps "not yet ready for prime time." He also worked to suppress his tendency to react to ideas with a sentence starting with the word "but." Instead, he tried to begin his responses with "and," which is more inclusive and constructive.

It can be helpful for leaders to be politically savvy and sensitive to the dynamics of influence within an organization. But leaders with a low need for agreeableness can also be too guarded and somewhat defensive, making it difficult for others to trust them. Consider the experience of a project director from the automobile industry: "By nature, I'm not the most open person," he told us. "But I've worked on lots of projects and I've found that unless I share what I'm thinking, it's very difficult to connect with new teams. They're wary. So at the start of a project, I always tell them something about myself, including my family situation, and some of the things I struggle with. I also make a joke about being German. It kick-starts the relationship."

Or you can be too considerate. Executives on the more agreeable end of the scale are both trusting and trustworthy. They are likely to promote collaboration and to be attentive to others' opinions, development needs and well-being. But agreeable executives can have difficulty delivering negative feedback or making decisions that risk upsetting others. Take the example of Sue Murray, executive director of the George Foundation and former CEO of the National Breast Cancer Foundation. When asked about her greatest weaknesses in the *Age*, she replied: "I can be too nice when tough decisions need to be made, which is not helpful to anyone. It just prolongs the inevitable."[14]

Highly agreeable executives must ask themselves: "Why do I have this need to be liked?" Of course, the answer may go deep into childhood, but posing the question at least launches the reflection process. More practically, we encourage these executives to switch mind-sets from "I want to be liked" to "I want to be perceived as fair." Research by organizational behavior

---

14   L. Mitchell, "Ten Things I Don't Put on My CV: Sue Murray," Age (Melbourne, Australia), Oct. 25, 2008, 3.

scholar Daan van Knippenberg and his colleagues has shown that fairness is the dominant concern when employees evaluate managers, not likability.[15]

5. Conscientiousness

How Much Focus is Too Much?

Conscientiousness reflects the extent to which we want to structure and organize our lives. Drive, reliability and persistence are important qualities for leaders, but they can prove dysfunctional if they are not properly channeled.

You can be too thorough. One risk for highly conscientious leaders is that their perfectionism can cause them to fuss over details while losing sight of the big picture. That can be a serious problem, as highlighted by the CEO of a family business we worked with. As he put it: "I have quite an appetite for details, so once I get to hear of a problem, I keep asking questions and I have difficulty letting go of it. That can distract me from the essentials. So I'm trying to be more selective about my deep involvement—but it's a work in progress."

Executives with this tendency need to ask themselves: "Is this a high-leverage activity—or could my time be better invested elsewhere?" They also need to authorize their direct reports to repeat this question whenever it seems like the executive is getting bogged down in time-wasting details. Perfectionism has another unfortunate consequence. Sensing that their boss is inclined to get too involved or to micromanage, employees may grow reluctant to flag issues. Perfectionist executives need to put on their coaching hats and switch to questioning mode, so that their input comes across as help, not control.

Beyond the professional harm that these preferences can cause, they can also wreak havoc in one's private life. Highly conscientious leaders can become workaholics, obsessive in their pursuit of goals, raising the risk of burnout and poor work-life balance. They can also struggle in situations calling for flexibility. A supply chain director in the telecom sector told us: "I can get overly focused sometimes. I feel an intense responsibility for my area to the extent that I just lose balance—I work too hard, I neglect my health and my family. And, of course, the less time I spend with my family, the less I feel like I belong with them—and the more I throw myself into the work. So that's a cycle I'm trying to break."

An unhealthy commitment to work is not something executives can change overnight. But one approach executives who have this tendency can take is to cut back the working day by 15 minutes. Then, the following week, shave off another 15 minutes, and so on each week until you reach a target workday length.

Or you can make decisions too quickly. While some leaders can be inclined to overanalyze before making up their minds, others realize that they tend to make decisions quickly, based on

---

15   D.L. van Knippenberg, D. De Cremer and B. van Knippenberg, "Leadership and Fairness: The State of the Art," European Journal of Work and Organizational Psychology 16, no. 2 (March 2007): 113–140.

instinct. For example, William Green, chairman of Accenture, told the *New York Times* that he has learned to become more methodical and less "seat of the pants" in his decision-making style as he rose through the ranks: "I have purposely tried to get better grounding in the analytics behind the decision making and used that to check to see if there was a huge disconnect between what my instinct told me and what the analytics told me."[16]

For executives low on decision-making caution, it can be helpful to appoint someone to play devil's advocate—someone who has full license from the executive to question his or her snap decisions without negative career consequences.

Becoming Self-Aware

Several of the preceding examples suggest ways of managing psychological preferences. The inevitable starting point is self-awareness. Without it, executives will find it hard to evolve or find coping strategies. In fact, a survey of 75 members of the Stanford Graduate School of Business Advisory Council rated self-awareness as the most important capability for leaders to develop.[17] Executives need to know where their natural inclinations lie in order to boost them or compensate for them. Self-awareness is about identifying personal idiosyncrasies—the characteristics that executives take to be the norm but actually represent the exception.

Sometimes self-awareness comes early in one's career, prompted by a comment from a trusted colleague or boss. In an article in *Fortune International*, Lauren Zalaznick, now chairman, Entertainment & Digital Networks and Integrated Media for NBC-Universal, recalled that the best advice she ever received was from her first boss, who told her: "Throughout your career, you're going to hear lots of feedback from show-makers and peers and employees and bosses. If you hear a certain piece of feedback consistently and you don't agree with it, it doesn't matter what you think. Truth is, you're being perceived that way."[18]

PepsiCo CEO Indra Nooyi has said that she benefited from feedback from mentors.

On her rise to the top, PepsiCo CEO Indra Nooyi has also benefited from constructive feedback: "I'm a pretty honest and outspoken person," she told the *Wall Street Journal Europe*. "So, you sit in a meeting and somebody presents a ... five-year plan. [Other executives] would say, 'You know, that's very interesting. But maybe you could think about this slightly differently.' I just said, 'That's crap. This is never going

---

16   A. Bryant, "68 Rules? No, Just 3 Are Enough," New York Times, Nov. 21, 2009, 2.

17   B. George, P. Sims, A.N. McLean and D. Mayer, "Discovering Your Authentic Leadership," Harvard Business Review 85, no. 2 (February 2007): 129–138.

18   L. Zalaznick, "The Best Advice I Ever Got," Fortune International (Europe), July 6, 2009, 35.

to happen.' I'm sure they were all thinking that, but they were saying it in a much more gentle way. I'd come out of the meeting, and one of the guys would pull me aside and say, 'You could have said the thing slightly differently.'"[19]

Over the past two decades, companies have increased the opportunities for executives to gain insight into their personalities and receive feedback from multiple sources. These instruments can even be distributed to friends and family, who may be only too pleased to enlighten their loved ones on how they come across. And self-awareness is one of the most frequently cited outcomes of leadership coaching.[20]

Cisco CEO John Chambers has said that, initially, it was not easy for him to learn to be more collaborative.

But some executives resist this process for a long time. Take the case of David Pottruck, the former CEO of Charles Schwab. Earlier in his career, he was summoned to his boss's office and told that his colleagues did not trust him. As Pottruck recalled in the *Harvard Business Review*, "That feedback was like a dagger to my heart. I was in denial, as I didn't see myself as others saw me. ... I had no idea how self-serving I looked to other people. Still, somewhere in my inner core the feedback resonated as true."[21]

Success in multiple roles is unlikely unless a leader can accept and overcome his or her blind spots. John Donaldson, former CEO of the Thomas Cook Group, testified to this in a book called *The Set-Up-to-Fail Syndrome:* "When I look back at the way I behaved when I was directing [one of the group's two business units], I am encouraged by the progress I have made. The journey is not over, but I've changed enough to say honestly that today, I would not employ a manager who behaves the way I did back then. If I was the CEO of the manager I was then, I think I'd fire myself!"[22]

Prisoners of our Personalities?

The objective is not to undergo a personality change. It is to be yourself, with more skill.[23] The point that comes across from many of the examples given in this article is that most successful leaders have had to work on themselves in order to manage or tone down potentially career-limiting traits. It required hard work and introspection. That is the bad news. The good news is that we are not prisoners of our personalities. Personality is about preferences — preferred ways

19   A. Murray, "PepsiCo's Indra Nooyi on the Trade-Offs She Made," Wall Street Journal Europe, April 12, 2011, sec. R, p. 5.
20   K. Ely, L.A. Boyce, J.K. Nelson, S.J. Zaccaro, G. Hernez- Broome and W. Whyman, "Evaluating Leadership Coaching: A Review and Integrated Framework," Leadership Quarterly 21, no. 4 (August 2010): 585–599.
21   George et al., "Discovering Your Authentic Leadership."
22   Manzoni and Barsoux, "The Set-Up-to-Fail Syndrome."
23   R. Goffee and G. Jones, "Why Should Anyone Be Led by You?" Harvard Business Review 78, no. 5 (September 2000): 62–70.

of behaving—and we can behave in ways that run contrary to our personality. Indeed, we all have to do this from time to time. Some people do it exceedingly well.

> In general, aspiring leaders need to become aware of their outlier ten-
> dencies and learn how they are perceived by others. Passion, hard work
> and intensity are vital traits for leaders, but those same traits can also be
> overwhelming. The lesson here is straightforward: The bundle of traits that
> work for you as a leader right now can become a source of problems on
> short notice."

Take the case of Richard Branson, who has dressed up in silly costumes to publicize the Virgin Group he founded. He told the *Independent:* "Every single time I am asked to do this sort of thing ... and make a spectacle of myself, there is always something in the pit of my stomach that turns."[24] Branson told *Strategy + Business* that his underlying personality bears little relation to his flamboyant public persona, but that he has learned to play the role: "Before we launched the airline, I was a shy and retiring individual who couldn't make speeches and get out there. ... I had to train myself into becoming more of an extrovert."[25]

Branson's example shows to what extent it is possible to expand our repertoire of behaviors beyond our underlying preferences. But such efforts take their toll. They are only sustainable if the person can figure out how to recover and recharge. Otherwise, there is a danger of burnout.

Sometimes, an executive who expands his or her repertoire of behaviors may allow new group dynamics to emerge as well. When Cisco's top management team decided to adopt a more collaborative approach, it was CEO John Chambers who found it trickiest to adapt. Accustomed to dominating meetings, he could not help stepping in to provide the answer. "It was hard for me at first to learn to be collaborative," he told the *Harvard Business Review.* "But when I learned to let go and give the team the time to come to the right conclusion, I found they made just as good decisions, or even better. ... I had to develop the patience to let the group think."[26]

It is worth investing effort into developing one's coaching skills. We mentioned this remedy in connection with the psychological tendencies to be too complex or too thorough. But it also applies to executives who may be too assertive or too competitive. The behavioral skills associated with coaching (asking questions, active listening, making suggestions, providing feedback) counteract several excesses simultaneously.

For executives who do not feel up to making such behavioral changes, self-awareness helps in two other ways. First, it allows us to share our particular foibles and shortcomings. This makes it easier for people to read us and to help us keep our extreme behaviors in check.

Second, self-awareness alerts us to activities and situations we are likely to find difficult. The simplest antidote is to find a complementary person who can act as a counterweight. If you

---

24   M. Harrison, "Space Is Not the Final Frontier for the Virgin Boss," Independent, Dec. 11, 2004, 61.

25   G. Rifkin, "How Richard Branson Works Magic," Strategy + Business 13 (November 1998): 53–59.

26   B. Fryer and T.A. Stewart, "Cisco Sees the Future," Harvard Business Review 86, no. 11 (fourth quarter, 2008): 72–79.

tend to be disorganized, find someone who is meticulous; if you tend toward the big picture, find a pragmatist; if you tend to be impulsive, find someone more risk averse; if you tend to be too trusting or open, find someone more skeptical or politically astute. At a joint coaching session we held with two executives from the packaging industry, a divisional director and his deputy, the former observed: "Looking at our scores, I can see how he complements me on several dimensions where I am a bit extreme—which may be something I sensed when I chose him [as deputy] and certainly explains some of our fights. I guess, the takeaway for me, is that those fights maybe save me from myself."

Consider, too, the example of the late Steve Jobs. According to an article in *Psychology Today*, he made little effort to curb his salient personality traits—narcissism, aesthetic sensibility, imagination, perfectionism, obsessive nature, faith in intuition—and indeed leveraged them to create innovative and visually pleasing tech products for the masses.[27] But he picked alongside him at Apple a partner capable of attenuating the potential liabilities of his own extreme personality. Tim Cook, Apple's CEO since August 2011, shares Jobs' intensity and workaholic tendencies. But in other respects he was a perfect foil. The most common observation about Cook, according to an article in *Fortune* called "Apple: The Genius Behind Steve," has been how temperamentally different he was from Jobs.[28] Cook is pragmatic, consistent and calm, and he never raises his voice. Jobs, of course, was none of the above—and he knew it.

In general, aspiring leaders need to become aware of their outlier tendencies and learn how they are perceived by others. Passion, hard work and intensity are vital traits for leaders, but those same traits can also be overwhelming. The lesson here is straightforward: The bundle of traits that work for you as a leader right now can become a source of problems on short notice. Where personality is concerned, executives must learn to adapt—and to watch out for too much of a good thing.

---

27 F. Carlin, "The Art of Influence," Psychology Today, Sept. 6, 2011, 64–69.
28 A. Lashinsky, "Apple: The Genius Behind Steve," Fortune, Nov. 24, 2008, 70–80.

Emotional Mastery

Seek to Excel in Four Dimensions

Daniel Goleman

Emotional intelligence has *immense practical applications* in leadership roles because beyond being smart intellectually (IQ), leaders need to excel in four domains of EQ:

1. ***Self-awareness.*** *Emotional self-awareness*—the ability to be aware of and understand your feelings—is critical for empathizing with the emotions of others (social awareness). Tuning in to *how you are feeling* plays a central role in *how you sense what someone else is feeling*. To make a good decision, you need to *have feelings about your thoughts*—connect your thoughts with emotional pros and cons to sense priorities and principles. And to more fully access your life experience on the matter, you need to access inputs from the basal ganglia: *when I did that, that worked well; when I said this, it bombed.* Your accumulated wisdom is stored in this primitive circuitry. The basal ganglia has connection to the verbal areas, and rich connections to the gastrointestinal tract—the gut. So in making the decision, *a gut sense of it being right or wrong is vital, too.* If the data doesn't fit what you're feeling, you should think twice about it. The best decision-makers are voracious consumers of any information that might bear on their decision. Then they all test their rational decision against their gut feeling. *If a deal doesn't feel right, they might not go ahead, even if it looks good on paper.* Answers often come to you via this gut sense. Then you put them into words.

2. ***Self-management.*** *Self-awareness* (awareness of your internal states) and *self-management* (management of those states) are the basis for *self-mastery* and high performance. Competencies like managing emotions, focused drive to achieve goals, adaptability, and initiative are based on self-management.

Self-regulation of *emotion* and *impulse* relies greatly on interaction between the prefrontal cortex—the brain's *executive center*—and the emotional centers in the amygdala. The prefrontal cortex, in a sense, is the brain's *good boss,* guiding you when you are at your best. The dorsolateral zone of the prefrontal area is the seat of cognitive control, regulating attention, decision-making, voluntary action, reasoning, and flexibility in response. The amygdala is a trigger point for emotional distress, anger, impulse, and fear. When this circuitry takes over, it acts as the *bad boss,* leading you to take actions you might regret later.

For the most part, you can't dictate *what emotions you will feel, when you'll feel them,* nor **how strongly you'll feel them**. Your choice comes once you feel a certain way. How do you express it? If your prefrontal cortex has its inhibitory circuits going full blast, you'll have a decision point that will make you more artful in guiding how you respond, and how you drive other people's emotions, for better or worse, in that situation.

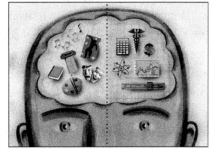

The amygdala is the brain's radar for threat. If it detects a threat, in an instant it can take over the rest of the brain—an amygdala hijack. You can't focus on what your job demands—you can only think about what's troubling you, what's relevant to the threat. You rely on habitual behaviors. You can't learn, innovate, or be flexible. You get the classic *fight-flight-or-freeze* response.

The problem is that the amygdala often makes mistakes. While it gets its data on what you see and hear in a single neuron from the eye and ear, it only receives a small fraction of the signals those senses receive. Most go to other parts of the brain that take longer to analyze the inputs—and get a more accurate reading. The amygdala gets a sloppy picture and reacts instantly. So you overreact in ways you later regret.

Here are the five top amygdala triggers in the workplace: 1) *condescension and lack of respect;* 2) *being treated unfairly;* 3) *being unappreciated;* 4) *feeling that you are not being listened to or heard;* and 5) *being held to unrealistic deadlines.*

How can you minimize hijacks? First, notice early when you experience one. Monitor what's going on in your mind. Reason with yourself; challenge what you tell yourself: "He isn't always unkind—maybe I should give him a chance." Or try some empathy, or use meditation or relaxation to calm down.

One value of self-mastery is being in the right brain state for the task at hand. Every internal state has its advantages and downsides. The plusses of being in a positive mood are that you are more creative, better at problem solving, and more efficient in decision making. The negatives include a tendency to be less discriminating, make decisions *too quickly,* or pay too little attention to detail.

3. **Social awareness.** *Social mastery* requires *social awareness* and *relationship management. Mindsight,* the term coined by Daniel Siegel, refers to the mind's ability to see itself. Our awareness of another person's inner reality and of our own, are both acts of empathy.

The social brain includes circuitry designed to attune to and interact with another person's brain. The brain is peppered with mirror neurons and they activate in us exactly what we see in the other person: Their emotions and movements, even intentions. In one study, people were given performance feedback. If given negative feedback in a positive tone, they felt good about it; if they were given positive feedback in a judgmental tone, they felt negative. So the emotional subtext is more powerful in many ways than the ostensible interaction. We are constantly impacting the brain states in other people.

4. *Relationship management.* You are responsible for *how you shape the feelings of those you interact with*—for better or for worse. In this sense, relationship skills have to do with managing brain states in other people. For peers, the sender tends to be the most emotionally expressive person. But when there are power differences, the most powerful person is the emotional sender, setting the emotional state for the team.

People pay most attention to what the leader, the most powerful person in that group, says or does. If the leader is in a *positive mood,* that spreads an *upbeat mood* to others and that *collective positivity enhances group performance.* A leader's *negative mood* hurts group performance. Such emotional contagion is found in groups making decisions and seeking creative solutions. This contagion happens because of the *mirror neuron system circuitry in our social brain.* Person-to-person emotional contagion operates automatically, instantly, unconsciously.

Social rapport has three elements: 1) *paying full attention* (both people need to tune fully to the other); 2) *being in synch non-verbally* (moves are almost choreographed, like a dance—such *synchrony* is orchestrated by neurons or oscillators, that regulate how our body moves in relationship to another body); and 3) *feeling positive* (like a micro-flow, an interpersonal high—moments of interpersonal chemistry, or *simpatico,* are when things happen at their best).

The core skill in social awareness is empathy—sensing what others are drinking and feeling, without them telling you in words. You continually send others signals about your feelings through your tone of voice, facial expression, gestures, and other nonverbal channels. People vary greatly in how well they can read these signals.

There are three kinds of empathy: 1) *cognitive empathy:* I know how you see things. Managers high in this empathy can put things in terms that people can understand and pick up the unspoken norms of a culture quickly—and that motivates people; 2) *emotional empathy:* I feel with you. People who excel in this empathy make good counselors, teachers, managers, and group leaders because they sense how others are re-acting; and 3) *empathic concern:* I sense you need some help, and I'm ready to give it. These are the good citizens who voluntarily help out as needed.

You need to sense what another person is going through, what they're feeling, to feel compassion and to engage in compassionate action. Narcissistic, Machiavellian, and sociopathic leaders can have *cognitive empathy,* but lack *emotional empathy* and *empathic concern.*

Developing EQ

To enhance you EQ, first **mobilize the motivating power**. Draw on your dreams. Work from *where you are now* to *what you might improve* to get *where you want to go*. Get 360-feedback on your EQ competencies and use it to determine what competencies you should strengthen.

Next, operationalize your goal at the level of a specific behavior. Make it *practical*. Know exactly *what to do* and *when*.

Then, do it over and over. As you persist, you form new circuitry. One day you'll do *the right thing* in *the right way* without a second thought. Also engage in mental rehearsal—it activates the same neural circuitry as real activity.

It's never too late to improve your EQ abilities and competencies.

Discussion Questions

1   What personality characteristics are associated with effective leadership?

2   Explain the contribution of intelligence to leaders' performance.

3   Describe gender differences in leadership. Do these differences justify the limited presence of women in top leadership positions in organizations worldwide?

4   Do you agree with the author's view that emotional intelligence can be learned and improved? What factors might limit people's ability to improve their emotional intelligence?

CHAPTER 3

Coming Across as an Effective Leader

Impression Management for Leaders

Andrew J. DuBrin

To be effective as a leader, a person needs a wide variety of personal attributes, including the right personality traits and cognitive skills. The leader also needs to work in a setting appropriate to these attributes. At the same time, the leader's combination of attributes must impress constituents that he or she is competent enough to carry out the role of a leader. As leadership researcher and theorist Bernard M. Bass notes, it is the leader's *perceived* competence that determines if he or she will be able to influence followers. For example, the leader must convince the group that he or she has the appropriate experience to help with the group task for his or her ideas to be accepted.[1] This is why self-confidence has long been associated with leadership effectiveness—the leader has to look the part of a person capable of being in charge.[2] Convincing others of one's skills and capabilities is one of the essential purposes of impression management.

The observation that creating a good impression is part of leadership does not mean that effective leadership consists mostly of creating a good impression. The effective leader has to be a good problem solver, think strategically, and implement plans, among many other attributes and skills.

In this chapter we describe two major topics intertwined with each other: how leaders project a leadership image, and how impression management contributes to charismatic leadership. The reader should recognize, however, that all other

---

1   Bernard M. Bass with Ruth Bass, *The Bass Handbook of Leadership: Theory, Research, & Managerial Applications*, 4th ed. (New York: The Free Press, 2008), p. 614.
2   George P. Hollenbeck and Douglas T. Hall, "Self-Confidence and Leader Performance," *Organizational Dynamics*, No. 3, 2004, p. 254.

WELL SUPPORTED BY EMPIRICAL RESEARCH	SUPPORTED MORE BY ANECDOTE AND OPINION
Implicit leadership theories and image projection	Acting skills required for winning over an audience: connecting; listening empathetically; improvising; radiating confidence; projecting discipline and toughness; and honesty
Being a servant leader	Influence tactics for projecting a leadership image
Impression management to create and maintain a charismatic identity (dramaturgy)	High self-esteem and high self-monitoring to project a leadership image
	Impression management behaviors of framing, scripting, staging, and performing

Figure 5.1 Topics and Subtopics Related to Impression Management for Leadership According to Basis of Support.

information about impression management presented in this book can also work in the service of being an effective leader. Unless you are able to impress people in the right way, you will not be able to lead them. Impression management must then be supported by many other leadership traits and competencies. Figure 5.1 organizes some of the major themes in this chapter based on amount of empirical support.

Projecting a Leadership Image

Projecting the image of a leader could be a subject without limits, depending on how *image* is interpreted. For example, developing a personal brand helps project a leadership image, as does demonstrating cognitive skills, displaying extraversion, and being well groomed. Therefore any discussion of impression management for leaders by projecting a leadership image can at best be illustrative. As outlined in Figure 5.2, here we concentrate on four approaches to projecting a leadership image that have been the subject of careful observation and research.

Acting Skills Required for Winning over an Audience

Political science professor Thomas E. Cronin argues that political leaders, in common with talented actors, develop skills to win over audiences. He notes that modern-day leaders must hone their self-promotion, likeability, and leadership attributes. At the same time they must not project the appearance of being pretenders or dissemblers. Most leaders need well-honed acting skills, yet being a skilled performer is only a means to effective leadership, not an end in itself.[3] Here we report on Cronin's observations but apply them to organizational leaders rather than those in the world of politics.

---

3   Thomas E. Cronin, "'All the World's a Stage ...' Acting and the Art of Political Leadership," *Leadership Quarterly,* August 2008, pp. 459–468.

Connecting with the Audience

An essential aspect of projecting the image of a leader is to connect with the audience, which translates into emotional rapport with group members. Based on the premise that wanting to connect is a basic human need, the actor intent on projecting a leadership image develops a phrase that facilitates this connection. A vision can be useful in creating the connection, as in "Everything we do will help provide better nutrition to the world." The connection will often be stronger when the leader focuses on specific benefits to the employees, as with the statement "Our best days of high profits and bonuses are ahead of us."

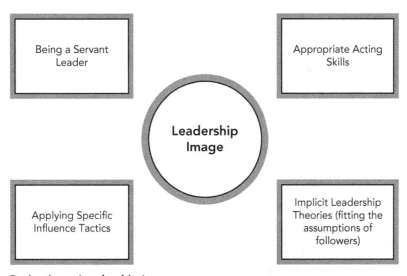

Figure 5.2   Projecting a Leadership Image.

A wide variety of behaviors and attitudes help a person project the image of being an effective leader, with those outlined in this figure having major significance.

Understanding and Exploiting Symbols

Political leaders in particular make references to symbols that are part of the culture, such as the Declaration of Independence, the Constitution, Franklin Delano Roosevelt, and Martin Luther King, Jr. Making references to these symbols is considered bipartisan rather than partisan because the symbols just presented are associated with *good* rather than *evil* by the vast majority of constituents. Organizational leaders have to search to find symbols related to their business considered positive by most of their employees. A heroic founder of the business will sometimes suffice. Wal-Mart managers can make reference to founder Sam Walton because the story (not necessarily false) widely circulates about the humanitarian values of Walton. A manager at UPS (United Parcel Services) can make reference to how the company has delivered valuable medical documents that saved lives.

An analysis prepared by Jeffrey Pfeffer further explains how the leader makes use of symbols to create a positive impression among constituents. He reasons that symbolic management operates fundamentally on the principle of illusion. By using *political language, ceremonies,* and *settings,* the leader effectively elicits powerful emotions in people, and these emotions interfere with rational analysis.[4] Keep in mind, however, that the leader might use symbols not to override rational analysis, but to create a positive impression so followers will take appropriate action. For example, a CEO might answer her own e-mails and drive a compact car to work to symbolize frugality—not to circumvent rational analysis by employees. An explanation of Pfeffer's three components of symbolic management is as follows:

- *Political language.* The intent of political language is to soften the impact of the more accurate term. By using political language, the leader can create a positive impression by not appearing harsh. Instead of referring to laying off thousands of people, the leader talks about "rightsizing the organization." Instead of referring to getting rid of costly American workers, the leader talks about the "importance of global outsourcing to remain competitive in the global marketplace."

- *Ceremonies.* The leader uses ceremonies as occasions to help organizational members feel better about doing what needs to be done. Among these ceremonies or ceremonial events are annual meetings, regional meetings, sales meetings, training sessions, offsite (or outdoor) training, award ceremonies, video conferences, and web seminars. Being the head or host of a ceremony is regarded as part of a leader's role, so conducting a ceremony well creates a positive impression among constituents.

- *Settings.* Physical space can be used as a tool for the exercise of power and influence. Simultaneously, physical space can be used to create an impression. To create the symbol of being a hands-on leader, some executives place their office among workers of lower rank. One example is Sergio Marchionne, the head of the combined Chrysler and Fiat companies. He placed his office in a manufacturing setting in Auburn Hills, Michigan to demonstrate his desire to be close to operations.

Another link between impression management and symbols is that mention of certain organizational symbols gives the leader an aura of being emotionally connected to the company and therefore worth following. For example, a Wal-Mart store manager might mention Sam Walton as a symbol of treating customers well, and being frugal.

Listening Empathetically

Listening to subordinates not only creates a good impression; the process is one of the major tactics of effective leadership. "Followers have a say in what they are being led to. A leader who neglects that soon finds himself (or herself) without followers," writes Gary Willis. "To sound

---

4   Jeffrey Pfeffer, *Managing with Power: Politics and Influence in Organizations* (Boston, MA: Harvard Business School Press, 1992), pp. 279–298.

a certain trumpet does not mean just trumpeting one's own certitudes. It means sounding a specific call to specific people capable of response."[5] A specific way in which listening creates a good impression is that the leader demonstrates a willingness to collaborate with group members by processing their input.

A standard approach for a newly appointed high-level organizational leader is to take a listening tour by such means as having interviews with a variety of people throughout the organization, often in a variety of locations. The listening tour creates a good impression for several reasons. First, it demonstrates that the new leader wants input from a variety of organizational members before taking action. Second, the tour demonstrates that the new leader respects the opinion of experienced workers.

Kim Simon was appointed as the first patient-advocacy director for Alexion Pharmaceuticals, a small biotechnology company. Simon met face to face with approximately one dozen colleagues in his first two weeks, picking up much information about politics at the company. Without the insights from his listening tour, he believes, "I might have been at a disadvantage on some projects." He also walked down the corridors at least twice a day to brainstorm and bond with the headquarters team.[6] Part of the success Simon has had in his position can be attributed to the positive impression he created by listening to colleagues and later involving them in his patient-advocacy initiatives.

Another mechanism for creating a good impression by listening is for the leader to make the rounds, sometimes referred to as *rounding* or *management by walking around*. During the rounds the leader can make a personal connection by asking about a key event in a subordinate's life, such as the health of a newborn. Describing follow-up action on an issue raised in a previous rounding creates a favorable impression. Giving workers a commitment to fixing problems they bring up during the rounds is another technique for the leader to create a good impression.[7] During her rounds a middle manager heard complaints from several employees about a heating and cooling system that often created conditions that were too warm during cold weather, and too cool during warm weather. After the manager worked diligently with the facilities department to resolve the problem her stature as a leader increased considerably.

Improvising

To project an impression of authenticity it is important for the leader not to appear fully scripted, meaning not to react to all problems with a response that appears rehearsed. By improvising responses, questions and problems, the leader gives the impression of wanting to really find answers and solutions. To appear stiff, wooden, or uncomfortable during interaction with constituents detracts from the leader's effectiveness.

---

5   Garry Willis, "What Makes a Good Leader?" *Atlantic Monthly*, April 1994, p. 67. As quoted in Cronin, "'All the World's a Stage ...'," p. 463.

6   Joann S. Lublin, "How You Can Ensure a Newly Created Job Has Staying Power," *The Wall Street Journal*, June 5, 2007, p. B1.

7   "'Making the Rounds' Like a Physician," *Manager's Edge*, February 2006, p. 8.

A leader will appear rehearsed when he or she explains losing money with a declaration of the nature "A weakening economy combined with low consumer demand created pressures for us." The same statement could be made to explain away all poor business results. A response that might create a better impression is: "We faced the same poor economy as everybody else. What we did particularly wrong was not to have the products that people would buy even during a poor economy. We will be working hard to fix that problem."

Radiating Confidence

As mentioned at the outset of the chapter, projecting confidence is an essential leadership characteristic. Even during bad times, followers want the leader to be optimistic and radiate confidence. United States presidents are sometimes given the label "the nation's First Optimist." A leader who projects pessimism is likely to lose credibility with his or her constituents. During an emergency planning session, an executive at Ford Motor Company told the group, "Ford is do-ing well in many areas. We have attractive new models coming down the pike. Our cost structure is in place, and we have a first-rate workforce. All we need is more sales." The comment provoked laughter, but also helped the executive gain currency. Should consumer demand increase, Ford would capitalize on the situation. Also, the automotive executive in question projected the image of a person with hope for the company and its employees.

Projecting Discipline and Toughness

A high-level leader will often create the impression of being effective by taking stern action when necessary to attain an important goal. A football coach who suspends a key player just before a big game for "having violated team rules" gains in credibility. Political leaders might call for war, or a one-time strike against another country, yet business leaders have to display discipline, toughness and sternness in other ways. Unfortunately for many employees and the economy as well, this toughness often takes the form of laying off thousands of employees to attain the goal of company survival. Mark Hurd of Hewlett-Packard (HP) is but one of many executives in recent years who have been responsible for the firing of over 30,000 employees to improve organizational efficiency. Yet he retains the image of being a capable executive who is a whiz at operations and cost effectiveness.

Another way in which a CEO can demonstrate toughness is to exit a business long associ-ated with the company. An extreme example was CEO Jeffrey R. Immelt at General Electric (GE) stating several years ago that he was considering getting the company out of the lightbulb and appliance businesses. Doing so reinforced Immelt's image as a bold executive whether or not GE does sell the lightbulb and appliance businesses.

Honesty

Few people expect political leaders to tell the truth all the time, yet the expectations for business leaders are high despite all the publicity about financial scandals. One such scandal several years ago involved leaders at a major investment bank authorizing the short selling of the same mortgage-backed securities they were simultaneously selling to clients as sound investments. By planning to sell short, the leaders were predicting that the price of the shares in these investments would decline substantially. These scandals aside, the leader who projects the image of honesty and trustworthiness is more likely to endure.

Martin Chemers writes that the primary goal of image management is to establish a legitimate basis for the leader's influence attempts. Competence and trustworthiness (or honesty) are key criteria for the leader's legitimacy. Other research has also found that the two most frequently cited characteristics of an outstanding leader are task competency and honesty. The leader who is competent and honest therefore projects the image of (and *is*) an effective leader.[8]

A concluding observation based on Cronin's analysis is that projecting the image of leadership is positive rather than manipulative and deceitful. Unless a leader gives the impression of being a leader, he or she cannot accomplish good deeds. Visualize a manager attempting to re-start a restaurant destroyed by a hurricane and a flood. Unless he or she projects the image of being composed and being able to build a path out of the crisis, the employees will most likely disband because they have no hope of the restaurant being restored.

Implicit Leadership Theories and the Projection of a Leadership Image

A personality-based perspective on how people create the impression of being a leader is that they do so by meeting the expectations people have of leaders. **Implicit leadership theories** are personal assumptions about the traits and abilities that characterize an ideal organizational leader. These assumptions, both stated and unstated, develop through socialization and past experiences with leaders. The assumptions are stored in memory and activated when group members interact with a person in a leadership position. Our assumptions about leaders help us make sense of what takes place on the job, and what kind of behavior we expect from a leader. Assume that Brett was raised in a household and neighborhood in which business leaders are highly respected and thought to be dedicated and intelligent. When Brett later works in a full-time professional job, he is most likely to be influenced by a supervisor he perceives to be dedicated and intelligent because this person fits Brett's preconceived notion of how a leader should behave. When a leader behaves in this manner, he or she impresses Brett.

According to implicit leadership theory, as part of making assumptions and expectations of leader traits and behaviors, people develop leadership prototypes and antiprototypes. *Prototypes* are positive characterizations of a leader, whereas *antiprototypes* are traits and behaviors people do not want to see in a leader. People have different expectations of what they want in a leader, yet research conducted with 939 subordinates in two different samples in British business organizations shows there is some consistency in implicit leadership theories. The study showed that these theories are consistent across different employee groups and are also stable trait-based stereotypes of leadership.[9] Another study in England showed that if the leader matches

---

8   Martin M. Chemers, *An Integrative Theory of Leadership* (Mahwah, NJ: Lawrence Erlbaum, 1997), p. 153.
9   Olga Epitropaki and Robin Martin, "Implicit Leadership Theories in Applied Settings: Factor Structure, Generalizability, and Stability over Time," *Journal of Applied Psychology*, April 2004, pp. 297–299.

employee assumptions about having the right traits, the leader–member exchange (LMX) will be more positive. In turn, the group member will be more readily impressed and influenced by the leader.[10]

Figure 5.3 lists the six traits group members want to see in a leader (prototypes), as well as the two traits they do not want to see in a leader (antiprototypes). Leaders who fit the prototypes are perceived to be effective leaders. The antiprototype of *masculinity* suggests that followers prefer a compassionate and relationship-oriented leader to a command-and-control leader. An implication of these data is that a leader who fits group members' prototypes is more likely to impress them than a leader who fits their antiprototype.

LEADERSHIP PROTOTYPE	LEADERSHIP ANTIPROTOTYPE
1. Sensitivity (compassion, sensitive)	1. Tyranny (dominant, selfish, manipulative)
2. Intelligence (intelligent, clever)	2. Masculinity (male, masculine)
3. Dedication (dedicated, motivated)	
4. Charisma (charismatic, dynamic)	
5. Strength (strong, bold)	
6. Attractiveness (well dressed, classy)	

Figure 5.3   Implicit Leadership Theory Dimensions.

Source: Gathered from information in Olga Epitropaki and Robin Martin, "Implicit Leadership Theories in Applied Settings: Factor Structure, Generalizability, and Stability over Time," *Journal of Applied Psychology,* April 2004, pp. 297–299.

Specific Influence Tactics for Projecting a Leadership Image

Influencing others is incorporated into most definitions of leadership, so when a leader makes effective use of influence tactics he or she will project the image of being an effective leader. The purpose of influence tactics is to facilitate subordinates attaining important goals. However, in the process of exerting influence, the leader's image is likely to be enhanced. Here we describe briefly six influence tactics that are likely to be perceived by group members as indicative of effective leadership: leading by example and respect; exchanging favors and bargaining; making an inspirational appeal; consultation with others; being a team player; and practicing hands-on leadership.

Leading by Example and Respect

A simple but effective way of influencing group members and projecting a positive leadership image is by **leading by example**, or acting as a positive role model. The ideal approach is to be a "do as I say and do" manager—that is, one whose actions and words are consistent. Actions and words confirm, support, and often clarify each other. Being respected facilitates leading by example because group members are more likely to follow the example of leaders they respect.

---

10   Olga Epitropaki and Robin Martin, "From Real to Ideal: A Longitudinal Study of Implicit Leadership Theories in Leader-Member Exchanges and Employee Outcomes," *Journal of Applied Psychology,* July 2005, pp. 659–676.

Leading by example is often interpreted to mean that the leader works long and hard, and expects others to do the same, with this type of behavior being prevalent among entrepreneurs who hire a staff. This approach to leading by example is more likely to project the image of a workaholic than an effective leader who coordinates the work of others.

Exchanging Favors and Bargaining

Offering to exchange favors if another person will help the leader achieve a work goal is another standard influence tactic. By making an exchange, the leader strikes a bargain with the other party and therefore projects the image of being fair. The exchange often translates into being willing to reciprocate at a later date. It might also be promising a share of the benefits if the other person helps the leader accomplish a task. For example, the leader might promise to place a person's name on a report to top management if that person will help him or her analyze the data and prepare the tables.

Making an Inspirational Appeal

A leader is supposed to inspire others, so it follows that making an inspirational appeal is an important influence tactic, as well as a way of creating a positive impression. As Pfeffer notes, "Executives and others seeking to exercise influence in organizations often develop skill in displaying, or not displaying, their feelings in a strategic fashion."[11] An inspirational appeal usually involves displaying emotion and appealing to group members' emotions. A moderating variable in the effectiveness of an inspirational appeal or emotional display is the influence agent's **personal magnetism**, or the quality of being captivating, charming, and charismatic. Possessing personal magnetism makes it easier for the leader to inspire people while at the same time projecting the image of what many constituents expect from an effective leader.

For an emotional appeal to be effective, the influence agent must understand the values, motives, and goals of the target. Often this means that the leader must explain how the group efforts will have an impact outside the company. A study concluded: "Business leaders tend to think in terms of bottom-line goals, like boosting revenues or profits. But they need to speak about their goals in terms of how they will make a positive difference in the world. If you can see a goal—if you can touch, feel, and smell it—it seems more doable."[12] Having established such a goal, the leader creates the image of an effective leader.

Consultation with Others

A large number of group members want to collaborate with the leader in making decisions. As a result, consulting with group members enhances a leader's image. The influence target becomes more motivated to follow the agent's request because the target is involved in the decision-making process. Consultation is most effective as an influence tactic when the objectives

---

11   Jeffrey Pfeffer, *Managing with Power: Power and Influence in Organizations* (Boston, MA: Harvard Business School Press, 1992), p. 224.
12   Cited in "Choose Words that Inspire," *Executive Leadership*, March 2001, p. 2.

of the person being influenced are consistent with those of the leader.[13] An example would be a business leader consulting with group members on how to reduce costs in order to increase both profits and year-end bonuses. In this situation the leader creates a good impression by consulting with group members about a goal important to them as well as the company.

Being a Team Player

To influence others by being a good team player is an important strategy for getting work accomplished. Also, at any level in the organization, the leader who pitches in creates a positive impression. An example would be an information technology team leader working through the night with team members to combat a virus attack on the company's computer network. Being a team player is a more effective influence tactic in an organizational culture that emphasizes collaboration than in one in which being tough-minded and decisive is more in vogue.

A study of CEO leadership profiles among buyout firms found that teamwork was less associated with success than traits such as persistence and efficiency. Leaders in buyout firms are strongly financially oriented and are much more concerned with making deals than building relationships.[14] In such firms, investing effort in building teamwork may not strongly enhance the leader's image.

Practicing Hands-On Leadership

A **hands-on leader** is one who gets directly involved in the details and processes of operations. Such a leader has expertise, is task oriented, leads by example, and will usually be considered a good team player. By getting directly involved in the group's work activities, the leader influences subordinates to hold certain beliefs and to follow certain procedures and processes. For example, the manager who gets directly involved in fixing customer problems demonstrates to other workers how he or she thinks such problems should be resolved, and therefore projects a positive image.

Hands-on leadership is usually expected at levels below the executive suite, yet many high-level executives are also hands-on leaders. An example is Steve Jobs, the legendary head of Apple Corp. and Pixar Animation Studios. The downside of being a hands-on leader is that if it is done to excess the leader becomes a micromanager, thereby detracting from his or her image as an effective leader.

Being a Servant Leader

When group members believe that a leader's major role is to help them attain their goals, the leader will create a strong impression by focusing his or her efforts on providing such assistance.

---

13   Gary Yukl, *Skills for Managers and Leaders: Texts, Cases, and Exercises* (Upper Saddle River, NJ: Prentice Hall, 1990), p. 65.

14   George Anders, "Tough CEOs Often Most Successful, a Study Finds," *The Wall Street Journal*, November 19, 2007, p. B3.

A **servant leader** emphasizes integrity and serves constituents by working on their behalf to help them achieve their goals, not the leader's own goals. The idea behind servant leadership, as formulated by Robert K. Greenleaf, is that leadership derives naturally from a commitment to service.[15] Serving others, including employees, customers, and community, is the primary motivation for the servant leader. And true leadership emerges from a deep desire to help others. A servant leader is therefore a moral leader. Servant leadership has been accomplished when group members become wiser, healthier, and more autonomous. Should a leader accomplish these ends, he or she would create a well-deserved positive impression. The following are key aspects of servant leadership:[16]

1 *Place service before self-interest.* A servant leader is more concerned with helping others than with acquiring power, prestige, financial reward, and status. The servant leader seeks to do what is morally right, even if it is not financially rewarding. He or she is conscious of the needs of others and is driven by a desire to satisfy them. Another aspect of service before self-interest is the leader focusing on helping subordinates grow and succeed through such means as making constructive suggestions for professional growth.

2 *Listen first to express confidence in others.* The servant leader makes a deep commitment to listening in order to get to know the concerns, requirements, and problems of group members. (As stated above, listening projects a positive image.) Instead of attempting to impose his or her will on others, the servant leader listens carefully to understand what course of action will help others accomplish their goals. After understanding others, the best course of action can be chosen. Through listening, for example, a servant leader might learn that the group is more concerned about team spirit and harmony than striving for company-wide recognition. The leader would then concentrate more on building teamwork than searching for ways to increase the visibility of the team.

3 *Inspire trust by being trustworthy.* Being trustworthy and ethical is a foundation behavior of the servant leader. He or she is scrupulously honest with others, gives up control, and focuses on the well-being of others. Usually such leaders do not have to work hard at being trustworthy because they are already quite moral. In support of this principle, a survey found that most employees want a boss who is a trusted leader, not a pal.[17]

---

15 Robert K. Greenleaf, *The Power of Servant Leadership* (San Francisco: Berrett-Koehler Publishers, 1998).

16 Based on Robert K. Greenleaf, Servant Leadership: *A Journey into the Nature of Legitimate Power and Greatness* (Mahwah, NJ: Paulist Press, 1997); Robert C. Liden, Sandy J. Wayne, Hao Zhao, and David Henderson, "Servant Leadership: Development of a Multidimensional Measure and Multi-Level Assessment," *Leadership Quarterly,* April 2008, pp. 161–177.

17 "Be a Leader, Not a Pal," *Manager's Edge,* March 2007, p. 3.

4   *Focus on what it is feasible to accomplish.* Even though the servant leader is idealistic, he or she recognizes that one individual cannot accomplish everything. So the leader listens carefully to the array of problems facing group members and then concentrates on a few. The servant leader thus systematically neglects certain problems. A leader might carefully listen to all the concerns and complaints of the constituents and then proceed to work on the most pressing issue. A good impression is created by accomplishing something tangible on the road to major improvements.

5   *Lend a hand.* A servant leader looks for opportunities to play the Good Samaritan. As a supermarket manager, he or she might help out by bagging groceries during a busy period. Or a servant leader might help dig up mud in the company lobby after a hurricane.

6   *Emotional healing.* A servant leader shows sensitivity to the personal concerns of group members, such as a worker being worried about taking care of a disabled parent. Showing sensitivity to the personal concerns of group members generates a strong impression because most people place heavy emphasis on wanting their own needs satisfied.

Carrying out the role of a servant leader would result in projecting a positive leadership impression for group members who expect the leader to be helpful. An example is college professors wanting the department head to take care of administrative work so they can concentrate on teaching, advising, and research. In contrast, being a servant leader might create a poor impression when the group members expected a leader to invest most of his or her time in external affairs such as making deals and landing customers.

Impression Management and Charismatic Leadership

Many of the strategies and tactics already described in the chapter contribute to creating the impression of a charismatic leader. Scholarly analysis, as well as observations in the media, indicates strongly that part of being charismatic is to generate the impression of a dynamic, magnetic person who can accomplish important goals for constituents as well as potential constituents. The effective charismatic leader creates a good impression, yet at the same time accomplishes much beyond creating an impression. Among the accomplishments of an effective charismatic leader would be to inspire subordinates to high performance, and to contribute to their job satisfaction by being warm and caring.

Our approach to understanding how impression management is an integral part of charismatic leadership is divided into two parts: definitions of charisma that include an element of impression management, and a model of how organizational actors use impression management to create and maintain a charismatic identity.

Definitions of Charismatic Leadership that Include an Element of Impression Management

Over the years, charisma has been defined in various ways. Nevertheless, there is enough consistency among these definitions to make charisma a useful concept in understanding and practicing leadership. The various definitions also help us to understand that impression management is an important part of projecting charisma. To begin, *charisma* is a Greek word meaning divinely inspired gift. In the study of leadership, **charisma** is a special quality of leaders whose purposes, powers, and extraordinary determination differentiate them from others.[18]

Part of these powers can be attributed to the compelling impression the leader makes on constituents. This is true because charisma is a positive and compelling quality of a person that makes many others want to be led by him or her. The term *many others* is carefully chosen because the charismatic leader does not create the same positive impression on all constituents. A case in point is Steve Jobs of Apple Corp. and Pixar, who inspires thousands with his technical acumen and visionary perspective about consumer electronics. In contrast, he is regarded as overbearing and conceited by some constituents and many business journalists.

The following definitions of charisma indicate directly or indirectly the impression management component of charisma and charismatic leadership:[19]

1   A certain quality of an individual personality by virtue of which he or she is set apart from ordinary people and treated as endowed with supernatural, superhuman, or at least specifically exceptional powers or qualities. (Observe that being treated as being endowed with exceptional powers or qualities suggests that the leader creates a strong impression.)

2   The process of influencing major changes in the attitudes and assumptions of organization members, and building commitment for the organization's objectives. (To exert influence, a leader would typically need to create a strong impression.)

3   Leadership that has a magnetic effect on people. (A magnetic effect is a function of the impression created.)

---

18   Jay A. Conger and Rabindra N. Kanungo, *Charismatic Leadership in Organizations* (Thousand Oaks, CA: Sage, 1998).

19   Several of these definitions stem from the literature review found in B. M. Bass, *The Bass Handbook of Leadership*, pp. 575–576. In order of their presentation here, the original citations are as follows: (1) Max Weber, *The Theory of Social and Economic Organization* (New York: The Free Press, 1924/1947), p. 358; (2) Gary A. Yukl, *Leadership in Organizations*, 3rd ed. (Upper Saddle River, NJ: Prentice Hall, 1994), p. 207; (3) James M. Kouzes and Barry Z. Posner, *The Leadership Challenge: How to Get Extraordinary Things Done in Organizations* (San Francisco, Jossey-Bass, 1987), p. 123; (4) Max Weber, *The Sociology of Religion* (Boston, MA: The Beacon Press, 1922/1963); (5) Robert J. House, "A 1976 Theory of Charismatic Leadership," in J. G. Hunt and L. L. Larson (Eds.), *Leadership: The Cutting Edge* (Carbondale, IL: Southern Illinois University Press, 1977); (6) Eric Fromm, *Escape from Freedom* (New York: Farrar & Rinehart, 1941); (7) C. J. Friedrich, "Political Leadership and the Problem of the Charismatic Power," *Journal of Politics*, Vol. 23, 1961, pp. 3–24; (8) D. E. Berlew, "Leadership and Organizational Excitement," in D. A. Kolb, M. Rubin, and J. M. McIntyre (Eds.), *Organizational Psychology* (Englewood Cliffs, NJ: Prentice-Hall, 1974).

4   A charismatic leader is a mystical, narcissistic, and personally magnetic savior with extraordinary capabilities and a doctrine to promote. (Being mystical and personally magnetic is based on the impression the leader creates.)

5   Charismatic leaders are those who exert various effects and influences on their followers. These include trust in the leader's beliefs, obedience and acceptance of the leader, identification of the leader, and emotional involvement with the leader's mission. (All of these ends depend on the leader creating a strong, positive impression on group members.)

6   A charismatic person exudes confidence, dominance, a sense of purpose, and the ability to articulate goals that the followers are predisposed to accept. (*Exuding* implies creating an impression.)

7   Inspirational leadership characterized by the charismatic having a call from God for his or her mission. (It takes a strong impression to inspire others, especially when the inspiration appears to be divine.)

8   Charismatic leadership takes place when there is confidence building, shared vision, and the creation of valued opportunities. (Confidence building is based on creating a strong impression.)

The basic reason that these definitions imply that the charismatic leader engages in self-presentation is that charisma is based on perceptions, and perceptions of others are based on the impressions they create.

Impression Management in the Service of Creating and Maintaining a Charismatic Identity

Image building has long been recognized as an important part of charismatic leadership. Impression management techniques bolster the image of the leader's competence, which helps build subordinate compliance and faith in them. Jay Conger and Rabindra N. Kanungo reason that charismatic leaders can be distinguished from other leaders partly because they use oral communication skills and impression management to inspire followers in pursuit of the vision.[20]

According to a model developed by William L. Gardner and Bruce J. Avolio, social (or organizational) actors rely on impression management behaviors to create and maintain identities as charismatic leaders. From this perspective, to be perceived as a charismatic leader depends on projecting the right impression. The Gardner and Avolio model is a comprehensive examination

---

20 Jay Conger and Ranbindra N. Kanungo, "Toward a Behavioral Theory of Charismatic Leadership in Organizational Settings," *Academy of Management Review*, 1987, pp. 637–647.

of the relationship between charismatic leaders and their followers. Here we focus on the links between impression management and charisma.[21]

Charismatic leaders use impression management to deliberately cultivate a certain relationship with group members. In other words, they take steps to create a favorable, successful impression, recognizing that the perceptions of constituents determine whether they function as charismatic leaders. Impression management could imply that these leaders are skillful actors in presenting a charismatic face to the world. But the behaviors and attitudes of truly charismatic leaders go well beyond superficial aspects of impression management, such as wearing fashionable clothing or speaking well. For example, a truly charismatic leader will work hard to create positive visions for group members.

The model Gardner and Avolio construct is based on **dramaturgy**, in which actors engage in performances in various settings for particular audiences in order to shape their definitions of the situation. Consistent with this perspective, the actor (leader) and audience (followers) play key roles in the charismatic performance. For example, unless the subordinates are looking to identify with and be impressed by a leader, charismatic influence will not occur. A charismatic relationship will most likely emerge during two conditions. First, the environment must be seen as turbulent; and, second, the organizational context is supportive of change. This proposition helps explain why earlier conceptions of charisma proposed that followers are most in need of a charismatic leader during a crisis.

The Role of High Self-Esteem and High Self-Monitoring

Charismatic leaders typically have high levels of self-esteem. As a result these leaders persist in portraying a confident image in public even when discouraged by repeated failures. The high self-esteem portrayed by the leader often triggers followers to elevate their own self-esteem. A relevant example is that the head of multilevel sales programs are often charismatic figures who engage the cooperation of many people with limited self-confidence to participate in selling their products. The "down-line distributors" feel better about themselves by identifying with the heroic figure at the top of the sales pyramid.

Charismatic leaders are also high self-monitors, which plays a useful role in understanding the type of image followers want to perceive. For example, if the charismatic leader detects that the group members are concerned about job security, the leader will frame messages pointing toward stability of employment. Similarly, the high self-monitoring tendencies of charismatic leaders help them respond to the values of group members. Messages can then be shaped to fit the dominant values. Assume that a chief operating officer of a food company detects that a large proportion of the workforce has developed green (environmentally friendly) values. To gain influence and leadership status with the group, the chief operating officer begins to frame many messages in terms of how the company is contributing to a healthy external environment.

---

21 William L. Gardner and Bruce J. Avolio, "The Charismatic Relationship: A Dramaturgical Perspective," *Academy of Management Review*, January 1998, pp. 32–58.

Self-monitoring includes the ability to understand the goals and dreams of subordinates. As a result the charismatic leader can shape visions that group members can identify with. The vision, in turn, is part of the impression the charismatic leader creates. John Chambers, the CEO and Chairman of Cisco Systems, has established a vision of Cisco becoming a highly recognizable brand. The vision Chambers has established for Cisco appears to be based in part on the rampant pride he detects among his employees.

Desired Identity Images

The identity images of trustworthy, esteemed, and powerful are highly valued by charismatic leaders because being perceived as charismatic is dependent on these images. As a result, the charismatic leader works hard at projecting these images. In some circumstances, highly unethical and criminal charismatic people work at establishing an image of trustworthiness to gain the confidence of their targets. Of note is the fact that many wealthy people who have been swindled by financial consultants were so surprised to learn that a person they perceived to be honest and caring proved to be a criminal.

Many charismatic leaders present themselves as being morally worthy, making many references to values and purposes in order to convince their constituents. So long as their self-presentations are true, these leaders retain their charismatic status. Another identity image favored by charismatic leaders is to be perceived as innovative, entrepreneurial, un-conventional, and as leaders who have a vision for radical change. As a result, the charismatic leader will sprinkle his or her messages with references to such matters as changing the organizational culture and rewarding entrepreneurial thinking by employees. A. G. Lafley, the esteemed former CEO of Procter & Gamble, made frequent reference to encouraging entrepre-neurial thinking among employees. As a result, many employees contributed ideas that have made their way into new products.

Specific Impression Management Behaviors

So far this section has described identity images and general approaches to impression manage-ment. Gardner and Avolio have also identified four specific impression management behaviors charismatic leaders employ to secure and obtain their identity images:

1. *Framing.* Charismatic leaders frame their visions to present the organization's (or organizational unit's) purpose in a manner that energizes followers. In other words, the vision creates a useful impression. An example is the vision formulated by top management at Google: "To make nearly all information accessible to everyone all the time."

2. *Scripting.* Framing provides general ideas, whereas scripts provide the details of the action to take place. Charismatic leaders provide a cast for the script when they define roles for themselves and others. One role for subordinates might be to help stave off

a competitor, such as a product developer at Nikon continually improving its high-end digital cameras to the point that lower-priced competitors are at a disadvantage. Another part of scripting is to develop a dialogue that can be invoked frequently to capture the imagination of constituents. Jeffrey R. Immelt, the CEO of GE, relentlessly delivers a message about the importance of growth in revenue, profits, and market share. In recent years GE has slipped from time to time, but the message still drives thousands of managers.

Charismatic leaders also emphasize nonverbal behavior to deliver the messages in their scripts. Leaders perceived to be charismatic project a powerful, confident, and dynamic presence by way of their body posture, speaking rate, gestures, smiles, eye contact, and non-sexual touching. Andrea Jung, the CEO and chairwoman of Avon, captivates her audience with her careful speech, stylish presence, and warm gestures, among other nonverbal cues. All of these behaviors may be easy for charismatic leaders to accomplish, yet they are also intended to strengthen the impression they create.

3 *Staging.* As in theater and selling a home, staging for the charismatic leader involves creating an appropriate scene and appearance. Charismatic leaders often manipulate their appearance for symbolic purposes, such as an executive at an investment banking firm wearing French cuffs or a luxury handbag to appear wealthy. Staging might also include a business leader taking part in television commercials to promote favorable corporate images, such as George A. Zimmer of Men's Warehouse. His warm, reassuring, and natural voice add to his credibility and charisma. Even when an executive is not particularly telegenic, appearing in a television commercial suggests his or her personal involvement in the business.

4 *Performing.* In the dramaturgical framework, *performing* refers to the enactment of scripted behaviors and relationships. Two specific impression management techniques for creating charismatic images are exemplification and self-promotion. Exemplification is the impression management strategy most closely linked to charisma. The attributions triggered by exemplification are associated with the desired identity images of trustworthiness and morality. As exemplifiers, charismatic leaders engage in self-sacrificing and high-risk behaviors that dramatically illustrate their commitment to the cause they espouse. An example here would include the turnaround manager who agrees to work for a first-year salary of $1 plus stock in the company. The leader's intent is to demonstrate that his or her compensation will be dependent on the success of the turnaround.

Self-promotion helps the leader appear credible, innovative, esteemed, and powerful. The successful charismatic leader will often self-promote in a subtle fashion, because blatant self-promotion can damage one's credibility. A subtle form of self-promotion might be for the business leader to let it be known that he or she has been appointed to a federal government position. In this way a second party has endorsed the leader's importance. A more typical form of self-promotion is for the leaders to take on challenges they know they can achieve. For example, a CEO might spearhead acquiring another company that is financially troubled and is looking for a suitor.

We reinforce the idea again that almost any strategy or tactic of impression management can be functional in terms of projecting charisma. The tactics of framing, scripting, staging, and performing provide a useful conceptual framework for understanding how charismatic leaders apply impression management.

Guidelines for Application and Practice

1   One of the most effective ways of projecting a leadership image is to satisfy assumptions followers make of how a leader should behave, as described in implicit leadership theory. The personality traits involved, if not already present in a leader, would take a long time to develop. However, most people are capable of making some progress in developing the following attributes: sensitivity, intelligence, dedication, charisma, strength, and attractiveness. A person might not be able to quickly elevate his or her intelligence, but people can learn to improve their intellect through disciplining themselves to think more carefully, and to acquire additional job-relevant information.

2   A recommended approach to asking for a favor is to give the other person as much time as feasible to accomplish the task, such as by saying, "Could you find ten minutes between now and the end of the month to help me?" Not pressing for immediate assistance will tend to lower resistance to the request. Giving a menu of options for different levels of assistance also helps lower resistance. For example, you might ask another manager if you can borrow a technician for a one-month assignment; then, as a second option, you might ask if the technician could work ten hours per week on the project.[22] To ensure that the request is perceived as an exchange, you might explain what reciprocity you have in mind: that you will mention your coworker's helpfulness to his or her manager.

3   Impression management tactics can be helpful in projecting the image of charisma, and therefore being perceived as charismatic. Conversely, behaving charismatically will project a positive impression in many situations. Following are several suggestions that will both enhance a person's charisma, as well as creating a positive impression:

   • *Create visions for others.* Being able to create visions for others will be a major factor in being perceived as charismatic. A vision uplifts and attracts others, as well as projecting the impression of a strong leader.

---

22   "You Scratch My Back ... Tips on Winning Your Colleague's Cooperation," *Working Smart*, October 1999, p. 1.

- *Be enthusiastic, optimistic, and energetic.* A major behavior pattern of charismatic people is their combination of enthusiasm, optimism, and high energy. Without a great amount of all three characteristics, a person is unlikely to be perceived as charismatic by many people.

- *Remember names of people.* Charismatic leaders, as well as other successful people, can usually remember the names of people they have seen just once or several times. Caring about people helps you remember their names, as does concentrating on the name when first introduced and then repeating the name.

- *Develop synchrony with others.* People tend to regard those in synchrony with them as charismatic. A practical method of being in sync with another person is to adjust your posture to conform to his or her posture. When the other person stands up straight, you do; when he or she slouches, you do also.[23]

Summary

Projecting the image of a leader could be a subject without limits, depending on how *image* is interpreted. Four approaches to projecting a leadership image described here are as follows: (1) using appropriate acting skills; (2) displaying the traits found in implicit leadership theories; (3) applying specific influence tactics such as leading by example and respect, and making an inspirational appeal; and (4) being a servant leader.

Impression management is an important part of projecting charisma. Various definitions of charisma point toward its link with impression management. One such definition is that charisma is a certain quality of an individual personality by which he or she is set apart from ordinary people and treated as endowed with supernatural, superhuman, or at least specifically exceptional powers or qualities.

Impression management helps create and maintain a charismatic identity. To be perceived as a charismatic leader depends on projecting the right impression. Charismatic leaders use impression management to deliberately cultivate a certain relationship with group members. A model presented here is based on dramaturgy, in which actors engage in performances in various settings for particular audiences in order to shape their definitions of the situation.

Charismatic leaders typically have high levels of self-esteem, and therefore persist in portraying a confident image in public even when discouraged by repeated failures. The high self-esteem portrayed by the leader often triggers followers into elevating their own self-esteem. Charismatic leaders are also high self-monitors, which facilitates understanding the type of image followers want to perceive.

---

23 Andrew J. DuBrin, *Leadership: Research Findings, Practice, and Skills* (Mason, OH: South-Western Cengage Learning, 2010), pp. 81–83.

The identity images of trustworthy, esteemed, and powerful are highly valued by charismatic leaders because being perceived as charismatic is dependent on these images. Also, many charismatic leaders present themselves as being morally worthy, making many references to values and purposes in order to convince their constituents.

Four specific impression management behaviors charismatic leaders employ to secure and obtain their identity images are (1) framing, (2) scripting, (3) staging, and (4) performing. Exemplification and self-promotion are two important techniques for performing.

Guidelines for application and practice presented here include: (1) a leadership image can be projected by satisfying assumptions made about how leaders should behave; (2) it is best to ask for a favor by giving the other person as much time as feasible to accomplish the task; (3) impression management tactics can help project charisma, and behaving charismatically will project a positive impression.

Neuroscience and Leadership

The Promise of Insights

Richard E. Boyatzis

R ichard Boyatzis is Distinguished University Professor, Case Western Reserve University. He is the author of six books, including *Primal Leadership* with Daniel Goleman and Annie McKee; *Resonant Leadership*, with Annie McKee; and *Becoming a Resonant Leader* with Annie McKee and Fran Johnston.

Emerging findings in neuroscience research suggest why inspiring and supportive relationships are important—they help activate openness to new ideas and a more social orientation to others. Insights such as these, this author writes, may move the primacy of a leader's actions away from the often proselytized "results-orientation" toward a relationship orientation. Readers will learn about this and other important findings in neuroscience that have the potential to tell us what we need to know to be good, even great leaders.

The quest for understanding leadership seems perpetual. Against the context of the daily news that is full of leadership failures and lost opportunities, it seems to be an area of mystery rather than understanding. Advances in neuroscience may help us understand the internal mechanisms that enable some people to be effective leaders, and some not. It will help us to know how some people can form effective leadership relationships, and some not. It will also help us to understand why some people can sustain their effectiveness and others can not. But we are not there yet.

Leaders engage and inspire others- that is how their work gets done. For the last 100 or so years, we have studied their personality, intelligence, values, attitudes and even behavior. But seldom has anyone ventured physiologically inside of leaders. Advances in fMRI (functional magnetic resonance imaging), access to people and machines, and interest in more holistic approaches to studying leadership have made this possible. This has become so popular and hot that a special issue of *Leadership Quarterly* is being reviewed right now on the Biology of Leadership (Senior, Lee & Butler, 2010). In this brief overview, I will use a few of our current studies to highlight some of the areas that seem to hold promise.

Building Relationships

Leaders need to build relationships that inspire and motivate others to do their best, innovate and adapt. In our earlier work, *Primal Leadership* (Goleman, Boyatzis & McKee, 2002) and *Resonant Leadership* (Boyatzis & McKee, 2005), we synthesized a great deal of research to support the idea that effective leaders build resonant relationships with those around them. At the same time, less effective leaders or those that are more one-sided seem to create dissonant relationships. We decided to explore this in one fMRI study.

A study was designed to explore the neural mechanisms invoked as a result of relationships with resonant, high-leader member exchange (i.e., LMX), high-quality relationship leaders, and dissonant, lo- LMX, low-quality relationship leaders (Boyatzis, Passarelli, Koenig, Lowe, Mathew, Stoller, & Phillips, in review). Middle-aged subjects were asked about critical incidents with leaders in their experiences. fMRI scans were conducted, with cues developed from these experiences.

In this exploratory study, preliminary observations revealed that recalling specific experiences with resonant leaders significantly activated 14 regions of interest in the brain, while dissonant leaders activated 6 and deactivated 11 regions. Experiences with resonant leaders activated neural systems involved in arousing attention (i.e., anterior cingulate cortex), the social or default network (i.e. right inferior frontal gyrus), mirror system (i.e., the right inferior parietal lobe), and other regions associated with approach relationships (i.e., the right putamen and bilateral insula). Meanwhile, dissonant leaders deactivated systems involved in social or default networks (i.e., the posterior cingulate cortex), the mirror system (i.e., the left inferior frontal gyrus), and activated those regions associated with narrowing attention (i.e., bilateral anterior cingulate cortex), and those associated with less compassion (i.e., left posterior cingulate cortex), more negative emotions (i.e., posterior inferior frontal gyrus).

With creative designs, future research can probe the neural activations that various relationships and people have had on us. We can begin to understand *how* they may be affecting our moods and cognitive openness.

Possible implications

In *Primal Leadership, Resonant Leadership,* and a more recent article in *Harvard Business Review* (Goleman & Boyatzis, 2008), we offered many examples of leaders who build resonant relationships with others around them—many others around them. And dissonant leaders who seem to turn people off, alienate them, and lose their motivation. The neuroscience findings emerging suggest a basic reason why inspiring and supportive relationships are important—they help activate openness to new ideas and a more social orientation to others.

These insights may move the primacy of a leader's actions away from the often proselytized "results-orientation" toward a relationship orientation. This does not preclude the concern with results, but could show why being first and foremost concerned about one's relationships may then enable others to perform better and more innovatively—and lead to better results. John Chambers of Cisco Systems and Oprah Winfrey of Harpo Productions are both driven to produce impressive results. But when people who work directly with them talk about their meetings, they walk out of them motivated and inspired by what they are doing and their commitment to each other.

Emotional Contagion and Empathy

While most people will acknowledge the role of empathy in understanding others, few appreciate how quickly impressions of others get formed or the neural mechanisms involved. For this we must look to the research on contagion. Prior research has explained mimicry and imitation (Hatfield, Cacioppo & Rapson, 1993). But recent studies, although somewhat controversial, offer three possibilities regarding emotional contagion: (1) emotional contagion spreads in milliseconds, below conscious recognition (LeDoux, 2002); (2) emotional arousal may precede conceptualization of the event (Iacoboni, 2009); and (3) neural systems activate endocrine systems that, in turn, activate neural systems (Garcia-Segura, 2009).

The mirror neuron system has been claimed to foster imitation and mimicry (Cattaneo & Rizzolatti, 2009). This system allows us to discern the: (a) *context of an observed action or setting;* (b) *the action;* and (c) *the intention of the other living being.* They help us to understand the sensing of the goals/intention of another's actions or expressions, and to link sensory and motor representation of them. Even the most recent approaches to emotional contagion that do not focus on the mirror system claim to show a sympathetic hemo-dynamic that creates the same ability for us to relate to another's emotions and intention (Decety & Michalaks, 2010).

Relevant to leadership, there are three implications of these observations: the speed of activation, the sequence of activation, and the endocrine/neural system interactions. The firing of the limbic system seems to occur within 8 milliseconds of a primary cognition *and* it takes almost 40 milliseconds for that same circuit to appear in the neocortex for interpretation and conceptualization (LeDoux, 2002). With this timing, our emotions are determining cognitive interpretation more than previously admitted. Once primary cognitions have occurred, secondary cognitions allow for the neocortical events (i.e., reframing) to drive subsequent limbic or emotional labeling. Our unconscious emotional states are arousing emotions in those with whom we interact before we or they know it. And it spreads from these interactions to others.

Research has suggested that negative emotions are stronger than positive emotions (Baumeister, Bratslavsky, Finkenauer, & Vohs, 2001). As a result, we would suspect that the contagion of negative emotion would ignite a stronger neural sequence than positive emotions. This may serve evolutionary functions but, paradoxically, it may limit learning. Arousal of strong negative emotions stimulates the Sympathetic Nervous System, which inhibits access to existing neural circuits and invokes cognitive, emotional, and perceptual impairment (Sapolsky, 2004; Schulkin, 1999; Dickerson and Kemeny, 2004).

The benefits of arousing positive emotions over negative ones have been demonstrated by Fredrickson and Losada (2004) and others. A contagion of positive emotions seems to arouse the Parasympathetic Nervous System, which stimulates adult neurogenesis (i.e., growth of new neurons) (Erickson et. al., 1998), a sense of well being, better immune system functioning, and cognitive, emotional, and perceptual openness (McEwen, 1998; Janig and Habler, 1999; Boyatzis, Jack, Cesaro, Passarelli, & Khawaja, 2010).

The sustainability of leadership effectiveness is directly a function of a person's ability to adapt and activate neural plasticity (please explain neural plasticity and why it's important). The SNS and PNS are both needed for human functioning. They each have an impact on neural plasticity. Arousal affects the growth of the size and shape of our brain. Neurogenesis allows the human to build new neurons. The endocrines aroused in the PNS allow the immune system to function at its best to help preserve existing tissue (Dickerson and Kemeny, 2004) (Please connect arousal, neurogenesis and endocrines).

Possible Implications

The most likely implication of these results is that leaders bear the primary responsibility for knowing what they are feeling and therefore, managing the contagion that they infect in others. It requires a heightened emotional self-awareness. This means having techniques to notice the feelings (i.e., know that you are having feelings and become aware of them), label or understand what they are (i.e., giving a label to vague or gnawing sensations), and then signal yourself that you should do something to change your mood and state. Merely saying to yourself that you will "put on a happy face" does not hide the fast and unconscious transmission of your real feelings to others around you.

You are infecting others around you with specific feelings. Some of those feelings help them to perform better and innovate and some are debilitating and inhibit adaptive thinking. Remember, negative feelings, even the unconscious ones, will easily overwhelm positive ones. The leader, because of his/her position of power, has a greater affect on others in a social or work environment. Being able to change your internal state might be one of the most powerful techniques you learn in becoming an effective leader—one who inspires others to learn, adapt and perform at their best.

Helping and Inspiring Others

Leaders should be coaches in helping to motivate and inspire those around them (Boyatzis, Smith & Blaize, 2006). But not any old form of coaching will help. Coaching others with compassion, that is, toward the Positive Emotional Attractor, appears to activate neural systems that help a person open themselves to new possibilities—to learn and adapt. Meanwhile, the more typical coaching of others to change in imposed ways (i.e., trying to get them to conform to the views of the boss) may create an arousal of the SNS and puts the person in a defensive posture. This moves a person toward the Negative Emotional Attractor and to being more closed to possibilities. We decided to test this difference.

In a study, sophomores were coached with each approach (Boyatzis, Jack, Cesaro, Khawaja & Passarelli, 2010). On the basis of two 30 minutes coaching sessions, one to the PEA (asking a person about their future dreams) and the other to the NEA (asking them how they are handling their courses and whether they are doing all of their homework), we found dramatic differences in neural activation. Using an fMRI to track neural activity, it showed significant differences in activation as a result of these two approaches to coaching. We found activation of the orbito-frontal cortex and nucleus accumbens to be positively related to PEA coaching. This also activated a part of the visual cortex in which a person can imagine and visualize something. These are associated with PNS arousal. Meanwhile, the NEA seemed to activate the Anterior Cingulate Cortex and Medial Prefrontal Cortex, both regions known for self-consciousness and reflections while feeling guilt.

These results were consistent with those from Jack, Dawson, Ciccia, Cesaro, Barry, Snyder & Begany (2010) showing that there is a network of brain regions activated when engaged in social activities (formerly called the Default Motor Network in the neuroscience literature). There is a dramatically different network that is activated when you are engaged in analytics or trying to solve a non-social problem. They showed that these two networks suppress each other. That is, when you are busy thinking about budgets, financial analysis, or product specifications, you will have turned off the parts of your brain that are key to social functioning—and visa versa!

Possible implications

If you believe that leadership involves inspiring others and motivating them to be their best and develop, learn, adapt and innovate, then activating the parts of their brain that will help requires arousing what we have called the Positive Emotional Attractor. To arouse the PEA, these studies are suggesting that we need to: (1) be social; and (2) engage the person in positive, hopeful contemplation of a desired future. The latter might also be stimulated when discussing core values and the purpose of the organization or project. All too often, people in leadership positions begin conversations about the financials or metrics and dashboard measures of the desired performance. These findings suggest that while important, this sequence confuses people and actually results in them closing down cognitively, emotionally and perceptually. If you want them to open their minds, you need to discuss the purpose of the activity (not merely the goals) and the vision of the organization or clients if a desired future were to occur. THEN, you can lead a discussion about the financials, metrics and measures. But you have made it clear that the measures follow the purpose, they have not become the purpose.

If this sounds like transformational leadership, versus its less effective sibling, transactional leadership, you have made an important connection. But our research shows that you need to arouse the PEA and the NEA to get sustained, desired change. The key appears to be, so far in our research, that you need to: (1) arouse the PEA first; and (2) arouse the PEA sufficiently such that it is about three to six times more frequent in the discussions than the NEA.

Findings such as these may help us to understand, if replicated, how to help others—and how to help us sustain our effectiveness as leaders.

References

Baumeister, R. F., Bratslavsky, E., Finkenauer, C., & Vohs, K. D. (2001). Bad is stronger than good. *Review of General Psychology*, 5: 323–370.

Boyatzis, R. E., Jack, A., Cesaro, R., Passarelli, A. & Khawaja, M. (2010). *Coaching with Compassion: An fMRI Study of Coaching to the Positive or Negative Emotional Attractor*. Presented at the Annual Meeting of the Academy of Management, Montreal.

Boyatzis, R. & McKee, A. (2005). *Resonant Leadership: Renewing Yourself and Connecting With Others Through Mindfulness, Hope, and Compassion*. Boston: Harvard Business School Press.

Boyatzis, R.E., Passarelli, A.P., Koenig, K., Lowe, M., Mathew, B., Stoller, J. & Phillips, M. (under review). Examination of the Neural Substrates Activated in Experiences with Resonant & Dissonant Leaders. *Leadership Quarterly*.

Boyatzis, R.E., Smith, M. and Blaize, N. (2006) "Developing sustainable leaders through coaching and compassion, *Academy of Management Journal on Learning and Education*. 5(1): 8–24.

Cattaneo, L. & Rizzolatti, G. (2009). The mirror neuron system. *Neurobiological Review, 66*(5), p. 557–560

Decety, J. & Michalska, K.J. (2010). Neurodevelopmental change in circuits underlying empathy and sympathy from childhood to adulthood. *Developmental Science. 13*: 6, 886–899.

Dickerson, S.S. & Kemeny, M.E. (2004). Acute stressors and cortisol responses: A theoretical integration and synthesis of laboratory research. *Psychological Bulletin*.130(3): 355–391.

Fredrickson, B. L., & Losada, M. (2005). Positive affect and the complex dynamics of human flourishing. *American Psychologist*. 60(7): 678–686. *Psychology*, 86(2): 320–333.

Garcia-Segura, L.M. (2009). *Hormones and brain plasticity*. NY: Oxford University Press.

Goleman, D., Boyatzis, R., & McKee, A. (2002). *Primal Leadership: Realizing the Power of Emotional Intelligence*. Boston: Harvard Business School Press.

Goleman, D. & Boyatzis, R. (September, 2008). Social intelligence and the biology of leadership. *Harvard Business Review*. 86:9, pp. 74–81.

Hatfield, E., Cacioppo, J.T., & Rapson, R.L. (1993). *Emotional contagion*. NY: Cambridge University Press.

Iacoboni, M. (2009). Imitaiton, empathy, and mirror neurons. *Annual Review of Psychology. 60*, p. 653–670.

Jack, A., Dawson, A., Ciccia, A. Cesaro, R., Barry, K., Snyder, A. & Begany, K. (2010). Social and Mechanical reasoning define two opposing domains of human higher cognition. Under review. Manuscript from Case Western Reserve University, Cleveland, Ohio.

Janig, W. & Habler, H-J. (1999). Organization of the autonomic nervous system: Structure and function. In O. Appendzeller (ed.). *Handbook of Clinical Neurology: The Autonomic Nervous System: Part I: Normal Function,* 74: 1–52.

LeDoux, J. (2002). *Synaptic self: How our brains become who we are.* NY: Viking.

McEwen, B. S. (1998). Protective and damaging effects of stress mediators. *New England Journal of Medicine.* 338: 171–179.

Sapolsky, R. M. (2004). *Why zebra's don't get ulcers (third edition).NY:* Harper Collins.

Schulkin, J. (1999). *Neuroendocrine regulation of behavior.* NY: Cambridge University Press.

Senior, C., Lee, N.L., & Butler, M. (2010). Organizational cognitive neuroscience. *Organization Science. On-line in advance of print,* 1–10.

Discussion Questions

1   Authentic leadership theory suggests that being genuine and exposing your real self to your followers will help you gain their trust. This chapter discusses the importance of impression management for leaders. Do you think authenticity and impression management represent contradictive principles? If you do, how can you resolve such contradiction as a leader?

2   What might be a possible side effect of attempting to project an image of a highly capable and successful leader who is never wrong or does not make mistakes?

3   What did you learn from this chapter about your leadership image? Identify three ideas that you could apply to your own leadership experience.

4   Describe the differences between resonant relationships and dissonant relationships. What does neuroscience research reveal in this regard?

PART III

MAIN LEADERSHIP THEORIES AND RESEARCH

CHAPTER 4

Contingency and Situational Leadership

Contingency Management and Situational Leadership Theories

JoAnn Danelo Barbour

Contingency management and situational leadership are two sides of the coin of belief that there is no one best way of managing or leading, the twin concepts I will address in this chapter. Sometimes there is overlap in use and meaning; sometimes the concepts veer in meaning or use. I will discuss the conceptual overlaps and differences as I describe the theories and discuss their original development, iterations, and uses and applications of the theories. I conclude with a discussion of the strengths of the theories and comments from critics of the theories.

From a somewhat evolutionary standpoint, management and leadership theorists wanted to expand beyond the early great man and trait theories and early behavioral theories. They wanted to address the criticism in management and leadership studies that did not take into account the contexts or situations in which managers and leaders make decisions. Contingency and situational theorists attempt to discuss management and leadership from both organizational and behavioral perspectives.

Embedded in open systems theory, both contingency and situational theories are influential in management and leadership theory development. In open systems theory, organizations are capable of self-maintenance based on environmental input or interaction, essential for open system functioning. From an organizational perspective within systems theory, contingency and situational theorists view administrative and leadership processes and choices as a condition of the particular character or nature of the organization itself, the environment of the organization at a given point in time, the nature of the key decision makers, and the specific task or tasks the organization seeks to accomplish within a particular timeframe.

Description

In coining the term, *contingency theory*, Lawrence and Lorsch (1967) argued that different environments place differing requirements on organizations, and, accordingly, on the leaders of those organizations (Scott, 1987). Consequently, theorists from a perspective grounded in behavioral theory contend that there is no one best way of leading or decision making, that a leadership style that is effective in some situations may not be successful in others. A major assumption, therefore, of contingency management and situational leadership is that one's ability to manage or lead is dependent upon or influenced by various situational factors, including the leader's preferred style and the capabilities and behaviors of organizational members (traditionally noted in the literature as followers), as well as other variables.

There are two conclusions one can draw based on this assumption. First, leaders and managers who may be effective at one place and time may become unsuccessful either when transplanted to another situation or when the factors around them change. Additionally, because manager and leader behavioral expectations will vary depending on the situations, managers and leaders will be more or less successful depending on their ability to change behaviors based on situational factors. A second conclusion, therefore, is that success as a leader or manager may depend upon one's ability to adapt and change one's behaviors as requirements and needs of situations change. As the theories evolved, they were characterized by two orienting sets of behaviors, one toward the task (initiating structure, concern for production) and one set toward interpersonal relations (consideration, concern for people).

As contingency theorists view organizational and management processes and choices as dependent upon a set of variables (nature of the organization, environment at a point in time, nature of key decision makers, and specific tasks to be accomplished), similarly, the major premise of situational leadership is that the best action of the leader depends on a range of situational factors. An effective leader does not fall into a single preferred style of decision making. Factors that affect situational decisions include motivation and capability of followers, factors that, in turn, are affected by particular issues, features or dynamic within the situational context, including the relationship between followers and the leader. One's perception of oneself, of the follower, of the tasks, and of the situation will often affect what a leader does rather than the truth or reality of the situation.

Development and Iterations of Contingency and Situational Theories

Although both contingency management and situational leadership theorists hold the assumption that there is no simple one right way to manage or lead, there are differences in the theories. Contingency theorists take a broader view that includes contingent factors about leader capability and other variables within the situation, whereas situational theorists tend to focus more on the behaviors that the leader should adopt when encountering factors within a given context or situation, for example follower behavior, environmental issues, or political concerns.

Situational and contingency theorists stress several key concepts. There is no universal or one best way to lead. There are, however, some universal principles of leadership that fit all situations. Organizationally, the design and its subsystems must be a fit for the leader; the organization, its subsystems and leader must have a proper fit with the environment; and each situation within the organizational environment is unique and therefore must be studied and treated as unique. The success of the leader is a function of various organizational contingencies in the form of subordinate, task, and/ or group variables.

Because the effectiveness of a given pattern of leader behavior is contingent upon the demands imposed by the situation, the leader's style is, of necessity, highly variable. For an individual leader, situational theorists assume that leadership is changeable and should be variable for different situations; thus, leaders use different styles of leadership appropriate to the needs created by different organizational situations. Tannenbaum and Schmidt (1973) suggest three elements produce a leader's action: factors or forces in the situation, capabilities or forces in the followers, and capabilities or forces in the leader. These elements are parts of four classic and frequently cited management and leadership contingency and situational models, which I will discuss next. The contingency model of leadership effectiveness and cognitive resource theory focuses on the leader's internal state and traits (Fiedler, 1967, 1972, 1973, 1974). Others focus on the leader's perceived behaviors, such as path-goal theory (House & Mitchell, 1974, 1997; and Tannenbaum & Schmidt, 1973), situational leadership theory (Hersey & Blanchard, 1974, 1993), and the normative decision making model (Vroom & Jago, 1988; and Vroom & Yetton, 1973).

Generally considered the father of leadership contingency theory, Fred Fiedler (1967, 1972, 1973, 1974) veered from traditional trait and behavioral models with his assertion that three organizational contingencies determine appropriate manager or leader behavior. These organizational contingencies include leader-member relations (the degree to which a leader is accepted and supported by group members), task structure (the extent to which tasks are structured and defined with clear goals and procedures), and leader positional power (the ability of a leader to control subordinates through reward and punishment). Fiedler argued that combinations of the three contingencies create favorable or unfavorable conditions for leadership, that is, situations in which the leader can exert influence over the group. High levels of leader-member relations, task structure and positional power provide the most favorable situation to exert influence over others; low levels of the three contingencies provide the least favorable leadership situation to exert influence. Fiedler determined that a task-oriented style is more effective in situations wherein the leader has very much or very little influence; a relationship-oriented leader is more effective in situations only moderately favorable to influence. Fiedler concluded that the organization should match up a particular manager or leader and style to the demands of the situation, or alter the variables within the situation, that is, the power that goes with the leadership position, so that the situation becomes more conducive to one's style of influence.

In other words, it may be easier for leaders to change a situation to achieve effectiveness, rather than change leadership style.

Variations to Fiedler's model include two examples of path-goal theory: those of House and Mitchell (1977, 1994) and Tannenbaum and Schmidt (1973). Influenced by expectancy theories of motivation, House and Mitchell developed the path-goal contingency model, asserting that the leader's behavior is acceptable to subordinates insofar as they view the leader's behavior as a source of immediate or future satisfaction. The leader is to observe and understand the situation and choose appropriate leadership styles and actions (paths) depending upon goals of subordinates and leader. The responsibilities of the leader, to offer rewards for achievement of performance goals, to clarify paths towards these goals, and to remove obstacles, are accomplished by adopting certain leadership styles according to the situation. The leader styles will be directive, supportive, participative, and achievement-oriented, depending on subordinate needs and abilities. Leadership behaviors are matched along a continuum of subordinate and environmental characteristics, from structured to unstructured situations; thus, if group members have a high need for motivation, directive leadership is provided, specific advice is given and ground rules are established to provide structure. If members have a low need for motivation, achievement-oriented leadership is provided and challenging goals are set with high performance encouraged while showing confidence in members' ability, a more unstructured situation.

Effective leaders adjust their leadership to fit these contingencies of group and environment and to motivate subordinates. To the House and Mitchell model, Tannenbaum and Schmidt (1973) add a range of behavioral patterns available to a manager or leader, from authoritarian (task-oriented) leadership to democratic (relationship-oriented) leadership. Leader action choices are connected to the degree of authority used by the leader and the amount of freedom available to the subordinates. Action choices begin on the left of the continuum with a high degree of control; the action choice on the farthest right of the continuum is a leader who delegates authority. Tannenbaum and Schmidt believe a leader should be flexible and adapt the leadership style to the situation.

Hersey and Blanchard (1974, 1993) developed the Situational Leadership Grid that contains two dimensions of leadership: task behavior and relationship behavior. More specifically, the effectiveness of four leadership behaviors (telling, selling, participating, and delegating) depends on whether the behaviors complement the subordinates' maturity. Hersey and Blanchard proposed that one's leadership style should be matched to the maturity of the subordinates' psychological maturity (willingness, self-confidence, motivation, and readiness to accept responsibility) and task maturity (education, skills, ability, technical knowledge, and experience). As the subordinate maturity increases, leaders should be more relationship-motivated than task-motivated. Leadership will vary with the situation and the leader may delegate to, participate with, sell ideas to, or tell subordinates what to do. Although the theory has a measure, the leadership effectiveness and adaptability description, to assess the leader's style, "many of the empirical studies on this model seem to use the Leader Behavior Description Questionnaire in measuring the leader's behaviors" (Ayman, 2004, p. 162).

Vroom and Yetton (1973) and Vroom and Jago (1988) developed a contingency model focused on the leader's decision strategy, a normative model that emphasizes leader behavior from authoritative to participative. With this model, the effectiveness of a decision depends upon a number of situational variables: (a) the importance of the decision quality and acceptance of the decision; (b) the amount of relevant information possessed by the leader and subordinates; (c) the likelihood that subordinates will accept an autocratic decision or collaborate in trying to make a good participative decision, and (d) the amount of disagreement among subordinates with respect to their preferred alternatives. The Vroom-Yetton leadership model (1973) includes the selection of one of five leadership styles for making a decision: (a) Autocratic 1 when the problem is solved using information already available; (b) Autocratic 2 when additional information is obtained from the group before the leader makes decision; (c) Consultative 1 when the leader discusses the problem with subordinates individually before making a decision; (d) Consultative 2 when the problem is discussed with the group before deciding, and (e) Group 2 when the group makes the decision with the leader simply acting as facilitator. The leadership style is chosen by progressing through seven questions at various nodes along the decision tree. Vroom and Yetton suggest that the overall effectiveness of a decision depends on two intervening variables: (a) decision quality—the objective aspects of the decision that affect group performance regardless of any effects mediated by decision acceptance, and (b) decision acceptance by followers—the degree of follower commitment in implementing a decision effectively. They maintain that both decision quality and acceptance are affected by follower participation during decision making.

Conclusions

One major strength in the contingency and situational models is that these scholars moved thinking beyond the *one best type of leader* assumption of the trait theorists and the *one best way to lead* model of the early behaviorists. The contingency and situational theorists began to conceptualize management and leadership theory within an organizational framework; thus, leader or manager style had to be discussed within an organizational context that includes the workers within the organization. Critics suggest, however, that contingency and situational theorists are limited in their conceptualization of leadership and the empirical strength to support the various arguments. While scholars might agree that the most effective leaders are those who are both task oriented and people oriented (that is, high-high leaders), the empirical research based on questionnaires, according to Yukl (1998), seems to provide limited support for the universal proposition that high-high leaders are more effective, and few studies have directly investigated whether the two types of leader behavior interact in a mutually facilitative way. In contrast, "The descriptive research from critical incidents and interviews strongly suggests that to be effective a leader must be able to guide and facilitate the work to accomplish task objectives while at the same time maintaining cooperative relationships and teamwork" (Yukl, 1998, p. 64).

Within an organizational context, contingency and situational theorists pay little attention to the structure of the organization—neither that over which the managers have control nor structural components to which managers have little control. These theorists oversimplify the options available to leaders and managers as well as the range of situations that they encounter. They pay little attention to cultural and symbolic aspects of the organization and the values of those who collectively lead, manage, and work within the organization; and pay no consideration to politics and the political climate within the organization and in the larger context outside and tangential to the organization (Blake & Mouton, 1969, 1985; Bolman & Deal, 2009; Hofstede, 1984; Morgan, 1997; and Schein, 1992). Additionally, they tend to overlook contextual factors such as hierarchical level, national culture, or leader-follower gender (Antonakis, Avolio, & Sivasubramaniam, 2003), and issues of paradoxical behavioral complexity (Denison, Hooijberg, & Quinn, 1995).

Effective leaders respond to situations by changing behaviors, by being perceived as behaving differently, or by choosing and then managing the situation (Ayman, 2004). Theoretically, contingency and situational approaches to management and leadership work because they are based on a person-to-situation fit concept. As a set of theories, contingency and situational theories are evolutionary. They help bridge a gap between trait theorists and the early behaviorists. The interactions of all organizational factors are very complex, however, and unpredictable; and, since circumstances do not stay fixed for long, a constant renegotiating of leadership behaviors and styles would have to occur.

References

Antonakis, J., Avolio, B. J., & Sivasubramaniam, N. (2003). Context and leadership: An examination of the nine-factor full-range leadership theory using multifactor leadership questionnaire (MLQ Form 5X). *Leadership Quarterly*, 14, 261–295.

Ayman, R. (2004). Situational and contingency approaches to leadership. In J. Antonakis, A. T. Cianciolo, & R. J. Stern-berg (Eds.), *The nature of leadership* (pp. 148–170). Thousand Oaks, CA: SAGE.

Blake, R., & Mouton, J. S. (1969). *Building a dynamic corporation through grid organizational development*. Reading, MA: Addison-Wesley.

Blake, R., & Mouton, J. S. (1985). *Managerial grid III*. Houston, TX: Gulf.

Bolman, L. G., & Deal, T. E. (2009). *Reframing organizations: Artistry, choice and leadership* (4th ed.). San Francisco, CA: Jossey-Bass.

Denison, D. R., Hooijberg, R., & Quinn, R. E. (1995). Paradox and performance: Toward a theory of behavioral complexity in managerial leadership. *Organization Science, 6*(5), 524–540.

Fiedler, F. E. (1967). *A theory of leadership effectiveness*. New York, NY: McGraw-Hill.

Fiedler, F. E. (1972). The effects of leadership training and experience: A contingency model interpretation. *Administrative Science Quarterly, 17*(4), 453–470.

Fiedler, F. E. (1973). The contingency theory and the dynamics of leadership process. *Advances In Experimental Social Psychology, 11*, 60–112.

Fiedler, F. E. (1974). The contingency model: New directions for leadership utilization. *Journal of Contemporary Business, 3,* 65–79.

Hersey, P., & Blanchard, K. H. (1974). So you want to know your leadership style? *Training and Development Journal, 2,* 1–15.

Hersey, P., & Blanchard, K. H. (1993). *Management of organizational behavior: Utilizing human resources* (6th ed.). Englewood Cliffs, NJ: Prentice Hall.

Hofstede, G. (1984). *Culture's consequences: International differences in work-related values.* Newbury Park, CA: SAGE.

House, R. J., & Mitchell, T. R. (1974). A path-goal theory of leader effectiveness. *Journal of Contemporary Business, 3,* 81–97.

House, R. J., & Mitchell, T. R. (1997). Path-goal theory of leadership. In R. P. Vecchio (Ed.), *Leadership: Understanding the dynamics of power and influence in organizations* (pp. 259–273). Notre Dame, IN: Notre Dame University Press.

Lawrence, P. R., & Lorsch, J. W. (1967). *Organization and environment: Managing differentiation and integration.* Boston, MA: Harvard University Graduate School of Business Administration.

Morgan, G. (1997). *Images of organization* (2nd ed.). Thousand Oaks, CA: SAGE.

Schein, E. H. (2004). *Organizational culture and leadership* (3rd ed.) San Francisco, CA: Jossey-Bass.

Scott, W. R. (1987). *Organizations: Rational, natural, and open systems* (2nd ed.). Englewood Cliffs, NJ: Prentice-Hall.

Tannenbaum, R., & Schmidt, W. H. (1973). How to choose a leadership pattern. *Harvard Business Review, 51*(3), 162–175, 178–180.

Vroom, V. H., & Jago, A. G. (1988). *The new leadership: Managing participation in organizations.* Englewood Cliffs, NJ: Prentice Hall

Vroom, V. H., & Yetton, P. W. (1973). *Leadership and decision making.* Pittsburgh, PA: University of Pittsburgh Press.

Yukl, G. (1998). *Leadership in organizations* (4th ed.) Upper Saddle River, NJ: Prentice-Hall.

Discussion Questions

1   Describe the differences between contingency and situational leadership.

2   What theories are included in the contingency and situational leadership approach? What do they suggest? In what ways are they different?

3   Fiedler's model is considered a prescriptive theory. What does Fiedler suggest with regard to establishing leadership effectiveness?

CHAPTER 5

Transactional and Transformational Leadership

Charismatic and Transformational Approaches

Karen Dill Bowerman and Montgomery Van Wart

My strong point is not rhetoric, it isn't showmanship, it isn't big promises—those things that create the glamour and the excitement that people call charisma and warmth.

—Richard M. Nixon, 1972

What is the leadership fire that ignites a follower's torch, heightening his commitment and drive for results? What is the spark that ultimately leads to a huge and purposeful flash of change for an organization? Is it primarily sound management practices in action? Is it the words of a leader, promising to give people what they want? Is it an authoritative personality that seems to charge the environment with electricity and stimulate people into action? Or is it uncommon personalities to which people are drawn because of that individual's ability to communicate a sense of magnetism, persuasion, and power? This chapter will examine these questions in depth.

Following years of prosperity after World War II, the U.S. economy waned and lost much of its preeminence by the 1970s, suffering from "stagflation" characterized by sluggish, or *stagnant*, output growth, high in*flation* rates, and rising unemployment. It is not a surprise that the field of leadership theory responded with new directions. In the 1980s, the new theories of leadership that emerged diverged markedly from those that grew out of the Ohio State and University of Michigan studies discussed in the previous chapter. There was a swell of interest in strong leaders who could provide boldness, incisive strategies, wide appeal, and sweeping changes when necessary.

It was widely felt that "the problem with many organizations, and especially the ones that are failing, is that they tend to be overmanaged and underled" (Bennis and Nanus 1985, 21).

The perspective of being **overmanaged and underled** was clearly articulated as early as 1977 in *Harvard Business Review* by Abraham Zaleznik, who taught the psychodynamics of leadership. At the time of his writing, the duty of management was seen as focusing on budgets and process, stability and control. In contrast, the business of leadership was seen as focusing on human aspects of inspiration and passion, vision and chaos. Management was a function with the ability to deal with complex systems and to keep the current system functioning. Leadership was about relationships that offered the ability to deal energetically with environmental change and to bring about purposeful transformation within the organization. Organizations were likened to individuals—when time was not spent on visionary growth and change, it tended to be used for routine day-to-day events or putting out immediate "fires."

In simple terms, overmanagement from the supervisor's perspective is spending too much energy making sure that things are done the way he or she wants them done. In a similar fashion, being underled, from the supervisor's perspective, results in spending too little time getting to the important matters at hand, such as inspiring positive change.

As true as Bennis and Nanus's observation is about being overmanaged and underled, another counterbalancing perspective is that an organization can be equally stifled by being overled and undermanaged. "In fact, there are far too many organizations today—both in government and the private sector—in which the person at the top *over*leads and *under*manages. All too often these organizations experience failure not because of a lack of ideas, goals and inspiration, but because they can't get their acts together and make it all happen. In the real world, leadership and management can't be split" (Kent 2001).

The point Kent makes is clear, that a careful balance of what we think of as management (e.g., organizing and controlling) and as leadership (e.g., planning with vision) is truly the ideal. Imagine, for instance, the medical director of Arrowhead Regional Medical Center, Dr. Dev GnanaDev, being without a well-rounded balance of management and leadership skills. As an MBA graduate, his leadership is strong, and he helped guide a visionary effort to build a solvent new San Bernardino County hospital in Colton, California. However, as an MD, he also kept sight of the fact that the medical leadership he provided had to present a clear-cut structure for hospital processes to control factors ranging from safety to disease management. In his endeavors to accomplish the task, Dr. GnanaDev was successful because he was trusted for his medical knowledge balanced with his good management background, and his strong, well-articulated vision as a leader (GnanaDev 2008).

Three major studies preceded and prepared for the theories that emerged in the mid-1980s. A classic and prominent approach was by Max Weber, the "father of bureaucracy," as discussed in Chapter 3. The brilliant German sociologist also provided insights into charismatic, or personality-based, leadership. He derived his interpretation of the concept from the Greek word *charisma*, meaning "the gift of God's grace," especially in religious contexts, to suggest divinely inspired talents. The person blessed with talents needed by a society or organization, particularly in crisis, would rise to the occasion, bringing radical solutions. Followers come along not only when they are attracted to an inspiring leader, but also when the leader's repeated success validates their transcendent powers. Initially, it may seem incongruous for the same theorist to talk on one hand about impersonal bureaucracy and on the other about personal charisma. Actually, the two notions are brought together by an understanding of Weber's perspective on the role of bureaucrats versus the role of the charismatics. Whereas bureaucrats administer to the day-to-day activity of an organization for its long-term stability, the charismatic leader emerges in the face of crisis to inspire major change. With new purpose and perhaps new principles established by the impact of the charismatic leader, the bureaucratic administration would then again emerge to guide the organization to an equilibrium of routine, predictable activity for the purpose of ensuring long-term stability. Of course, the two approaches to organizational life are not always followed in tandem, whereby one operates in lieu of the other as the engine that drives the organization. Charismatics are not only the top executive leaders, but also they can be found at the middle and even bottom levels of large bureaucracies. Charismatics can be invaluable at the divisional or unit level when they inspire significant change because of their personal power among peers.

Given the significance of the word "gift" in the meaning of charisma in business today, one could say that scholarly focus is shifting from *who is gifted* (i.e., leaders are born) to *the gifts that charismatic leaders employ* in order to bring change (i.e., leadership can be learned).

In 1977, Robert House published a book with a chapter titled "A 1976 Theory of Charismatic Leadership." Charismatic leaders were said to be those who, having extraordinary effects on followers, cause them to perform beyond conventional expectations. Organizations perform at higher levels as a result of cohesion, inspiration, and a strong sense of values, all of which can be imparted by a charismatic leader. House, Spangler and Woycke (1991) later wrote that charisma "refers to the ability of a leader to exercise diffuse and intense influence over the beliefs, values, behavior, and performance of others through his or her own behavior, beliefs, and personal example." As if from a divine source, charismatics emanate a sense of power that few can resist. People with great communication skills and/or great power often take on significant charismatic elements. However, the pervasive nature of television and the invasive nature of modern reporting may make the aura of charisma more difficult to sustain, since charisma has a tendency to be diminished by overexposure.

It was James McGregor Burns, however, who emphasized somewhat different aspects and popularized the term transformational leadership (1978). It is appropriate to group charismatic and transformational theories together because of their strong similarities, but they are so distinctive that a student of leadership should understand where they tend to diverge as well.

Charismatic approaches are leader-focused and tend to focus specifically on the personality and emotional communication of vision by the leader; they thus show strong interest in leaders' qualities and character. On the other hand, transformational theories are organization-focused and tend to center on leaders triggering tremendous change. Transformational leaders have extraordinary effects not only on their followers in meeting organizational or social needs, but also on organizations or social and political structures themselves. As the major theories from the two approaches have been revised and expanded, they tend to merge more and more into a single approach rather than the reverse, particularly when the leader is involved with orchestrating significant change, such as the type of change required by the U.S. economy in the 1970s or the 2010s (see Chapter 11).

A brief sketch of the charismatic Lee Iacocca, the former president of Chrysler whose leadership inspired a company turnaround in the 1980s, provides an example of the complexity of extracting a large personality out of a great change process, or vice versa. It comes as no surprise that in his 2007 book on leadership—*Where Have All the Leaders Gone?*—Iacocca's description of the nine Cs of leadership included charisma (along with curiosity, creativity, communication, character, courage, conviction, competence, and common sense). The Biggest C, he wrote, is crisis because leaders are made in times of crisis.

Conger and Kanungo's Charismatic Leadership Theory

Based in part on House's early work on charismatic leadership, Conger and Kanungo proposed a theory of **charismatic leadership** in 1987, which they later refined in book-length treatments (1987, 1998). Their focus is on *how* charisma is attributed to leaders. What is it about the leader's context in conjunction with the leader's personality and behavior that produces the perception of charisma? The account of Lee Iacocca in Exhibit 8.1 illustrates many of the concepts of Conger and Kanungo's theory. For example, Iacocca accepted a symbolic salary of $1 a year as he worked to achieve the vision he championed. One factor in the theory of charismatic leadership is that people are more likely to attribute charisma to a leader when the leader self-sacrifices or takes personal risks while working to achieve a vision.

The context, according to Conger and Kanungo, has to be problematic in some way for the emergence of charismatic leadership. The stronger the sense of crisis or emergency, the more likely that charismatic leadership can emerge, and do so flamboyantly. "In some cases, contextual factors so overwhelmingly favor transformation that a leader can take advantage of them by advocating radical changes for the system .... [Yet] during periods of relative tranquility, charismatic leaders play a major role in fostering the need for change by creating the deficiencies or exaggerating existing minor ones" (Conger and Kanungo 1998, 52–53). Some "negative charismatics" may even create a sense of crisis or deficiencies for personal advancement, even when real crises do not exist. Thus, the situational demand for charismatic leadership is a moderating factor; long-term disappointments, outright failures, and debacles all substantially increase the chance for charismatic leadership but guarantee neither its emergence nor its success.

Even if the environment has major deficiencies or is in a state of crisis, followers are likely to attribute charismatic characteristics only to leaders who have certain traits and behave in certain ways. First, charismatic leaders are dissatisfied with the status quo and are interested in changing it, sometimes through unconventional means. Leaders with charisma frequently have

Exhibit 8.1

Charismatic or Transformer: Lee Iacocca

When great change occurs, there is inevitably a big personality (or two) involved. Often it is difficult to separate the personality from the change itself and to accurately assess the significance of force of personality—convictions and charisma—from the technical and political skills of a "change master." Some would say that the role of happenstance is difficult to separate out also, although happenstance of the overall situation generally does little more than push one leader into the spotlight more than another because of that individual's expertise relative to the environment. The 1979 case of Lee Iacocca is a timeless example of a transformational leader highly focused on bringing about tremendous change and being the "trigger" of that change. There is no doubt that he was also a "big personality," in the best sense of the words.

Lido Anthony Iacocca was born in 1924 and joined Ford Motor Company as a student engineer in 1946. He soon moved into sales and headed marketing by age thirty-three. In 1960 he became general manager of the Ford Division and by 1970, as president, he was second only to Henry Ford II. Within six years, the company showed a profit of $1.8 billion, but by 1978, the two men were embroiled in a battle of trying to outmaneuver each other, and Iacocca was fired.

As fate would have it, the tenth largest corporation in the United States, Chrysler, was headquartered in the same city. It was unprofitable, inefficient, losing market share, and heavily debt-ridden. In the middle of a fuel crisis, Chrysler found itself specializing in gas-guzzling cars. On the brink of bankruptcy, Chrysler aggressively went after Iacocca and hired him as its chair. At the helm of the failing company, Iacocca communicated his radical plans, closing plants and laying off workers. He approached Congress in 1979, asking for a loan guarantee, saying that the government had bailed out the airlines and the railroads, and now it must do the same for the automobile manufacturer. He was successful; both the House and the Senate approved $1.5 billion loan guarantees, and Iacocca used the infusion of money to release the company's first compact, fuel efficient, front-wheel-drive cars. Iacocca hired an engineer (who had also been fired by Ford) who then released Chrysler's first minivan. Adding further to the benefits of good product, Iacocca obtained discounts from suppliers and wage concessions from his workers.

By now Iacocca had gained the reputation of a can-do executive. He took an annual salary of $1 per year to make the point that everyone must sacrifice for the good of Chrysler in order for the company to survive. There was no question in Iacocca's mind that the No. 3 automaker must successfully pull through. Iacocca was heard saying in ads, "If you can find a better car, buy it!" Saving Chrysler became a personal battle for Iacocca and a patriotic battle for the nation. In turn, the company began to rebound. In turn, that began to reshape the corporation's culture. The loans Iacocca had secured were due in 1991, but under his leadership, Chrysler paid them back in 1984, less than four years after receiving them and fully seven years early! He appeared on television saying, "Chrysler borrows money the old-fashioned way. We pay it back." Iacocca and Chrysler were inseparable in the public's mind. From that time on, until his retirement in 1992, Iacocca was a celebrity, a national hero, and an American patriot. The country loved what Iacocca had accomplished through his fight for America, his hard work ethic, and gutsy independence.

After those celebratory years, the situation changed again, along with the times. The automotive industry and the economy were subjected to yet another round of influences. But that, as they say, is another story.

vision, which in turn makes their leadership more compelling to followers. **Vision** is an image of what the organization can become and its effective position in its environment; vision points to an image of the desired future of the organization. *Vision* is future-oriented as opposed to *mission* which is oriented to the current organizational purpose.

Charismatic leaders may have an idealized vision of the future that is highly discrepant from the current and projected state of affairs, but they are able to communicate with confidence and enthusiasm about their vision or proposal. Charismatic leaders are willing to articulate their bold notions of how things could be, and they are interested in leading others to a better future. Generally, they tend to elicit inspirational effects by communicating emotionally as opposed to using a participative management style. Because of their opposition to the status quo, charismatic leaders are willing to be perceived by many (initially) as unconventional or proposing values different from those that have prevailed. Indeed, their advocacy is so passionate that they are willing to take personal risks or make personal sacrifices. As Conger and Kanungo note, "because of their emphasis on deficiencies in the system and their high levels of intolerance for them, charismatic leaders are always seen as organizational reformers or entrepreneurs" (1998, 53).

Many leaders respond to situations that allow or encourage charismatic behaviors, and in fact exhibit those behaviors, but are still not successful because their execution of them is flawed. In opposing the status quo, charismatic leaders must propose an alternate vision. That vision should be based on external assessments, such as the needs of constituents or the market, rather than the internal needs of the leader. It should also include a realistic assessment of the resources available to achieve the vision. Frequently, the environment shifts even as a plan or vision is being crafted; leaders who are inflexible about adapting to changing needs may doom their enterprise. Because changing cultures and traditions calls for unconventional behaviors and new values, they invariably create some opposition; if charismatic leaders create too much opposition at any one time, however, they are likely to fail or lose power. Charismatic leadership is also based on the leader's passion, confidence, and exceptional ability to persuade and sway people. But these same abilities may also predispose the leader toward a variety of dysfunctional behaviors over time: excessive egoism, contempt for superiors who withhold agreement, a tendency to turn nonsupporters into a hostile out-group, a propensity to turn supporters into sycophants, dismissal of contravening information, and encouragement of overreliance on the leader rather than an emphasis on subordinate development. Because such leaders enjoy not only position and expert power but also enormous personal power, opportunities to use their power in self-serving ways are enormous, often leading to unconscious temptations. Conger and Kanungo also describe the leader who is charismatic but in a negative way:

> Charismatic leaders can be prone to extreme narcissism that leads them to promote highly self-serving and grandiose aims. As a result, the leader's behaviors can become exaggerated, lose touch with reality, or become vehicles for pure personal gain. In turn, they may harm the leader, the followers, and the organization. An overpowering sense of self-importance and strong need to be at the center of attention can cause charismatic leaders to ignore the viewpoints of others and the development of leadership ability in followers. (1998, 211–239)

The causal-chain implicit in charismatic leadership is outlined in Exhibit 8.2.

An enormous strength of charismatic leadership theory is that it is descriptive of the world around us. It acknowledges that some impactful leaders—such as Margaret Thatcher, Charles DeGaulle, Nelson Mandela, and George Patton—are charismatic, while other leaders equally effective in terms of impact—such as Bill Gates or Paul Volcker—are noncharismatic. A charismatic leader who is ethical uses power to develop and serve others. The spotlight is shared with others in a spirit of interdependence rather than usurped by one who may be dwelling in the light of narcissism.

Not all charismatic leaders are famous, like Lee Iacocca or John F. Kennedy. Some are renowned only in their town or region or industry sector. Take, for instance, the leadership of Tom Slide, president of his high school senior class in Topeka, Kansas, and star basketball player on his college team. After earning a marketing degree at a top business school in the East, Tom decided to go back to Topeka and start his own firm, Slide Marketing. The road to ownership and success was not easy. Employees were aware that he was willing to sacrifice for the business by mortgaging his home to provide sufficient capital to grow the business. Tom honed his public speaking skills, and in his personal relations he came across as humble, although he always claimed to offer a vision of organizational success through marketing that was radically different from any other approach. The company webpage cited how Tom's expertise was championed in business magazines and blogs. Employees were loyal to the man, and he became a local hero of sorts, frequently interviewed in the media on virtually any regional business issue. Though not famous outside his community, Tom Slide embodies the spirit of a charismatic business leader.

Exhibit 8.2
Charismatic Leadership Causal Chain

Leadership styles
- Noncharismatic (lack of charismatic style)
- Good charismatic (ideal style)
  - Opposes the status quo and strives to change it
  - Has idealized vision that is highly discrepant from the status quo
  - Articulates strong and/or inspirational articulation of future vision and motivation to lead
  - Unconventional or counternormative
  - Exercises passionate advocacy
  - Is willing to incur great personal risk and cost
- Bad charismatic (misuse of charismatic style)

Ideal conditions
- Need for change and/or higher goals

Success of charismatic behaviors by leader
- Vision based on external assessments rather than projections of personal needs
- Realistic estimate of environment
- Realistic estimate of resource estimates and constraints
- Ability to see recognize shifts in the environment that call for a change in one's vision
- Ability to inspire trust and confidence and avoid excessive alienation
- Avoidance of the use of self-serving power, etc.

Performance goals
- Follower satisfaction with leader
- Follower trust in leader
- Group cohesion
- External alignment and organizational change

Source: Conger and Kanungo (1998).

Whether famous or not, it is clear that charismatic leaders can be effective agents of change. Their method is more than flashing a winning personality or an appealing visualization of the future. Research suggests that charismatic leaders employ consistent communication strategies for bringing about change, recognizing that there is great power in language for shaping norms and attitudes One study, for example, empirically analyzed speeches of twentieth-century presidents and found that during the stages for change there are "consistent communication strategies for breaking down, moving, and re-aligning the norms of their followers" (Fiol, Harris, and House 1999, 450). Differences in speech patterns help to explain why charismatic leaders are effective during the stages for change. The use of "negation, inclusion, and abstraction [occurred] more frequently during the middle phase of their tenure as leaders than in the earlier and later phases" (470) and also occurred more frequently during the most critical stage of change: moving (472–473).

Charismatic leadership is not without its flaws. Researchers such as Rakesh Khurana (2002) have found that if struggling companies looking for a new CEO seek a charismatic executive, their troubles may become worse. When corporate performance sags, directors in search of new leadership who succumb to pressure, fire the CEO, and hire a "savior" may enjoy only a brief period of satisfaction. Executive charisma does not necessarily result in organizational performance. Charisma may inspire awe, but not necessarily on-time delivery or quality output.

Khurana reports that "charisma leads companies to overlook many promising candidates and to consider others who are unsuited for the job" (2002). He cites the 1993 example of Kodak's directors, who made much ado about firing CEO Kay Whitmore. Two months later, they appointed Motorola's CEO, George Fisher. They envisioned Fisher as the savior who would soar into the Kodak picture with a flourish and right everything in due course. The fact was, however, that the company had not adopted digital imaging when it should have, so it was behind the curve when compared to its competition. Even a charismatic CEO could not change that history. After six turbulent years of cutbacks, restructurings, and a free fall in operating profits following an initial appearance of market gain, Fisher stepped down as CEO.

Kodak's next CEO, Daniel Carp, worked five years on the serious adaptation to digital imaging. In 2007, Kodak experienced a profit—the year when the company completed the transition to digital technology and the new CEO, Antonio Perez, claimed a compensation package of over $11 million. This example illustrates how a corporate board, hailing a charismatic leader selected from the outside, misinterpreted the allure of charisma and expected it to be the antidote to the strategic errors of its past. The energizing leader who ignites followers to venture in new directions in a different setting may not always be the wise choice simply because of the ability to inspire awe.

Charismatic leadership theory recognizes that for every good charismatic, it is possible to have a negative charismatic as well. There have been Roosevelts and Hitlers, Gandhis and Saddam Husseins, Mother Teresas, and Jim Joneses. In the case of many **negative charismatics**, the leader's focus shifts from organization to self.

One example of a negative charismatic that illustrates the shift in focus from organization to self is collections manager Walter Pavlo. "By the time he was 40, Walter A. Pavlo Jr. had graduated with a master's degree in business from Mercer University, worked as a manager at MCI, concocted a $6 million money laundering scheme, served a two-year sentence in federal prison, and was divorced, unemployed, and living again with his parents. It's a story that should scare any MBA straight" (Porter 2008). Pavlo, whose conservative upbringing belied his subsequent behavior, was a charismatic, energetic young collections manager who was under corporate pressure to show profits in the billing of $1 billion per month for MCI's carrier division. Without proper oversight, he began to cook the books and ultimately brought down with him others who were attracted to his charismatic style. At some point, Pavlo admitted that his focus shifted from the organization to himself. In fact, at a low point, he began to hate the organization as if to give himself psychological permission to use customers in his schemes (Pavlo and Weinberg 2007). After prison, he told his tragic tale at business schools so that future leaders would not make the unethical choices that he did. One of Pavlo's important messages was that leaders must supervise managers who are admired by others, have access to money, and are under pressure to produce "unfeasibly high" results. This does not mean that the charismatic manager is not to be trusted, but rather that no employee should be allowed free rein without oversight. Pavlo's message regarding proper supervision of charismatics is consistent with guidelines for effective delegation in any situation—supervisors at any level of the organization who delegate responsibility with commensurate authority must retain their own authority as well as knowledge of the work being done.

Other leaders with charm who are viewed as charismatic may be hollow when it comes to substance. According to ChangingMinds.org (1998), "A typical experience with them is that whilst you are talking with them, it is like being bathed in a warm and pleasant glow, in which they are very convincing. Yet afterwards, as the sunbeam of their attention is moved elsewhere, you may begin to question what they said (or even whether they said anything of significance at all)."

There can be flawed charismatics such as Bill Clinton, Oliver North, or Mao Zedong. Charismatic leadership theory has also significantly expanded our understanding of negative charismatics. It is important to understand the negative syndromes as well as the positive ones if one is to have a robust understanding of leadership.

Charisma, like other personality characteristics, is itself neither noble nor bad; it can be used for good or evil. Great generals and great heads of state often acquire charismatic qualities, even if they were not innate, such as Alexander the Great, Charlemagne, Joan of Arc, Elizabeth I, Napoleon, George Washington, Winston Churchill, and Mahatma Gandhi. Cult founders often espouse these charismatic qualities as well. A famous example of negative charisma is cult leader Jim Jones, who triggered mass suicide among his followers at Jonestown, Guyana, in 1978 (Exhibit 8.3). This case is a complete counterpoint to the earlier example of Lee Iacocca, except for the fact that others saw charisma in both of these leaders.

Charismatic leadership theory is not without its problems, of course. It is certainly not a comprehensive leadership theory inasmuch as it acknowledges but largely ignores noncharismatics

Exhibit 8.3

Negative Charisma: The Case of James Warren Jones

The charisma of cult leader Jim Jones became evident when an investigation into his alleged cures for cancer and arthritis threatened his message to followers, causing them to leave Indiana en masse for Redwood Valley, California (which he selected when *Esquire* magazine listed Ukiah as one of nine cities in the United States that could survive a nuclear war). In 1977, when an investigation into Jones's church for tax evasion threatened its tax-exempt status, followers then left California for a so-called utopian community dubbed Jonestown (named for Jim Jones himself) in Guyana, South America. A mix of religious and social ideas, combined with the charisma of James Warren Jones, ultimately led to the planned mass suicide of 909 cult members of the People's Temple church in Guyana in 1978.

Jim Jones was born in 1931 and died in the mass suicide from a gunshot to his head. He was described by people who knew him when he was young as an isolated, withdrawn child who killed animals so he could preside over their funerals (Bates 2006). A neighbor took him to the Pentecostal Church as a child, where some thought that he might have found acceptance. Jones sold pet monkeys to raise the money needed to found a church in Indianapolis in 1955, a church that eventually became known as the People's Temple. By 1960, the People's Temple became affiliated with the Disciples of Christ and Jones was listed as its ordained pastor, even though he had no formal education in theology. He initially invoked the Bible but later wrote a booklet titled "The Letter Killeth," highlighting what he thought were absurdities and lies in the Bible. Jones soon began invoking his own texts, along with the Communist Party newspaper Pravda. Probably influenced by his mother, he promoted racial equality and social justice as central principles of the People's Temple, and about 70 percent of Jonestown residents were black and impoverished. Jones felt that when residents called him "Father" and, on demand, sent him notes and letters of support addressed "Dear Dad," it was proof of his acceptance.

Life in the jungle of Guyana was very difficult. On top of long workdays, residents had numerous meetings and even Russian language classes at night. Jones made it clear to his interracial residents that they were building the Promised Land in order to escape racial injustice in the United States. Perhaps because of the pressures, Jones began taking drugs, often to excess. Some days he had difficulty speaking coherently and would ramble on to his followers over the public address system, preventing them from sleeping well. When Jones's top assistant deserted the flock of follow-ers, he claimed that Jones brainwashed the residents and held them there as if in a concentration camp. Some defectors who feared for their kin called themselves the Concerned Relatives and repeatedly appealed to congressional representatives for assistance.

In the 1970s, Jones's charisma continued on the path to corruption as he punished members who were not fully loyal to him. In the mid-1970s, loyalty tests were given at Jonestown: some members of the leadership were given a drink that they were first told was poison. As members one by one fell to the ground, faking affliction, the drink was given to others to test their loyalty before everyone was told it was only a check to make certain they were ready to die for the cause of the People's Temple.

Deeper investigation did not begin until November 18, 1978, when Representative Leo Ryan of California, along with media representatives and several Concerned Relatives, went to Jonestown to investigate charges of abusive behavior. Although loyal members of the flock greeted the investigators with a standard message of the wonderment of their life, over the course of a day, sixteen members asked to return to the United States with Congressman Ryan. As the departing party made its way to the airstrip several miles from the compound and were preparing to board their two airplanes, gunshots rang out, killing Representative Ryan and four others.

Later that same day, Jones gathered the remaining residents together, announcing that the outside world had forced them into "revolutionary suicide," a term borrowed (albeit not accurately) from Huey Newton of the Black Panther Party. Residents presumably understood Jones's call and lined up obediently. Parents and children alike drank from a vat of purple Flav-R-Aid, similar to Kool-Aid, which was laced with cyanide, sedatives, and tranquilizers. A heavy aura of pure, negative charisma ruled the scene, with very few followers taking the path of independent thinking. Almost one-third of the 909 who died at Jonestown were children. Another third were senior citizens, many of whom may have been injected with poison.

and leadership situations that are not particularly built around crises or significant change. If anything, it is moderately dismissive of noncharismatic leaders even though they may be more numerous and extremely necessary in the daily operations of organizations. This may be because charismatic leaders are "called upon" to do greater things, and their force of personality—derived from superb communication skills, excellent talent for drawing vivid images, and ability to persuade others—is relatively uncommon. President Barack Obama became known during the 2008 Democratic campaign for the presidency for his stirring rhetoric for change as well as a contagious drive for hope. His charisma led many to believe that if "called upon" to do great things, he would be uniquely equipped to come through as a leader.

Finally, the emphasis of charismatic leadership theory is essentially on personality-based leadership, and when the focus is broadened to skills that charismatic leaders employ in order to bring change, the theoretical base shifts only slightly to interpersonal communication and influence. Useful and important though these perspectives are, the study of charisma does not give a full picture of leadership because of its emphasis on both heroic and despotic leadership types. We next examine transformational leadership theory, which frequently involves a charismatic leader, but is more organizationally based and less personality-based, although still considered change-oriented leadership.

Transformational Leadership Theory

Transformational leadership theory may or may not involve an extraordinary charismatic leader at its center. But **transformational leadership** always results in follower commitment to organizational objectives along with increased follower skills and self-confidence, often resulting from empowerment. A variety of forms of transformational leadership have been put forward. We will review three—first Tichy and Devanna's model, then Kouzes and Posner's—and finally Bass's "full range theory."

Tichy and Devanna's Transformational Leadership Model

Researchers have found that charismatic leadership is not an essential ingredient for major organizational change. Instead, leaders of organizations achieving major change use transformational behaviors and may or may not be identified as charismatic individuals. A model by Tichy and Devanna (1990) emphasizes organizational needs first and examines the cascading behavioral needs second. They assert that "more than ever the key to global competitiveness will be widespread capability of institutions around the world to continuously transform." In addition, "increasingly excellence is the condition not just for dominance but for survival." Therefore, "transformational leadership is about change, innovation, and entrepreneurship" (1990, iv, xii). Their model also emphasizes the *temporal phases of change* reminiscent of Lewin, who proposed that change requires unfreezing, changing, and refreezing the organization (1951). However, they use a three-act play as their metaphor for the temporal phases, linking both organizational and individual needs to each of those acts.

Tichy and Devanna provide only two alternate styles: a managerial style and a transformational style. They assert that managers are relatively commonplace but that transformational leaders are rarer and increasingly critical to organizational success. Managers are "individuals who maintain the balance of operations in an organization, relate to others according to their role, are detached, impersonal, seek solutions acceptable as a compromise among conflicting values, and identify totally with the organization." Leaders—transformational leaders, that is—are "individuals out to create new approaches and imagine new areas to explore; they relate to people in more intuitive and empathetic ways, seek risk where opportunity and reward are high, and project ideas into images to excite people" (1990, xiii).

The transformational leader must change organizations and people in successive stages. The first stage is *recognizing the need for revitalization*. Because of the competitive environment and the speed of responsiveness required in that environment, the need for revitalization is nearly ubiquitous. The second stage is *creating a new vision*. New ways of doing business must be contemplated, refined, rehearsed, and widely articulated. The third stage is *institutionalizing change*. As the new vision is understood and accepted, new structures, mechanisms, and incentives must be put in place. This requires a creative destruction and reweaving of the social fabric of the organization. Keeping the motivation of individuals high remains key so that they continue their inner realignment and adaptation to new internal scripts.

The inclination of the leader to induce change is the intervening variable; the moderating variables are the "triggers" for change. Thus, like most transformational models, Tichy and Devanna are less interested in specifying the exact conditions under which the preferred style is useful than they are in articulating the general set of behaviors that has universal utility. The causal-chain model representing their theory is presented in Exhibit 8.4.

Kouzes and Posner's Leadership Practices Theory

The leadership practices theory employed by Kouzes and Posner (1987) represents another approach in the transformational school. Rather than starting with a chronological approach, as did Tichy and Devanna, they started with an empirical approach. They asked: *According to leaders themselves, what leads to excellent leadership based on their personal experiences?* Kouzes and Posner originally surveyed 1,330 individuals using a critical incident methodology focusing exclusively on "personal best" experiences. They assert that the five major practices they identified, each composed of two "commitments," covered more than 70 percent of respondents' descriptions of personal best scenarios. Subsequently, they designed a leadership instrument called the Leadership Practices Inventory (LPI) (1993), which has been highly popular in the training sphere, as have their writings. Both the instrument and their framework are pragmatic but largely atheoretical. That is, they are based on survey research about actual trends, but the explanation of how the practices all fit together is weak, even though each of the practices they advocate is consistent with research findings. Like Tichy and Devanna, Kouzes and Posner focus exclusively on the transformational style. They omit laissez-faire, directive, and achievement styles, for the most part, while they emphasize supportive, participative, and inspirational styles. (See Chapter 2 for an in-depth discussion of styles.)

Like other transformational theorists, Kouzes and Posner (1987, 1993) use a universal approach. Their critical-incident methodology does not discriminate based on level of leadership within the organizational hierarchy (supervisor, middle manager, or executive) or types of situations. The only moderating factors, then, are the quality of implementation of the five practices themselves.

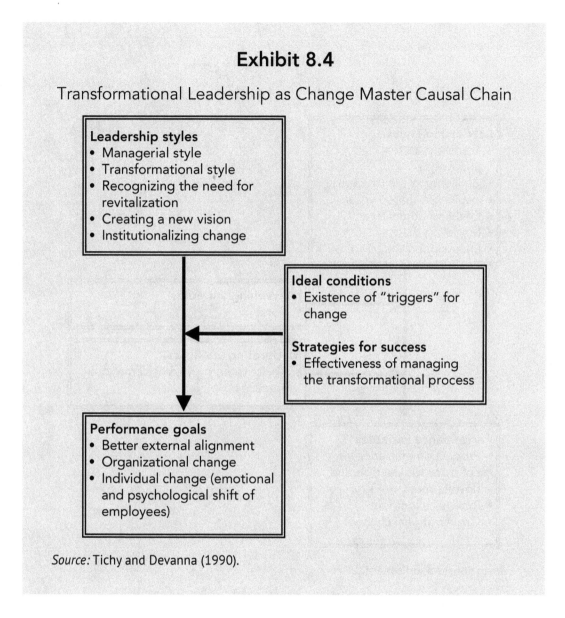

Exhibit 8.4

Transformational Leadership as Change Master Causal Chain

Leadership styles
- Managerial style
- Transformational style
- Recognizing the need for revitalization
- Creating a new vision
- Institutionalizing change

Ideal conditions
- Existence of "triggers" for change

Strategies for success
- Effectiveness of managing the transformational process

Performance goals
- Better external alignment
- Organizational change
- Individual change (emotional and psychological shift of employees)

Source: Tichy and Devanna (1990).

As the first practice, they assert that successful leaders must "challenge the process," a type of leadership emphasizing quest and courage. In turn, the two supporting practices are, first, searching for opportunities, and second, experimenting and taking risks. The second practice involves "inspiring a shared vision" composed of the commitment to envision the future and to enlist others in a common vision by appealing to their values, interests, hopes, and dreams. This inclusion of other people's ideas and dreams flows into the third practice, "enabling others to act," which is a type of participative style. It consists of fostering collaboration and strengthening others. Kouzes and Posner assert that other researchers found this to be the most important practice, and one that leaders themselves mentioned in 91 percent of the cases they studied

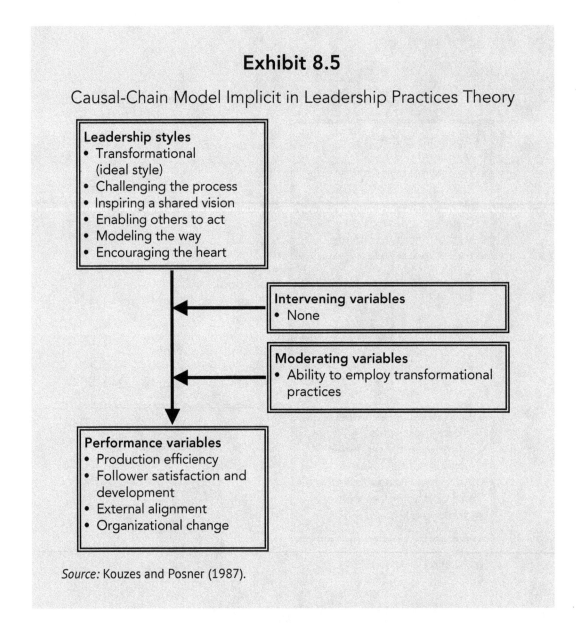

Exhibit 8.5

Causal-Chain Model Implicit in Leadership Practices Theory

Leadership styles
- Transformational (ideal style)
- Challenging the process
- Inspiring a shared vision
- Enabling others to act
- Modeling the way
- Encouraging the heart

Intervening variables
- None

Moderating variables
- Ability to employ transformational practices

Performance variables
- Production efficiency
- Follower satisfaction and development
- External alignment
- Organizational change

Source: Kouzes and Posner (1987).

(1987, 10). The fourth practice involves "modeling the way," which is composed of setting the example and planning small wins. The final practice involves "encouraging the heart." It is a supportive style composed of recognizing contributions and celebrating accomplishments. The causal-chain model based on their theory is shown in Exhibit 8.5.

Because it is based on real practices culled from more than 1,000 managers, Kouzes and Posner's Leadership Practices Inventory has pragmatic appeal. What do leaders need to do to be excellent? Indeed, it is clear that Kouzes and Posner have identified and loosely amalgamated the important inspirational, supportive, and participative styles. This has led to the popularity of the approach, which has been greatly enhanced by especially readable and dynamic books aimed largely at a nonscholarly audience. However, the weaknesses of the approach are also significant. Most importantly, although the approach tells a persuasive and rational story, the LPI has weak discriminant validity, making it ineffective for specifying verifiable transformational leader behaviors (Carless 2001). Moreover, the theory should not be mistaken for a comprehensive theory of leadership.

Bass's Full-Range Theory

The next theory we review is the most comprehensive of the transformational approaches. If Tichy and Devanna excel at providing a good articulation of transformational leadership as a process over time, and Kouzes and Posner excel at providing pragmatic microcompetencies, Burns and Bass (1978 and 1985) excel at providing a solid theoretical framework that resulted in the "**full-range leadership**" theory. Bass credits Burns with being the first to provide a comprehensive theory explaining how transactional and transformational leaders differ; Bass cites Burns' description of the transactional leader as one who approaches followers for the purpose of exchanging one thing for another, such as jobs for votes (1990, 23). The idea of the "transforming leader" grew from Burns' description of the leader who lifted followers from petty preoccupations to common goals. Bass extended Burn's approach, developing a typology of leadership behaviors with the "full range" extending from transformational leaders who are charismatic and motivate through inspiration, to transactional leaders who motivate by exchanging rewards for achievement, to laissez-faire leaders whose approach is to avoid active involvement. Laissez-faire or nonleadership normally provides haphazard or unpredictable results; transactional leadership provides conventional results; and transformational leadership provides, as Bass' book title indicates, "performance beyond expectations." When Bass extended Burns' earlier research, he suggested that leadership can simultaneously display both transformational and transactional characteristics and that the approaches are not mutually exclusive; rather, transformational leadership augments transactional leadership. The additive nature of his theory is portrayed in Exhibit 8.6.

Understanding differences between transactional leadership and transformational leadership is an important distinction, because both can establish appropriate goals and coordinate goal achievement. However, the transactional leader works less to change the framework within which she leads than does the transformational leader. The transactional leader focuses on watchful guidance, or management, within a closed system, or organization, which as a result may become increasingly out of touch with the environment, while the transformational leader will work without those boundaries, attempting to turn the tide to link the organization externally for strategic opportunities to change in response to its environment. One of the world's most famous businessmen, Walt Disney, is attributed with saying that "there are three types of people in the world today. There are 'well poisoners,' who discourage you and stomp on your creativity and tell you what you cannot do. There are 'lawn mowers,' people who are well intentioned but self-absorbed; they tend to their own needs, mow their own lawns, and never leave their yards to help another person. Finally, there are 'life-enhancers,' people who reach out to enrich the lives of others, to lift

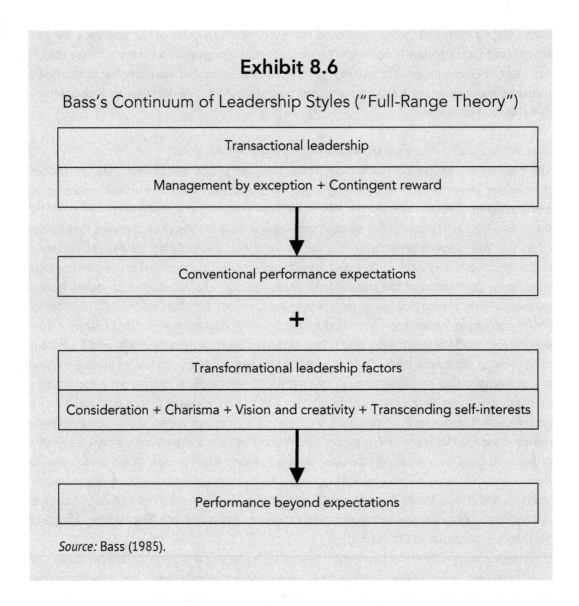

Exhibit 8.6

Bass's Continuum of Leadership Styles ("Full-Range Theory")

| Transactional leadership |
| Management by exception + Contingent reward |

↓

| Conventional performance expectations |

+

| Transformational leadership factors |
| Consideration + Charisma + Vision and creativity + Transcending self-interests |

↓

| Performance beyond expectations |

Source: Bass (1985).

them up and inspire them" (Maxwell 2008, 19). The transformational leader is the last, enriching others by raising expectations and inspiring them, thinking beyond the organization itself and perhaps even achieving revolutionary change. But meanwhile, it is transactional leadership that probably constitutes the bulk of most leader behavior and research on leadership.

In transactional leadership, rewards and benefits to followers are exchanged for their fulfillment of agreements with the leader. The more progressive and positive half of transactional leadership is contingent reward. Managers using contingent reward find out what employees value and vary the incentives that they offer accordingly An employee willing to take on one assignment may be released from another. A high-performance employee may get a large raise or a promotion. Such leadership is at its best, generally, when the work and incentives are negotiated and mutually agreed upon in advance. While contingent reward is a fundamental part of most organizational systems and represents a practical reality—people expect rewards for hard work—it does have its weaknesses. First, by itself, contingent reward systems can easily lead to extensive tit-for-tat systems where only what is specifically rewarded gets done. Second, contingent rewards generally apply to individual workers and thus do not directly account for group achievements. Furthermore, an exclusive reliance on contingent rewards may leave many, perhaps most, managers and executives with few leadership options when resources are extremely scarce or diminishing and yet the organizational needs are critical or increasing.

Management-by-exception is one use of leadership as contingent reinforcement; the approach calls for a leader to respond only to mistakes or deviations from standards, viewing them as corrective opportunities, which in turn emphasizes negative feedback. In the more lax or passive form of management-by-exception, the manager intervenes and takes corrective action only after a mistake has been made or a problem has become obvious. An active management-by-exception style indicates that the manager is monitoring more closely and intervening prior to problems going outside the unit. Neither of these approaches is necessarily bad in itself. However, Bass holds that it is generally an inferior style that should be used sparingly because the feedback given signals employees to maintain the status quo. Extensive use of this style may create intimidation and discourage initiative and creativity.

Transformational leadership was described in general earlier in this chapter. Bass asserts that transformational leadership is a widespread phenomenon across levels of management, types of organizations, and around the globe. It is therefore a universal theory without contingency factors for performance results, whereby followers are motivated to perform beyond even their own expectations as a by-product of trust and respect for the leader. As with other transformational theories, it assumes that both the quality of the transformational factors executed and the number of styles or factors used will have a moderating effect on the performance. That is, there is a substantial additive effect of the styles that invokes higher-level needs in followers.

Bass identified four elements of transformational behaviors based on his behavior description questionnaire called the Multifactor Leadership Questionnaire. The activation of these four elements—individualized consideration, idealized influence, inspirational motivation, and intellectual stimulation—engenders follower motivation.

The first behavioral element designated as transformational by Bass and others in the transformational school, called **individualized consideration**, refers to coaching, professional and personal support, individualized treatment based on specific needs, increased delegation as employees mature professionally, and so forth. In short, it boils down to respect and empathy. It is highly similar to the supportive roles proposed in **transactional theories** as discussed previously.

Bass's second element, **idealized influence**, is very similar to the concept of charisma. Those who exhibit idealized influence function as powerful role models for their followers. Followers identify with the leaders' goals and emulate their actions. This requires a perception by followers of a high level of integrity and wisdom.

The third behavioral element in Bass's taxonomy is **inspirational motivation**—in a sense, the most critical element of a transformational style. When leaders successfully use inspirational motivation, their followers are able to transcend their self-interests long enough to become passionate about organizational pride, group goals, and group achievements. Through enhanced team spirit, leaders are able to motivate followers to pursue higher standards or to make sacrifices without reliance on extrinsic incentives. Although the greater good is expected to redound to followers at some point in the future, there is generally not an exact commitment or transaction contract because of the uncertainty or abstractness of the goals.

The fourth element, **intellectual stimulation,** is the behavior of transformational leadership that encourages people to create new opportunities, to solve problems in new ways, and to envision a different ability to reexamine competing values. This style emphasizes techniques such as information sharing, brainstorming, vision articulation, and employee development targeted at specific organizational improvements. Leaders who invoke intellectual stimulation to transform an organization are often thought of as idea people or visionaries.

Later versions of Bass's theory include laissez-faire leadership as a third category distinguished from transformational and transactional. Starting with an essentially nonleadership style, laissez-faire takes a hands-off approach to leadership, as we discussed in Chapter 2. Laissez-faire leaders in this approach are largely uninvolved in operations, often slipshod about details for the situation at hand, resistant to participation in problem-solving, lax in decision-making, negligent in providing feedback, and indifferent to their subordinates' needs. The theory does not account for those occasions when the style is used purposefully, as when competing demands necessitate overlooking a particular area of responsibility or when indifference is appropriate.

The causal chain implied in Bass's model is illustrated in Exhibit 8.7.

All four transformational elements are generally present in concert in successful change initiatives, but that is not to say that the leader must supply all of them. Colleagues may supply their own consideration; low-key trust may successfully substitute for brassier charisma; young, highly motivated professionals in the group may provide the intellectual stimulation; and inspirational motivation may be largely the result of a rich and proud tradition as well as a professional indoctrination instilling strong ethical values.

Of all the transformational theories, Bass's is the most highly researched and has a good deal of positive support. Further, one gets the sense that Bass's approach builds on earlier transactional theory, even though the earlier theory and concepts are somewhat downplayed. It has its weaknesses, however. One of the most obvious is its universality, which in turn implies that transformational leadership is superior to transactional or other approaches in all leadership levels and situations. This flies in the face of the day-to-day reality of many leaders, especially those working at operational levels where stability is critical. Second, the overlap of transformational concepts with other leadership topics is problematic. Part of the problem is structural, however, because higher-level human motivations that are associated with transformational leadership are abstract and complex. Additionally, the nomenclature of the concepts is not always easy to understand. Even though Bass's transformational factors have the mnemonic of all starting with

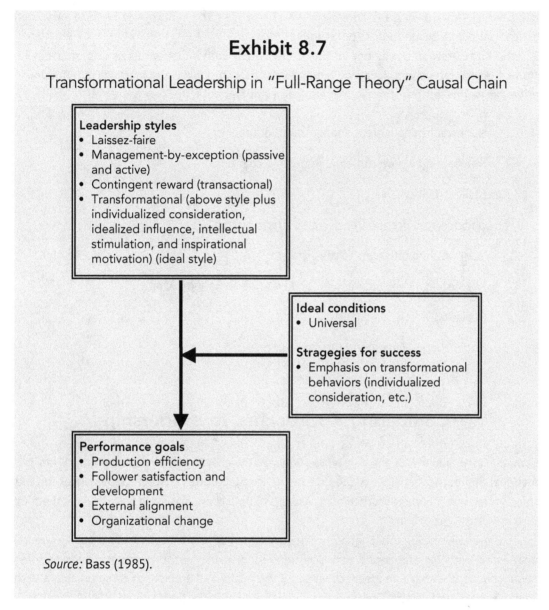

Exhibit 8.7

Transformational Leadership in "Full-Range Theory" Causal Chain

Leadership styles
- Laissez-faire
- Management-by-exception (passive and active)
- Contingent reward (transactional)
- Transformational (above style plus individualized consideration, idealized influence, intellectual stimulation, and inspirational motivation) (ideal style)

Ideal conditions
- Universal

Stragegies for success
- Emphasis on transformational behaviors (individualized consideration, etc.)

Performance goals
- Production efficiency
- Follower satisfaction and development
- External alignment
- Organizational change

Source: Bass (1985).

the letter *i*, differences between concepts such as those between individualized consideration and idealized influence have to be explained and memorized.

Regardless of the particular transformational theory followed, the executive who is bringing momentous change to an organization is supported by informative writings on the specific steps to take in transforming an organization. When these steps are not followed, they become the errors that explain why the transformation effort failed. In the previous explanation of the stages of transformation, and the steps that undergird these stages, focus is on the vision for change along with sufficient communication of that vision to all involved. Without the vision being sufficiently known, transformational effort may seem to employees to be little more than a lot of projects without purpose or meaning.

John Kotter, recognized as one of the world's great authorities on leadership after having studied leadership up and down the hierarchy for over thirty years, advised that the following errors be avoided for transformational effort to be successful (2007).

1   Not establishing a great enough sense of urgency

2   Not creating a powerful enough guiding coalition

3   Lacking a vision

4   Undercommunicating the vision by a factor of ten

5   Not removing obstacles to the vision

6   Not systematically planning for and creating short-term wins

7   Declaring victory too soon

8   Not anchoring changes in the corporation's culture

Comparing Approaches to Leadership

Comparing the similarities and differences between the charismatic, transactional, and transformational approaches provides a good means of concluding this chapter. Coming later in time, transformational theories absorbed many aspects of both charismatic and transactional theories, thus creating some overlap.

At the beginning of this chapter, we mentioned that charismatic leaders are frequently dissatisfied with the status quo and may be willing to use unconventional means to bring about change. They have an idealized vision of the future and are able to communicate it with confidence and enthusiasm. They may be markedly similar to the transformational leader in their ability to elicit inspirational effects by communicating emotionally as opposed to using a style that emphasizes the status quo. Although charisma is not an essential ingredient of transformation, charisma is frequently considered a component of transformational leadership. Whereas the relationship between subordinates and a charismatic leader may inspire love or hate, they are rarely bland. If leader-subordinate relationships are excessively bland, the possibility of inspiring transformation of the organization is doubtful. Thus, charismatics are less frequently associated with transactional leadership.

The theoretical emphasis of transactional leadership focuses on supervisors in a closed system. Researchers are interested in keeping variables limited and testable. Transformational researchers are more interested in executives, political leaders, and social leaders in relatively open systems. Such leaders function as the nexus between the external economic and political environment and the internal organizational environment, and they have to adjust the latter to conform to the former. Because of the wider perspective that transformational researchers seek to explain, they either use a larger number of variables or must be more abstract in their explanations.

Transactional leaders rely heavily on certain types of power: legitimate (power from formal appointed authority), reward, and punishment. As formal managers, transactional leaders have the mantle of authority and the ability to administer and adjust incentives. Moreover, transactional researchers have frequently assumed expert power and tend to ignore referent power (power based on personality and likability). Transformational researchers, on the contrary, emphasize expert and referent power. To make a major impact, for good or ill, leaders have to be perceived as wise and brilliant, and they must have enough personal appeal to sell their ideas and be trusted. Such leaders can use their power indirectly through emotional appeal and at a distance through ideological appeal.

Transactional researchers were originally highly influenced by economic perspectives, such as social exchange and expectancy theory. The basic self-interests and immediate needs of followers are the focus, ranging from pay to clear instructions to adequate resources and working conditions. Follower motivation is considered largely a rational, calculative process. On the other hand, transformational researchers emphasize stimulating individuals' interest in group productivity and organizational success. Transformational researchers frequently examine followers' motivations to emulate or idolize leaders for personal or ideological reasons. Follower motivation is a more symbolic process based on ideology, inspiration, and the intellectual belief that past patterns are no longer functional.

In transactional settings, organizational conditions are assumed to be stable, or, at the very least, the leader is responding to the organizational condition as if it were stable. Problems in organizations involve adjustments, exceptions, or refinements in properly functioning systems. In transformational settings, the assumption is that change is inevitable, constant, and healthy. This is particularly true in the new economy in which the U.S. market must contend with vigorous global competition. Of particular interest to transformational researchers are the roles of crisis, organizational collapse, and other dramatic forms of system deterioration.

Performance expectations in transactional theories tend to emphasize "good" performance. To be reasonable, efficient, effective, sustainable, and consistent, performance should be engineered by management with the substantial input of employees. Good performance is the goal in systems that have already been well designed. Transformational theories tend to assume that standards or quality has stagnated or languished, or that adaptation to new processes, technologies, changing environments, or organizational structures is required. Exceptional performance is necessary for organizational success, whether that entails higher productivity levels, a greater contribution in adaptation and innovation, or effective organizational transformation.

Leader behaviors in transactional theories strongly emphasize the task- and people-oriented domains (see Chapters 5 and 6). In particular, they emphasize monitoring, operations planning, clarifying roles, informing, delegating, problem-solving, consulting, personnel planning, developing staff, and motivating. Leader behaviors in transformational theories strongly emphasize organizational-oriented behaviors (see Chapters 8 and 9) as well as people-oriented behaviors. They do not completely neglect, but certainly downplay, task-oriented behaviors. They emphasize environmental scanning, strategic planning, vision articulation, networking, decision-making, and managing organizational change, as well as informing, delegating (empowering), managing technical innovation, consulting, developing staff, motivating, building teams, and managing personnel change. A rough comparison of these differences between transactional and transformational theories is displayed in Exhibit 8.8.

Exhibit 8.8   A Rough Comparison of Transactional Theories and Transformational or Charismatic Theories

	TRANSACTIONAL	TRANSFORMATIONAL
Theoretical emphasis	Supervisors	Executives
	Closed system	Open system
	Narrow range of variables	Broad range of variables
Leader's type of power	Legitimate, reward, punishment	Expert, referent
	Direct influence at close range	Indirect influence, including influence at a distance
Follower motivation	Self-interests such as pay; immediate needs such as resources, group compatibility	Group interests such as organizational success; psychic satisfaction such as emulation of leader
	Rational processes (calculative)	Symbolic processes based on ideology or breaking with the past
Facilitating conditions	Stable; refinement of functioning systems	Unstable; need for change; crisis
Performance expectations	Good performance	Exceptional performance either in terms of quantity or adaptation
Leader behaviors emphasized	Monitoring, operations planning, clarifying roles, informing, delegating, problem-solving, consulting, personnel planning, developing staff, and motivating	Environmental scanning, strategic planning, vision articulation, networking, decision-making, managing organizational change as well as informing, delegating (empowering), managing innovation, consulting, developing staff, motivating, building teams, and managing personnel change

Note: Because of the tremendous variety of transactional and transformational theories, there are some exceptions to these general trends.

Conclusion

Charismatic leaders have extraordinary effects on their followers. Under their leadership that brings inspiration and a strong sense of values, followers often perform at higher levels. Transformational leaders are triggers of extraordinary organizational change. Under their leadership, organizations or political and social entities may undergo significant structural change. Charismatic and transformational leadership frequently have agents in common, but actually the two notions are distinct. The former involves a magnetic quality of the leader and the latter involves a type of change that can be brought about by various types of leader, whether charismatic or not.

Conger and Kanungo focus on how charisma is attributed to leaders. They contend that for charismatic leadership to emerge, the context has to be sufficiently problematic to allow for dissatisfaction with the status quo and for radical change to be acceptable. Charismatic leaders may be known locally or throughout a nation. Charisma can lead to positive or negative outcomes. Charismatic leadership is not for every situation. For example, charisma is not a substitute for solid management that brings continuous improvement.

Tichy and Devanna focus on transformational leadership, with the belief that charismatic leadership is not required in order to bring about major organizational change. They examine leadership over time; before institutionalizing change, transformational leaders first recognize the need for revitalization and then create a new vision. The leadership practices theory by Kouzes and Posner is another mechanism for examining transformational leadership and recommending competencies or practices. By interviewing individuals on their "personal best" experiences, they advocate practices consistent with their findings—challenging the process and searching for opportunities, inspiring a shared vision, enabling others to act by fostering collaboration in a participative style, modeling the way, and, finally, "encouraging the heart" with a supportive style.

The full-range leadership theory by Bass provides a good visualization on a continuum from laissez-faire nonleadership to transactional leadership to transformational leadership. The approaches are not thought of as mutually exclusive, but as one approach augmenting another. Transactional leadership, constituting most leadership behavior, is not revolutionary, but brings incremental improvements by offering incentives to employees for achieving desired results. Transformational leadership involves behaviors or elements Bass calls individualized consideration, or coaching and personal support; idealized influence, which is similar to charisma; inspirational motivation, which allows followers to transcend self-interest in favor or organizational achievement; and intellectual stimulation, which supports people creating new opportunities and solving old problems in new ways.

Key Terms

charismatic leadership

full-range leadership

idealized influence

individualized consideration

inspirational motivation

intellectual stimulation

management-by-exception

negative charismatics

overmanaged and underled

transactional theories

transformational leadership

vision

Resources

Bernard Bass has heard his detractors question the morality of transformational leadership. He and coauthor Steidlmeier make it clear in this paper that real transformational leadership must be grounded in a moral and ethical foundation.

- Bernard M. Bass and Paul Steidlmeier, "Ethics, Character, and Authentic Transformational Leadership," September 24, 1998. www.vanguard.edu/uploadedFiles/Faculty/RHeuser/ETHICS,%20MORAL%20CHARACTER%20AND%20AUTHENTIC%20TRANSFORMATION-AL%20LEADERSHIP.pdf.

Bill Gates was cited in this chapter as a "noncharismatic" individual. Draw your own conclusions about this icon's charisma by reading an in-depth article on Gates, such as the following one. You will read about a man known for an aggressive and confrontational style, shown by actions such as firing Microsoft's first president after he had been on the job for less than a year. Yet Gates and his wife have used their wealth to establish a foundation to benefit primarily minority students' education and global health issues.

- "Bill Gates," Answers.com. www.answers.com/topic/bill-gates?cat=biz-fin.

Walt Pavlo was discussed in this chapter as a charismatic, successful manager who gave in to pressures for personal gain. Until recently, he lectured at many universities to tell business students that there are—and should be—dire consequences for surrendering personal ethics. Hear him speak in several short videos by searching YouTube.com for his name; be sure to include the NightLine broadcast that is posted at www.youtube.com/watch?v=sPUuHn5_L1g ("CON Walter Pavlo Corporate Manager Steals $6 Million," October 9, 2007).

Discussion Questions

1   Describe the differences and similarities between charismatic and transformational leadership.

2   What were the precursors to charismatic and transformational theories?

3   Discuss Conger and Kanungo's theory of charismatic leadership.

4   Many business, political, and religious leaders who are cultural icons have been "good" charismatics. Discuss the appropriateness of "good" charismatic leadership in business. What type of charismatic leader is best for an organization? Should charismatic leaders be in lower-level supervisory roles as well as at the top of the organization? Do you think that all leaders must be somewhat charismatic to be effective? Do you think you are or can be a charismatic leader?

5   Explain Bass's additive model of high-performance leadership. Which factor does he claim for the transformational arena that was formerly subsumed under transactional approaches?

    Assuming for a moment that Bass's theory of leadership is correct, why is there so little successful transformational leadership anywhere, including in the public and nonprofit sectors? Why is it so difficult to be a high-performing transformational leader in today's organizational environment?

    Compare and contrast the differences between transactional and transformational approaches.

6   Kotter used this quip to highlight differences between leadership and management: "No one has yet figured out how to manage people effectively into battle—they must be led." Have you encountered a leader who could, figuratively speaking, lead people effectively into battle? What effect did that person have on you?

7   Would Kotter's eight mistakes to avoid come naturally to a charismatic leader who is attempting to bring transformation? Defend your position by referring to the central meaning of Kotter's points and to the description of a charismatic leader.

8   Which single leadership theory do you feel you can use to best explain organizational change? (Refer to this chapter and prior chapters.)

Classroom Activity

This classroom activity is based on Exhibit 8.3. In groups of about five students, prepare to answer the following questions and discuss with the class as a whole. Before the discussion, students are encouraged to read some of the excellent analyses available of the events in Jonestown and to use those readings in their responses. In the context of this chapter's focus on negative charismatics, discussions should downplay the many conspiracy theories that abound and emphasize instead the phenomenon of ultimate commitment to a cause and to its leader. For example, the Department of Religious Studies at San Diego State University hosts a site with summaries, transcripts, and audiotapes of hundreds of survivors of the People's Temple as well as those who later committed suicide. The government documents section of the university library holds transcripts of the 1979 hearing held by the U.S. House of Representatives Committee on Foreign Affairs. There are also many books on the topic, including some with extensive commentary on Jones's personality and charisma.

1   Why did Jim Jones have power over his followers? Is that power the same thing as "charisma"?

2   Why was Jim Jones's influence over 900 people in Jonestown so strong even though he was so clearly negative in his influence?

3   The visit of Congressman Ryan was a precipitating event in the mass suicide. If he had not visited Jonestown, what does your group hypothesize would have been the future of the People's Temple? Why?

Case Analysis 1

Devon sat there and thought about the next phase of his marketing plan. It had been a whirlwind experience so far, and he knew it was not going to get easier. Nonetheless, he had high hopes for himself and was ready to take appropriate risks to bring the marketing department's staff in alignment with ambitious goals. He did not have the same flair as his predecessor, but he thought he had what it takes to make a big difference through hard work and competence.

His predecessor, Randy, quit within five months on the job. As a department head within the marketing division, Randy had been an outsider, hired to test market a new product line for the company, a sleek electric car called Green and Gorgeous. He had interviewed brilliantly. He was highly articulate; he knew an enormous amount about doing customer surveys and how to leverage that information in order to secure additional resources to "get product to market," as he called it; he exuded confidence and enthusiasm. Initially he was popular and operations went very well. He encouraged people to work harder for the common good, successfully got the funds for a major customer survey, and was seen everywhere. The problems started when Randy presented the results of the customer survey to senior management staff at their request. He did not provide a preview of his remarks to the marketing division VP, who assumed that the initial overview would reveal findings relative to the one new product line of Green and Gorgeous, not recommendations on various lines for which Randy was not responsible. Because of the extensiveness of the data (a forty-page booklet filled with statistics, graphs, and pie charts on multiple product lines), Randy concentrated on only a few highlights and his recommendations. The data clearly indicated to Randy that there was great interest in Green and Gorgeous, at the expense of other current priorities. Randy had recommended a phase-out of funding on test marketing other lines in order to increase funding for a new marketing campaign in his own area.

The reactions were varied. The marketing division VP was shocked and chagrined. How dare Randy make product recommendations outside of his own product area without reviewing them with her first and getting her approval! Of the six other members of the senior management staff, three were very taken with Randy and his ideas. Two members had no major reactions except that they wanted to study the data before taking any stand. One member was angry because he had received the study only two days before and had not had any opportunity to shape the recommendations before they were presented. He was, after all, directly involved with product lines that had been negatively evaluated by Randy through the survey, although what he said was that he liked Randy's ideas but was steadfast in fiscal constraint for building up unproven lines at this point. Also, when Randy's recommendations leaked outside of the senior management team, one marketer involved with a different product line said that he wanted equal time to do a competing study.

Despite a great beginning, things disintegrated rapidly after that. The VP reprimanded Randy, and because Randy was not aware of the impending trouble that he had stirred up, he was unapologetic. Unconcerned with the political patchwork and financial limitations of the company, he wanted to proceed with alacrity and continued to push hard. Meanwhile, Randy's aggressive and bold style had started to polarize the department. When he failed to act on an egregious sexual harassment allegation against a line employee, he was put on administrative leave and quit shortly thereafter.

Devon, as Randy's successor, had stabilized the situation. He had investigated the sexual harassment allegation as required by law and likely avoided a lawsuit against the company. He had also spent time with everyone in the department so that employees were not demoralized. However, he could tell that the luster and excitement that the division experienced briefly with Randy was gone. Also, when Devon took a tough look at the other lines' marketing plans, he realized that they were mediocre. Ideas and initiative did not seem to percolate up anywhere, and the overall mentality was "what a lot of work," and "that's good enough." Yet Devon did not want a mediocre division. Although he did not want to make the same mistakes that Randy had made, he did want to take advantage of some of his ideas and recreate some of the excitement.

Discussion Questions

1   Use charismatic theory to describe what happened to Randy.

2   Use transformational theory to describe steps that Devon needs to take to be more than mediocre.

3   How effective would transactional leadership be in helping Devon move the division forward? Why?

Case Analysis 2: A Case of Transformational Leadership

In 2010, Stater Bros. was a chain of 167 supermarkets, with annual sales of $3.77 billion, 19,000 employees, a new 2.1 million square foot office and distribution center, and the largest privately owned supermarket chain in Southern California. But it was not always that big. How did that growth come about? A significant part of the vision was achieved in 1999 when chair and CEO Jack Brown acquired forty-three former Albertsons and Lucky stores to add to Stater's existing 112 supermarkets.

On August 9, 1999, an amazing communication went out from the office of Jack Brown: "Stater Bros. Markets, the largest locally owned supermarket chain in Southern California, has announced that the former Albertsons supermarket in Temecula will reopen at 9:00 A.M. on Tuesday, August 10, as a Stater Bros. supermarket." The store closed Friday night as Albertsons and, remarkably, opened Tuesday morning as Stater Bros.

The Temecula store was the trial run for Jack Brown and his executive team. Jack had a thirty-five-year veteran in Donald Baker (2009), who headed operations as executive VP and senior VP of store operations. Don had strong relationships within the food industry and was dedicated to helping bring Jack's shared vision to reality. Following Jack's leadership, Don assembled the operations team that would oversee key aspects of the planning and implementation.

Jack, Don, and the team assessed strategy, scanned the organizational environment, and mapped out transformations. They strategized, deciding to tackle the new stores by area utilizing what they learned in their trial run. They met with future employees and explained what they were doing and why it was worthwhile. Jack told them, "I'm going to adopt you—your same pay, same hours, same store, same benefits, same seniority. There is a place at the table for everyone to join our Stater family." It would have been easy for employees to find the transformation overwhelming, but under Jack's influence, the organizations being acquired were ready to buy in, face any problems, and identify new opportunities.

In successful acquisitions, leaders must deal with many detailed operational issues while planning the execution of change. Transformation mandates that leaders seek to benchmark and learn from others' successes and failures. To that end, the top management team turned to an industry peer and long-time personal friends. Stater Bros. leased two jets to take fifteen employees to meet with their counterparts at a Missouri-based grocer, Schnucks. The Schnucks employees shared invaluable experiences. They warned in particular about the challenges of integrating front-end (checkout) systems. At the outset Schnucks had not bought new cashiering and inventory equipment for its stores and later had to perform a costly installation, interrupting operations. Buying and installing new equipment before each store reopening would save Stater Bros. thousands of dollars.

In order to spur his employees to perform beyond conventional expectations, Jack expressed his vision clearly in an emotional appeal to his employees so that the talent needed would rise to the occasion. Over 800 employees and suppliers became enthusiastically involved. For twenty-five days, two stores a day were tackled in thirty-six-hour transformations until all forty-three were completed. While one crew worked on new checkout systems, another trained front-end staff. Cranes hoisted new banners. Entire stores were cleaned top to bottom. An attorney who oversaw legal issues of the merger described the timing of the accomplishment as nothing short of amazing given the legal risk and legal protections involved in connection with corporate merger or acquisition transactions.

Jack led the process throughout, as changes in the organizational culture and environment of the stores being acquired were addressed. The leadership team figured out how all 36,000 items in each store would be remerchandised within a twenty-four-hour window. Prices were lowered by 10 percent. Where work ethics differed, clarifications were spelled out. All Stater employees—new and old—would dress the same and thus appear cohesive to the public. Employees in parking lots would don bright safety vests. Customers were to be greeted.

Job duties were altered overnight. The three employee unions involved were supportive and helpful. Two former managers were chosen to join the new team. Hundreds of employees from multiple stores at one time were given essential training in the few hours before each store reopened under the Stater name.

Jack says that in this case study, some people would see only a case of acquisitions done right, without realizing that "if there is a story here, it is about the people. I think companies make a mistake. They think they're just acquiring assets, but they're really acquiring the responsibility for people and their futures" (Brown 2010).

Discussion Questions

1 What evidence do you see in this case as to why Jack Brown is described in the region served by Stater as a "charismatic leader?" What attributes prescribed by Conger and Kanungo would apply?

2 In your judgment, did the charisma of the leader contribute to a successful transformation of the organization?

3   Apply the characteristics of transformational leadership as described in this chapter to the case. What was transformed beyond the forty-three stores that were purchased?

4   We noted in this chapter that transformational leadership results in follower commitment to organizational objectives along with increased follower skills and self-confidence. What was done by the leadership in this case to illustrate how follower commitment to Stater's organizational objectives was achieved?

References

Baker, D. 2009. Interview with K. Bowerman, San Bernardino, California, February 17.

Bass, B. M. 1985. *Leadership and Performance Beyond Expectations*. New York: Free Press.

_____. 1990. *Bass and Stogdill's Handbook of Leadership*. 3rd ed. New York: Free Press.

Bennis, W., and Nanus, B. 1985. *Leaders: Strategies for Taking Charge*. New York: Harper and Row.

Brown, J. 2010. Interviews with K. Bowerman, San Bernardino, California, January 21 and April 1.

Burns, J. M. 1978. *Leadership*. New York: Harper and Row.

Carless, S. 2001. "Assessing the Discriminant Validity of the Leadership Practices Inventory." *Journal of Occupational and Organizational Psychology* 74: 233–239.

ChangingMinds.org. 1998. "Charismatic Leadership." www.changingminds.org/disciplines/leadership/styles/charismatic_leadership.html.

Conger, J. A., and Kanungo, R. N. 1987. "Toward a Behavioral Theory of Charismatic Leadership in Organizational Settings." *Academy of Management Review* 12: 637–647.

Conger, J. A., and Kanungo, R. N. eds. 1998. *Charismatic Leadership in Organizations*. Thousand Oaks, CA: Sage.

Fiol, C. M., Harris, D., and House, R. 1999. "Charismatic Leadership: Strategies for Effecting Social Change." *Leadership Quarterly* 10 (3): 449–482.

GnanaDev, D. 2008. Interviews with K. Bowerman, Colton, California, February 20 and April 4.

House, R. J., Spangler, W. D., and Woycke, J. 1991. "Personality and Charisma in the U.S. Presidency: A Psychological Theory of Leader Effectiveness." *Administrative Science Quarterly* 36 (September): 364–396.

Iacocca, L. 2007. *Where Have All the Leaders Gone?* New York: Scribner.

Kent, R. H. 2001. "You Can't Lead Without Managing." ManagerWise.com. www.managerwise.com/article.phtml?id=138.

Khurana, R. 2002a. *Searching for a Corporate Savior: The Irrational Quest for Charismatic CEOs*. Princeton, NJ: Princeton University Press.

Khurana, R. 2002b. "The Curse of the Superstar CEO." *Harvard Business Review* (September): 60–66.

Kotter, J. P. 2007. "Leading Change: Why Transformation Efforts Fail." *Harvard Business Review*, Special Issue (The Tests of a Leader) January: 96–101. (Best of HBR, originally published in spring 1995).

Kouzes, J. M., and Posner, B. Z. 1987. *The Leadership Challenge: How to Get Extraordinary Things Done in Organizations*. San Francisco: Jossey-Bass.

_____. 1993. *The Leadership Practices Inventory*. San Diego, CA: Pfeiffer.

Lewin, K. 1951. *Field Theory in Social Science*. New York: Harper.

Maxwell, J. 2008. *Encouragement Changes Everything: Bless and Be Blessed*. Nashville, TN: Thomas Nelson, Inc.

Pavlo, W., Jr., and Weinberg, N. 2007. *Stolen Without a Gun: Confessions from Inside History's Biggest Accounting Fraud: The Collapse of MCI Worldcom*. Encino, CA: Etika Books.

Porter, J. 2008. "Using Ex-Cons to Scare MBAs Straight." *Business Week*, April 24.

Tichy, N. M., and Devanna, M. A. 1990. *The Transformational Leader*. New York: Wiley.

Weber, Max. 1968 [1921]. *Max Weber on Law in Economy and Society*, ed. Max Rheinstein, trans. E. Shils and M. Rheinstein. New York: Simon & Schuster.

Zaleznik, A. 1977. "Managers and Leaders: Are They Different?" *Harvard Business Review* 55 (5): 67–78.

Discussion Questions

1   What are the similarities and differences between transformational and transactional leadership?

2   Describe the main characteristics of charismatic leadership. Can you think of 3-5 things you can do to improve your charisma?

3   Can charisma be used in a negative way? Think about three notorious leaders who were highly charismatic. Do you think that their charisma enabled them to cause more destruction and damage?

CHAPTER 6

Leadership as a Relationship

Leader–Member Exchange Theory

Peter G. Northouse

Description

Most of the leadership theories discussed thus far in this book have emphasized leadership from the point of view of the leader (e.g., trait approach, skills approach, and style approach) or the follower and the context (e.g., Situational Leadership® and path–goal theory). Leader- member exchange (LMX) theory takes still another approach and conceptualizes leadership as a process that is centered on the *interactions* between leaders and followers. As Figure 9.1 illustrates, LMX theory makes the *dyadic relationship* between leaders and followers the focal point of the leadership process.

Before LMX theory, researchers treated leadership as something leaders did toward all of their followers. This assumption implied that leaders treated followers in a collective way, as a group, using an average leadership style. LMX theory challenged this assumption and directed researchers' attention to the differences that might exist between the leader and each of the leader's followers.

Early Studies

In the first studies of exchange theory, which was then called vertical dyad linkage (VDL) theory, researchers focused on the nature of the *vertical linkages* leaders formed with each of their followers (Figure 9.2). A leader's relationship to the work unit as a whole was viewed as a series of vertical dyads (Figure 9.3).

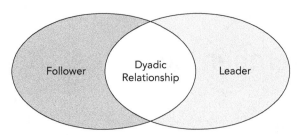

Figure 9.1 Dimensions of Leadership

Source: Reprinted from *Leadership Quarterly, 6*(2), G. B. Graen & M. Uhl-Bien, "Relationship-Based Approach to Leadership: Development of Leader-Member Exchange (LMX) Theory of Leadership Over 25 Years: Applying a Multi-Level, Multi-Domain Perspective" (pp. 219–247), Copyright © 1995, with permission from Elsevier.

Note: LMX theory was first described 28 years ago in the works of Dansereau, Graen, and Haga (1975), Graen (1976), and Graen and Cashman (1975). Since it first appeared, it has undergone several revisions, and it continues to be of interest to researchers who study the leadership process.

In assessing the characteristics of these vertical dyads, researchers found two general types of linkages (or relationships): those that were based on expanded and negotiated role responsibilities (extra-roles), which were called the *ingroup,* and those that were based on the formal employment contract (defined roles), which were called the *out-group* (Figure 9.4),

Within an organizational work unit, followers become a part of the in-group or the out-group based on how well they work with the leader and how well the leader works with them. Personality and other personal characteristics are related to this process (Dansereau, Graen, & Haga, 1975). In addition, membership in one group or the other is based on how followers involve themselves in expanding their role responsibilities with the leader (Graen, 1976). Followers who are interested in negotiating with the leader what they are willing to do for the group can become a part of the in-group. These negotiations involve exchanges in which followers do certain activities that go beyond their formal job descriptions, and the leader, in turn, does more for these followers. If followers are not interested in taking on new and different job responsibilities, they become a part of the out-group.

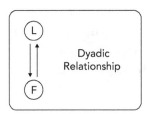

Figure 9.2 The Vertical Dyad

Note: The leader (L) forms an individualized working relationship with each of his or her followers (F). The exchanges (both content and process) between the leader and follower define their dyadic relationship.

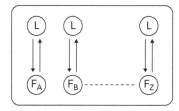

Figure 9.3   Vertical Dyads

Note: The leader (L) forms special relationships with all of his or her followers (F). Each of these relationships is special and has its own unique characteristics.

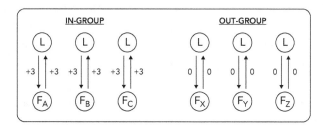

Figure 9.4   In-Groups and Out-Groups

Note: A leader (L) and his or her followers (F) form unique relationships. Relationships within the in-group are marked by mutual trust, respect, liking, and reciprocal influence. Relationships within the out-group are marked by formal communication based on job descriptions. Plus 3 is a high-quality relationship, and zero is a stranger.

Followers in the in-group receive more information, influence, confidence, and concern from their leaders than do out-group followers (Dansereau et al., 1975). In addition, they are more dependable, more highly involved, and more communicative than out-group followers (Dansereau et al., 1975). Whereas in-group members do extra things for the leader and the leader does the same for them, followers in the out-group are less compatible with the leader and usually just come to work, do their job, and go home.

Later Studies

After the first set of studies, there was a shift in the focus of LMX theory. Whereas the initial studies of this theory addressed primarily the nature of the differences between in-groups and out-groups, a subsequent line of research addressed how LMX theory was related to organizational effectiveness.

Specifically, these studies focus on how the quality of leader-member exchanges was related to positive outcomes for leaders, followers, groups, and the organization in general (Graen & Uhl-Bien, 1995).

Researchers found that high-quality leader–member exchanges produced less employee turnover, more positive performance evaluations, higher frequency of promotions, greater organizational commitment, more desirable work assignments, better job attitudes, more attention and support from the leader, greater participation, and faster career progress over 25 years (Graen & Uhl-Bien, 1995; Liden, Wayne, & Stilwell, 1993).

In a meta-analysis of 164 LMX studies, Gerstner and Day (1997) found that LMX was consistently related to member job performance, satisfaction (overall and supervisory), commitment, role conflict and clarity, and turnover intentions. In addition, they found strong support in these studies for the psychometric properties of the LMX 7 Questionnaire. For purposes of research, they highlighted the importance of measuring LMX from the perspective of both the leader and the follower.

Based on a review of 130 studies of LMX research conducted since 2002, Anand, Hu, Liden, and Vidyarthi (2011) found that interest in studying leader–member exchange has not diminished. A large majority of these studies (70%) examined the antecedents and outcomes of leader–member exchange. The research trends show increased attention to the context surrounding LMX relationships (e.g., group dynamics), analyzing leader–member exchange from individual and group levels, and studying leader–member exchange with non-U.S. samples.

For example, using a sample of employees in a variety of jobs in Israeli organizations, Atwater and Carmeli (2009) examined the connection between employees' perceptions of leader–member exchange and their energy and creativity at work. They found that perceived high-quality leader-member exchange was positively related to feelings of energy in employees, which, in turn, was related to greater involvement in creative work. LMX theory was not directly associated with creativity, but it served as a mechanism to nurture people's feelings, which then enhanced their creativity.

Ilies, Nahrgang, and Morgeson (2007) did a meta-analysis of 51 research studies that examined the relationship between LMX and employee citizenship behaviors. Citizenship behaviors are discretionary employee behaviors that go beyond the prescribed role, job description, or reward system (Katz, 1964; Organ, 1988). They found a positive relationship between the quality of leader–member relationships and citizenship behaviors. In other words, followers who had higher-quality relationships with their leaders were more likely to engage in more discretionary (positive "payback") behaviors that benefited the leader and the organization.

Researchers have also studied how LMX theory is related to empowerment. Harris, Wheeler, and Kacmar (2009) explored how empowerment moderates the impact of leader–member exchange on job outcomes such as job satisfaction, turnover, job performance, and organizational citizenship behaviors. Based on two samples of college alumni, they found that empowerment and leader–member exchange quality had a slight synergistic effect on job outcomes. The quality of leader–member exchange mattered most for employees who felt little empowerment. For these employees, high-quality leader–member exchange appeared to compensate for the drawbacks of not being empowered.

In essence, the aforementioned findings clearly illustrate that organizations stand to gain much from having leaders who can create good working relationships. When leaders and followers have good exchanges, they feel better and accomplish more, and the organization prospers.

Leadership Making

Research of LMX theory has also focused on how exchanges between leaders and followers can be used for leadership making (Graen &. Uhl-Bien, 1991). Leadership making is a prescriptive approach to leadership emphasizing that leaders should develop high-quality exchanges with all of their followers rather than just a few. It attempts to make every follower feel as if he or she is a part of the in-group and, by so doing, avoids the inequities and negative implications of being in an out-group. In general, leadership making promotes partnerships in which the leader tries to build effective dyads with all followers in the work unit (Graen & Uhl-Bien, 1995). In addition, leadership making suggests that leaders can create networks of partnerships throughout the organization, which will benefit the organization's goals and the leader's own career progress.

Graen and Uhl-Bien (1991) suggested that leadership making develops progressively over time in three phases: (1) the stranger phase, (2) the acquaintance phase, and (3) the mature partnership phase (Table 9.1). During Phase 1, the stranger phase, the interactions in the leader–follower dyad generally are rule bound, relying heavily on contractual relationships. Leaders and followers relate to each other within prescribed organizational roles. They have lower-quality exchanges, similar to those of out-group members discussed earlier in the chapter. The follower complies with the formal leader, who has hierarchical status for the purpose of achieving the economic rewards the leader controls. The motives of the follower during the stranger phase are directed toward self-interest rather than toward the good of the group (Graen & Uhl-Bien, 1995).

In a study of the early stages of leader–member relationship development, Nahrgang, Morgeson, and Ilies (2009) found that leaders look for followers who exhibit enthusiasm, participation, gregariousness, and extraversión. In contrast, followers look for leaders who are pleasant, trusting, cooperative, and agreeable. Leader extraversión did not influence relationship quality for the followers, and follower agreeablenes did not influence relationship quality for the leaders. A key predictor of relation hip quality for both leaders and followers was behaviors such as performance.

Phase 2, the acquaintance phase, begins with an offer by the leader or the follower for improved career-oriented social exchanges, which involve sharing more resources and personal or work-related information. It is a testing period for both the leader and the follower to assess whether the follower is interested in taking on more roles and responsibilities and to assess whether the leader is willing to provide new challenges for followers. During this time, dyads shift away from interactions that are governed strictly by job descriptions and defined roles and move toward new ways of relating. As measured by LMX theory, it could be said that the quality of their exchanges has improved to medium quality. Successful dyads in the acquaintance phase begin to develop greater trust and respect for each other. They also tend to focus less on their own self-interests and more on the purposes and goals of the group.

Table 9.1 Phases in Leadership Making

	PHASE 1 STRANGER	PHASE 2 ACQUAINTANCE	PHASE 3 PARTNERSHIP
Roles	Scripted	Tested	Negotiated
Influences	One way	Mixed	Reciprocal
Exchanges	Low quality	Medium quality	High quality
Interests	Self	Self and other	Group
		Time	

→

Source: Adapted from "Relationship-Based Approach to Leadership: Development of Leader–Member Exchange (LMX) Theory of Leadership Over 25 Years: Applying a Multi-Level, Multi-Domain Perspective," by G. B. Graen and M. Uhl-Bien, 1995, *Leadership Quarterly. 6*(2), 231.

Phase 3, mature partnership, is marked by high-quality leader–member exchanges. People who have progressed to this stage in their relationships experience a high degree of mutual trust, respect, and obligation toward each other. They have tested their relationship and found that they can depend on each other. In mature partnerships, there is a high degree of reciprocity between leaders and followers: Each affects and is affected by the other. For example, in a study of 75 bank managers and 58 engineering managers, Schriesheim, Castro, Zhou, and Yammarino (2001) found that good leader–member relations were more egalitarian and that influence and control were more evenly balanced between the supervisor and the follower. In addition, during Phase 3, members may depend on each other for favors and special assistance. For example, leaders may rely on followers to do extra assignments, and followers may rely on leaders for needed support or encouragement. The point is that leaders and followers are tied together in productive ways that go well beyond a traditional hierarchically defined work relationship. They have developed an extremely effective way of relating that produces positive outcomes for themselves and the organization. In effect, partnerships are transformational in that they assist leaders and followers in moving beyond their own self-interests to accomplish the greater good of the team and organization.

The benefits for employees who develop high-quality leader–member relationships include preferential treatment, increased job-related communication, ample access to supervisors, and increased performance-related feedback (Harris et al., 2009). The disadvantages for those with low-quality leader–member relationships include limited trust and support from supervisors and few benefits outside the employment contract (Harris et al., 2009). To evaluate leader–member exchanges, researchers typically use a brief questionnaire that asks leaders and followers to report on the effectiveness of their working relationships. The questionnaire assesses the degree to which respondents express respect, trust, and obligation in their exchanges with others. At the end of this chapter, a version of the LMX questionnaire is provided for you to take for the purpose of analyzing some of your own leader–member relationships.

How Does LMX Theory Work?

LMX theory works in two ways: It describes leadership, and it prescribes leadership. In both instances, the central concept is the dyadic relationship that a leader forms with each of the leader's followers. Descriptively, LMX theory suggests that it is important to recognize the existence of in-groups and out-groups within a group or an organization.

The differences in how goals are accomplished by in-groups and out-groups are substantial. Working with an in-group allows a leader to accomplish more work in a more effective manner than he or she can accomplish working without one. In-group members are willing to do more than is required in their job description and look for innovative ways to advance the group's goals. In response to their extra effort and devotion, leaders give them more responsibilities and more opportunities. Leaders also give in-group members more of their time and support.

Out-group members act quite differently than in-group members. Rather than trying to do extra work, out-group members operate strictly within their prescribed organizational roles. They do what is required of them but nothing more. Leaders treat out-group members fairly and according to the formal contract, but they do not give them special attention. For their efforts, out-group members receive the standard benefits as defined in the job description.

Prescriptively, LMX theory is best understood within the leadership-making model of Graen and Uhl-Bien (1991). Graen and Uhl-Bien advocated that leaders should create a special relationship with all followers, similar to the relationships described as in-group relationships. Leaders should offer each follower the opportunity to take on new roles and responsibilities. Furthermore, leaders should nurture high-quality exchanges with their followers. Rather than focusing on the differences between in-group and out-group members, the leadership-making model suggests that leaders should look for ways to build trust and respect with all of their followers, thus making the entire work unit an in-group. In addition, leaders should look beyond their own work unit and create high-quality partnerships with people throughout the organization.

Whether descriptive or prescriptive, LMX theory works by focusing our attention on the special, unique relationship that leaders can create with others. When these relationships are of high quality, the goals of the leader, the followers, and the organization are all advanced.

References

Anand, S., Hu, J., Liden, R.C. and Vidyarthi, P.R. (2011) Leader-Member Exchange: Recent Research Findings and Prospects for the Future. *The Sage Handbook of Leadership,* 309–323.

Atwater, L., & Carmeli, A. (2009). Leader-member exchange, feelings of energy, and involvement in creative work. *Leadership Quarterly,* 20(3), 264–275.

Dansereau, F., Graen, G. B., & Haga, W. (1975). A vertical dyad linkage approach to leadership in formal organizations. *Organizational Behavior and Human Performance,* 13, 46–78.

Graen, G. B. (1976). Role-making processes within complex organizations. In M.D. Dunnette (Ed.), *Handbook of industrial and organizational psychology* (pp. 1202–1245). Chicago: Rand McNally.

Graen, G. B., & Cashman, J. (1975). A role-making model of leadership in formal organizations: A developmental approach. In J. G. Hunt & L. L. Larson (Eds.), *Leadership frontiers* (pp. 143–166). Kent, OH: Kent State University Press.

Graen, G. B., & Uhl-Bien, M. (1991). The transformation of professionals into self-managing and partially self-designing contributions: Toward a theory of leadership making. *Journal of Management Systems,* 3(3), 33–48.

Graen, G.B., & Uhl-Bien, M. (1995). Relationship-based approach to leadership: Development of leader-member exchange (LMX) theory of leadership over 25 years: Applying a multi-level, multi-domain perspective. *Leadership Quarterly,* 6(2), 219–247.

Gerstner, C. R., & Day, D. V. (1997). Meta-Analytic review of leader-member exchange theory: Correlates and construct issues. *Journal of Applied Psychology,* 82(6), 827–844.

Harris, K. J., Wheeler, A. R., & Kacmar, K. M. (2009). Leader-member exchange and empowerment: Direct and interactive effects on job satisfaction, turnover intentions, and performance. *Leadership Quarterly,* 20(3), 371–382.

Ilies, R., Nahrgang, J. D., & Morgeson, F. P. (2007). Leader-member exchange and citizenship behaviors: A meta-analysis. *Journal of Applied Psychology,* 92(1), 269–277.

Katz, D. (1964). The Motivational Basis of Organizational Behavior. *Behavioral Science,* 9, 131–133.

Liden, R.C., Wayne, S.J., & Stilwell, D. (1993). A longitudinal study on the early development of leader-member exchange. *Journal of Applied Psychology,* 78, 662–674.

Organ, D. W. (1988). Issues in organization and management series. Organizational citizenship behavior: The good soldier syndrome. Lexington, MA, England: Lexington Books/D. C. Heath and Com.

Nahrgang, J. D., Morgeson, F. P., & Ilies, R. (2009). The development of leader-member exchanges: Exploring how personality and performance influence leader and member relationships over time. *Organizational Behavior and Human Decision Processes,* 108(2), 256–266.

Schriesheim, C.A., Castro, S.L., Zhou, X., & Yammarino, F.J. (2001). The folly of theorizing "A" but testing "B": A Selective level-of-analysis review of the field and a detailed leader-member exchange illustration. *Leadership Quarterly,* 12, 515–551.

Communication and Conflict Resolution Skills

Andrew J. DuBrin

Learning Objectives

After studying this chapter and doing the exercises, you should be able to:

- Describe how leaders use communication networks to accomplish their tasks.

- Describe the basics of inspirational and emotion-provoking communication.

- Describe key features of a power-oriented linguistic style.

- Describe the six basic principles of persuasion.

- Describe the challenge of selective listening, and the basics of making the rounds.

- Be sensitive to the importance of overcoming cross-cultural barriers to communication.

- Identify basic approaches to resolving conflict and negotiating.

Chapter Outline

Communication Networks for Leaders
Face-to-Face Communication Networks
Social Media Networks
Inspirational and Powerful Communication
Speaking and Writing

The CEO of David Yurman, Glen Senk, has been a successful retailing executive. Yurman jewelry is sold at high-end retailers such as Neiman-Marcus and Saks Fifth Avenue, with big-name actors and actresses among its wearers. Senk began his retailing career at Bloomingdales, but he is best known for his two decades with Urban Outfitters, beginning in 1994, and becoming CEO in 2007. Urban Outfitters Inc. is a company that includes five retail brands: Anthropologle, Free People, Terrain, BHLDN, and Urban Outfitters. The company has 400 locations and projects a hip, funky Image, and its offerings include luxury brands. During Senk's tenure, Urban Outfitters was highly successful.

As a leader, Senk strongly emphasizes the Importance of effective communication. During a leadership conference, he pointed to the Importance of recruiting and developing a team that is a good fit for the corporate culture. After the team is assembled, it is essential to listen to what employees have to say, even when the feedback isn't always positive. Senk says, "When you are the CEO, everybody wants to 'yes' you: no one wants to give you bad news. But I have to pull the bad news out of them. I need to know what I'm doing wrong." Communicating consistent objectives to employees is also an important success factor the company.

Senk said that the willingness of managers to debate with him and each other drove the success of Urban Outfitters while he was CEO. He remembered that in 2000, an Anthropologle executive asked for funding to create a company website. Senk initially dismissed the notion, arguing that the brand's customers were unlikely to shop online. Yet, Senk listened to the executive and was Impressed by the number of hits the website received when it went live.

Senk believes also in the importance of communicating with customers. He once commented that social networking is word of mouth on steroids. He pointed out that if Urban Outfitters was doing its job, and constantly focused on wowing the customer, then the company would not have to worry about what is said on blogs and social media posts.

Senk holds an undergraduate degree in business from New York University and an MBA from the University of Chicago. While at school, he decided he wanted a career in retail, partly because of its theater and excitement.[1]

The executive leader just described acts on an obvious truth that many leaders ignore—open communication between company leaders and group members helps an organization overcome problems and attain success. Effective managers and leaders listen to employees, and open communications contribute to leadership effectiveness. John Hamm notes that effective communication is a leader's most essential tool for executing the essential job of leadership: inspiring organizational members to take responsibility for creating a better future.[2]

Effective communication skills contribute to inspirational leadership. Chapter 3 describes how charismatic leaders are masterful oral communicators. This chapter expands on this theme and also covers the contribution of written, persuasive, and nonverbal communication. In addition, this chapter describes the leadership use of communication networks, how the ability to overcome cross-cultural communication barriers enhances leadership effectiveness. Finally, because leaders spend a substantial amount of communication time resolving conflicts, the chapter also discusses conflict resolution and negotiating skills.

To focus your thinking on your communication effectiveness, complete Leadership Self-Assessment Quiz 10.1.

Communication Networks for Leaders

A major feature of communication by leaders is to rely on networks of contacts both in-person and electronically. Without being connected to other people, leaders would find it almost impossible to carry out their various roles. Communication researchers Bruce Hoppe and Claire Reinelt note that leadership networks are a response to a rapidly changing world in which interconnectedness is important because it facilitates learning and solving complex problems. Networks provide resources and support for leaders. With networks, leaders have more impact because they influence more people.[3] Many of these contacts are within the organization, but

---

1   Original story created from facts and observations in the following sources: "Urban Outfitters' Glen Senk: Look for the Right Culture, Diverse Opinions and 'Bad News,'" *Knowledge@Wharton* (http://knowledge.wharton.upenn.edu), May 25, 2011, pp. 1–3; Erin Carlyle, "Glen Senk Out, Richard Hayne in as Urban Outfitters CEO," *Forbes* (www.forbes.com), January 10, 2012, pp. 1–2; Margaret Case Little, "Talking With ... Urban Outfitters CEO Glen Senk," http://blog.shop.org, August 17, 2010, pp. 1–3; Adrianne Pasquarelli, "David Yurman Taps Senk as CEO," *Crain's New York Business* (www.crainsnewyork.com), January 11, 2012, p. 1.

2   John Hamm, "The Five Messages Leaders Must Manage," *Harvard Business Review,* May 2006, p. 116.

3   Bruce Hoppe and Claire Reinelt, "Social Network Analysis and the Evaluation of Leadership Networks," *The Leadership Quarterly,* August 2010, p. 600.

Leadership Self-Assessment Quiz 10.1

A Self-Portrait of My Communication Effectiveness

Instructions: The following statements relate to various aspects of communication effectiveness. Indicate whether each of the statements is mostly true or mostly false, even if the most accurate answer would depend somewhat on the situati on. Asking another person who is familiar with your communication behavior to help you answer the questions may improve the accuracy of your answers.

	MOSTLY TRUE	MOSTLY FALSE
1. When I begin to speak in a group, most people stop talking, turn toward me, and listen.	☐	☐
2. I receive compliments on the quality of my writing, including my e-mail messages and social media postings.	☐	☐
3. The reaction to the outgoing message on my voice mall has been favorable.	☐	☐
4. I welcome the opportunity to speak in front of a group.	☐	☐
5. I have published something, including a letter to the editor, an article for the school newspaper, or a comment in a company newsletter.	☐	☐
6. I have my own website, and have received at least two compliments about its effectiveness.	☐	☐
7. The vast majority of my written projects in school have received a grade of B or A.	☐	☐
8. People generally laugh when I tell a joke or make what I think is a witty comment.	☐	☐
9. I stay informed by reading newspapers, watching news on television, or reading news websites.	☐	☐
10. I have heard such terms as enthusiastic, animated, colorful, or dynamic applied to me.	☐	☐
11. The text messages I send look a little better in terms of spelling and grammar than most of the text messages I receive.	☐	☐
Total score:		

Scoring and Interpretation: If eight or more of these statements are true in relation to you, it is most likely that you are an effective communicator. If three or fewer statements are true, you may need substantial improvement in your communication skills. Your scores are probably highly correlated with charisma.

Skill Development: The behaviors indicated by the ten statements in the self-assessment exercise are significant for leaders because much of a leader's impact is determined by his or her communication style. Although effective leaders vary considerably in their communication style, they usually create a positive impact if they can communicate well. Observe some current business leaders on CNBC news or a similar channel to develop a feel for the communication style of successful business leaders.

many are also external, such as communicating with a customer, supplier, government official, or union official.

Here we describe briefly how organizational leaders use face-to-face (or in-person) as well as social media networks to communicate. Recognize, however, that the categories often overlap. A leader might be chatting with a colleague from another department in the company cafeteria, and then continue the communication that evening by tweeting the network member.

Face-to-Face Communication Networks

Developing networks of live interpersonal contacts remains an essential method for a leader building relationships, motivating others, and attaining collaboration. Even the most smartphone-obsessed executives who carry several mobile devices with them at the same time supplement their electronic messages with some personal contacts. A major reason that face-to-face communication networks are vital is that leaders achieve more engagement and credibility when they participate in genuine conversation with the subordinates and coworkers. A *conversation* in this sense is a frank exchange of ideas and information with an agenda specified or unspecified.[4] An example would be a product designer at an automotive manufacturer talking with the CEO about how the company emphasizing fuel-efficient vehicles might make sense for the environment but could be losing sales. The designer might allude to the fact that the latest growth in vehicles sales is for pickup trucks and SUVs, not small-size vehicles. The two people would talk about the issue rather than the CEO delivering as stern message about obeving his or her orders.

According to the research in organizations of Boris Groysberg and Michael Slind, one major factor behind the importance of conversations is *organizational change*. As organizations have become flatter and less hierarchical, and frontline employees are more involved in value-creating work, lateral and bottom-up communication has attained the importance of top-down communication. Another major factor favoring conversations is *generational change*. As young

---

4   Boris Groysberg and Michael Slind, "Leadership Is a Conversation," *Harvard Business Review,* June 2012, p. 79.

people have gained a foothold in organizations, they expect that coworkers and superiors alike to engage in two-way communication with them?[5]

Various types of leadership networks have been identified, with four of these types being particularly relevant. First is the *peer leadership network* that is a system of social ties among leaders who are connected through shared interests and commitments, as well as shared work. Network members share information, provide advice and support, engage in mutual learning, and sometimes collaborate together. Members of the leader's network are perceived as providing resources that can be trusted.[6]

The *operational network* is aimed at doing one's assigned task more effectively. It involves cultivating stronger relationships with coworkers whose membership in the network is clear. Some of these relationships may be part of the formal structure, such as getting cost data from a member of the finance department. *Personal networks* engage cooperative people from outside the organization in a person's effort to develop personally and advance. This type of networking might involve being mentored on how to deal with a challenge, such as dealing with the problem of sexual harassment by a senior manager. (The personal network has much in common with the peer network, except that it might include people who are not peers.)

Strategic networks focus networking on attaining business goals directly. At this level, the manager creates a network that will help identify and capitalize on new opportunities for the company, such as breaking into the African market[7] Even when the manager's own company has good resources for identifying business opportunities, speaking to external people can provide a fresh and useful perspective.

Social Media Networks

An important use of the social media is for the leader to build and maintain a professional network, much like being a member of LinkedIn. The productive leader is more likely to focus on contacts of relevance or *density* rather than focus on accumulating hundreds of superficial network members. The websites used for networking can be external (or public) as well as internal. Most consulting and management services firms, such as Accenture, have widely internal social media websites.

The *strength-of-ties* perspective explains the difference between strong and weak ties.[8] The quality of a contact in the network is particularly important for social media networks because so many contacts can be of dubious value. A key part of the theory is that there are different densities in different parts of the network. A high-density network consists of close friends or

---

5   Boris Groysberg and Michael Slind, "Leadership Is a Conversation," pp. 80, 81.
6   Bruce Hoppe and Claire Reinelt, "Social Network Analysis," p. 601.
7   Networks three, four, and five are from Herminia Ibarra and Mark Hunter, "How Leaders Create and Use Networks," *Harvard Business Review*, January 2007, pp. 40–47.
8   Mark Granovetter, "The Strength of Weak Ties: A Network Theory Revisited," *Sociological Theory*, vol. 1, 1983, pp. 201–233.

associates linked together, such as CEOs in the same industry exchanging information. In contrast, a low-density network consists of acquaintances linked together.

The relationships among the different actors in a network can be broadly classified into two major types: strong versus weak ties and direct versus indirect ties. An acquaintance would be a weak tie, whereas a close friend would be a strong tie. Strength of ties would ordinarily be measured by frequency of contact, yet some contact could be relatively superficial and others might be more emotional and intimate. Melissa might ask Trevor for status reports on his prediction about currency fluctuation, whereas she talks to Sylvie about her career and her relationship with her boss. (The conversation about the relationship with the boss would probably only take place on a social media website if it could not be observed by others.)

Direct versus indirect ties relate to whether you are directly connected to a person because of a contact you developed, or indirectly, such as a friend of a friend. Your direct contact might be Mike, but Mike is connected to Sally, so Sally is an indirect contact.

A caution about internal social networking sites such as Yammer and Chatter is that the leader or other worker will communicate in the same brash, insulting, and overly casual manner often found on public social networking sites. The result is that the leader or other worker will appear unprofessional, thereby detracting from his or her leadership image. Noshir Contractor, a professor of behavioral sciences at Northwestern University, warns that people can fall into the trap of being too informal on internal social media sites. "When you're considered for a promotion ... anything you said on Yammer will be used in some case to determine if you're qualified," said Contractor.[9]

Inspirational and Powerful Communication

Information about communicating persuasively and effectively is extensive. Here we focus on suggestions for creating the high-impact communication that contributes to effective leadership. Effective communication is frequently a criterion for being promoted to a leadership position. U.S. Senator and former mayor of Newark, N.J., Cory Booker, reminds us that the real communicators are those who can motivate people to act and ultimately lead themselves.[10] In this section, suggestions for becoming an inspirational and emotion-provoking communicator are divided into the following two categories: (1) speaking and writing, and (2) nonverbal communication. We also discuss six basic principles of persuasion.

---

9   Quoted in Jim Alev and Brian Bremmer (eds.), "Trouble at the Virtual Water Cooler," *Bloomberg Businessweek,* May 2-May 8, 2011, P-31.

10   Cary Booker, "How to Get People to Listen," *Bloomberg Businessweek,* April 15-April 21, 2013, p. 61. (As told to Devin Leonard.)

Speaking and Writing

You are already familiar with the basics of effective spoken and written communication. Yet, the basics—such as writing and speaking clearly, maintaining eye contact, and not mumbling—are only starting points. The majority of effective leaders have an extra snap or panache in their communication style, both in day-by-day conversations and when addressing a group. The same energy and excitement is reflected in both speaking and writing. Suggestions for dynamic and persuasive oral and written communication are presented next and outlined in Table 10.1.

Table 10.1   Suggestions for Inspirational Speaking and Writing

---

A. A Variety of Inspirational Tactics

1. Be credible.
2. Gear your message to the listener.
3. Sell group members on the benefits of your suggestions.
4. Use heavy-impact and emotion-provoking words.
5. Use anecdotes to communicate meaning.
6. Back up conclusions with data (to a point).
7. Minimize language errors, junk words, and vocalized pauses.
8. Write crisp, clear memos, letters, and reports, including a front-loaded message.
9. Use business jargon in appropriate doses.

B. The Power-Oriented Linguistic Style

Included here are a variety of factors such as downplaying uncertainty, emphasizing direct rather than indirect talk, and choosing an effective communication frame.

Be Credible Attempts at persuasion, including inspirational speaking and writing, begin with the credibility of the message sender. If the speaker is perceived as highly credible, the attempt at persuasive communication is more likely to be successful. The perception of credibility is influenced by many factors, including those covered in this entire section. Being trustworthy heavily influences being perceived as credible. A leader with a reputation for lying will have a difficult time convincing people about the merits of a new initiative such as outsourcing. Being perceived as intelligent and knowledgeable is another major factor contributing to credibility.

Gear Your Message to the Listener, Including His or Her Needs An axiom of persuasive communication is that a speaker must adapt the message to the listener's interests and motivations. The company CEO visiting a manufacturing plant will receive careful attention—and build support—when he says that jobs will not be outsourced to another country. The same CEO will receive the support of stockholders when he emphasizes how cost reductions will boost earnings per share and enlarge dividends.

In order to gear your message to the listener, it is usually necessary to figure out what he or she wants, or deal with the other person's perceived self-interest.[11] Visualize the head of a customer support center who believes strongly that more funding is necessary to meet the demands placed on the department. To be convincing, the woman needs to figure out what the CEO really expects from a customer support center. Careful listening might indicate that the CEO is mainly interested in customers not asking for refunds and/or badmouthing the company face-to-face as well as online. The customer support head can then direct her pitch for more funding in terms of how an expanded department can reduce merchandise returns and customer complaints.

The average intelligence level of the group is a key contingency factor in designing a persuasive message. People with high intelligence tend to be more influenced by messages based on strong, logical arguments. Bright people are also more likely to reject messages based on flawed logic.[12]

Sell Group Members on the Benefits of Your Suggestions A leader is constrained by the willingness of group members to take action on his or her suggestions and initiatives. As a consequence, the leader must explain to group members how they can benefit from what he or she proposes. For example, a plant manager attempting to sell employees on the benefits of recycling supplies as much as possible might say, "If we can cut down enough on the cost of supplies, we might be able to save one or two jobs."

Use Heavy-Impact and Emotion-Provoking Words Certain words used in the proper context give power and force to your speech. Used comfortably, naturally, and sincerely, these words will project the image of a self-confident person with leadership ability or potential. Two examples of heavy-impact phrases are "We will be outsourcing those portions of our knowledge work that are not mission critical" and "We will be leading edge in both product development and business processes." However, too much of this type of language will make the leader appear that he or she is imitating a Dilbert cartoon (a long-running cartoon satire about managers and businesspeople).

Closely related to heavy-impact language is the use of emotion-provoking words. An expert persuasive tactic is to sprinkle your speech with emotion-provoking—and therefore inspiring—words. Emotion-provoking words bring forth images of exciting events. Examples of emotion-provoking and powerful words include *"outclassing* the competition," *"bonding* with customers," *"surpassing* previous profits," *"capturing* customer loyalty," and *"rebounding* from a downturn."

Communications specialist Frank Lunt found that five words resonate in the current business world: consequences, impact, reliability, mission, and commitment. A leader who incorporated

---

11   Carlin Flora, "The Art of Influence," *Psychology Today,* September/October 2011, p. 67.
12   Stephen P. Robbins and Phillip L. Hunsaker, *Training in Interpersonal Skills: Tips for Managing People at Work* (Upper Saddle River, N.J.: Prentice Hall, 1996), p. 115. (These findings are still valid today.)

these words into his or her business vocabulary would therefore be influential.[13] It also helps to use words and phrases that connote being modem. Those now in vogue include *virtual organization, transparent organization,* and *seamless organization.*

A large vocabulary assists using both heavy-impact and emotion-provoking words. When you need to persuade somebody on the spot, it is difficult to search for the right words in a dictionary or thesaurus—even if you access the Internet with your smartphone. Also, you need to practice a word a few times to use it comfortably for an important occasion.

Use Anecdotes to Communicate Meaning Anecdotes are a powerful part of a leader's kit of persuasive and influence tactics, as already mentioned in this chapter and in Chapter 3 about charismatic leadership. Although storytelling is an ancient art, it is more in vogue than ever as a method for leaders to influence and inspire others. A carefully chosen anecdote is also useful in persuading group members about the importance of organizational values. So long as the anecdote is not repeated too frequently, it can communicate an important message.

Zippo is a consumer products company that has hundreds of anecdotes to share about how those sturdy steel cigarette lighters saved somebody's life by deflecting a bullet. It seems that the stories originated in World War II but have continued into modem times, such as how a Zippo in the pocket of a police worker prevented a criminal's bullet from killing the officer. Zippo leaders can inspire workers with such heroic tales starring the Zippo lighter. In recent years, Zippo has shifted into many nonsmoking-related products, but the anecdotes are still inspiring for the nonsmoker.

Back Up Conclusions with Data You will be more persuasive if you support your spoken and written presentations with solid data. One approach to obtaining data is to collect them yourself—for example, by conducting an online survey of your customers or group members. Published sources also provide convincing data for arguments. Supporting data for hundreds of arguments can be found in the business pages of newspapers, in business magazines and newspapers, and on the Internet. The Statistical Abstract of the United States, published annually, is an inexpensive yet trusted reference for thousands of arguments.

Relying too much on research has a potential disadvantage, however. Being too dependent on data could suggest that you have little faith in your own intuition. For example, you might convey an impression of weakness if, when asked your opinion, you respond, "I can't answer until I collect some data." Leaders are generally decisive. An important issue, then, is for the leader to find the right balance between relying on data and using intuition alone when communicating an important point.

Minimize Language Errors, Junk Words, and Vocalized Pauses Using colorful, powerful words enhances the perception that you are self-confident and have leadership qualities. Also, minimize

---

13   Frank Luntz, "Words That Pack Power," *BusinessWeek,* November 3, 2008, p. 106.

the use of words and phrases that dilute the impact of your speech, such as "like," "y know," "you know what I mean," "he goes" (to mean "he says"), and "uh." Such junk words and vocalized pauses convey the impression of low self-confidence, especially in a professional setting, and detract from a sharp communication image.

An effective way to decrease the use of these extraneous words is to video-record your side of a phone conversation and then play it back. Many people are not aware that they use extraneous words until they hear recordings of their speech.

An effective leader should be sure always to write and speak with grammatical precision to give the impression of being articulate and well informed, thereby enhancing his or her leadership stature. Here are two examples of common language errors: "Just between you and I" is wrong; "just between you and me" is correct. "Him and I," or "her and I," are incorrect phrases despite how frequently they creep into social and business language. "He and I" and "she and I" are correct when used as the subjects of a sentence. "Him and me" or "Her and me" are correct when used as the objects of a sentence. For example, "She and I greeted the client" and "The client greeted her and me" are both correct.

Another very common error is using the plural pronoun *they* to refer to a singular antecedent. For example, "The systems analyst said that *they* cannot help us" is incorrect. "The systems analyst said *she* cannot help us" is correct. Using *they* to refer to a singular antecedent has become so common in the English language that many people no longer make the distinction between singular and plural. For example, nowadays most people say, "Everyone placed their order," when actually "Everyone placed his (or her) order" is the grammatically correct statement. Staff at Facebook systematically confuse singular and plural with such statements as "What does Jessica do in *their* spare time?" Some of these errors are subtle and are made so frequently that many people do not realize they are wrong; but again, avoiding grammatical errors may enhance a person's leadership stature.

Perhaps the most common language error business leaders make is to convert hundreds of nouns into verbs. Many nouns do become legitimate verbs, such as using the noun *phone* for a verb, such as "I will phone you later." The leader has to set a limit, and perhaps not use such verb-to-noun conversions such as, "Facebook me tonight," "Focus-group this problem," and "Skype me a message." Yet, the hip leader will correctly use nouns that have been recently been converted into dual use as a verb and noun, such as "Google some potential customers for this product." Judgment is called for with respect to which nouns should be used as verbs to avoid sounding silly, and therefore weak.

When in doubt about a potential language error, consult a respected dictionary. An authoritative guide for the leader (and anyone else) who chooses to use English accurately is *The Elements of Style* by William Strunk Jr. and E. B. White.[14] First published in 1918, the book has its critics but has sold millions of copies.

---

14   William Strunk Jr., E. B. White, and Maira Kalman, *The Elements of Style,* Sixth Edition (Boston: Allyn and Bacon, 2007).

Use Business Jargon in Appropriate Doses Business and government executives and professionals make frequent use of jargon. (Only athletic coaches exceed businesspeople in the heavy use of jargon and clichés.) Often the jargon is used automatically without deliberate thought, and at other times jargon words and phrases are chosen to help establish rapport with the receiver. A vastly overused phrase these days is "at the end of the day," with "buckets" fighting for second place. "The end of the day" has come to replace "in the final analysis," and "buckets" replace "categories." Many businesspeople say "at the end of the day" twice in the same few sentences.

Six major executives and management professors were asked which buzzwords they would ban from conversation in the boardroom, office, and beyond: The six disliked buzzwords, or jargon words, were "push the envelope," "de-layering" (in place of downsizing), "dynamic resilience," "out-of-the-box thinking," "passionate," and "viral."[15]

Sprinkling business talk with jargon does indeed help establish rapport and adds to a person's popularity. But too much jargon makes a person seem stereotyped in thinking, and perhaps even unwilling to express an original thought—and therefore lacking power.

Write Crisp and Clear Memos, Letters, and Reports that Include a Front-Loaded Message Business leaders characteristically write easy-to-read, well-organized messages, both in e-mail and in more formal reports. Writing, in addition to speaking, is more persuasive when key ideas are placed at the beginning of a conversation, e-mail message, paragraph, or sentence.[16] Front-loaded messages (those placed at the beginning of a sentence) are particularly important for leaders because people expect leaders to be forceful communicators. A front-loaded and powerful message might be "Cost reduction must be our immediate priority," which emphasizes that cost reduction is the major subject. It is clearly much more to the point than, for example, "All of us must reduce costs immediately."

One way to make sure messages are front-loaded is to use the active voice, making sure the subject of the sentence is doing the acting, not being acted upon. Compare the active (and front-loaded) message "Loyal workers should not take vacations during a company crisis" to the passive (not front-loaded) message "Vacations should not be taken by loyal workers during a company crisis." Recognize, however, that less emphasis is placed on the active voice today than several years ago. Also, the passive voice may be necessary for front-loading, as in "Cloud backups are recommended by cybersecurity experts."

Suggestions for effective business writing continue to evolve, and many of these tips are worthy of a leader's or potential leader's attention. For example, there is much less emphasis using "Dear" in a salutation, particularly in the United States. Yet, "Hello" beats "Hey" for appearing dignified.

---

15 "Which Buzzwords Would You Ban?" *The Wall Street Journal,* January 2, 2014, p. B4.
16 Sherry Sweetham, "How to Organize Your Thoughts for Better Communication," *Personnel,* March 1986, p. 39.

Use a Power-Oriented Linguistic Style A major part of being persuasive involves choosing the correct **linguistic style,** a person's characteristic speaking pattern. According to Deborah Tannen, linguistic style involves such aspects as the amount of directness, pacing and pausing, word choice, and the use of such communication devices as jokes, figures of speech, anecdotes, questions, and apologies.[17]

Linguistic style is complex because it includes the culturally learned signals by which people communicate what they mean, along with how they interpret what others say and how they evaluate others. The complexity of linguistic style makes it difficult to offer specific prescriptions for using one that is power oriented. Many of the elements of a power-oriented linguistic style are included in other suggestions made in this section of the chapter, including using heavy-impact words. Nevertheless, here are several components of a linguistic style that would give power and authority to the message sender in many situations, as observed by Deborah Tannen and other language specialists:[18]

- Speak loudly enough to be heard by the majority of people with at least average hearing ability. Speaking too softly projects an image of low self-confidence.

- Use the pronoun *I* to receive more credit for your ideas. (Of course, this could backfire in a team-based organization.)

- Minimize self-deprecation with phrases such as "This will probably sound stupid, but ..." Apologize infrequently, and particularly minimize saying, "I'm sorry."

- Make your point quickly. You know you are taking too long to reach a conclusion when others look bored or finish your sentences for you.

- Emphasize direct rather than indirect talk: Say, "I need your report by noon tomorrow," rather than, "I'm wondering if your report will be available by noon tomorrow."

- Weed out wimpy words. Speak up without qualifying or giving other indices of uncertainty. It is better to give dates for the completion of a project rather than say "I'll get it to you soon" or "It shouldn't be a problem." Instead, make a statement like "I will have my portion of the strategic plan shortly before Thanksgiving. I need to collect input from my team and sift through the information."

- Know exactly what you want. Your chances of selling an idea increase to the extent that you have clarified the idea in your own mind. The clearer and more committed you are at the outset of a session, the stronger you are as a persuader and the more powerful your language becomes.

---

17   Deborah Tannen, "The Power of Talk: Who Gets Heard and Why?" *Harvard Business Review,* September–October 1995, pp. 138–148.

18   Deborah Tannen, "The Power of Talk: Who Gets Heard and Why?" pp. 138–148; "How You Speak Shows Where You Rank," *Fortune,* February 2, 1998, p. 156; "Speak Like You Mean Business," *Working Smart* (www.nibm.net), March 2004; "Weed Out Wimpy Words: Speak Up Without Backpedaling, Qualifying," *Working SMART,* March 2000, p. 2.

- Speak at length, set the agenda for a conversation, make jokes, and laugh. Be ready to offer solutions to problems, as well as to suggest a program or plan. All of these points are more likely to create a sense of confidence in listeners.

- Strive to be bold in your statements. As a rule of thumb, be bold about ideas, but tentative about people. If you say something like "I have a plan that I think will solve these problems," you are presenting an idea, not attacking a person.

- Frame your comments in a way that increases your listener's receptivity. The *frame* is built around the best context for responding to the needs of others. An example would be to use the frame, "Let's dig a little deeper," when the other people present know something is wrong but cannot pinpoint the problem. Your purpose is to enlist the help of others in finding the underlying nature of the problem.

Despite these suggestions for having a power-oriented linguistic style, Tannen cautions that there is no one best way to communicate. How you project your power and authority is often dependent on the people involved, the organizational culture, the relative rank of the speakers, and other situational factors. The power-oriented linguistic style should be interpreted as a general guideline.

The Six Basic Principles of Persuasion

Persuasion is a major form of influence, so it has gained in importance in the modern organization because of the reason described in Chapter 8: Managers must often influence people for whom they have no formal responsibility. The trend stems from leaner corporate hierarchies and the breaking down of division walls. Managers must persuade peers in situations where lines of authority are unclear or do not exist. One way to be persuasive is to capitalize on scientific evidence about how to persuade people. Robert B. Cialdini has synthesized knowledge from experimental and social psychology about methods for getting people to concede, comply, or change. These principles can also be framed as influence principles, but with a focus on persuasion.[19] The six principles described next have accompanying tactics that can be used to supplement the other approaches to persuasion described in this chapter.

1 ***Liking: People like those who like them.*** As a leader, you have a better chance of persuading and influencing group members who like you. Emphasizing similarities between you and the other person and offering praise are the two most reliable techniques for getting another person to like you. The leader should therefore emphasize similarities, such as common interests with group members. Praising others is a powerful influence technique and can be used effectively even when the leader finds something relatively small to compliment. Genuine praise is the most effective.

---

19   Robert B. Cialdini, "Harnessing the Science of Persuasion," *Harvard Business Review,* October 2001, pp. 72–79.

2   ***Reciprocity: People repay in kind.*** Managers can often influence group members to behave in a particular way by displaying the behavior first. The leader might therefore serve as a model of trust, good ethics, or strong commitment to company goals. In short, give what you want to receive.

3   ***Social proof: People follow the lead of similar others.*** Persuasion can have high impact when it comes from peers. If you as the leader want to influence a group to convert to a new procedure, such as virtually eliminating paper records in the office, ask a believer to speak up in a meeting or send his or her statement of support via e-mail. (But do not send around paper documents.)

4   ***Consistency: People align with their clear commitments.*** People need to feel committed to what you want them to do. After people take a stand or go on record in favor of a position, they prefer to stay with that commitment. Suppose you are the team leader and you want team members to become more active in the community as a way of creating a favorable image for the firm. If the team members talk about their plans to get involved and also put their plans in writing, they are more likely to follow through. If the people involved read their action plans to each other, the commitment will be even stronger.

5   ***Authority: People defer to experts.*** The action plan here is to make constituents aware of your expertise to enhance the probability that your plan will persuade them. A leader might mention certification in the technical area that is the subject of influence. For example, a leader attempting to persuade team members to use statistical data to improve quality might mention that he or she is certified in the quality process Six Sigma (is a Six Sigma Black Belt).

6   ***Scarcity: People want more of what they can have less of.*** An application of this principle is that the leader can persuade group members to act in a particular direction if the members believe that the resource at issue is shrinking rapidly. They might be influenced to enroll in a course in outsourcing knowledge work, for example, if they are told that the course may not be offered again for a long time. Another way to apply this principle is to persuade group members by using information not readily available to others. The leader might say, "I have some preliminary sales data. If we can increase our sales by just 10 percent in the last month of this quarter, we could be the highest performing unit in the company."

The developer of these principles explains that they should be applied in combination to multiply their impact. For example, while establishing your expertise you might simultaneously praise people for their accomplishments. It is also important to be ethical, such as by not fabricating data to influence others.[20]

---

20   Ibid., p. 79.

Nonverbal Communication Including Videoconferencing and Telepresence

Effective leaders are masterful nonverbal as well as verbal communicators. Nonverbal communication is important because leadership involves emotion, which words alone cannot communicate convincingly. A major component of the emotional impact of a message is communicated nonverbally.

A self-confident leader not only speaks and writes with assurance but also projects confidence through body position, gestures, and manner of speech. Not everybody interprets the same body language and other nonverbal signals in the same way, but some aspects of nonverbal behavior project a self-confident leadership image in many situations.[21]

- Using an erect posture when walking, standing, or sitting. Slouching and slumping are almost universally interpreted as an indicator of low self-confidence.

- Standing up straight during a confrontation. Cowering is interpreted as a sign of low self-confidence and poor leadership qualities.

- Patting other people on the back while nodding slightly.

- Standing with toes pointing outward rather than inward. Outwardpointing toes are usually perceived as indicators of superior status, whereas inward-pointing toes are perceived to indicate inferiority. Also, opening limbs at 18 inches or more expresses power and dominance.

- Speaking at a moderate pace, with a loud, confident tone. People lacking in self-confidence tend to speak too rapidly or very slowly.

- Smiling frequently in a relaxed, natural-appearing manner.

- Maintaining eye contact with those around you, with the ideal gaze lasting about seven to ten seconds. The ability to make eye contact has multiplied in importance as a sign of leadership because so many people are accustomed to looking at their mobile devices at every possible moment, and therefore lack skill in looking directly at people.

- Gesturing in a relaxed, nonmechanical way, including pointing toward others in a way that welcomes rather than accuses, such as using a gesture to indicate, "You're right," or "It's your turn to comment."

- Having a big desk or big chair helps project a powerful image, yet the opportunities for having such trappings of power are diminishing in organizations. Related to this finding is that taking up a lot of space, which might include extending the arms, conveys power and confidence.

---

21   Several of the suggestions here are from Sue Shellenbarger, "Strike a Powerful Pose: Posture Can Determine Who's a Hero, Who's a Wimp; Bad News for Phone Users," *The Wall Street Journal,* August 21, 2013, pp. D1, D2; Shellenbarger, "Just Look Me in the Eye Already," *The Wall Street Journal,* May 29, 2013, p. D1; *Body Language for Business Success* (New York: National Institute for Business Management, 1989), pp. 2–29; Andy Yap et al., "The Ergonomics of Dishonesty: The Effects of Incidental Posture on Stealing, Cheating, and Traffic Violations," *Psychological Science,* November 2013, pp. 2281–2289.

A general approach to using nonverbal behavior that projects confidence is to have a goal of appearing self-confident and powerful. This type of autosuggestion makes many of the behaviors seem automatic. For example, if you say, "I am going to display leadership qualities in this meeting," you will have taken an important step toward appearing confident.

Your external image also plays an important role in communicating messages to others. People pay more respect and grant more privileges to those they perceive as being well dressed and neatly groomed. Even on casual dress days, most effective leaders will choose clothing that gives them an edge over others. Appearance includes more than the choice of clothing. Self-confidence is projected by such small items as the following:

- Neatly pressed and sparkling clean clothing

- Freshly polished shoes

- Impeccable fingernails

- Clean jewelry in mint condition

- Well-maintained hair

- Good-looking teeth with a white or antique-white (or off-white) color

What constitutes a powerful and self-confident external image is often influenced by the organizational culture. At a software development company, for example, powerful people might dress more casually than at an investment banking firm. Leadership at many law firms is moving back toward formal business attire for the professional staff. Your verbal behavior and the forms of nonverbal behavior previously discussed contribute more to your leadership image than your clothing, providing you dress acceptably.

Videoconferencing places extra demands on the nonverbal communication skills of leaders, managers, and other participants. A recent advance in video-conferencing, referred to as *telepresence,* places even more demands on nonverbal communication skills because it appears closer to human presence. For example, the illumination highlights the facial features of the people sitting in the telepresence studio. Some telepresence systems are custom-built meeting rooms equipped with a bank of high-definition screens and cameras. Other systems take the form of humanoid robots that are used outside of meeting rooms. Etiquette tips for making a strong nonverbal presence during a videoconference or telepresence conference include the following (and are similar to nonverbal communication suggestions in general):

- Choose what you wear carefully, remembering that busy (confusing and complex) patterns look poor on video. Also do not wear formal attire mixed with running shoes because you might move into full camera view.

- Speak in crisp conversational tones and pay attention. (The tone and paying attention are the nonverbal aspects of communication.)

Leadership Skill-Building Exercise 10.1

Feedback on Verbal and Nonverbal Behavior

Ten volunteers have one week to prepare a three-minute presentation on a course-related subject of their choice. The topics of these presentations could be as far-reaching as "The Importance of Investing in Gold" or "My Goals and Dreams." The class members who observe the presentations prepare feedback slips on 3 x 5 cards, describing how well the speakers communicated powerfully and inspirationally. One card per speaker is usually sufficient. Notations should be made for both verbal and nonverbal feedback.

Emphasis should be placed on positive feedback and constructive suggestions. Students pass the feedback cards along to the speakers. The cards can be anonymous to encourage frankness, but they should not be mean-spirited.

Persuading and inspiring others is one of the main vehicles for practicing leadership. Knowing how others perceive you helps you polish and refine your impact.

- Never forget the video camera's powerful reach, such as catching you rolling your eyes when you disagree with a subordinate, or sending and receiving text messages during the conference.

- Avoid culturally insensitive gestures including large hand and body gestures that make many Asians feel uncomfortable. Asians believe that you should have long-term relationships before being demonstrative.[22]

An effective way of sharpening your videoconferencing and telepresence nonverbal skills, as well as other nonverbal skills, is to be videotaped several times. Make adjustments for anything you don't like, and repeat what you do like. Feedback on your behavior from another observer can be quite helpful.

Now that you have refreshed your thoughts on effective verbal and nonverbal communication, do Leadership Skill-Building Exercise 10.1.

Listening as a Leadership Skill

Listening is a fundamental management and leadership skill. Listening also provides the opportunity for dialogue and conversation, in which people understand each other better by

---

22   Cited in Joann S. Lublin, "Some Dos and Don'ts to Help You Hone Videoconference Skills," *The Wall Street Journal,* February 7, 2006, p. B1.

taking turns having their point of view understood. For a leader to support and encourage a subordinate, active listening (as described in the discussion of coaching) is required. Also, effective leader–member exchanges require that each party listen to one another. The relationship between two parties cannot be enhanced unless each one listens to the other. Furthermore, leaders cannot identify problems unless they listen carefully to group members. Multitasking is a major deterrent to listening carefully to subordinates because the leader who is involved in another task at the moment, such as glancing at a tablet computer, is not paying full attention to the speaker.

An effective approach to develop good listening habits is to remember to ask questions—and then listen to the answers. Bill Kanarick, the senior vice president and chief marketing officer of Sapient Crop., a global services company, believes that the organizational culture contributes to effective listening. He says that it is incumbent upon the company to create an environment that welcomes exploration and questioning.[23]

Two major impediments face the leader who wants to be an effective listener. First, the leader is so often overloaded with responsibilities, including analytical work, that it is difficult to take the time to carefully listen to subordinates. Second is the speed difference between speaking and listening. The average rate of speaking is between 110 and 200 words per minute, yet people can listen in the range of 400 to 3,000 words per minute. So the leader, as well as anybody else, will often let his or her mind wander.

Here we look at three leadership aspects of listening to supplement your general knowledge of listening, acquired most likely in other courses: showing respect, selective listening to problems, and making the rounds.

Show Respect

A foundation tactic for a leader to become an effective listener is to show respect for others. Consultant Bernard T. Ferran provides the case in point of the COO of a large medical institution. He told Ferran that he could not run an operation as complex as a hospital without gathering input from staff members at all levels—from the chief of surgery to the custodial crew. The chief operating officer let everyone know that he believed each one of them had something unique to contribute. As the executive drew out the critical information, he attentively processed what he heard. Part of the COO's being liked and admired stemmed from his listening approach.[24]

Selective Listening to Problems

Organizational leaders are so often bombarded with demands and information that it is difficult to be attentive to a full range of problems. So the leader makes an intentional or unintentional decision to listen to just certain problems. Erika H. James notes that despite how our brains

---

23   "A Conversation with Bill Kanarick: The Art of Asking Questions," *Executive Leadership,* January 2014, p. 3.
24   Bernard T. Ferran, "The Executive's Guide to Better Listening," *McKinsey Quarterly* (www.mckinseyquarterly), February 2012, p. 2.

ordinarily work, success is dependent on staying open to all incoming information.[25] The busy leader must avoid listening to limited categories of information such as good news, bad news, or financial news. A CEO with a propensity to listen only to financial results might ignore any word of problems so long as the company is earning a profit.

Making the Rounds

A robust communication channel for the leader/manager is to engage in face-to-face communication with direct reports and others, with an emphasis on listening. **Making the rounds** refers to the leader casually dropping by constituents to listen to their accomplishments, concerns, and problems and to share information. *Rounding* is a well-established concept from health care in which the physician talks to patients and other health care workers to observe problems and progress firsthand.[26] Through rounding, vital information is gathered if the physician or manager listens carefully. Making the rounds is also referred to as *management by wandering (or walking) around,* yet rounding seems more focused and systematic.

From the perspective of listening, the leader stays alert to potential problems. Assume that a subordinate is asked, "How are things going?" and he or she replies, "Not too terrible." This response begs a little digging, such as, "What is happening that is a little terrible?"

Leadership Skill-Building Exercise 10.2 gives you an opportunity to try out the fundamental leadership skill of listening.

Discussion Questions

1 Does LMX theory enrich your understanding of leadership? If so, what would you consider its main contribution?

2 As a leader, how can you establish high-quality leader–member relationships? Identify three things you can improve in your current leadership practice to better your relationships with subordinates.

3 What can you do to improve your communication skills? Why is that important?

---

25 Erika H. James, "Selective Hearing Can Lead to a Blind Eye," *The Darden Perspective in First Person,* published in *The Wall Street Journal,* December 4, 2007, p. A16.
26 Linda Dulye, "Get Out of Your Office," *HR Magazine,* July 2006, pp. 99–100; " 'Making Rounds' Like a Physician," *Manager's Edge,* February 2006, p. 8.

PART IV

DESTRUCTIVE LEADERSHIP

CHAPTER 7

When Leadership Goes Wrong

The Nature, Prevalence, and Outcomes of Destructive Leadership

A Behavioral and Conglomerate Approach

Ståle Einarsen, Anders Skogstad, and Merethe Schanke Aasland

The present article presents a definition and a taxonomy of destructive leadership based on a behavioral approach in opposition to the approach traditionally taken in leadership research where a one-sided emphasis on the personality of these "dark leaders" is the rule. Destructive leadership is then defined as any repeated behaviors that may undermine or sabotage either the organization itself or the subordinates of the leader. Building on these two dimensions, organizational directed behaviors and subordinate directed behaviors, that both may range from being highly pro to highly anti, a model is created that pinpoint four basic forms of destructive leadership; Laissez-faire leadership, Derailed leadership, Tyrannical leadership and Supportive but disloyal leadership. The model further implies that a leader may display both constructive as well as destructive behaviors, as leaders often face the dilemma of siding either with the goals or interests of the organization or with the goals and interests of their subordinates. Hence, the present article argues for a conglomerate perspective on leadership behaviors in order to understand the full nuances in leaders' behaviors, making it difficult to distinguish between pure 'good' and pure "bad" leaders. The latter is also pinpointed by data on the prevalence of destructive leadership presented showing that destructive leadership is quite common in working life, at least in its more passive and less severe forms. Data are then presented showing that all the above mentioned forms of destructive leadership have significant negative relationships with both subordinate and organizational outcomes.

Introduction

Two important biases exist in leadership research and writings. First of all, leadership research often equates a leader with a good and efficient leader (Kellerman, 2004). Hence, most writings on leadership are based on the implicit assumption that to improve leadership it is sufficient to do more of what is already regarded as positive and productive. Furthermore, one sees leaders as inherently good people that do not need to worry about whether or not they at times may behave badly or commit mistakes. This position is exemplified by all those text-books that ignore the issue of potential bad or unwanted behaviors among leaders. For instance, the very popular and informative book of Yukl (2010) *Leadership in Organizations* does not include the terms "abusive supervision" or "destructive leadership" in its subject index. The same is true for Peter G. Northouse's (2007) book *Leadership: Theory and Practice*.

Second, writings that do exist on destructive forms of leadership have traditionally, explicitly or at least implicitly, equated destructive leadership with a "dark side" of the individual leader's personality. Hence, many studies have tried to identify personality traits in those leaders who fail or who derail from the path of constructive and effective leadership. This tradition of looking for the "evil within" has a long tradition in social psychology; although much evidence talks to the opposite (see Zimbardo, 2004). For instance, the work of Adorno and colleagues gave us the notion of the "authoritarian personality" (Adorno, Frenkel-Brunswik, Levinson, & Sanford, 1950). Later, Kets de Vries (1979) studied destructive leaders with a psychoanalytic perspective, focusing on the so-called "narcissistic" leaders. The concepts of "the dark side of leadership" (Conger, 1990; Hogan, Raskin, & Fazzini, 1990; Howell, 1988) substantiates that not all charismatic leaders focus on the common good of the organization and their followers. Rather, some leaders obviously have their own personal needs and interest at heart. Studies have shown that these leaders are characterized by an exaggerated and dysfunctional need for power, by narcissism, an authoritarian personality, and with a tendency for blaming others when failing themselves (House & Howell, 1992). Later on, concepts such as "toxic leaders" (Lipman-Blumen, 2005) and "crazy bosses" (Bing, 1992), among many others, likewise, have such connotations of personality flaws embedded.

Yet, such a focus on leaders traits in the search for negative aspects of leadership may have some problematic implications, not at least in applied settings. First of all, such a focus may lead to leaders being either seen as "white angels" (the rule) or as "black demons" (the anomaly), while few are seen as what they probably are, namely "grey suites" who portray all kinds of both good and bad behaviors depending on the situation and the systems that govern their everyday life

(Skogstad, 2008). One may easily underestimate the risk factors and dilemmas leaders inherently face in their leadership role and within any kind of position of power, organizational structure and culture, appropriately illustrated with the words of Philip G. Zimbardo (2004):

> While a few bad apples might spoil the barrel (filled with good fruit/people), a vinegar barrel will always transform sweet cucumbers into sour pickles—regardless of the best intentions, resilience, and genetic nature of those cucumbers. So does it make more sense to spend our resources on attempts to identify, isolate and destroy a few bad apples or to learn how vinegar works so that we can teach cucumbers how to avoid undesirable vinegar barrels? (p. 47)

The management of destructive leadership then becomes a search for those very few and very bad "apples in the barrel," alienating the issue of bad leader behaviors from most training and development programs. Hence, one may train presumably good leaders to become even better, without an adequate focus on those pitfalls which most leaders probably will encounter sooner or later.

To avoid a one-sided emphasis on personality we will argue that there is a strong need for a firm behavioral approach to the study of destructive leadership. The question of personality traits as antecedents then becomes an empirical and not a definitional issue. Only by a behavioral approach may we enlighten and train leaders in the full range of possible behaviors that they may need and show in the role as a leader; only then may we create fair and safe early-detection systems for destructive leadership; only then may we fully discover the forces within the organization that act to shape such behaviors in the first place; only then may we train employees to be aware of and report safely those instances where one or more leaders behave in ways that they should not, be it in terms of inefficiency, in terms of legal aspects or in terms of ethics.

The present chapter will provide such a behavioral framework for the study of destructive leadership by presenting a definition and a taxonomy of destructive leadership behaviors based on two theoretically derived dimensions found in many theories and models of group dynamics and organizational behaviors. We will also show how a leader may display both constructive as well as destructive behaviors, as leaders often face the dilemma of siding either with the goals or interests of the organization or with the goals and interests of their subordinates, which at times may differ. Hence, the present article will show how we need a conglomerate perspective on leadership behaviors in order to understand the full nuances in leaders' behaviors. A conglomerate perspective on organizational behaviors implies that an actor, in our case a leader, may portray different kinds of behaviors that may occur simultaneously or that may occur in sequence (van de Vliert, Euwema, & Huismans, 1995). A leader may portray behavior that in some respects must be considered constructive while simultaneously may be considered as destructive from another point of view. Alternatively, the leader has a repertoire of behaviors including both destructive and constructive elements. In the following, we will also summarize some results from studies in our ongoing research on the nature, prevalence and outcomes of destructive leadership based on such a behavioral and conglomerate approach, building on the notion that to be able to identify and combat destructive leadership, we need to know what it is in terms of nuanced behavioral descriptions.

The Nature of Destructive Leadership Behaviors

A Definition of Destructive Leadership

Different concepts have been introduced to describe destructive leadership behaviors such as "petty tyranny" (Ashforth, 1994), "abusive supervision" (Tepper, 2000), and "toxic leadership" (Lipman-Blumen, 2005). These concepts describe leaders who behave in a destructive manner towards followers, and may include behaviors such as intimidating followers, belittling or humiliating them in public, or exposing them to aggressive nonverbal gestures (Aryee, Sun, Chen, & Debrah, 2007; Ashforth, 1994; Tepper, 2000). Studies have shown such behaviors to be destructive for the motivation, efficiency and health of followers and thereby possibly also pose a problem for the organization (e.g., Tepper, 2007). Yet, leaders may also behave destructively in a way that primarily effects the organization (Einarsen, Aasland, & Skogstad, 2007; Kellerman, 2004; Lipman-Blumen, 2005; Vredenburgh & Brender, 1998). Concepts proposed in the literature to describe such anti-organizational behaviors include, for example, "flawed leadership" and "impaired managers" (Lubit, 2004). Leaders may, for instance, hamper the execution of tasks, reduce the quality of work performed in the department, reduce the efficiency of subordinates, or more directly act in a way that hamper relationships with customers and clients (Padilla, Hogan, & Kaiser, 2007). The behavior of leaders may undermine or sabotage the organization's goals, tasks, resources, and effectiveness both directly through their own behaviors and through their potential negative effect on the behavior of subordinates. In extreme cases, leaders may in this way also perform illegal acts such as stealing resources from the company. As mentioned above, leaders may have their own best interests at heart more so than the best interest of the company. Hence, there are clearly both a subordinate and an organizational dimension in destructive leadership (see also Einarsen et al., 2007).

In addition, the lack of initiative and the lack of appropriate responses by leaders may also pose a problem. Leaders' passiveness and lack of appropriate leadership, exemplified by laissez-faire leadership (see e.g., Bass & Riggio, 2006) have been shown to be associated with negative consequences for followers and leader effectiveness (Hinkens & Schriesheim, 2008; Judge & Piccolo, 2004; Skogstad, Einarsen, Aasland, Torsheim, & Hetland, 2007). Passive leadership represents a leadership style where the leader has been nominated and still exists physically in the leadership position, but in practice has abdicated from the responsibilities and duties designated to him/her (Lewin, Lippitt, & White, 1939), implying that the leader did not accomplish legitimate expectations from subordinates or from superiors and the owners of the organization (Skogstad et al., 2007). With their concept of "poor leadership," distinguishing between an active and a passive component, Kelloway and colleagues (Kelloway, Sivanathan,

Francis, & Barling, 2005) argue that passive leadership is both *distinct from* active leadership and has negative effects *beyond* those attributed to a lack of transformational leadership. Hence, leaders may be experienced as destructive both by doing things they should not be doing and by not doing what they are expected to do.

Building on the notion that leaders may undermine or sabotage both followers and the organization itself, we have earlier proposed the following definition of destructive leadership behavior;

> the systematic and repeated behavior by a leader, supervisor or manager that violate the legitimate interest of the organization by undermining and/or sabotaging the organization's goals, tasks, resources, and effectiveness and/or the motivation, well-being or job satisfaction of subordinates. (Einarsen et al., 2007, p. 208)

The definition emphasizes that destructive behaviors may be directed towards both followers as well as towards the organizations itself, or towards both. Further, to be defined as destructive the behaviors have to be repeated and systematic as opposed to single behaviors such as an isolated outburst of anger. Here we side with Tepper (2000) who defined abusive supervision as "subordinates perceptions of the extent to which supervisors engage in the sustained display of hostile verbal and nonverbal behaviors, excluding physical contact" (p. 178). A single mistake or a single instance of incivility by a leader is not sufficient to evaluate such leadership as destructive. Single mistakes are human and to be expected. Multiple mistakes are also human, but may still pose a serious problem to the organization. Hence, if incivility becomes repeated it represents destructive leadership, irrespectively of its intentions or causes.

An important feature of the proposed definition is that it excludes any reference to "intent" or "motive," thus embracing instances where there is a clear intent to cause harm as well as instances of thoughtlessness or the lack of skills (see also Einarsen et al., 2007). Hence, we employ a strict behavioral definition where underlying constructs such as intent, is of no relevance to the determination of whether or not a destructive behavior has occurred. Intent may only be verified by the focal leader, hence being of little relevance in applied settings and difficult to verify in scientific terms (see also Buss, 1961 for a discussion on intent in interpersonal aggression). Including intent in the definition may only provide the leader with a final saying regarding the nature of the behavior exhibited, as compared to followers' or observers' perceptions of destructive leadership. Furthermore, it really does not matter why a leader acts as he or she does if their behavior is repeated and of a kind that will likely harm either the organization or it's employees. Thus, the main issue is the actual behaviors and their potential consequences, rather than their underlying psychological intentions and motivations.

As compared to Tepper's definition, we broaden the domain of behavior to include all kinds of inadequate or bad leader behaviors, physical as well as verbal, active as well as passive and indirect as well as direct (see also Buss, 1961). Accordingly, destructive leadership consists of any kind of repeated and systematic behavior that undermines or sabotages either the motivation, the well-being or the job satisfaction of followers or the goals, resources or effectiveness of the organizations.

Further, destructive leadership is about that what violates or is in opposition to the *legitimate interest* of the organization (see also Sackett & DeVore, 2001) and their definition of "counterproductive workplace behavior"). The term "legitimate interest" narrows down the range of behaviors to those that may be seen as illegal, immoral, or otherwise counterproductive from an organizational point of view. Yet, by employing the concept of legitimate interest, we restrict what an organization can and cannot expect from it's leaders to what can be considered as legal, reasonable and justifiable within a given cultural context. Hence, the perception of destructive leader behavior will vary between different cultures and societies over time, and even, to some extent, between organizations depending on their legitimate goals within a given society. For example, in times of war, exposing soldiers to a risk of dying can probably not be defined as destructive leadership, while doing so in times of peace probably would. Including this term in the definition also prohibits those leaders who defer from joining an illegal or unethical management culture to be considered destructive even if their behavior is deviant as seen by the company norm. In such cases, a leader refusing to obey such norms would actually represent constructive leadership. Employers as well as employees are obligated to behave in accordance with norms, laws, and agreements that exist in the given culture.

A Taxonomy of Destructive Leadership Behaviors: The Destructive and Constructive Leadership Model

Based on the above definition we have developed a model of leadership behavior that includes both constructive and destructive elements and that incorporates both active behaviors and the lack of appropriate behavior. The model is based on three assumptions, that is; that destructive leadership is about two main classes for behaviors; those mainly directed at subordinates and those mainly directed at the organization (see also Bass, 1990 for a description of such basic dimensions in leadership theory). Second, it is based on the assumption that a leader's behaviors on both dimensions may range from being highly pro to being highly anti, hence departing from most models of leadership which mainly see leadership on dimensions from "low" to "high," from "little" to "much" or from "ineffective" to "effective," for example, as found in *The Managerial Grid* by Blake and Mouton (1985). A range of studies have shown leaders to bully and harass their subordinates, that is, showing a high level of behaviors directed at subordinates but in a manner that are "anti" regarding the motivation and well-being of these subordinates. Similarly, a leader committing fraud is actively managing the organizations assets, but in an "anti" way. Only looking at behaviors on a continuum from "low" to "high," would not necessarily detect the behaviors of such leaders (see Figure 11.1). Third, by cross-cutting the two dimensions we provide four quadrants of leadership with different combinations of destructive and constructive behavior, assuming that leaders are not necessarily either "good" or "bad," but rather may show conglomorated behaviors. According to the logic of the model, a leader may be seen as being constructive on one of the two dimensions (pro), while behaving in breach with the legitimate interest of the organization (anti) on the other dimension, providing a conglomerate perspective on the behaviors of leaders. Again, conglomerate behaviors are different kinds of behaviors that may occur simultaneously or that may occur in sequence (van de Vliert, Euwema, & Huismans, 1995). In addition to a broad category of constructive leadership behaviors where the leaders show a conglomerate of behaviors that are constructive regarding both subordinates as well as the organization, the model contains three basic kinds of destructive leadership where the leader is behaving badly on at least one of the dimensions;

- Tyrannical behavior (pro-organization combined with anti-subordinate behavior),
- Supportive disloyal (pro-subordinate combined with anti-organizational behavior)
- Derailed behavior (anti-subordinate combined with anti-organizational behavior).

In addition, the model contains a category of "laissez-faire" leadership where the leader avoids fulfilling the legitimate expectancies embedded in the role of a leader, hence being passive on both dimensions.

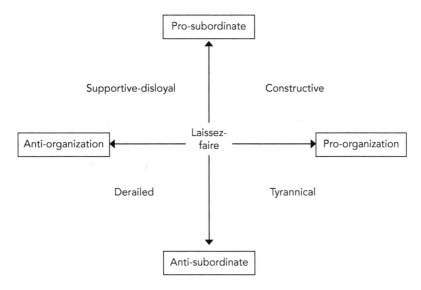

Figure 11.1 The destructive and constructive model of leadership behaviors.

Constructive leadership is about leaders who display pro-organizational as well as pro-subordinate behaviors. The leader then acts in accordance with the legitimate interests of the organization, supporting and working towards the strategy of the organization, while simultaneously motivating and supporting their followers through considerate behaviors, inspiration and the involvement and participation in decision processes. Hence, constructive leadership reflects both transformational and transactional forms of leadership as described in the "Full Range Leadership Model" (see Bass & Riggio, 2006), and may be seen as a parallel to the "high-high" leader, and what is called "Team Management" in Blake and Mouton's (1985) *The Managerial Grid*. Even though such a broad conceptualization do not do justice to the abundant and varied body of research on constructive forms of leadership (see also Avolio & Gardner, 2005; Bass, 1990), it does pinpoint the main ingredients of all forms of constructive leadership; supporting and motivating subordinates while focusing on the optimal use of organizational resources to achieve legitimate organizational goals. What is the focus of most leadership research is how a leader may accomplish this in the most optimal and effective way.

Tyrannical leadership behavior is manifested when a leader combines pro-organizational and anti-subordinate behaviors. Being pro-organizational, these leaders may behave in accordance with the legitimate goals, tasks, and strategies of the organization. They may even be superior strategists or high performing leaders in terms of technical skills or in terms of task related efficiency. However, they frequently obtain results at the cost of subordinates, not through their willing cooperation (Ashforth, 1994; Einarsen et al., 2007). Being anti-subordinate, tyrannical leaders manipulate, humiliate and intimidate subordinates in order to "get the job done" (e.g., Ashforth, 1994; Kile, 1990; Lombardo & McCall, 1984). Hence, what upper-management may view as an efficient focus on task completion by a leader, may simultaneously be viewed as abusive leadership or even as bullying by subordinates (Einarsen et al., 2007). Leaders who harass their subordinates may nevertheless perform well on other assignments, for example, through specialized skills or competencies (Brodsky, 1976). Leaders who behave destructively towards subordinates may not necessarily be destructive in other interpersonal relationships, be it with customers or business partners or in relation to the upper-management (Skogstad, 1997). Ma, Karri, and Chittipeddi (2004) define this phenomenon as "the paradox of managerial tyranny," arguing that tyrannical leadership may lead to extraordinary performance, even when subordinates suffer, at least in the short run. Yet, abusing subordinates is not in the legitimate interest of the organization, hence defining tyrannical leadership as a certain type of destructive leadership. Tyrannical is then a kind of abusive supervision conducted by a leader who in other respects is taking good care of the organizations by fulfilling its tasks and missions.

Derailed leadership behavior is about portraying both anti-organizational as well as anti-subordinate behaviors. These leaders are anti-subordinate though behaviors such as bullying, humiliation, manipulation and deceiving (see e.g., Ashforth, 1994; Kile, 1990; Lombardo & McCall, 1984), while at the same time conducting anti-organizational behaviors like absenteeism, work withdrawal, shirking, committing fraud, or otherwise by stealing resources (be it financial, time or material resources) from the organization (Einarsen et al., 2007; Lubit, 2004; McCall & Lombardo, 1983). An example would be leaders who use their charismatic qualities for personal gains while exploiting followers as well as their employer (Conger, 1990). Such leader characteristics are also prominent in descriptions of pseudo-transformational leadership as compared to authentic transformational leadership (Bass & Riggio, 2006) and in the concept of narcissistic leadership with characteristics such as arrogance, insatiable need for recognition, anger, lack of empathy, irrationality, and inflexibility (Rosenthal & Pittinsky, 2006). Accordingly, derailed leaders violate the legitimate interest of the organization, both by working against organizational goals and, concurrently, by undermining or sabotaging subordinates. Hence, these leaders may be seen as not only abusive towards subordinates but also towards the organization.

In *Supportive-disloyal leadership behavior* a leader combines pro-subordinate with anti-organizational behaviors. Hence, such leaders may motivate, stimulate and support their subordinates, for example, through inspirational motivation and individualized consideration (Bass & Riggio, 2006). However, these leaders may simultaneously deprive resources from the organization, be it consumption of working hours, material resources or economical resources (Altheide, Adler, Adler, & Altheide, 1978; Ditton, 1977; Einarsen et al., 2007). They may grant their employees more benefits than appropriate and encourage low work ethic or even misconduct. Accordingly, supportive-disloyal leaders direct their subordinates towards inefficiency, or towards other goals than those of the organization, at the same time behaving in a comradely and friendly manner. This leadership style has some features in common with what Blake and Mouton (1985) termed "Country Club Management" as both styles represent an overriding concern with establishing camaraderie with subordinates. Yet, supportive-disloyal leaders are combining this with behaviors that are not in the best and legitimate interest of the organization; theft, fraud, and embezzlement being widespread problems in today's business world even among leaders that are well liked by their subordinates (e.g., the scandals that hit WorldCom and Enron in the first years of the twenty-first century). The intention of the supportive-disloyal leader may not necessarily be to harm the organization; he or she may simply be acting upon a different "vision" or strategy working in support of other values or goals than that of the organization, even believing that he or she acts with the organization's best interest at heart (e.g., narcissistic leadership). By directing and motivating followers to work hard, but in a direction contrary to organizational goals, supportive-disloyal leaders behave contrary to the legitimate interest of the organization.

Yet, destructive forms of leadership are not limited to such active and manifest behaviors as described above. Destructive leadership may also be a function of *passive direct* and *passive indirect* behaviors (see Buss, 1961). Passive and avoiding leadership has frequently been referred to as *laissez-faire leadership*, and as such constituting one of three main types of leadership in the "Full Range Leadership model" (Bass & Riggio, 2006). Bass and Avolio (1990), who are frequently cited in definitions of laissez-faire leadership, describe this type of leadership as

> With Laissez-faire (Avoiding) leadership, there are generally neither transactions nor agreements with followers. Decisions are often delayed; feedback, rewards, and involvement are absent; and there is no attempt to motivate followers or to recognize and satisfy their needs. (p. 20)

Laissez-faire leadership does not merely represent nonbehaviors and nontransactions, as the formal leader position triggers legitimate expectations among both subordinates and superiors, which, when left unfulfilled, may have destructive consequences for subordinates as well as for the organization. Accordingly, metastudies (Bass & Avolio, 1990; Judge & Piccolo, 2004) show that laissez-faire leadership behavior negatively is associated with leader job performance, leader effectiveness and follower satisfaction with the leader. A study by Skogstad and colleagues (2007) showing systematic relationships between laissez-faire leadership behavior and role stress and interpersonal conflict, which in turn predicted bullying at work and distress among subordinates, supports the assumption that *laissez-faire* is a type of leadership which is associated with negative consequences, for subordinates as well as for the organization. Hence, laissez-faire leadership is not a zero-type of leadership. As it is impossible to not communicate (see see Watzlawick, Beavin, & Jackson, 1967) one may also argue that a leader cannot avoid to lead. Doing nothing is also to do something. Hence, by doing nothing a leader would, at least in the long run, run the risk of undermining or sabotaging one's followers or the organization itself.

The Prevalence of Destructive Leadership Behavior

While some researchers claim that destructive or abusive leadership constitutes a low base-rate phenomenon (e.g., Aryee, Sun, Chen, & Debrah, 2007), others believe it to be a substantial problem in many organizations, in terms of both its prevalence and consequences (Burke, 2006; Hogan, Raskin, & Fazzini, 1990). Yet, in empirical terms we really do not know. Few if any studies have so far investigated the *prevalence* of such destructive leadership in contemporary working life. We will therefore now summarize the results of such a study conducted in a representative sample of the Norwegian work force where the prevalence of the above described forms of destructive leadership were investigated employing subordinate ratings (see Aasland, Skogstad, Notelaers, Nielsen, & Einarsen, 2009). In this study, a representative sample of Norwegian workers were asked, in a paper and pencil questionnaire, to rate the behavior of their immediate supervisor employing four items on each of the four types of destructive leadership described. In addition, six items were included measuring constructive leadership behavior, in which two items measured person-oriented, two task-oriented and two change-oriented leadership behaviors, respectively. These items were scattered among the destructive items to avoid any kind of response style or a "horns effect" where the leader is only seen in negative terms.

The results first of all showed that constructive leadership was by far the most prevalent form of leadership behavior reported by the subordinates, as should be expected. Results also showed that all three kinds of constructive behaviors loaded on the same factor indicating a conglomerate type of constructive leadership where the leader combines task-oriented, subordinate-oriented and change-oriented behaviors. Hence, most leaders behave constructively most of the time.

Second, destructive and constructive behaviors were portrayed quite simultaneously by many leaders as the correlation between constructive leadership and the destructive forms of leadership behavior were modest at best (that is $r -.29$, ($p <.001$) between constructive leadership and derailed leadership). Hence, many leaders, at least over a period of 6 months showed both constructive and destructive forms of leadership, even if there is a tendency that the best leaders are less destructive than are the second or third best leaders.

Third, experiences of destructive leadership behaviors were very common, at least according to the responses of Norwegian employees. As many as 83.7% in the sample (N = 2539) reported exposure to one *or more* of tyrannical, derailed, supportive-disloyal or laissez-faire leadership behavior during the last 6 months. According to an operational criterion focusing on repeated experiences, 33.5% of the respondents reported exposure to at least one destructive leadership behavior "quite often" or "very often or nearly always" during the last 6 months. Based on the same criterion, 21.2% were exposed to one or more instances of laissez-faire leadership behavior, while 11.6% reported one or more instances of supportive-disloyal leadership behavior. Furthermore, the corresponding numbers for derailed leadership behavior was 8.8%, while the prevalence rate of tyrannical leadership behavior was reported to be 3.4%. Hence, exposure to some form of destructive leadership is quite common, with laissez-faire leadership and supportive-disloyal leadership being the most prevalent ones.

The observed prevalence rates in Aasland and colleagues' study (2009) are far higher than those reported in two somewhat comparable studies conducted by Schat and colleagues (Schat et al., 2006) and Hubert and van Veldhoven (2001). Schat and colleagues reported that, during the last 12 months, 13.5% of the respondents were exposed to aggression from their superior, while Hubert and van Veldhoven found an average prevalence rate of about 11%. However, these two studies are only partially comparable with the Norwegian study as they only investigated *one* form of destructive leadership behavior, namely *aggressive* behavior. Consequently, they neither investigated passive forms of destructive leadership nor destructive forms of leadership that may also include constructive elements (cf. popular-disloyal and tyrannical leadership behaviors). Furthermore, these studies did not measure destructive behavior targeting the organization. Hence, there is a need to assess a broader range of destructive leadership behavior, as was the case in the presented study (Aasland et al., 2009), as this will yield a more nuanced picture of prevalence rates. Accordingly, studies including all the four forms of destructive leadership in the presented model (see Figure 11.1) will probably yield considerable higher prevalence rates than measuring a narrower range of behaviors, as in studies on abusive supervision (see Tepper, 2007 for a review) who mainly look at behaviors on the subordinate dimension in the above presented model.

The Occurrence of Conglomerate Destructive Behaviors

In line with a conglomerate perspective of organizational behavior (see Van de Vliert, 1997) different kinds of leadership behavior may occur simultaneously or sequentially, a perspective seldom taken in leadership research. The prevalence rates of the four types of destructive leadership described above are in itself indicators that such conglomerate behaviors exist among many leaders making it more difficult to distinguish between "good" and "bad" leaders. Hence, many leaders are both good and bad. Another indicator of conglomerate behavior is the intercorrelations between the different forms of destructive leadership. The highest intercorrelations were found between tyrannical leadership and derailed leadership (r =.60), reflecting that both forms consist of anti-subordinate behavior (Aasland et al., 2009). Laissez-faire leadership showed a comparable relationship with derailed leadership (r =.54) substantiating that laissez-faire leadership is, indeed, a destructive form of leadership, and that it is highly related to derailed leadership (as illustrated in Figure 11.1). Accordingly, laissez-faire leadership showed a relatively high positive correlation (r=.38) with tyrannical leadership. However, the relationships between supportive-disloyal leadership and the other forms of destructive leadership were very weak or insignificant in a negative direction, indicating that this type of destructive leadership do not concur together with the three other forms (Aasland et al., 2009). However, the intercorrelation between supportive-disloyal leadership and constructive leadership was reported to be relatively high (r =.35) substantiating the pro-subordinate characteristics of supportive-disloyal leadership. Again, the study showed moderate negative correlations between different forms of destructive leadership behaviors and *constructive* leadership behavior (Aasland et al., 2009). Hence, destructive leadership is not a phenomenon that exists apart from constructive leadership, but is probably an integrated part of the behavioral repertoire of most leaders.

We may draw a similar conclusion from an English study on harassment by managers (Rayner & Cooper, 2003) where, of 72 managers evaluated by subordinates, only 11.1% were exclusively perceived as being a 'tough manager' where all employees reported bullying behaviors from that manager, and correspondingly only 9.7% of the managers were exclusively perceived as "angels" with no reports of bullying behaviors toward any of the included subordinates. The same study showed that about 28% of the managers were evaluated as either "tough managers with supporters," "middlers with victims," or as "angels with victims." Thus, the authors conclude that leadership consists of conglomerate behavior, representing different behavior and different combinations of behavior in relation to different subordinates, who again may react differently (Rayner & Cooper, 2003).

In order to look more closely into such conglomerate destructive behaviors by leaders, Aasland and colleagues (2009) reanalyzed their representative sample of subordinates ratings of their immediate leaders behavior by the use of a latent class cluster analysis (LCC) (Magidson & Vermunt, 2004). LCC was used to classify the respondents into mutually exclusive but homogeneous groups based on similarities in their ratings of their immediate leader, taking both the frequency and the nature of their experiences into account (see also Notelaers, Einarsen, De Witte, & Vermunt, 2006). Based on the probability to report the behaviors of the leaders in a certain way, Aasland and colleagues (2009) could investigate how the subordinates saw their leaders in a more nuanced way than was the case with the operational criterion method. Compared to the latter method, as employed in the results summarized above, this procedure could, first, indentify reports of systematic and repeated but low frequency behaviors, as when a leader shows many different kinds of behaviors infrequently but where these behaviors aggregated to quite an amount of destructive behaviors. Second, this procedure made it possible to investigate if conglomerate behaviors exist regarding destructive leadership where a subordinate describes his or her leader to portray more than one kind of destructive leadership behaviors.

The results showed that six separate clusters of destructive leadership behavior existed. One group of respondents labelled as "no-destructiveness" and consisting of 39% of the respondents in the sample, was characterized by a high conditional probability of answering "never" to any of the items measuring the four kinds of destructive leadership behavior. Hence, these subordinates claim that their immediate supervisor exhibited no systematic destructive behavior what so ever. This would also mean, then, that 60% of all Norwegian employees do perceive such systematic behaviors in their leaders, even in quite a few of the constructive ones. A second group of respondents, labeled "laissez-faire" constituting 19% of the respondents, had an increased conditional probability of reporting exposure to items measuring laissez-faire leadership combined with a low probability to report any kind of tyrannical, derailed or supportive-disloyal leadership behavior. Yet, another group, consisting of 17% was labeled "sometimes laissez-faire and sometimes supportive-disloyal"; reporting that their superiors showed a conglomerate of both these kinds of behavior. Another group of respondents, comprising ten per cent of the respondents, reported exposure to "supportive-disloyal" leadership behavior only, as they had a low probability to report any other kind of destructive behavior in their immediate superior. A fifth group of respondents were labeled "sometimes destructive" as these subordinates faced destructive leadership behavior in a variety of forms, be it laissez-faire, tyrannical or derailed leadership, however on an occasional basis. These comprised 11% of the total sample. Finally, a sixth group of respondents existed that were labelled "highly abusive" as these respondents reported high exposure to both laissez-faire, tyrannical as well as derailed leadership behavior. The latter group comprised 6% of the respondents in the sample.

Hence, the study by Aasland et al. (2009) showed that exposure to destructive leadership is frequent, at least according to subordinates, but that it represents a complex phenomenon where laissez-faire leadership behavior stands out as the most frequent type. Furthermore laissez-faire leadership behavior is reported, all together, in three different forms; a stand-alone phenomenon, in combination with supportive-disloyal leadership behavior, or as part of a conglomerate in which subordinates report exposure to a combination of both tyrannical and derailed leadership behavior, as well as to laissez-faire leadership (Aasland et al., 2009). The latter seems to come in two forms, an infrequent and a highly frequent form. Furthermore, the results of this study indicate that a pure form of tyrannical behavior seldom occur. This may raise the hypothesis that this is a destructive form of leadership that, at least in the long run, more and more may turn into or are being seen as derailed leadership. Probably, tyrannical leadership only leads to good results in the short run, while its destructive potential concerning the motivation and performance of followers only becomes apparent in the long run when it also impairs organizational goal attainment.

Noteworthy is also the fact that supportive-disloyal behaviors occur quite frequently, even as seen by subordinates, again either as a stand a lone phenomenon or in combination with laissez-faire leadership. Hence, the "black demons" seems to be few in numbers at least in Norwegian working life, while "Grey suits" and the "do—nothings" (Skogstad, 2008) are many.

The study by Aasland and colleagues (2009) investigated subordinates' experiences of destructive leadership behavior over a 6-month period. Hence, the exposures may be experienced simultaneously as well as sequentially. Further, over time, laissez-faire leadership behavior may develop into more active forms of destructive leadership in the same way that tyrannical leadership behavior may evolve into derailed leadership behavior (Ma et al., 2004). Thus, the study substantiates our assumption that destructive leadership represents conglomerate behavior with different classes of behavior occurring simultaneously or sequentially. Studying one single class of destructive leader behavior, for example, leader aggression (Hubert & van Veldhoven, 2001; Schat et al., 2006) or abusive supervision (Tepper, 2007) only, may therefore result in a too constricted focus, resulting in a partial picture of a complex phenomenon.

Outcomes of Destructive Leadership Behaviors

Various empirical studies have shown that experiencing a destructive leader may have serious negative effects on the subordinates' well-being. Studies on abusive supervision have been linked with several indicators of psychological distress, including anxiety (Tepper, 2000), depression (Tepper, 2000), diminished self-efficacy (Duffy, Ganster, & Pagon, 2002), somatic health complaints (Duffy et al., 2002; Kile, 1990), burnout (Tepper, 2000; Yagil, 2006), and job strain (Harvey, Stoner, Hochwarter, & Kacmar, 2007). Yet, fewer studies have investigated the effects of conglomerate behaviors or the effects of behaviors that are mainly destructive regarding the organization.

In a study employing the same representative sample of the Norwegian work force as described in the study above, the present authors found a range of relationships between exposure to the destructive forms of leadership presented in the destructive and constructive leadership model and well-being outcomes as reported by subordinates (Einarsen, Aasland, & Skogstad, 2008). In Figure 11.2, we show how the six groups of respondents described above rate their own job satisfaction. A one-way analysis of variance showed a systematic relationship between the exposure of destructive leadership and job satisfaction ($F = 51,71$, df (5/2107), $p < .001$). As can be seen in the figure, a clear relationship between the form and severity of the exposure and the reported level of job satisfaction exist. Yet, subordinates exposed to "supportive-disloyal" behaviors (group 2) alone or in combination with laissez-faire behavior (group 3) did not report any different from the group not reporting exposure to destructive leadership behavior (group 1). Yet, those reporting exposure to "sometimes till often laissez-faire" leadership differed significantly from the three first clusters, and significantly and more pronounced reduced level of job satisfaction was revealed by those exposed to the two most severe patterns of destructive leadership (group 5 and 6). The results again substantiate that laissez-faire leadership, at least when reaching a certain threshold, is not only a type of zero-leadership but constitutes a passive form of destructive leadership (see also Skogstad et al., 2007). Yet, a relatively high exposure to destructive leadership behavior represented by high levels of tyrannical, derailed as well laissez-faire leadership was clearly associated with the lowest levels of job satisfaction. Accordingly, extant research substantiate that abusive supervision is associated with lowered job satisfaction (Tepper, 2000; Tepper, Duffy, Hoobler, & Ensley, 2004). Likewise, a metastudy (Judge & Piccolo, 2004) shows that laissez-faire leadership is negatively and consistently associated with job satisfaction.

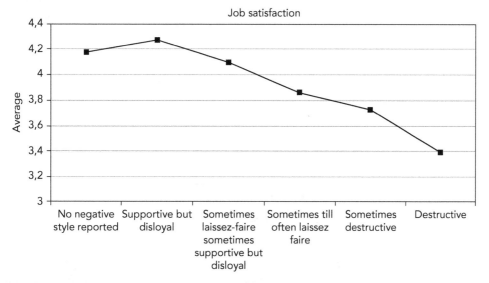

Figure 11.2   Reported job satisfaction in six groups of respondents with different experiences regarding their exposure to destructive leadership behavior by their immediate leader.

Figure 11.3 also shows how the same respondents report in regard to mental health complaints in the form of reporting symptoms of anxiety and depression. Again, systematic relationship were revealed ($F = 48,36$, $df(5/2180)$, $p < .001$) (see Figure 11.3), and again the cluster with no exposure to destructive leadership behavior reported the best mental well-being with a low level of mental health complaints and, again, the cluster reporting exposure to supportive-disloyal leadership (cluster 2) did not report different than did those nonexposed. Yet, all other groups (clusters 3 to 6) reported significantly higher levels of health complaints than those nonexposed. Comparable findings have been found among targets of bullying. A study among 199 subordinates who had experienced bullying from one or more of their superiors identified systematic relationships between "tyrannical leadership," but also partly between "supportive-disloyal" and "laissez-faire leadership" behavior, and symptoms of posttraumatic stress (Nielsen, Matthiesen, & Einarsen, 2005). Likewise, in an interview-based study of 50 teachers in the United States who had been mistreated by school principals over a long period of time (6 months to 9 years), revealed that the respondents experienced shock, disorientation, humiliation, loneliness, and injured self-esteem (Blase & Blase, 2004). The principals' abuse of teachers was also associated with severe emotional problems, including chronic fear, anxiety, anger, and depression (Blase & Blase, 2004). Passive-avoidant leadership, defined as leaders avoiding their responsibility, and in many cases showing an absence of leadership behaviors, has also been positively associated with exhaustion and cynicism, which are key components in the burnout syndrome (Hetland, Sandal, & Johnsen, 2007; Maslach, Schaufeli, & Leiter, 2001).

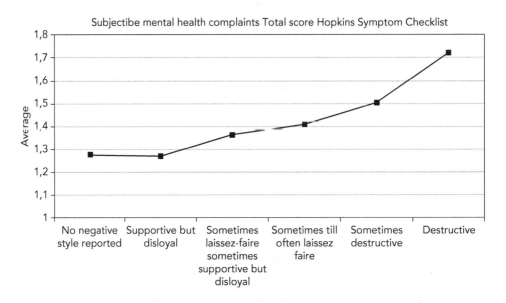

Figure 11.3 Reported mental health complaints in six groups of respondents with different experiences regarding their exposure to destructive leadership behavior by their immediate leader.

In studies of abusive supervision a positive association has also been found with intentions to quit (Tepper, 2000, Tepper, Carr, Breaux, Geider, Hu, & Hua, 2009). Likewise, in a qualitative study among Swedish PhD students who had dropped out of the program, Frischer and Larsson (2000) identified supervisors' laissez-faire behavior to be the main reason for this "drop-out."

Analysis of the representative Norwegian sample (Einarsen et al., 2008) also revealed significant associations between exposure to destructive leadership and intentions to leave the organization within the next 12 months (see Figure 11.4). The patterns of relationships between groups are the same as those reported for job satisfaction and mental health complaints. There were significant differences between those nonexposed (cluster 1) and all other groups except for those reporting "supportive-disloyal" leadership (cluster 2). In line with the proposed model of destructive and constructive leadership behaviors, supportive disloyal leadership behavior does not seem to portray a particular problem for subordinates, at least not in its pure form. Yet, it is worth noticing that it is not associated with positive outcomes. Hence, one may argue that leaders manifesting this type of leadership are seen very differently by their subordinates, probably based on whether or not the subordinates acknowledge the destructive aspects of their behavior on the organizational dimension.

Yet, experiencing systematic supportive but disloyal behavior by ones immediate boss is related to subordinates' report of work-withdrawal (Skogstad, Notelaers, & Einarsen, 2009). In a study employing a second wave of data collection among the same Norwegian representative sample (*N* = 1452) four groups of subordinates where discovered again employing latent class cluster analysis; no exposure; exposure to some laissez-faire leadership, exposure to supportive but disloyal leadership combined with some laissez-faire, and exposure to both tyrannical, derailed and laissez-fair leadership. This study (see also Figure 11.5) showed that those subordinates that where exposed to supportive but disloyal leadership (in combination with laissez-faire) were related to elevated levels of work withdrawal in the form of increased absenteeism and tardiness and reduced job input (Skogstad, Notelaers, & Einarsen, 2009).

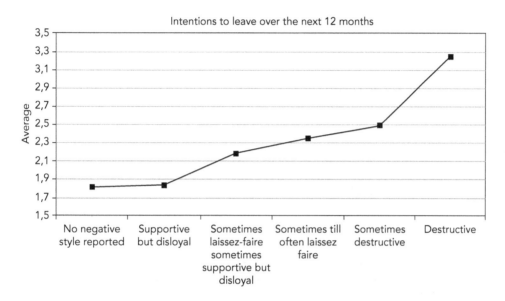

Figure 11.4   Intentions to leave during the next 12 months among 6 groups of respondents with different experiences regarding their exposure to destructive leadership behavior by their immediate leader.

The level of work withdrawal among those experiencing supportive disloyal leadership was as high as among those employees who reported extensive abuse behaviors in the form of a combination of tyrannical, derailed and Laissez-faire behaviors. Hence, a ripple effect may follow from leaders behaving in an anti-organizational way. It may also be that those exposed to tyrannical and derailed behaviors may perceive threats from their leader resulting in subordinates not daring to withdraw from their work as much as they may want to. In his metastudy Tepper (2007) documented that abusive supervision may result in various resistance behavior by part of the subordinates, such as resisting to behave according to supervisor's requests, as well as to substance abuse. Systematic relationships between abusive supervision and organizational deviance were also found by Tepper and colleagues in a later study (Tepper et al., 2009). In line with these studies, a study by Harris, Kacmar, and Zivnuska (2007) found that abusive supervision was negatively related to self-rated and leader-rated job performance. Hence, it is substantiated that destructive forms of leadership, including those where the target is mainly the organization are associated with reduced subordinate performance or contraproductive behavior. However, it is reason to believe that personality factors among subordinates as well as situational factors may play additional roles in explaining these relationships between destructive forms of leadership and outcomes (see also Tepper, Carr, Breaux, Geider, Hum, & Hua, 2009).

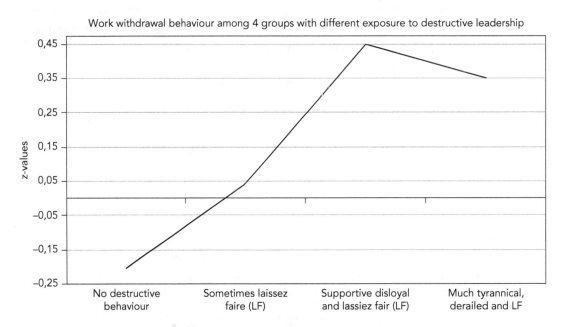

Figure 11.5 Work withdrawal among four groups of employees with different exposure to destructive leadership, employing z-scores (Skogstad, Notelaers & Einarsen, 2009).

Conclusions and Implications

The present chapter has described the very nature of destructive leadership building on a behavioral and a conglomerate approach. Based on this approach we conclude that destructive leadership behaviors come in many shapes and forms, in both passive and active variants, along two basic dimensions; pro-organizational versus anti-organizational behavior, and, pro-subordinate versus anti-subordinate behavior (see also Aasland, Einarsen, & Skogstad, 2008; Einarsen et al., 2007). Based on our definition of destructive leadership and the following taxonomy of destructive leadership behaviors, we may infer that many leaders portray both constructive as well as destructive behaviors, a claim supported by empirical data from a representative sample of the Norwegian work force (Aasland et al., 2009). Furthermore, this empirical study also showed that destructive leadership behaviors are quite prevalent, at least as seen by subordinates, as only a minority of those surveyed had no observations of such systematic behaviors in their immediate leader. As seen by followers, destructive leadership is quite frequent, at least in passive and less intense forms. Hence, destructive leadership is not to be seen as a 'deviant' phenomenon represented by a few "dark leaders" only, as most leaders may show such behaviors from time to time. Hence, it may be a better characterisation to define leaders in general as "grey suits" characterized by many constructive as well as some destructive behaviors, rather than being either "white angels'" or "black demons" (Skogstad, 2008).

The conclusions drawn above have important theoretical, methodological and applied implications. From a theoretical perspective, the presented destructive and constructive leadership model and the reported empirical findings imply that destructive leadership in the future should be viewed as an integral part of what constitutes leadership behavior in general. Including this "dark" side of leadership in models and theories of leader behaviors has the potential of providing a more accurate and nuanced understanding of the very phenomenon of leadership than what has been typical in the leadership literature so far. Adopting a conglomerate perspective on leadership behavior will also open a range of new avenues for the analysis of leadership behavior, as well as its antecedents and consequences. First, a conglomerate perspective on leadership invites us to investigate how constructive and destructive aspects of leadership are related, and to question how and why such behaviors co-occur. Second, antecedents of both destructive leadership in particular, and leadership in general, should be investigated in a nuanced way where different kinds of leader behaviors may have quite different antecedents. Third, different types of destructive leadership may also have quite different consequences (see also Hershcovis & Barling, 2009), as shown above where supportive disloyal leadership behaviors were not related to subordinate job satisfaction or mental health problems as were more abusive forms of destructive leadership. Yet, at the same time the former showed to be related to counterproductive behaviors among subordinates, making it a rather destructive form of leadership from the perspective of the organization.

From a methodological perspective, the measurement of leadership should clearly cover constructive as well as destructive leader behaviors. In addition, methods of measurement as well as statistical techniques taking a conglomerate perspective on leadership behaviors into consideration should be developed and tested.

Regarding applied implications, organizations should be prepared to investigate and manage cases where employees complain or blow the whistle on alleged leader destructive behaviors. Hence, organizations need policies with preventive as well as restorative elements (see also Einarsen & Hoel, 2008). Organizations must realise that a leader may behave destructively for a number of reasons, including personality factors, a stressful work situation, lack of competence, inherited role expectations, or even the adherence to predominant but "noxious" values in the organizational culture. In line with this, behavior is always a result of a complex interplay between a wide range of internal and external factors. Yet, although scientifically of profound interest, we will argue that the "why" is of less importance than the "how" and "what" when dealing with destructive leadership in real world organizations. While dispositions per definition are difficult to change, behaviors are necessarily not. Training, proper instructions, empirically based feedback, rewards, and sanctions are what may be needed to retain constructive leader behavior and to alter behaviors that are destructive. By taking a behavioral and conglomerate approach as presented above one may avoid the "witch-hunting" of supposedly "dark" leaders, taking a more balanced position where a variety of constructive as well as destructive leader behaviors are considered to be within a "normal" range of leader behaviors, which are changeable, as opposed to an unchangeable "dark" leader.

References

Aasland, M. S., Skogstad, A., Notelaers, G., Nielsen, M. B., & Einarsen, S. (2009). The prevalence of destructive leadership behaviour. *British Journal of Management*. DOI: 10.1111/j.1467-8551.2009.00672.x

Adorno, T. W., Frenkel-Brunswick, E., Levenson, D. J., & Sanford, R. N. (1950). *The autortitarian personality*. New York: Harper & Row.

Altheide, D. L., Adler, P. A., Adler, P., & Altheide, D. A. (1978). The social meaning of employee theft. In J. M. Johnson, & J. D. Douglas (Eds.), *Crime at the top: Deviance in business and the professions*. Philadelphia, PA: J. B. Lippincott.

Aryee, S., Chen, Z. X., Sun, L.-Y., & Debrah, Y. A. (2007). Antecedents and outcomes of abusive supervision: Test of a trickle-down model. *Journal of Applied Pscyhology, 92*(1), 191-201.

Ashforth, B. (1994). Petty tyranny in organizations. *Human Relations, 47*, 755–778.

Avolio, B., & Gardner, W. L. (2005). Authentic leadership development. Going to the root of positive forms of leadership. *Leadership Quarterly, 16*, 315–338.

Bass, B. M. (1990). *Bass & Stogdill's Handbook of leadership: Theory, research and managerial applications* (Vol. 3). New York: The Free Press.

Bass, B. M., & Avolio, B. J. (1990). *Transformational leadership development: Manual for the Multifactor Leadership Questionnaire*. Palo Alto, CA: Consulting Psychologists Press.

Bass, B. M., & Riggio, R. E. (2006). *Transformational leadership*. Mahwah, NJ: Erlbaum.

Bing, S. (1992). *Crazy bosses: Spotting them, serving them, surviving them*. New York: Morrow.

Blake, R. R., & Mouton, J. S. (1985). *The Managerial Grid III*. Houston, TX: Gulf.

Blase, J., & Blase, J. (2004). The dark side of school leadership: Implications for administrator preparation. *Leadership and Policy in Schools, 3*(4), 245–273.

Brodsky, C. M. (1976). *The harassed worker*. Lexington, MA: Lexington Books.

Buss, A. H. (1961). *The psychology of aggression*. New York: Wiley.

Burke, R. (2006). Why leaders fail: Exploring the dark side. *Int. Journal of Manpower, 27*, 91–100

Conger, J. A. (1990). The dark side of leadership. *Organizational Dynamics, 19*(2), 44–55.

Ditton, J. (1977). *Part-time crime: An ethnography of fiddeling and pilferage*. London, England: Billings.

Duffy, M. K., Ganster, D., & Pagon, M. (2002). Social undermining in the workplace. *Academy of Management Journal, 45*, 331–351.

Einarsen, S., Aasland, M. S., & Skogstad, A. (2007). Destructive leadership behaviour: A definition and conceptual mode. *The Leadership Quarterly, 18*, 3, 207–216.

Einarsen, S., Aasland, M. S., & Skogstad, A. (2008, April). *The nature, prevalence and consequences of destructive leadership*. Paper presented at SIOP San Fran-cisco, CA.

Einarsen, S., & Hoel, H. (2000). Dullying and mistreatment at work: How managers may prevent and manage such problems. In A. Kinder, R. Hughes, & C. L. Cooper (Eds), *Employee well-being support. A workplace resource* (pp. 161–173). Chichester, England: Wiley.

Frischer, J., & Larsson, K. (2000). Laissez-faire in research education—an inquiry into a Swedish doctoral program. *Higher Education Policy, 13*, 131–155.

Harris, K. J., Kacmar, K. m., & Zivnuska, S. (2007). An investigation of abusive supervision as a predictor of performance and the meaning of work as a moderator of the relationship. *Leadership Quarterly, 18*, 252–263.

Harvey, P., Stoner, J., Hochwarter, W., & Kacmar, C. (2007). Coping with abusive supervision: The neutralizing effects of ingratiation and positive affect on negative employee outcomes. *The Leadership Quarterly, 18*, 264–280.

Hetland, H., Sandal, G. M., & Johnsen, T. B. (2007). Burnout in the Information Technology sector: Does leadership matter? *European Journal of Work and Organizational Psychology, 16*(1), 58–75.

Hershcovis, S., & Barling, J. (2009). Towards a multi-foci approach to workplace aggression: A meta-analytic review of outcomes from different perpetrators. *Journal of Organizational Behaviour.* DOI: 10.1002/job.621

Hinkens, T. R., & Schriesheim, C. A. (2008). An examination of "non-leadership." *Journal of Applied Psychology, 93*, 1234–1248.

Hogan, R., Raskin, R., & Fazzini, D. (1990). The dark side of charisma. In K. E. Clark & M. B. Clark (Eds.), *Measures of leadership*. West Orange, NJ: Leadership Library of America.

House, R. J., & Howell, J. M. (1992). Personality and charismatic leadership. *Leadership Quarterly, 3*, 81–108.

Howell, J. M. (1988). Two faces of charisma: Socialized and personalized leadership in organizations. In J. A. Conger & R. N. Kanungo (Eds.), *Charismatic leadership: The elusive factor in organizational effectiveness*. San Francisco: Jossey-Bass.

Hubert, A. B., & van Veldhoven, M. (2001). Risk sectors for undesirable behaviour and mobbing. *European Journal of Work and Organizational Psychology, 10*, 415–424.

Judge, T. A., & Piccolo, R. F. (2004). Transformational and transactional leadership: A meta-analytic test of their relative validity. *Journal of Applied Psychology, 89*(5), 755–768.

Kellerman, B. (2004). *Bad leadership. What it is, how it happens, why it matters*. Boston: Harvard Business School Press.

Kelloway, E. K., Sivanathan, N., Francis, L., & J. Barling. (2005). Poor leadership. In J. Barling, E. K. Kelloway, & M. R. Frone (Eds.), *Handbook of Work Stress*. Thousand Oaks, CA: SAGE.

Kile, S. M. (1990). *Helsefarlige ledere—og medarbeidere* [Health endangering leaders and employees]. Oslo, Norway: Hjemmets Bokforlag.

Kets de Vries, M. F. R. (1979, July-august). Managers can drive their subordinates mad. *Harvard Business Review*, 125–134.

Lewing, K., Lippitt, R., & White, R. K. (1939). Patterns of aggressive behaviour in experimentally created social climates. *Journal of Social Psychology, 10*, 271–301.

Lipman-Blumen, J. (2005). *The allure of toxic leaders. Why we follow destructive bosses and corrupt politicians—and how we can survive them*. Oxford, England: Oxford University Press.

Lombardo, M. M., & McCall, M. W. (1984). *Coping with an intolerable boss* (Special Report). Greensboro, NC: Center for Creative Leadership.

Lubit, R. (2004, March/April). The tyranny of toxic managers: Applying emotional intelligence to deal with difficult personalities. *Ivey Business Journal*, 1–7.

Ma, H., Karri, R., & Chittipeddi, K. (2004). The paradox of managerial tyranny. *Business Horizons, 4*(4), 33–40.

Magidson, J., & Vermunt, J. K. (2004). Latent class models. In D. Kaplan (Ed.), *The SAGE Handbook of Quantitative Methodology for the Social Sciences*. Thousand Oaks, CA: SAGE.

McCall, M. W. J., & Lombardo, M. M. (1983). *Off the track: Why and how successful executives get derailed* (report No. 21). Greensboro, NC: Center for Creative Leadership.

Maslach, C., Schaufeli, W. B., & Leiter, M. P. (2001). Job burnout. *Annual Review of Psychology, 52,* 397–422.

Nielsen, M. B., Matthiesen, S. B., & Einarsen, S. (2005). Ledelse og personkon-flikter: Symptomer på posttrau-matisk stress blant ofre for mobbing fra ledere [Leadership and interpersonal conflicts: Symptoms of posttraumatic stress among targets of bullying from supervisors]. *Nordisk Psykologi, 57*(4), 391–415.

Notelaers, G., Einarsen, S., De Witte, H., & Vermunt, J. (2006). Measuring exposure to bullying at work: The validity and advantages of the latent class cluster approach. *Work & Stress, 20*(4), 288–301.

Northouse, P. G. (2007). *Leadership: Theory and practice.* London, England: SAGE.

Padilla, A., Hogan, R., & Kaiser, R. B. (2007). The toxic triangle: Destructive leaders, susceptible followers, and conducive environments. *The Leadership Quarterly, 18,* 176–194.

Rayner, C., & Cooper, C. L. (2003). The black hole in "bullying at work" research. *International Journal of Management and Decision Making, 4*(1), 47–64.

Rosenthal, S. A., & Pittinsky, T. L. (2006). Narcissistic leadership. *The Leadership Quarterly, 17,* 617–633.

Sackett, P. R., & DeVore, C. J. (2001). Counterproductive behaviours at work. In N. Anderson, D. S. Ones, H. K. Sinangil, & C. Viswesvaran (Eds.), *Handbook of Industrial, Work & Organizational Psychology* (Vol. 1, pp. 145–164). London: SAGE.

Schat, A. C. H., Frone, M. R., & Kelloway, E. K. (2006). Prevalence of workplace aggression in the u.s. workforce: Findings from a national study. In E. K. Kelloway, J. Barling, & J. J. Hurrell (Eds.), *Handbook of Workplace Violence* (pp. 47–90). Thousand Oaks, CA: SAGE.

Skogstad, A. (2008, November). *Nuances in destructive leadership. Theoretical and methodological issues.* Paper presented at The Nordic Network meeting on Bullying at the Workplace, Reykjavik, Iceland.

Skogstad, A. (1997). *Effects of leadership behaviour on job satisfaction, health and efficiency.* Doctoral thesis, faculty of psychology. University of Bergen, Norway.

Skogstad, A., Einarsen, S., Torsheim, T., Aasland, M., & Hetland, H. (2007). The destructiveness of Laissez-faire leadership behaviour. *Journal of Occupational Health Psychology, 12*(1), 80–92.

Skogstad, A., Notelaers, G., & Einarsen, S. (2009, May). *Exposure to destructive leadership: Relationships with job satisfaction, work-withdrawal and intentions to leave.* Paper presented at the 14th European Congress of Work and Organizational Psychology, Santiago de Compostela, Spain.

Tepper, B. J. (2000). Consequences of abusive supervision. *Academy of Management Journal, 43*(2), 178–190.

Tepper, B. J. (2007). Abusive supervision in work organization: Review, synthesis, and research agenda. *Journal of Management, 33*(3), 261–281.

Tepper, B. J., Carr, J. C., Breaux, D. M., Geider, S., Hu, C., & Hua, W. (2009). Abusive supervision, intention to quit, and employees' workplace deviance: A power/dependence analysis. *Organizational Behaviour and Human Decision Processes, 109*(2), 156–167.

Tepper, B. J., Duffy, M. K., Hoobler, J., & Ensley, M. D. (2004). Moderators of the relationship between coworkers' organizational citizenship behaviour and fellow employees' attitudes. *Journal of Applied Pscyhology, 89,* 455–465.

Van de Vliert, E. (1997). *Complex interpersonal conflict behaviour: Theoretical frontiers.* Hove, England: Psychology Press.

Vredenburgh, D., & Brender, Y. (1998). The hierarchical abuse of power in work organizations. *Journal of Business Ethics, 17*(12) 1337–1347.

Watzlawick, P., Beavin, J. H., & Jackson, D. D. (1967). *Pragmatics of human communication. A study of interactional patterns, pathologies, and pradoxes.* New York: W. W. Norton.

Yagil, D. (2006). The relationship of abusive and supportive workplace supervision to employee burnout and upward influence tactics. *Journal of Emotional abuse, 6*, 49–65.

Yukl, G. (2010). *Leadership in organizations*. New York: Pearson.

Zimbardo, P. G. (2004). A situationist perspective on the psychology of evil: Understanding how good people are transformed into perpetrators. In A. Miller (Ed.), *The social psychology of good and evil: Understanding our capacity for kindness and cruelty* (pp. 21–50). New York: Guildford.

Van del Vliert, E., Euwma, M. C., & Huismans, S. E. (1995). Managing conflict with a superior or a subordinate: Effectiveness of a conglomerated perspective. *Journal of Applied Psychology, 80*(2), 271–281.

The Corporate Reflecting Pool

Antecedents and Consequences of Narcissism in Executives

Dean B. McFarlin and Paul D. Sweeney

When leadership goes wrong in an organization, it's important to understand why that occurs and what can or should be done about it. As illustrated by the previous chapters, there are many types of bad leadership. In our chapter, we focus on narcissistic leadership. Excessive narcissism is characterized by a profound sense of importance, the pursuit of grandiose fantasies, a pre-occupation with attention and an unwillingness or inability to consider the perspective of others, among other things. At the same time, narcissists can be charming and charismatic, at least for a time. We review a growing body of empirical literature has taken this person-based and clinical focus and placed it squarely in a work and interpersonal setting. We begin by exploring the roots of excessive narcissism, including personal and situational antecedents. Next, we assess the state of the art when it comes to research on narcissism, especially in corporate leadership and any impact on employee, company, and firm performance. Finally, we present steps that firms can take to reduce the odds of hiring narcissistic executives as well as minimize the damage caused by narcissists already in leadership ranks. This includes our effort to extend the research into specific actions that can be taken by organizations and individuals alike to deal with narcissism.

Introduction

Leadership will always be the subject of intense study. Already one of the most researched topics in all of social science, a recent search for leadership-related articles in a popular business research database generated over 80,000 "hits" since 1980. If your interests turn more toward the popular, then you could scan through the roughly 20,000 titles that Barnes and Noble now has for sale on leadership. Clearly, people want to know what makes leaders tick. And many, particularly in the business world, want to become better leaders—someone with the bold visions, strategic insights, and motivational talents that produce corporate as well as personal success.

Indeed, much of the popular literature on leadership has a "how to" or "here's how I did it" quality to it, with advice distilled down into the all-too-familiar sets of "10 laws," "20 principles," or "5 secrets" for successful leadership. These approaches tend to be relentlessly positive, which clearly strikes a chord with many people—apparently even Atilla the Hun was "up tone" about leadership (Roberts, 1990).

Yet an irony is that for many employees their superiors do anything but lead. Many employees feel their bosses are focused on personal agendas, if not personal enrichment—often at the expense of organizational success. This can help explain why large numbers of employees report that they have had a "bad" boss in their career and why the direct supervisor is a pernicious and consistent cause of employee stress and turnover (Hogan, Raskin, & Fazzini, 1990, 1994; McFarlin & Sweeney, 2002). Hogan et al. (1990), for example, estimate that the prevailing rate of leader incompetence approaches 70%!

Why Study Narcissistic Leaders?

Today, some might feel that 70% figure is too low. A global economic crisis is staring us in the face, driven, at least in part, by hubris and greed among executives who apparently didn't know what they were doing. In the process, business leadership has been knocked off its high horse. Look at the numbers. Trust in corporations and in anything CEOs say has dropped precipitously between the end of 2007 and the end of 2008, especially in the United States. According to one recent survey, by December 2008 only 17% of some 4,500 college-educated Americans reported that they trusted corporate CEOs as credible sources of information. Put simply, attitudes toward corporate leadership in the United States are at all time lows, Enron and the dot-com bust of several years ago notwithstanding (Edelman, 2009).

Those earlier scandals also remind us that we've been through this before, with spasms of executive greed, indulgence, and corrosive abuse of power periodically provoking outrage before dying down again (Lipman-Blumen, 2005). Today, the popular press is again full of articles fulminating about the risks to companies and employees of projecting too much charisma, infallibility, dependence, wisdom—you name it—onto senior executives (cf. Schopen, 2009).

Consequently, this is an opportunity to more closely examine bad leadership in corporations—to understand why it occurs, when it occurs, and what can or should be done about it.

Of course, there are many types of bad bosses. But we focus in this chapter on narcissistic leadership—a phenomenon that is especially pernicious. Excessive narcissism is characterized by, among other things, disproportionate self-focus, the pursuit of grandiose fantasies, and the need to project power and dominance. This is especially dangerous when combined with the apparent charm and charisma that many narcissistic leaders project—something that attracts followers. But, they are also preoccupied with getting attention and are unwilling or unable to consider the perspectives of others. Their profound sense of importance goes hand in hand with feelings of entitlement. They appear to have high esteem, but it is either a façade or built on a weak foundation. As a result, narcissistic individuals feel vulnerable underneath their positive veneers and are constantly on guard: they dismiss feedback, externalize blame, and can turn aggressively on those who challenge them. Consider the corporate leader who is excessively narcissistic—he or she can literally ride the company off the tracks into oblivion, blaming and abusing employees who offer criticisms or who otherwise get in the way of their flawed visions and overwhelming feelings of entitlement (McFarlin & Sweeney, 2002).

Based on this description, it is tempting to disparage any attention given to narcissistic leaders in business as narrow, misplaced, and nonscientific—better treated by psychotherapists than serious social scientists. We disagree with this view. Of all the types of "bad bosses" we are interested in narcissists for three reasons. First, narcissism is not narrowly confined to a few isolated individuals. Narcissism seems to be common, if not replete, in senior executive ranks—the literature is full of examples of narcissistic leaders in corporations. Indeed, narcissism is more common and more difficult to extinguish than one might expect (McFarlin & Sweeney, 2002). In one study of a large fortune 500 company, it was estimated that about half of management was inept (Millikin-Davies, 1992, as cited in Hogan et al., 1990). Among the most common complaints was that these managers tyrannized their subordinates and stole their ideas. These behaviors are commonly associated with narcissism in the literature (McFarlin & Sweeney, 2002).

Second, it is important not to underestimate the potential negative impact of narcissism in the executive ranks of today's organizations. While it is true that the behavior of executives is constrained by many factors inside and out of the firm, studies show that senior leaders still have a good deal of latitude for their strategic choices—let alone their treatment of others (Finkelstein, Hambrick, & Cannella, 2009). And latitude attracts narcissistic managers to do what they do best—serve their personal needs for attention and control. Interest in narcissism is not misplaced—if anything, it may be underemphasized.

Third, attention to executive narcissism has grown dramatically among social scientists and the boundaries of our understanding have expanded considerably, especially in the last decade. We know, for example, that it is important to not only understand a narcissistic leader's tendencies and styles, but also the organizational conditions under which narcissism flourishes. Recent work on narcissism reflects individual difference variables as well as contextual factors—research that shares much of the contingency-oriented approach found in the broader literature on leadership, motivation, decision-making and related topics (e.g., Morf & Rhodewalt, 2001).

Chapter Preview

We begin by exploring the roots of excessive narcissism, including both dispositional and situational antecedents. Next, we assess the state of the art when it comes to research on narcissism, especially in corporate leadership. What are the behavioral consequences of narcissism and what impact does it have on employee, company, and firm performance? Finally, we present steps that firms can take to reduce the odds of hiring narcissistic executives as well as minimize the damage caused by any narcissistic leaders already in the workforce. In addressing this last point, we try to extend research into specific actions that can be taken by organizations and individuals dealing with narcissism.

Defining Narcissism and Its Antecedents

Narcissism is essentially a personality trait—one that, as it increases in intensity, can produce attributes that have negative impacts on others. For narcissistic individuals, life is "an arena" in which they strive for admiration, success, and status. And when narcissistic people engage in reality distortion to protect their overblown self-images, pursue grandiose plans for success, and attack or abuse anyone who dares to challenge them, the results—especially when they hold executive roles—are typically destructive (Campbell, Bush, Brunell, & Shelton, 2005).

The mythical figure Narcissus fell in love with his own beautiful reflection in a pool of water and was unable to stop gazing at his image before wasting away. This extreme example aside, having some level of self-love helps us attend to our own legitimate needs in a variety of areas (Kets de Vries, 1995). Without some level of self-focus, we would not get out of bed in the morning. Indeed, narcissism exists on a continuum—from functional to problematic. Some, such as Kets de Vries and Miller (1985), suggest that there may be thresholds in the continuum of narcissism that could serve as demarcation points defining the "healthy" and "unhealthy" narcissist. The metaphor of a race car captures this idea—up to a point speed wins races. But past a certain point, the driver loses control—too much speed kills. Likewise, executives who can harness or limit their narcissism may achieve positive results, but those who cannot may destroy their companies and wreak havoc with employees in the process.

In this chapter, our focus is on excessive levels of narcissism. Yes, there is arguably a level of hubris that is productive, if not essential, for senior corporate leaders—a "healthy" narcissism that produces confident, bold executives who can inspire based on visions that have been thought through rather than reflect grandiose flights of fancy. These executives have real confidence and have the ability to be empathetic as well as introspective (Kets de Vries, 1995). But an analysis of many ineffective corporate leaders suggests that they have crossed the proverbial line—that their problems were rooted in excessive narcissistic tendencies which produced counterproductive behaviors, a lack of integrity, and ultimately, failure (Allio, 2007; Rosenthal & Pittinsky, 2006).

The roots of narcissism are complex and have been discussed and debated in the clinical psychology literature for decades. Some experts argue that narcissism has a genetic component. Others suggest that parenting styles play a major role in the development of narcissistic adults (Kets de Vries, 1995). For them, narcissism in adulthood is a reaction to parents who were conditional in their affection and approach. Some experts have suggested that parents who were aloof or who offered children excessive praise can foster the development of narcissistic personality traits (Kets de Vries, 1995; Otway & Vignoles, 2006; Vogel, 2006). The broader point is that parenting practices may sow the seeds of self-doubt and rage, with narcissistic tendencies developing to protect the individual from resulting insecurities. These tendencies to pursue grandiose fantasies combined with the need to exert dominance over others, both protects the self and provides an outlet for pent-up rage and hostility toward parents. In turn, these twin needs then become self-fulfilling prophecies which feed and strengthen the inflated self-images held by narcissists (Kets de Vries & Miller, 1985; Morf & Rhodewalt, 2001).

This pattern also acts to strengthen behaviors that keep personal fantasies going (e.g., exhibitionism, excessive impression management and attention-seeking, flawed visions). It also helps maintain the dominance that narcissists often crave by ruthlessly exploiting, manipulating, and raging at those around them, especially when challenged. In this way, they avoid facing their inner demons and craft a façade of infallibility, superiority, and entitled self-importance for the world around them to see and applaud. Indeed, given their closeted insecurities, narcissistic individuals constantly crave adoration because of their inner fragility. Moreover, that fragility prompts obsession with slights, criticism, or negative feedback, real or imagined—anything that may compromise their crafted self-images will be ferociously attacked, further reinforcing dominance needs (see Bogart, Benotsch, & Pavlovic, 2004; Kets de Vries, 1995; Morf & Rhodewalt, 2001; Wallace & Baumeister, 2002).

What We Know About Narcissism in Management

As we have just noted, the narcissism concept originated in the clinical literature (cf. Otway & Vignoles, 2006), but yet took roots in other, more empirical fields. Narcissism among managers, especially those in the executive suite, has been subject to systematic study for at least 25 years, with Kets de Vries being a leading early example of someone whose work has continued to have an impact (e.g., Kets de Vries & Miller, 1985; Kets de Vries, 1995). And, the study of narcissism has increasing momentum among researchers in the organizational sciences, perhaps in response to recent executive excesses. As a result, our knowledge about the effects of narcissism in the workplace has expanded considerably. In this chapter, we will examine this work, focusing on that which might translate more directly into the workplace and employee relations with management. Specifically, we will discuss research on (a) the characteristics of narcissists, including measurement and identification issues; (b) the consequences of narcissism on the workforce; and (c) the performance of narcissistic managers. In the process, we will also examine some contextual factors (e.g., role of followers, organizational features) that might exacerbate or buffer the negative effects of excessive narcissism. We will finish with a section on dealing with the narcissist and their effects in an organization.

Personal Characteristics of Narcissists

To unambiguously determine the effects of narcissism, we must be able to measure the construct and accurately identify individuals. We turn our attention to this topic first before reviewing research on specific characteristics of narcissists.

Pinpointing Narcissism

Narcissists can be difficult to identify in organizations, especially without extended interaction. Indeed, holding aside the ample negatives of the narcissist that become clearer over repeated interactions (Hogan & Kaiser, 2005; Paulhus, 1998), brief encounters with narcissistic leaders can sometimes be pleasant experiences. After all, narcissism involves projecting a positive view of the self—and people can find such confidence attractive (Campbell, Rudich, & Sdeikides, 2002; John & Robins, 1994; Rhodewalt & Morf, 1995). Plus, narcissism is also linked with extroversion—narcissistic leaders can be exciting, charming, and engaging. They are also said to be bold and decisive—traits many are drawn to (Deluga, 1997; Paulhus, 1998).

As a result, identifying narcissistic leaders can prove challenging, as can convincing others who only view the leader from a narrow or distant perspective. In fact, distant observers may only see the narcissistic leaders' positives and attribute the problems that a close subordinate perceives to the subordinate's own foibles (McFarlin & Sweeney, 2002). Moreover, the positive features many narcissistic leaders possess, at least on the surface, often help them rise to prominent positions (Finkelstein et al., 2009). And, once there, narcissists may rate themselves higher in leader effectiveness as well as receive higher ratings of effectiveness from others (Paulhus, 1998). While this assessment from others may well dissipate over time, especially as narcissistic leaders' weaknesses become more apparent, it underscores why many of us should expect to run into, if not work for, a narcissistic leader at some point in our careers. In short, narcissistic people frequently find their way into senior management positions and are adept at staying there.

Are there Narcissistic Subtypes?

We just noted that many narcissistic people display positive or at least apparently positive behaviors. And given the right circumstances, these attributes and behaviors might be seen as very useful to organizations. This would make it very difficult for organizations to take preventative measures against harmful effects of narcissistic leadership. For example, Khurana (2002) claims that troubled companies tend to look for narcissistic "saviors" to lead their turnaround efforts. In these situations, employees often prefer visible leaders who take bold and decisive action—again characteristic of many narcissistic personalities. Leaders displaying such behavior have been called "productive" narcissists (Maccoby, 2000), or "constructive" narcissists (Kets de Vries & Miller, 1985).[1]

Making distinctions among various "types" of narcissism is appealing, but this notion has not been clearly established empirically. Most contemporary research on narcissism uses a scale to pre-identify individuals and then studies their reactions to or behavior with others. Development and use of the Narcissistic Personality Inventory (NPI) scale, the most commonly used instrument, has brought the study of the concept from solely a clinical disorder to a personality dimension on which individuals are assigned scores (see Emmons, 1984; Raskin & Hall, 1979). Research provides extensive support for the psychometric quality of this scale, including among non-clinical populations (e.g., Corry, Merritt, Mruq, & Pamp, 2008; Emmons, 1984; Emmons, 1987; Raskin & Terry, 1988) and this scale has fostered a great deal of new research, much in the social psychology and organizational science areas.

Nevertheless, this research has essentially sidestepped the issue of narcissistic types, preferring instead to look at (linear) associations of NPI scores with various dependent variables. If Kets de Vries and Miller (1985) and others are correct, then there may be thresholds in the distribution of narcissism scores that could serve as demarcation points defining the "healthy" and "unhealthy" narcissist. But those demarcation points are ambiguous, especially since narcissism has usually been treated as a personality dimension on a continuum. Only a few studies have examined such nonlinear effects and those were generally not supportive of different types of narcissism, much less their differential effects.

Chatterjee and Hambrick (2007), for example, did *not* find nonlinear effects of narcissism in their study of CEO decision making and performance. This is an important finding because the argument that only a subset of narcissists has the unique mix of qualities that make them "productive" or "healthy" was not supported. Instead, their data showed that the full range of narcissism was associated with impacts on their dependent variables. We must be cautious about drawing too many conclusions from Chatterjee and Hambrick's findings—especially since so few studies have tested for nonlinear effects of narcissism. That said, we are aware of only three studies that have tested for "threshold effects" of narcissism—and none have found supportive results (i.e., Chatterjee & Hambrick, 2007; Sedikides, Rudich, Gregg, Kumashiro, & Rusbult, 2004; Zuckerman & O'Laughlin, 2008).

We recommend that future researchers embrace more non-linear tests and do more to address what we feel are definition problems in the narcissism literature. For instance, Rosenthal and Pittinsky (2006) alert us to the fact that it is sometimes hard to know where narcissism begins and ends. Some authors include confidence and assertiveness in their definition of narcissism, while also claiming narcissists can be thoughtful when dealing with others, realistic, and able

---

1 Another distinction made in the literature is between a covert and an overt narcissist (Wink, 1991). The overt type is said to be characterized by openly expressed power, manipulativeness, and a strong need for admiration. Covert narcissism, on the other hand, reflects defensiveness, hostility toward others and low self-confidence and insecurity. This distinction is unrelated to these other views in that (presumably) both covert and overt narcissism are not a pattern likely to lead to success in most situations.

to laugh at themselves (see Kets de Vries & Miller, 1985; Maccoby, 2000). Yet some might argue that these latter characteristics (e.g., thoughtful, etc.) should *exclude* someone being considered excessively narcissistic (Rosenthal & Pittinsky, 2006).

In fact, we would make that argument ourselves. However, there is little doubt that narcissism is associated with projected confidence and high self-regard—something we will discuss in more detail later. For now, we note that self-esteem—even if that is fragile or unstable—is regularly associated with narcissism. We located over 65 separate studies of this relationship and found a weighted average correlation of.29 between the two constructs.[2] Many of these studies also found that narcissism had an impact on interpersonal reactions and performance after self-esteem was statistically controlled. Likewise the impact of narcissism did not go from good to bad as one might predict from the "distinct type" hypothesis.

In short, while narcissists may have some appealing features such as projecting self-confidence, those features often help them maintain their narcissistic self-views (Morf & Baumeister, 2001). So far there is relatively little evidence of "healthy" and "unhealthy" types of narcissism. It is possible that the set of features they possess could be advantageous in some situations— thereby appearing "healthy."[3] But situations change—sometimes rapidly, with those "healthy" advantages quickly becoming liabilities (Chatterjee & Hambrick, 2007; Paulhus, 1998).

Another empirical approach to identify distinct types of narcissism—possibly including "healthy/unhealthy" or "productive/unproductive"—is to examine the multidimensionality of the construct. Emmons (1984) was among the first to do so using the NPI scale, finding four distinct factors—*entitlement/exploitativeness* (e.g., "I'll never be satisfied until I get all that I deserve"), *leadership/authority* ("I have a natural talent for influencing other people"), *superiority/arrogance* ("I am a born leader") and *self-absorption/admiration* ("I think I am a special person"). These four factors were moderately correlated with one another. Distinctive in the study were the correlations of narcissism with abasement and aggression toward others, dominance and exhibitionism. Scores were also highly correlated with self-monitoring tendencies and social anxiety. The only positive or productive dimensions associated with narcissism were self-esteem and extroversion. Narcissism was also negatively correlated with self-ideal discrepancy. Apparently, narcissists are happy with the way they are and see little room for improvement (see also Emmons, 1987; Raskin & Terry, 1988; Rhodewalt & Morf, 1995). Self-esteem aside, a somewhat negative overall picture of narcissists is painted, without a great deal of upside. All in all, while interesting, the work of Emmons and others on the multidimensionality of narcissism doesn't really provide clear evidence of "types" of narcissistic personalities.

That said, more recent research has provided stronger evidence for a two-factor structure (Corry et al., 2008; Kubarych, Deary, & Austin, 2004). Kubarych et al. found support for the first two factors identified by Emmons (1984, 1987), a finding that was replicated by Corry et al.

---

2   We assembled these studies from the literature here for this review. We would be happy to share this list of studies— as well as others mentioned below—to interested readers.

3   Our reference to a characteristically "healthy" narcissist uses this term from the existing literature and it refers to the impact on organizations rather than physical or mental health per se.

Both studies found that these factors of Leadership/Authority and Entitlement/ Exhibitionism were highly correlated. Each factor was positively associated with extroversion, was negatively correlated with agreeableness, and was unrelated to openness to experience. The Leadership/ Authority factor also correlated negatively with neuroticism and positively with conscientiousness ("I work hard to accomplish my goals"). While both factors predicted some positive personality features and revealed some negative ones, the factors acted similarly on these other constructs (see also Brunell, Gentry, Campbell, Hoffman, Kuhnert, & DeMarree, 2008; Judge, LePine, & Rich, 2006; and others).

Once again, this is evidence that increasing levels of narcissism are associated with negative features (e.g., lack of agreeableness) as well as some positive features (e.g., self-esteem, extroversion). But this leaves us with little empirical evidence for two distinct types of narcissism (for an exception, see Rhodwalt & Morf, 1995—where both narcissism factors were highly correlated but produce some different effects).

Some have suggested our inability to detect narcissistic subtypes is limited because most studies focus on "normal" narcissists. In other words, examining more extreme or pathological levels of narcissism would allow possible subtype effects to emerge more clearly. Yet Buss and Chiodo (1991) found that narcissistic acts in the everyday life of students corresponded well to the seven elements used by the DSM-III-R manual to define clinical levels of narcissism. These, in turn, tended to correlate with scores on the NPI scale used in most published research. In short, narcissism may well have adaptive and maladaptive aspects that co-occur and vary in intensity, as any one-dimensional trait might (Rhodewalt & Morf, 1995). Moreover, a given context may determine whether an individual's narcissistic behaviors and tendencies pay dividends or not— at least in the short term. We can also envision specific circumstances where some narcissistic attributes may appear to help (e.g., extroversion when starting a new executive role) and other circumstances where different attributes could prove useful initially (e.g., extreme assertiveness, single-mindedness, and a sense of superiority may help enact change quickly in a crisis).

In essence, we are saying that a different set of narcissistic types may exist. A related possibility is that subtypes are blurred because of the intersection between behavioral tendencies and the situation that narcissists find themselves in. Helpful behaviors in one context might be harmful in another. Moreover, the impact of those behaviors could vary over time—starting out helpful but becoming increasingly toxic, particularly as circumstances change. For now, however, we have relatively little evidence for separate types of narcissists—either because we need more sophisticated research or because the notion of a "healthy" and "unhealthy" narcissist is simply not viable.

Characteristics Associated With Narcissism

As just illustrated, there are plenty of studies addressing the personal characteristics associated with narcissism, with many relying on student samples (see summaries by Rhodewalt & Morf, 1995; Morf & Rhodewalt, 2001). We will not review all of these here, focusing instead on work that can generalize to leaders and followers in organizational settings.

In short, research shows that narcissists think a lot of themselves, a view that's not completely shared by others. And, as noted, narcissism is correlated with self-esteem and extroversion across large number of studies (see Brunell et al., 2008; Rhodewalt & Morf, 1995; others). Narcissists are often socially skilled individuals, especially at initiating relationships, during which others find them entertaining, warm, and interesting during those early (but not later) encounters.

In an interesting study, Paulhus (1998) had subjects interact with others in a group setting for only 20 minutes. Peer ratings of outgoingness, happiness and adjustment—among others—were significantly related to narcissism scores. Apparently, however, narcissists can convey an initial positive impression in even less time. Oltmanns, Friedman, Fiedler, and Turkheimer (2004) took 30 second videos of Air Force recruits' answers to the simple question "what do you like doing?" Later, a set of observers rated the degree of likableness and attractiveness of their personality. Ratings of these "thin slices" slices of behavior were significantly correlated with recruits' narcissism scores.

To convey a positive impression quickly, narcissists rely on their apparent self-confidence (Farwell & Wohlwend-Lloyd, 1998; John & Robins, 1994; Judge et al., 2006), sometimes— particularly in task domains—to the point of being objectively overconfident (Campbell, Goodie, & Foster, 2004; Farwell & Wohlwend-Lloyd, 1998; Gabriel et al., 1994). They are more likely than others to self-nominate and self-promote (Hogan et al., 1990). In conversation and extemporaneous speeches, narcissism is positively correlated with the number of first person pronouns used and negatively related to use of "we" (Raskin & Shaw, 1988). Narcissists view themselves as smart and attractive (Campbell, Rudich, & Sedikides, 2002), more so than others around them do and more than objective measures indicate (Gabriel et al., 1994). Overall, it appears that narcissists rate themselves especially high on "agentic" features (e.g., intellectual pursuits, outgoingness) and are less concerned with their "communal" features such as agreeableness and conscientiousness (Campbell, Rudich, & Sedikides, 2002).

As they approach a variety of tasks, narcissists possess and express very high expectations for success (Farwell & Wohlwend-Lloyd, 1998; Gabriel et al., 1994; Wallace & Baumeister, 2002). This perception is regularly sustained by their reactions to feedback on those tasks—not necessarily the performance level itself. For example, Kernis and Sun (1994) studied how high and low narcissistic subjects reacted to positive and negative feedback about their social skills. The narcissistic respondents gave much more credence and credibility to the positive feedback, but felt negative feedback resulted from a much poorer measure that was produced by a less competent evaluator (see also Smalley & Stake, 1996). Bogart, Benotsch, and Pavlovic (2004) reported that feedback resulting from upward comparisons experienced in everyday life increased hostility among narcissists, but that downward comparisons bolstered their self-esteem and positive affect.

Likewise, Rhodewalt and Morf (1995, Study 1) found that narcissism was associated with internal and enduring aspects about the self after success but not failure. Farwell and Wohlwend-Lloyd (1998) also found that narcissism was correlated positively with internal attributions (ability and effort) for a successful performance, but not with attributions about a partner's performance (see also Campbell, Reeder, Sedikides, & Elliott, 2000; Hartouni, 1992; Ladd, Welsh, Vitulli, Labbe, & Law, 1997; Rhodewalt & Morf, 1998; Rhodewalt, Tragakis, & Finnerty, 2006; and Stucke, 2003, for other attribution studies showing similar effects). These results might explain why narcissists don't seem to adjust their future performance expectations downward after a poor performance, often indicating they are pleased with the way they are and see little room for improvement (Emmons, 1984, 1987; Raskin & Terry, 1988; Rhodewalt & Morf, 1995).

Such chronic self-confidence is often unjustified (Farwell & Wohlwend-Lloyd, 1998; John & Robins, 1994) relative to narcissists' actual performance. And while they try to attribute away negative feedback, they can react to it with more hostility and aggression than those low in narcissism (Kernis & Sun, 1994; McCann & Biaggio, 1989; Rhodewalt & Morf, 1998; Raskin & Novacek, 1989; Stucke, 2003). Likewise, despite their emotional and negative reactions to social rejections (Twenge & Campbell, 2003), narcissists can bounce back to their high-confidence selves, probably by virtue of the self-maintenance processes they chronically engage in (Morf & Rhodewalt, 2001). In short, they can simultaneously fend off potential threats to the self and take personal advantage of opportunities they see for themselves in social situations.

One major casualty from all this defensiveness, self-focus, and unabashed self-enhancement is that the initial positive impressions narcissists generate are often fleeting once people see through them after extended interactions. Earlier, we discussed the Paulhus (1998) study of peer group members' ratings of narcissists—they were generally positive even after just 20 minutes. But Paulhus also found that the rating advantage that narcissists enjoyed in the early, initial meetings, generally deteriorated once these 20 minute interactions were extended to weekly meetings over 2 months. In several cases, the ratings reversed themselves—peers ratings went from agreeable to disagreeable, from happy/adjusted to maladjusted, and from performance-oriented to self-oriented. A second study replicated this pattern and was able to trace these negative trends to bragging, defensiveness, and ability overestimation on the part of narcissists (Paulhus, 1998).

Are we Becoming More Narcissistic?

Of course, rising into senior management takes time. Consequently, a question arises about the relationship between narcissism and age. A related temporal issue to consider is whether we are become more narcissistic over the last decades and subsequent generations—something that may somehow connect to what appears to be an increase in executive scandals and decision-making debacles in recent years. Needless to say, these are very complex issues, as our brief research discussion below will demonstrate.

One position is that narcissism declines as people age (Foster, Campbell, & Twenge, 2003). For instance, Americans are very individualistic (Hofstede, 2001) and some experts suggest that younger Americans have become progressively more self-focused in recent decades (Lasch, 1979; Baumeister, 1987). Indeed, one might expect younger people generally to be more narcissistic since as the years pass and experience is gained with failure, people may generally become other/feedback sensitive. To test this reasoning, Foster et al. (2003) used an internet survey method to collect data from nearly 3,500 participants. Among other items, respondents completed the popular NPI measure described earlier. They found a modest, but significant decline in NPI scores with age—an effect that strengthened when certain controls (e.g., income, gender) were added. Foster et al. (2003) suggested future studies were needed to pinpoint the source of any age effects—such as developmental changes, socialization practices, and birth cohort differences.

In fact, the authors took their own advice in a subsequent study. In that research, they conducted a cross-temporal meta-analysis of narcissism scores from 1979–2006 (Twenge, Konrath, Foster, Campbell, & Bushman, 2008a). All known studies of college students who completed the same narcissism scale across this 27-year period were collected and summarized. In total, 85 different samples comprising over 16,000 participants were located. Twenge et al. (2008a) found that narcissism scores among college students actually rose during this generational period, with scores of the most recent set of students being almost two-thirds above scores among students in 1979–1985.

Critics have suggested, however, that birth cohort or generational effects have not clearly supported the view that a "Generation Me" exists (Trzesniewski, Donnellan, & Robins, 2008a; Trzesniewski, Donnellan, & Robins, 2008b). One objection to the Twenge et al. (2008a) approach is their use of temporal meta-analyses to uncover population-level cohort effects by examining studies relying on small, convenience samples not designed to make such inferences.

Trzesniewski et al. (2008b) addressed is critique empirically. They obtained a large sample of data collected across time from students at University of California (UC) campuses—NPI data was collected in 1988, 1996, and annually from 2002 through 2007 (Raskin & Terry, 1988). Overall, this data set (n = 26,000) was significantly larger than the total number of participants across the 85 samples summarized in Twenge et al. (2008a). Analyses of this larger UC sample found that narcissism levels appeared stable over time. This is important, if for no other reason than it represents a strong test of generational effects. After all, California is the geographic epicenter of the self-esteem movement and should evince a "Generation Me" attitude. The authors also obtained a national probability sample of high school seniors, a study conducted annually since 1976. This study included a measure of self-esteem (Trzesniewski et al., 2008a, 2008b). That data showed no increase in self-esteem scores among those high school seniors (n = 180,000) across a 30-year period (cf. Twenge & Campbell, 2001). Finally, in both data sets, a "self-enhancement" index (difference measures of self-rated intelligence vs. objective/self-report indicators of intelligence) showed no appreciable changes over time.

As a response to the UC results, Twenge, Konrath, Foster, Campbell, and Bushman (2008b) suggested that demographic shifts in California college student populations which occurred after Proposition 209 passed (prohibiting race or ethnicity in admissions decisions)—accounted for the results reported by Trzesniewski et al. (2008a, 2008b). Specifically, they claimed that Proposition 209 led to large increases in Asian populations at the UC campuses starting in 1997 (freshmen were 30% Asian in 1996, increasing to 43% in 2006). This is important because Asian Americans are said to be more self-enfacing and score lower on measures reflecting individualistic views (e.g., self-esteem and presumably narcissism) than other groups. They argued that since these demographic shifts were unique to California, they could mask a broader generational shift toward greater narcissism. To address this possibility, Twenge et al. (2008b) used their 85 study meta-analysis to compare samples collected in California to those from other states. They replicated the finding of no difference in mean narcissism scores in California reported by Trzesniewski et al. (2008a, 2008b), apparently supporting their "Asian influence" hypothesis. Additionally, the remaining non-California studies in their meta-analysis still showed significant annual increases in narcissism.

Our assessment of this controversy favors the Trzesnieski et al. conclusions over Twenge et al. claims for several reasons. First, Twenge et al.'s (2008a, 2008b) data showed the biggest national-level jumps in narcissism *before* 1997 (when the California law took effect), yet little to no increases in California. Second, they report no drop in narcissism scores after 1997 in the California data, something we would expect if Asians entered the sample in large numbers as they suggest (see their Figure 1, p. 920). Both these facts are inconsistent with their explanation. Also, a close look at the admissions data for UC-Davis (the source of Trzesnieski et al. [2008b] data) after the passage of Proposition 209 is informative.[4] Indeed, it is noteworthy that Asian students only increased 1.9% between the years of 2002 and 2007 on the UC-Davis campus. On an average sample size of 4,792 enrolled students, this translates into only 91 more Asian students enrolled in 2007 than did in 2002—the first and last years of UC-Davis data reported by Trzensnieski et al. (2008b).

Moreover, we noted earlier that Twenge et al. (2008b) recalculated their estimates, removing their California data. It would have also been valuable to recalculate their own estimates, adding in the very large California samples of Trzesniewski et al. (2008b). We estimated some of these values and they dramatically reduce the effects reported in Twenge et al. (2008a).[5] Consider the effects reported in light of their dependent variable—the 40 item forced-choice NPI scale. The difference reported by Twenge et al. (2008a) indicates respondent selected only 1.67 more items out of 40 over a 20-year period, itself not an impressive, practical difference. But, the change drops to less than a half an item (.44) when we include the effect of the Trzesniewski (2008b) data, hardly a signature effect of a new generation. Overall, we believe this a compelling finding, especially when taking the size of the Trzesniewski et al. (2008b) sample (approximately 25,000)

4   We obtained these admissions data from: http://statfinder.ucop.edu/ default.aspx. Using overall number of freshman and the number of Asian/ Filipino/Pacific Islanders, we simply calculated the percent of "Asian" freshman. While these data include more than Asians, admissions data were not separated at UC. Regardless, this is a conservative number since we "over-count" Asians, thus deflating the mean NPI score as per Twenge et al.'s (2008b) argument.

5   We used Twenge et al.'s (2008a) equation (p. 883) to calculate mean NPI scores from 1988 (15.62) to 2006 (17.29). This increase represents the endorsement of 1.67 more NPI items (out of 40 total) over these 2 decades. We factored in estimates of these differences using the means reported in Trzesniewski et al (2008b). The study sample sizes are 16,475 versus 25,849, respectively; or what would be 36.3% of the data versus 63.7% if added together. We used these values to weight the means of the two studies in 1988 and 2006 before averaging them. The resulting estimate was an increase in means from 15.58 (1988) to 16.02 (2006)—a new difference of only.44. This is less than ½ item change in the 40 item NPI scale over a nearly 20-year period. Our estimate does not permit a significance test or effect size calculation worth much. Yet, a difference of so little on a 40 item scale does not seem of value practically, especially as it may characterize resulting behavior of the latest generation.

and its degree of consistency (uniformity in student features, survey administration, etc.) into account.[6]

Overall, our assessment is that there are only some small differences across decades in narcissism. While narcissism might be more common than a casual observer might think, it is not clear whether a pattern of increasing narcissism will characterize the latest generation of those entering the business world. That said, it may be more accurate to say that the corporate world, for whatever reason (e.g., runaway growth in pay and power in the last 30 years), has done more to attract narcissists even if the overall level of narcissism in the population or in specific demographic cohorts, has not changed in any major way. In other words, narcissistic people may have increasingly come to view the business world as an attractive "arena" in which to play out their narcissistic fantasies. Perhaps this could help explain why the ranks of corporate executives seem to have no shortage of excessively narcissistic individuals. Naturally, this is yet another thesis that falls to future research to tease out in more detail.

Performance of Narcissists

One of the most important topics to study in this area is the performance of narcissists, especially given the signals that narcissists send in their interactions with others. If you exude self-confidence and esteem, tell others you think highly of yourself, and make moves to assume leadership positions, you have set a high bar for yourself and drawn a great deal of attention in the process. Of course, attention is what the narcissist wants—they seek out opportunities to display their talents and document their superiority over others (Morf, Weir, & Davidov, 2000; Wallace & Baumeister, 2002).

On balance, it is fair to say that the inflated self-assessments that characterize narcissists are *not* borne out in their performance. For example, earlier we noted that narcissists tend to be overconfident, especially relative to others' views. John and Robbins (1994) studied MBA students' performance in a simulated management committee meeting about employee evaluation and compensation. They found that while narcissism correlated strongly with self-rated performance

---

6   Self-enhancement analyses reported in Trzensniewski et al. (2008b) were also contested by Twenge et al. (2008b). They suggested that lack of changes were due to the use of two self-report items included in the large Monitoring the Future (MTF) dataset. This is important—after all, the opportunity to inflate one's self is the playground of narcissists. At the same time, Twenge et al. (2008b) did not comment on a similar lack of changes in the UC-Davis sample that compared objective indicants (SAT and GPA). Also, Twenge acknowledged the lack of self-esteem changes in the large sample MTF (n = 170,000), pointing out that this replicated their earlier results (Twenge & Campbell, 2001) based on a large sample meta-analysis. There, they found no increase in self-esteem over high school, but increases in elementary and college student self-esteem, and suggested that the social forces of high school might mask birth cohort changes. This results in a very complicated set of predictions regarding increases in the self-views of generations, and like Twenge et al. (2008a, 2008b) we believe is very deserving of future research. We believe it is fair to summarize all this work by saying that the there are at least some small differences across decades in narcissism, up and down patterns regarding self-esteem, not just between elementary, high school, and college, but then linear declines as one ages (Twenge & Campbell, 2003). These differences may be as small as less than ½ item endorsement on a 40 item scale, and we are uncertain as to how this might translate into actual, observable behavior. Self-enhancement effects seem stable across generations (even setting aside the MTF data).

(presenting the case for a raise), ratings by peers and trained observers not privy to narcissism scores showed no relation with performance on the task. Robins and John (1997) also found that objective measures of quality of performance of an oral argument showed no difference between low and high narcissists, even though the latter group rated themselves much higher than the former. A set of studies by Campbell, Goodie, and Foster (2004) found similar effects. First, narcissism was significantly related to confidence on a general knowledge test, but unrelated to student's actual performance on the test. In study 2, betting and confidence in one's bet was used as a proxy for risk taking behavior. Again, narcissism was associated with overconfidence and this resulted in poorer performance—in this case more lost bets. These effects were largely replicated in a third study—where narcissists' predictions of future performance were based on their expectations rather than on how they actually performed.

And those expectations are quite high indeed. In fact, Gabriel, Critelli, and Ee (1994) found that while narcissism was significantly correlated with self-reported intelligence, no correlation was found with actual performance on an intelligence test. Two other studies also found no impact of narcissism on performance on a cognitive ability task (Paulhus & Williams, 2002) or on a factual judgment task by working MBA students (Ames, Rose, & Anderson, 2006). Yet both studies showed that narcissism was associated with overestimation of actual performance.

A similar pattern of effects, in a different domain and study setting, was observed by Brunell et al. (2008). As noted earlier, these researchers had groups of people work on a task that involved significant interaction. Each group member was given a separate profile of a candidate seeking a job. After some time to read their materials, members began discussing the qualifications of the person they represented, with the goal being to convince the group that their candidate was the best. Brunell et al. found that while narcissism predicted both self and peer-rated leadership, it did not predict successful advocacy of the job candidates; narcissism did not reliably correlate whose candidate was forwarded by the groups.

Judge et al. (2006) examined the relationship between narcissism and task performance among beach patrol officers. They studied several forms of performance and assessed those using supervisor ratings and self ratings. Two performance types were measured—*task* performance was assessed using a multi-item in-role scale (e.g., "adequately completes responsibilities") and *contextual* performance was measured using a popular organizational citizenship scale. This measure looks at the performance of behaviors that are not necessarily part of the job description or evaluation system, but yet are valuable to an organization (e.g., talking up the organization to others; being conscientious with customers, etc.). They found that narcissism was not related to self-reports of contextual behavior but was negatively related to supervisor evaluations. Narcissism was also not related to supervisor ratings of actual performance or to self-ratings. Nor did using two subfactors of the NPI scale predict performance.

While most studies assessing narcissism show either no performance advantage or a negative one, not all do. Raskin (1980) found that narcissism was positively correlated with self-reports of creativity and performance on objective tests of creativity. Likewise, Farwell and Wohlwend-Lloyd (1998) found that narcissistic students were more likely to overestimate current and future course grades than their non-narcissistic peers. They also found that while narcissism and actual course grades were not related in their first study, a positive relation was reported in their second study. Ames and Kammrath (2004) also found that MBA students scoring high in narcissism overestimated their performance on several social judgment tasks, but that narcissism was not correlated with actual performance.

Finally, an interesting study by Wallace and Baumeister (2002) also speaks to this issue. These researchers reasoned that narcissism would either be an impetus or drag on performance, depending on the degree of scrutiny of their output. In particular, they argued that the relation between narcissism and performance would be moderated by the perceived degree of self-enhancement opportunity. In four carefully designed experiments, different manipulations of self-enhancement opportunity and tasks were examined. On tasks where the "glory" had to be shared (i.e., self-enhancement opportunities were reduced), narcissists performed worse than they did when their individual performance stood out. They rose to the challenge and performed best when social comparison information showed the task at hand to be difficult, but did poorly when it was not challenging. Those low in narcissism did not show this differential level of performance—they were not as motivated to seek admiration from others as were the narcissists.

It is important to note, however, that across all of the four studies reported by Wallace and Baumeister (2002) narcissism was not significantly associated with overall performance. The narcissist's good performance in the self-enhancement conditions was offset by their poor performance in the other conditions. Consequently, situational opportunities for recognition drove performance effects.

By extension, one might think that performances observed by superiors (versus subordinates) might activate this concern studied by Wallace and Baumeister (2002). After all, part of the job of a supervisor is to monitor and evaluate their employee's performance and important decisions about organizational resources are involved. Therefore, the opportunity to show off is greater while interacting with supervisors than with subordinates. This issue was indirectly studied by Blair, Hoffman, Helland (2008). These researchers examined the relationship of supervisor and subordinate evaluations of managers in several different performance domains. For each of the practicing managers in their study, Blair et al. (2008) had immediate supervisors and several subordinates complete evaluation forms that asked for ratings of the managers' performance in several different domains, including *conceptual* (judgment, decision making, planning), *interpersonal* (e.g, degree of interpersonal effectiveness, team building, participation), and *integrity* behavior (e.g., "does not misrepresent him/herself for personal gain"). The results showed differences between the two categories of raters. For interpersonal and integrity behaviors (but not conceptual), a correlation was found between narcissism and supervisors' ratings of performance but not between narcissism and subordinates' evaluations.

These findings are consistent with Wallace and Baumeister's hypothesis that the opportunity for recognition or glory sensitizes narcissists to more closely monitor their performance and to "kick it up a notch." In this study, however, while the supervisors did indeed take notice (as apparently intended by the narcissists), they were not duly impressed. In fact, their ratings of performance and integrity were negatively correlated with the managers' degree of narcissism.

One domain of managerial performance that is easily observed and relatively unambiguous in form is the area of sales production. A study by Soyer, Rovenpor, and Kopelman (1999) examined the narcissism—performance link in salespeople. This group was chosen for study for several reasons, all of which might promote better performance among narcissists in that field. For one, narcissists may be attracted in greater numbers to sales in the first place because the job typically has fewer levels of bureaucracy and permits more autonomous actions. Plus, the many visible markers of status and importance (e.g., travel, expense accounts, cars, computers, etc.) should be attractive to the narcissist as would the fact that high performers are often publicly recognized. Finally, their strong extroversion might fit well with the job requirements. In short, a narcissist may have many things in their favor in a sales role.

Soyer et al.'s (1999) results did indeed show that narcissists were satisfied with a job in sales and their narcissism scores were significantly higher than respondents who never had a sales job. Nevertheless, narcissism did not significantly correlate with any of the four measures of sales performance (e.g., average performance to quota, income, etc.). Interestingly, another personality variable, need for achievement, did significantly predict three of the four sales performance measures.

Earlier, we briefly mentioned an interesting study by Chatterjee and Hambrick (2007). This article also speaks to the performance issue, especially among highly visible, practicing leaders of organizations. These researchers conducted a very careful study of the strategic actions and behavior of CEOs in the computer hardware and software industries from 1992 through 2004. Not surprisingly, the response rate of CEOs to requests from researchers is low, even when studying topics of some interest to their business (Cycyota & Harrison, 2006). Getting this group to reply to personality questionnaires is harder still.

Accordingly, Chatterjee and Hambrick (2007) used a clever set of unobtrusive proxies to index the level of narcissism among the CEOs. For example, they obtained press releases and interviews conducted with the CEOs of these firms. The protocols were coded for the relative prominence of the CEO in those publicity pieces as well as the number of first-person singular pronouns stated in those documents. They also obtained the firm's annual reports and coded other indirect indictors of narcissism, such as the prominence of the CEO photograph(s) in those documents. In all, five such measures were calculated, each showing a significant amount of variance. These were summed to create a narcissism index. As a check on the quality of their measure, Chatterjee and Hambrick had security analysts who specialized in the computer in- dustry rate the personality of a subsample of the CEOs. The analysts had covered the industry for an average of 10 years and had interacted with those CEOs in formal, informal, and other settings. The correlation between the analysts' ratings and the unobtrusive narcissism index was .82, adding to the construct validity of their narcissism measure.

After controlling for a number of factors, Chatterjee and Hambrick (2007) looked at the effect of narcissism on several variables including: (a) company performance extremes (e.g., total shareholder returns, TSR and return on assets, ROA); (b) fluctuation of these performance measures across years; and (c) changes in resource deployment (e.g., acquisitions). The findings were interesting and provocative.

First, CEO narcissism was positively associated with the number and size of acquisitions. This is important because researchers have observed that most acquisitions reduce shareholder value (Roll, 1986), with some even turning to the use of executive "hubris" as an explanation for this strategic grandiosity (Hayward & Hambrick, 1997). The Chatterjee and Hambrick (2007) study points to a source of that hubris—narcissism. They also found that fluctuation of firm performance (ROA) was predicted by the CEO's level of narcissism. In other words, those higher in narcissism favored bolder action that would attract attention. Those actions resulted in both big wins and big losses—with wild swings in between.

A final set of analyses showed that CEO narcissism was not related to firm performance—they did not generate better (or worse) performance than those low in narcissism. As Chatterjee and Hambrick (2007) note and we discussed earlier, some have speculated that "productive" narcissism should be more likely to occur in an unstable and dynamic industry because that situation calls for bold strategies (cf. Maccoby, 2007). Accordingly, this study in the software/hardware industry should be considered a strong—but disconfirming—test of the productive narcissist hypothesis. Chatterjee and Hambrick went on to speculate that given their findings, perhaps narcissism may even have a negative effect in less dynamic or stable industries.

In summary, the relation between narcissism and performance in the literature is a lot like narcissists themselves—there is a lot of bluster, some promise, and unreliable success, with only a high self-opinion surviving. The majority of research shows no positive relation between performance and level of narcissism. The issue of whether there are thresholds or tipping points of degrees of narcissism that might produce better or much better (Maccoby, 2007) performance could be an area of future study. Right now, it is fair to say that despite their expectations and statements to the contrary, narcissists are not better performers; indeed, on some occasions the research shows they are poor performers.

Promise also exists in the area of situational drivers of narcissistic motivation, such as the pressure, visibility, or attention available to the narcissist's performance (Chatterjee & Hambrick, 2007; Wallace & Baumeister, 2002). In the Chatterjee and Hambrick study, however, performance was defined in several ways, including the number and size of acquisitions—a good proxy of visibility and a lighting rod for attention by the financial community. Likewise, in a supplementary analysis, they showed that narcissists were attracted to a challenge (they joined poorly performing companies) and the admiration it would bring if they rose to it. Nevertheless, more direct measures of business visibility and challenge in future studies might provide additional insights and value.

Effects on Others in the Organization

The work by Paulhus (1998) underscores an important component of narcissistic behavior—the impact it has on others in at work. The popular literature concerning business leaders overlaps with the often attractive components of the narcissistic personality. For example, it is often said that confidence is contagious and if so, this is one strong asset of the narcissist. Likewise, a popular conception of leadership is that of a take-charge hero who makes bold decisions quickly and is comfortable on stage—whether in a boardroom or on CNN.

Indeed, it is fair to say that narcissists want to lead others. They often think about power (Raskin, Novacek, & Hogan, 1991) and want to assert their dominance over others (McFarlin & Sweeney, 2002). Moreover, they see themselves as leaders and are often viewed as leaderly as well. For instance, Raskin and Terry (1988) had observer's rate people's performance in leaderless discussion groups. Narcissism was significantly related to observers' ratings of assertiveness, extent of participation in group discussion, exhibitionism, and tendency to criticize others. On the other hand, narcissism was unrelated to both the quality of people's performance as well as their level of cooperativeness.

Along the same lines, Judge et al. (2006) found that narcissism was related to both self and peer ratings of leadership, although the effect was three times as strong for self ratings than for peer ratings. In their second study, however, only self-ratings were positively correlated with leadership behavior; other ratings were negatively related to narcissism. Among military cadets, other researchers found a significant correlation between peer ratings of being a "born leader" and positive aspects of narcissism (high self-ratings) but not negative features of narcissism such as being manipulative (Paunonen, Lonnqvist, Verkasalo, Leikas, & Nissinen, 2006). Finally, Brunell et al. (2008) observed groups involved in simulated managerial decisions. Narcissism was significantly associated with self-ratings and their peers' ratings of leadership. Moreover, the self-ratings of leadership were significantly higher than the ratings of others.[7]

Collectively, these studies show that narcissists can, at the minimum, be seen as leaders or someone with leadership potential—not simply in their own minds, but often in that of others as well. But studies finding significant correlations between leader ratings and narcissism tend to produce those relationships in ad hoc groups that spend little time together. Things might be different in a workplace where extended interactions between employees occur and are expected to continue. Indeed, Judge et al. (2006) found a negative relation between narcissism and confidential leadership ratings provided by superiors in the workplace. Clearly, this latter group has had ample opportunity to observe and form impressions of the narcissist—more than the "thin slices of behavior" that occurred in the other studies.

Interestingly, Paunonen et al. (2006) found leader ratings to be positively related to "egoistic" features of narcissism, but unrelated to more self-centered sides of the construct. These cadets studied by Paunonen et al. had spent nearly six months together in situations where leadership features could be observed. In Brunell et al. (2008), when positive and distinctive individual characteristics were controlled for (e.g., extraversion, agreeableness), others' ratings of leadership were no longer correlated with narcissism. These two studies suggest that the narcissistic tendency to be assertive early in group interactions can mask some seamier attributes of

---

7 We conducted these analyses using the means and standard errors provided in the Brunell et al. (2008) studies.

narcissism—attributes that may become clearer over time. All of this underscores the important issue of how much continuing interaction exists when sizing up the impact of narcissists on others in the organization.

That said, it may not take a good deal of interaction with a narcissist to conclude that they are not all they seem to be. We found 12 studies showing that others can quickly identify narcissists and narcissistic behavior. Indeed, the empirical literature shows that people who interact with narcissists—even for short periods of time as in the Brunell et al. study—generally do not share the positive view that narcissists have of themselves, even if they are seen as having some leadership potential. We found at least 19 studies which show a difference between narcissists' self-assessments and those of others about a wide variety of characteristics and behavior. In all cases, narcissists' self-assessments were more positive. Said differently, others have a less than ideal view of narcissists—at least from the narcissist's perspective.

Not surprisingly, this disconnect can prove problematic. For example, in their quest for self-enhancement, narcissists are willing to step over others (Campbell et al., 2000; Gosling, John, Raik, & Robins, 1998; Morf & Rhodewalt, 2001). They may be unrealistic about their level of empathy (Ames & Kammrath, 2004) or oblivious to the perspectives of others because of selfishness (Campbell, Bush, Brunell, & Shelton, 2005; Watson, Grisham, Trotter, & Biderman, 1984). Narcissists tend to assume they are better than others (Campbell, Reeder, Sedikides, & Elliot, 2000; Raskin & Terry, 1988; Paulhus, 1998), may be motivated to demonstrate their superiority (Morf, Weir, & Davidov, 2000), and often fail to acknowledge the positive input of others (Campbell et al., 2000; John & Robins, 1994).

And if narcissists perceive threats to their ego, they respond with aggression toward others (Bushman & Baumeister, 1998). Combine all this with the fact that they commonly brag and otherwise draw attention to themselves (Buss & Chiodo, 1991) and it is easy to see why they upset others in work interactions. Narcissists appear to use relationships with others as an opportunity to feed their need for self-enhancement and, consequently, have trouble in sustaining those relationships (Campbell, 1999; Campbell & Foster, 2002). All in all, a narcissist is the antithesis of "a team player."

Another line of research that speaks to effects of narcissism on others in organizations is work on ethics and counternormative practices by employees. Soyer, Rovenpor, and Kopelman (1999), for instance, asked salespeople and managers questions about their degree of comfort with work behavior that might be questionable (e.g., "A good salesperson is part informant, part con artist," "People will believe most anything if you appear confident and knowledgeable"). Narcissism was significantly correlated with the salespersons' comfort with questionable behavior.

Recently, several additional studies have been conducted, most showing similar effects. Penney and Spector (2002) found that narcissism scores were related to counterproductive work behavior (CWB) such as stealing on the job or doing work incorrectly. They also found that narcissism moderated the relationship between job constraints and CWB. Specifically, when employees experience multiple barriers and frustrations on the job, they were more likely to engage in CWB if they scored high in narcissism.

Likewise, another study found modest correlations between narcissism and a variety of honesty tests (Mumford, Connelly, Helton, Strange, & Osburn, 2001). Similarly, Campbell, Rudich, and Sedikides (2002) found that narcissism scores were negatively related to a scale of self-reported ethical characteristics (e.g., honest, moral, deceptive). Also, Paunonen et al. (2006) found that honesty ratings by peers of military cadets were negatively correlated with a manipulative aspect of narcissism. These findings parallel Brown's (2004) finding that narcissism was related to vengefulness (e.g., "I don't get mad, I get even," and "It's important for me to get back at people who've hurt me"), even after controlling for self-esteem.

Adding to the above findings was a study by Judge et al. (2006) of beach patrol officers and their bosses who were asked about deviant workplace behaviors (e.g., I have taken property from work without permission."). Narcissism was positively and significantly related to supervisors' ratings of employee deviance, but not correlated with self-ratings. Blair, Hoffman, and Helland (2008) also surveyed a set of employed MBA students, as well as their bosses and subordinates. A number of interesting variables were assessed, including narcissism and integrity (e.g., "Does not misrepresent him/herself for person gain"). Their results showed that while supervisor ratings of integrity were negatively correlated with narcissism, this was not true for subordinates.

This finding is noteworthy because narcissists do tend to be viewed by most people, including subordinates, in less than positive ways. Blair et al. (2008) addressed this point and were careful to show that these items were viewed in the same way by both bosses and subordinates; this particular artifact can not explain the results. They did point out that the MBA students themselves chose the subordinate who they wanted to solicit feedback from. Consequently, MBA students could have selected subordinates with whom they had the most affinity. These subordinates may also have been fearful of retribution for poor ratings, even if they were assured confidentiality. Moreover, Blair et al. note that the MBA students' bosses may have viewed them in a more complex or experienced way ("wild-eyed thinker with no detail orientation") than their subordinates. The idea that the observer's vantage point matters in terms of how narcissists are evaluated is an interesting one to explore in future research. On a somewhat related note, a study by Davis, Wester, and King (2008) found that narcissism was predictive of a self-reported tendency to compromise research ethics (e.g., inappropriate authorship; unethical reviewing, etc.) for professors, but not for doctoral students.

A final fascinating study in this area, by Blickle, Schlegel, Fassbender, and Klein (2006), looked at personality correlates of white-collar crime. Not content to examine self-reports of ethical lapses in behavior, these researchers went directly to those who actually committed and were convicted of white collar crimes in Germany. In particular, they sampled from inmates at correctional institutions who were former high-level managers and executives. Each had been convicted of white-collar crimes—these included embezzlement, fraud, tax evasion, and bribery, with the financial damage to their respective firms averaging over $3.5 million. Blickle et al. (2006) also obtained a second, matched set of managers who were currently employed in similar companies with equivalent levels of responsibility. The results showed that narcissism predicted respondent's status (i.e., criminal vs. noncriminal), even after controlling for social desirability. Overall, narcissism is closely related to poor attitudes and behavior concerning ethical practices in organizations.

Dealing with Managerial Narcissism

While we obviously know quite a bit about narcissism, it's equally clear that many unanswered questions remain. Indeed, as we have seen, the literature about narcissism presents a murky picture in many respects (e.g., about the different "types" of narcissism and the impact of contextual factors, just to name a few). So there is no doubt that the need for more research exists—perhaps now more than ever in these difficult times where the need for leaders with integrity is acute.

Yet the response we have always received from a "need more research" refrain from people in corporations is this—"we can't wait for all the scientific questions to be resolved, we need help now!" Consequently, in this final section we present action suggestions based on our current, albeit limited, understanding of narcissistic leaders. We break these suggestions into two basic parts: personal and organizational. First, we focus on employees who find themselves—all too frequently—in the position of working for an excessively narcissistic boss or leader. In a nutshell, these personal suggestions will involve raising employee self-awareness and diagnostic skills as well as presenting specific tactics for responding to narcissistic leaders.

After presenting these person-level suggestions, we conclude this chapter by presenting some ideas, policies, and strategies that companies should embrace to keep narcissistic people from running wild through their top management ranks. In essence, companies should take steps to preclude narcissists from getting a foothold and create an environment where it is difficult for narcissists to operate in positions of power.

How Employees Can Deal With Their Narcissistic Leaders

Dealing with Narcissistic Exploitation and Manipulation

A common problem many employees face when working for narcissistic leaders is their tendency to exploit and manipulate to advance or protect themselves. The narcissistic leader may lie, distort or withhold information, engage in blaming, and play any number of psychological games with subordinates. Perhaps the first challenge employees must rise to when it comes to exploitation and manipulation is detecting it in the first place. This is no small task. In essence, employees must determine whether they are actually dealing with a narcissistic boss and, if so, then assess the damage that is being inflicted (e.g., does being blamed for the narcissist's own flaws have negative career implications?).

Next, employees must evaluate their options for responding—which depend on the seriousness of the situation and whether others are experiencing manipulative behavior and are willing to step forward. In any case, options range from short-run avoidance (i.e., staying away from the narcissist as much as possible—impractical over the long term) to filing complaints with higher ups to forming coalitions to resist the narcissistic leader. Regardless, we advocate creating a log of any incidents experienced and maintaining a library of any e-mails or documents received that might attest to the narcissists' manipulative behavior. Naturally, all options have drawbacks. A coalition typically has a better chance of exposing narcissistic malfeasance, but coalitions can be notoriously difficult and time-consuming to build, especially if subordinates are afraid of retribution. Likewise, filing complaints with Human Resources or other senior leaders can expose subordinates to scrutiny and narcissistic revenge. But if employees have strong performance records and can present themselves as being interested in helping the company rather than trashing their boss, written complaints can work (McFarlin & Sweeney, 2002).

Dealing With Narcissistic Tantrums

One of the themes we have touched on throughout this chapter is the narcissist tendency to exert power and dominate others. This can produce explosive temper tantrums and inappropriate rages in narcissistic leaders, especially when they feel they are being threatened or criticized. Typically, being passive or cowering in the face of such tantrums ultimately feels reinforcing to the narcissist (i.e., their explosions "work" to crush opposition). For subordinates, all of the options we have mentioned for dealing with manipulation are also relevant here—as are their respective drawbacks. That said, these suggestions do not directly address how employees should behave when they are on the receiving end of a narcissistic tantrum.

Consequently, we suggest employees try to display strength instead of weakness when facing narcissistic tantrums. For instance, employees should literally stand their ground, maintaining direct eye contact and speak firmly in response to the narcissist. They can also use interruption tactics to disrupt a narcissistic tantrum (e.g., by asking for more information, restating issues, disagreeing, or stating one will leave the interaction unless the narcissist calms down). After the incident passes, subordinates should write down the details and begin a paper trail with the narcissist to create a record. For instance, subordinates can send the narcissist an e-mail to solicit additional information, to officially disagree with the narcissist's points, or to raise concerns about how they were treated. Subordinates also should be ready to escalate their complaints up the line if the narcissistic leader retaliates (McFarlin & Sweeney, 2002).

Dealing With Narcissistic Impression Management

Another insidious problem with narcissistic leaders is that their self-aggrandizing tendencies often result in excessive impression management behavior. This can include a variety of self-promotional behavior, ingratiation with higher-ups, and, what really rankles subordinates, credit-stealing. Like manipulative and exploitative behavior, a key for subordinates with impression management abuse is to be able to recognize it when they see it. In essence, subordinates need to be attuned to impression management tactics and contextual factors that create impression management opportunities. Dealing with credit-stealing is a particular challenge and subordinates should look for ways to communicate their contributions (e.g., via the grapevine or written efforts) to correct the record. Longer term, subordinates may want to put roles, responsibilities, and credit-sharing activities in writing prior to starting on major tasks or projects. This may help blunt any credit-stealing efforts by narcissistic superiors (McFarlin & Sweeney, 2002).

Dealing With Narcissistic Visions

Narcissistic leaders tend to have grandiose self-regard and often see themselves as infallible. And when narcissists occupy the executive suite, personal monument-building and vision-based excesses are common. For instance, narcissists may pursue risky gambits and expensive dreams as a testament to their own superiority (e.g., in the form of over-the-top acquisitions, new business launches, and so on).

Moreover, narcissistic visions tend to encourage rather than discourage dependency. After all, narcissists want adoring and subservient followers—something a lofty and inspiring vision can bolster. Once again, subordinates need to educate themselves about the clues that suggest a corporate vision is the product of narcissistic fantasies. For instance, red flags should go up if the vision being pushed is somehow wrapped up in the leader's reputation, persona, or past achievements. Likewise, if the vision seems overly bold and ignores obvious implementation risks, external factors, or costs, subordinates should be wary. To combat all of this, subordinates should document and investigate their concerns, perhaps with the help of outside experts willing to share their assessment with the rest of the management team (McFarlin & Sweeney, 2002).

Stepping back for a moment, it is important to underscore the role subordinates often play in enabling flawed narcissistic visions—as well as putting up with other narcissistic abuses. As Lipman-Blumen (2005) has pointed out, anxiety, fear, and self-doubt among subordinates create the kind of dependency that many flawed leaders crave. This is what can cause subordinates to suspend disbelief or not question their leaders—no may how crazy their ideas are. Recognizing that their anxieties may encourage the embrace of false visions will help subordinates see things as they really are and embolden them to speak out. And taking the initiative to do so cuts to the core of what good leadership really is. On a broader level, this means followers need to abandon their roles as passive, dependent servants of leaders and become proactive, independent employees who desire stronger leadership skills and take responsibility for the firm. Only in this way will followers learn to "kick their addition" to the lofty, illusory visions that narcissistic leaders often present (Lipman-Blumen, 2005; McFarlin & Sweeney, 2002).

Taking on Narcissistic Leaders: A Positive View of the Process

Before we leave this section, we want to end on a "glass is half full" note. Employees who must combat narcissism in their companies often find it a difficult, dangerous, and depressing chore—where the odds are long and there seems to be little upside (short of leaving the firm). Consequently, it may be helpful for beaten-down subordinates to reframe what they are facing. In other words, we would encourage subordinates to look for what Lipman-Blumen (2005) argues are the "opportunities" in working for a toxic leader like a narcissist. Specifically, working for a narcissist may be an excellent opportunity for subordinates to: (1) exercise leadership themselves, at least on an informal basis, to counteract the leader; (2) learn from a negative role model about how not to behave; (3) become more aware of their own moral superiority, building self-esteem in the process; (4) vent about the leader's excesses and foibles in ways that build espirit de corps across the firm; and (5) learn how to build coalitions to organize and fight back (a theme we have revisited repeatedly in this section).

How Organizations Can Deal With the Challenge of Narcissistic Leaders

We turn our attention in this final section to some steps and strategies that organizations may want to adopt to combat narcissism in their ranks. This process starts, we believe, by adopting hiring practices that will make it harder for narcissists to get inside the firm and cause trouble. Granted, that will always be an imperfect solution. Consequently, we will also discuss things firms can do to bolster their internal defenses against narcissism in the ranks.

Job One: Avoid Hiring Narcissists in the First Place

The bottom line is that many screening techniques used when firms hire managers are tailor-made for narcissists. In other words, interview processes are often tilted toward self-presentation skills. Interviewees who project charm, confidence, assertiveness, and charisma—while taking personal credit for every success and attributing problems elsewhere—often do quite well. And, put simply, schmoozing and pumping themselves up are what narcissistic leaders often do very well indeed. Once exposed, narcissists often have an easy time moving on to the next unsuspecting company, propelled forward by syrupy recommendations designed to offload the narcissist somewhere else as soon as possible.

Fortunately, firms can put hiring practices into place that will minimize the ability of narcissists to avoid detection. First, companies need to embrace a philosophy that looks for the predictors of failure (like narcissism) instead of focusing exclusively on superficial factors that are believed to correlate with leadership success. Moreover, managerial candidates should be asked about how they approached conflict, hardships, or difficult challenges they have encountered on the job, with the interview team focusing on anything in the answers that might reveal narcissistic tendencies. For instance, blaming subordinates, castigating rivals, or attributing success to only personal characteristics may all be worrisome signs. Interviewers should also be trained to be cautious and avoid falling under the charm offensive narcissistic managers may unleash. Finally, the screening process could include personality instruments designed to detect narcissism (McFarlin & Sweeney, 2002).

Adopt Policies That Promote Subordinate Development and Succession Planning

Naturally, the hiring process is not foolproof and firms should assume that some narcissistic individuals will end up on the payroll. And unfortunately, once in management ranks, most narcissistic individuals have little interest in developing their subordinates or planning for succession. After all, doing so would mean creating competent (and threatening) rivals who might push them out of the limelight. The nasty succession battles we often read about in the business press are undoubtedly driven by narcissism in many cases. Narcissistic CEOs want to keep their jobs while undermining potential successors. Likewise, narcissistic successors often covet the CEO role and will do what they can to get it (McFarlin & Sweeney, 2002).

But companies are not helpless. They can enact policies to encourage better succession planning and employee development. Indeed, this arguably should start at the top with the board of directors—something that is especially important when times are tough. And when companies get into trouble, boards of directors sometimes turn to narcissistic, imperial leaders to serve as CEO in the mistaken belief that imposing a "strong will" on the firm will turn things around. Current board practices remain problematic in many cases. For instance, by some estimates, over 60% of CEOs in American corporations are also serving as board chair, putting too much power in one person's hands. To limit cronyism that can provide a free pass for narcissistic executives, especially in difficult times, board director terms should be limited. Moreover, boards should take steps to ensure that strong leadership development and succession plans are implemented and rigorous performance measurements for the CEO are in place (Allio, 2007).

Other recommendations for board-level improvements in succession planning efforts would be to work to ensure that the board is comprised of independent directors not tied to the CEO. An independent board will engender much more confidence in developing and running succession plans for the company. Boards may also want to tie CEO pay to succession planning (i.e., to grade the CEO on well he or she helps identify and develop potential successors).

Develop Cultural Values That Discourage Narcissism

The bottom line is that boards can also play a key role in fostering a corporate culture that values employee development and succession planning (McFarlin & Sweeney, 2002). For example, boards can encourage executives to cultivate cultural values that focus on honesty and integrity. That means creating explicit norms and codes of conduct, with positive behaviors rewarded and negative behaviors punished. Over time, integrity-related values will become institutionalized in the firm, making it less vulnerable to narcissistic excesses (Allio, 2007; see also Appelbaum & Roy-Girard, 2007).

Speaking of which, companies should be creative in their quest to adopt values systems that combat narcissism. And that means looking far and wide for alternative approaches to management. For instance, consider the African management concept of *Ubuntu*. The Ubuntu philosophy is about "connective leadership," with everyone's well-being and humanity in the firm expressed through others. Embracing the communal orientation of many African societies, Ubuntu stresses responsibility—on the part of everyone in the corporate community—to support and nurture all members of that community. At its core, Ubuntu rests on mutuality of purpose and interdependent concern—the essence of the village. Consequently, Ubuntu arguably represents the antithesis of the "me, myself, and I" culture found in many American corporations—a culture that appeals to narcissistic leaders (see Lipman-Blumen, 2005; McFarlin, Coster, & Mogale-Pretorius,

1999; McFarlin & Sweeney, 2002). Perhaps some variant of this approach, Westernized through the corporate family concept, could have some promise.

Summary

The study of narcissism has moved from a focus on clinical classification and analysis to a social/organizational empirical analysis over the last several decades. This shift has provided useful information about the features that characterize the narcissistic personality, the impact of this style on performance, and how they appear and impact others in organizations. We also looked closely at how peers, subordinates and organizations themselves can deal with the challenges presented by narcissistic leadership. More research conducted in functioning organizations is needed and will likely appear over the next decades. Hopefully this work will provide more specific, empirically grounded advice about how to take advantage of or temper this complex narcissistic style of some leaders.

References

Allio, R. J. (2007). Bad leaders: How they get that way and what to do about them. *Strategy & Leadership, 35*(3), 12–17.

Ames, D. R., & Kammrath, L. K. (2004). Mind-reading and metacognition: Narcissism, not actual competence, predicts self-estimated ability. *Journal of Nonverbal Behavior, 28,* 187–209.

Ames, D. R., Rose, P., & Anderson, C. P. (2006). The NPI-16 as a short measure of narcissim. *Journal of Research in Personality, 40,* 440–450.

Appelbaum, S. H., & Roy-Girard, D. (2007). Toxins in the workplace: Affect on organizations and employees. *Corporate Governance, 7*(1), 17–28.

Baumeister, R. F. (1987). How the self became a problem: A psychological review of historical research. *Journal of Personality and Social Psychology, 52,* 163–176.

Blair, C. A., Hoffman, B. J., & Helland, K. R. (2008). Narcissism in organizations: A multisource appraisal reflects different perspectives. *Human Performance, 21*(3), 254–276.

Blickle, G., Schlegel, A., Fassbender, P., & Klein, U. (2006). Some personality correlates of business white-collar crime. *Applied Psychology: An International Review, 55,* 220–233.

Bogart, L. M., Benotsch, E. G., & Pavlovic, J. D. (2004). Feeling superior but threatened: The relation of narcissism to social comparison. *Basic and Applied Social Psychology, 26,* 35–44.

Brown, R. P. (2004). Vengeance is mine: Narcissism, vengeance, and the tendency to forgive. *Journal of Research in Personality, 38,* 576–583.

Brunell, A. B., Gentry, W. A., Campbell, W. K., Hoffman, B. J., Kuhnert, K. W., & DeMarree, K. G. (2008). Leader emergence: The case of the narcissistic leader. *Personality and Social Psychology Bulletin, 34,* 1663–1676.

Bushman, B., & Baumeister, R. F. (1998). Threatened egotism, narcissism, self esteem, and direct and displaced aggression: Does self-love or self-hate lead to violence? *Journal of Personality and Social Psychology, 75,* 219–229.

Buss, D. M., & Chiodo, L. M. (1991). Narcissistic acts in everyday life. *Journal of Personality, 36,* 543–545.

Campbell, W. K. (1999). Narcissism and romantic attraction. *Journal of Personality and Social Psychology, 77,* 1254–1270.

Campbell, W. K., Bush, C. P., Brunell, A. B., & Shelton, J. (2005). Understanding the social costs of narcissism: The case of the tragedy of the commons. *Personality and Social Psychology Bulletin, 31,* 1358–1368.

Campbell, W. K., Goodie, A. S., & Foster, J. D. (2004). Narcissism, confidence, and risk attitude. *Journal of Behavioral Decision Making, 17,* 297–311.

Campbell, W. K., & Foster, C. A. (2002). Narcissism and commitment in romantic relationships: An investment model analysis. *Personality and Social Psychology Bulletin, 28,* 484–495.

Campbell, W. K., Reeder, G. D., Sedikides, C., & Elliot, A. J. (2000). Narcissism and comparative self-enhancement strategies. *Journal of Research in Personality, 34,* 329–347.

Campbell, W. K., Rudich, E. A., & Sedikides, C. (2002). Narcissism, self-esteem, and the positivity of self-views: Two portraits of self-love. *Personality and Social Psychology Bulletin, 28,* 358–368.

Chatterjee, A., & Hambrick, D. C. (2007). It's all about me: Narcissistic chief executive officers and their effects on company strategy and performance. *Administrative Science Quarterly, 52,* 351–386.

Corry, N., Merritt, R. D., Mrug, S., & Pamp, B. (2008). The factor structure of the narcissistic personality inventory. *Journal of Personality Assessment, 90*(6), 593–600.

Cycyota, C. S., & Harrison, D. A. (2006). What (not) to expect when surveying executives: A meta-analysis of top manager response rates and techniques over time. *Organizational Research Methods, 9,* 133–160.

Davis, M. S., Wester, K. L., & King, B. (2008). Narcissism, entitlement, and questionable research practices in counseling: A pilot study. *Journal of Counseling & Development, 86,* 200–210.

Deluga, R. J. (1997). Relationship among American presidential charismatic leadership, narcissism, and rated performance. *Leadership Quarterly, 8,* 49–65.

Edelman, R. (2009). *2009 Edelman Trust Barometer Executive Summary & Edelman Trust Barometer–Paradise Lost.* Retrieved from www.edelman.com

Emmons, R. A. (1984). Factor analysis and construct validity of the narcissistic personality inventory. *Journal of Personality Assessment, 48,* 291–300.

Emmons, R. A. (1987). Narcissism: theory and measurement. *Journal of Personality and Social Psychology, 52,* 11–17.

Farwell, L., & Wohlwend-Lloyd, R. (1998). Narcissistic processes: Optimistic expectations, favorable self-evaluations, and self-enhancing attributions. *Journal of Personality, 66,* 65–83.

Finkelstein, S., Hambrick, D. C., & Cannella, A. A. (2009). *Strategic leadership: Theory and research on executives, top management teams, and boards.* London, England: Oxford University Press.

Foster, J. D., Campbell, W. K., & Twenge, J. M. (2003). Individual differences in narcissism: Inflated self-views across the lifespan and around the world. *Journal of Research in Personality, 37,* 469–486.

Gabriel, M. T., Critelli, J. W., & Ee, J. S. (1994). Narcissistic illusions in self-evaluations of intelligence and attractiveness. *Journal of Personality, 62,* 143–155.

Gosling, S. D., John, O. P., Craik, K. H., & Robins, R. W. (1998). Do people know how they behave? Self-reported act frequencies compared with on-line codings by observers. *Journal of Personality and Social Psychology, 74,* 1337–1349.

Hartouni, Z. S. (1992). Effects of narcissistic personality organization on causal attributions. *Psychological Reports, 71,* 1339–1346.

Hayward, M., & Hambrick, D. C. (1997). Explaining the premiums paid for large acquisitions: Evidence of CEO hubris. *Administrative Science Quarterly, 42,* 103–107.

Hofstede, G. (2001). *Culture's consequences: Comparing values, behaviors, institutions, and organizations across cultures.* Thousand Oaks, CA: SAGE.

Hogan, R., Curphy, G. J., & Hogan, J. (1994). What we know about leadership effectiveness and personality. *American Psychologist, 49,* 493–504.

Hogan, R., & Kaiser, R. B. (2005). What we know about leadership. *Review of General Psychology, 9,* 169–180.

Hogan, R. Raskin, R., & Fazzini, D. (1990). The dark side of charisma. In K. E. Clark & M. B. Clark (Eds.), *Measures of leadership* (pp. 343–354). West Orange, NJ: Leadership Library of America.

John, O. P., & Robins, R. W. (1994). Accuracy and bias in self-perception: Individual differences in self-enhancement and the role of narcissism. *Journal of Personality and Social Psychology, 66,* 206–219.

Judge, T. A., LePine, J. A., & Rich, B. L. (2006). Loving yourself abundantly: Relationship of the narcissistic personality to self- and other perceptions of workplace deviance, leadership, and task and contextual performance. *Journal of Applied Psychology, 91,* 762–776.

Kernis, M. H., & Chien-Ru, S. (1994). Narcissism and reactions to interpersonal feedback. *Journal of Research in Personality, 28,* 4–13.

Kets de Vries, M. F. R. (1995). *Life and death in the executive fast lane.* San Francisco: Jossey-Bass.

Kets de Vries, M. F. R., & Miller, D. (1985). Narcissism and leadership: An object relations perspective. *Human Relations, 38,* 583–601.

Khurana, R. (2002). *Searching for a corporate savior: The irrational quest for charismatic CEOs.* Princeton, NJ: Princeton University Press.

Kubarych, T. S., Deary, I. J., & Austin, E. J. (2004). The narcissistic personality inventory: Factor structure in a non-clinical sample. *Personality and Individual Differences, 36,* 857–872.

Ladd, E. R., Welsh, M. C., Vitulli, W. F., Labbe, E. E., & Law, J. G. (1997). Narcissism and causal attribution. *Psychological Reports, 80,* 171–178.

Lasch, C. (1979). *The culture of narcissism: American life in an age of diminishing expectations.* New York: Norton.

Lipman-Blumen, J. (2005). *The allure of toxic leaders.* New York: Oxford University Press.

Maccoby, M. (2000, Jan.-Feb.). Narcissistic leaders: The incredible pros, the inevitable cons. *Harvard Business Review,* 92–101.

Maccoby, M. (2007). *Narcissistic leaders: Who succeeds and who fails?* Boston: Harvard Business School Press Books.

McCann, J. T., & Biaggio, M. K. (1989). Narcissistic personality features and self-reported anger. *Psychological Reports, 64,* 55–58.

McFarlin, D. B., Coster, E. A., & Mogale-Pretorius, C. (1999). Management development in South Africa: Moving toward an Africanized framework. *Journal of Management Development, 18,* 63–78.

McFarlin, D. B., & Sweeney, P. D. (2002). *Where egos dare: The untold truth about narcissistic leaders—and how to survive them.* London, England: Kogan Page.

Morf, C. C., & Rhodewalt, F. (2001). Unraveling the paradoxes of narcissism: A systematic self-regulatory processing model. *Psychological Inquiry, 12,* 177–196.

Morf, C. C., Weir, C., & Davidov, M. (2000). Narcissism and intrinsic motivation: The role of goal congruence. *Journal of Experimental Social Psychology, 36,* 424–438.

Mumford, M. D., Connelly, M. S., Helton, W. B., Strange, I M., & Osburn, H. K. (2001). On the construct validity of integrity tests: Individual and situational factors as predictors of test performance. *International Journal of Selection and assessment, 9,* 240–257.

Oltmanns, T. F., Friedman, J. N. W., Fiedler, E. R., & Turkheimer, E. (2004). Perceptions of people with personality disorders based on thin slices of behavior. *Journal of Research in Personality, 38,* 216–239.

Otway, L. J., & Vignoles, V. L. (2006). Narcissism and childhood recollections: A quantitative test of psychoanalytic predictions. *Personality and Social Psychology Bulletin, 32*(1), 104–116.

Paulhus, D. L. (1998). Interpersonal and intrapsychic adaptiveness of trait self-enhancement: A mixed blessing? *Journal of Personality and Social Psychology, 74,* 1197–1208.

Paulhus, D. L., & Williams, K. M. (2002). The dark triad of personality: Narcissism, Machiavellianism and psychopathy. *Journal of Research in Personality, 36,* 556–563.

Paunonen, S. V., Lonnqvist, J., Verkasalo, M., Leikas, S., & Nissinen, V. (2006). Narcissism and emergent leadership in military cadets. *Leadership Quarterly, 17,* 475–486.

Penny, L. J., & Spector, P. E. (2002). Narcissism and counterproductive work behavior: Do bigger egos mean bigger problems? *International Journal of Selection and Assessment, 10,* 126–134.

Raskin, R. (1980). Narcissism and creativity: Are they related? *Psychological Reports, 46,* 55–60.

Raskin, R., & Hall, C. S. (1979). A narcissistic personality inventory. *Psychological Reports, 45,* 590.

Raskin, R., & Novacek, J. (1989). An MMPI description of the narcissistic personality. *Journal of Personality Assessment, 53,* 66–80.

Raskin, R., & Shaw, R. (1988). Narcissism and the use of personal pronouns. *Journal of Personality, 56,* 393–404.

Raskin, R., & Terry, H. (1988). A principal-components analysis of the narcissistic personality inventory and further evidence of its construct validity. *Journal of Personality and Social Psychology, 54,* 890–902.

Rhodewalt, F., & Morf, C. C. (1995). Self and interpersonal correlates of the Narcissistic Personality Inventory: A review and new findings. *Journal of Research in Personality, 29,* 1–23.

Rhodewalt, F., & Morf, C. C. (1998). On self-aggrandizement and anger: A temporal analysis of narcissism and affective reactions to success and failure. *Journal of Personality and Social Psychology, 74,* 672–685.

Rhodewalt, F., Tragakis, M. W., & Finnerty, J. (2006). Narcissism and self-handicapping: Linking self-aggrandizement to behavior. *Journal of Research in Personality, 40,* 573–597.

Roberts, W. (1990). *Leadership secrets of Atilla the Hun.* New York: Grand Central Publishing.

Robins, R. W., & John, O. P. (1997). Effects of visual perspective and narcissism on self-perception: Is seeing believing? *Psychological Science, 8,* 37–42.

Roll, R. (1986). The hubris hypothesis of corporate takeovers. *Journal of Business, 59,* 197–216.

Rosenthal, S. A., & Pittinsky, T. L. (2006). Narcissistic leadership. *The Leadership Quarterly, 17,* 617–633.

Schopen, F. (2009, January 28). Leadership is about more than charisma. *The Times Online.* Retrieved from http://timesonline.co.uk

Sedikides, C., Rudich, E. A., Gregg, A. P., Kumashiro, M., & Rusbult, C. (2004). Are normal narcissists psychologically healthy?: Self-esteem matters. *Journal of Personality and Social Psychology, 87,* 400–416.

Soyer, R. B., Rovenpor, J. L., & Kopelman, R. E. (1999). Narcissism and achievement motivation as related to three facets of the sales role: Attraction, satisfaction and performance. *Journal of Business and Psychology, 14,* 285–304.

Smalley, R. L., & Stake, J. E. (1996). Evaluating sources of ego-threatening feedback: self-esteem and narcissism effects. *Journal of Personality and Social Psychology, 62,* 1036–1049.

Stucke, T. S. (2003). Who's to blame. Narcissism and self-serving attributions following feedback. *European Journal of Personality, 17,* 465–478.

Trzesniewski, K. H., Donnellan, M. B., & Robins, R. W. (2008a). Is "Generation Me" really more narcissistic than previous generations? *Journal of Personality, 76,* 903–917.

Trzesniewski, K. H., Donnellan, M. B., & Robins, R. W. (2008b). Do today's young people really think they are so extraordinary? An examination of secular trends in narcissism and self-enhancement. *Psychological Science, 19*(2), 181–188.

Twenge, J. M., & Campbell, W. K. (2001). Age and birth cohort differences in self-esteem: A cross-temporal meta-analysis. *Personality and Social Psychology Review, 5,* 321–344.

Twenge, J. M., & Campbell, W. K. (2003). "Isn't it fun to get the respect that we're going to deserve?" Narcissism, social rejection, and aggression. *Personality and Social Psychology Bulletin, 29,* 261–272.

Twenge, J. M., Konrath, S., Foster, J. D., Campbell, W. K., & Bushman, B. J. (2008a). Egos inflating over time: A cross-temporal meta-analysis of the narcissistic personality inventory. *Journal of Personality, 76,* 875–901.

Twenge, J. M., Konrath, S., Foster, J. D., Campbell, W. K., & Bushman, B. J. (2008b). Further evidence of an increase in narcissism among college students. *Journal of Personality, 76,* 919–927.

Vogel, C. (2006, Jan/Feb.). A field guide to narcissism. *Psychology Today,* 68–74.

Wallace, H. M., & Baumeister, R. F. (2002). The performance of narcissists rises and falls with perceived opportunity for glory. *Journal of Personality and Social Psychology, 82,* 819–834.

Watson, P. J., Grisham, S. O., Trotter, M. V., & Biderman, M. D. (1984). Narcissism and empathy: Validity evidence for the Narcissistic Personality Inventory. *Journal of Personality Assessment, 48,* 301–305.

Wink, P. (1991). Two faces of narcissism. *Journal of Personality and Social Psychology, 61,* 590–597.

Zuckerman, M., & O'Loughlin, R. E., (2009). Narcissism and well-being: A longitudinal perspective. *European Journal of Social Psychology, 39,* 957–972.

Discussion Questions

1   How does thinking about destructive leadership from a personality perspective different from thinking about destructive leadership from a behavior perspective?

2   Why do you think laissez-faire leadership is destructive?

3   Constructive leadership is described as pro-subordinate and pro-organization. Can you explain these terms? What does a constructive leader do to maintain effectiveness?

4   What are the main problems associated with narcissistic leadership?

What can the organization do to discourage narcissism among its members?

PART V

POWER AND POLITICS

CHAPTER 8

Introduction to Power and Politics in Organizations

Power, Politics, and Influence

Andrew J. DuBrin

Chapter Outline

The Meaning of Power, Politics, and Influence

Sources of Individual and Subunit Power

Empowerment of Group Members

Organizational Politics

Organizational Influence Tactics

The Control of Dysfunctional Politics and Ethical Considerations

Implications for Managerial Practice

Learning Objectives

After reading and studying this chapter and doing the exercises, you should be able to:

1   Identify sources of power for individuals and subunits within organizations.

2   Describe the essence of empowerment.

3   Pinpoint factors contributing to, and examples of, organizational politics.

4   Differentiate between the ethical and unethical use of power, politics, and influence.

5   Identify and describe a variety of influence tactics.

6   Explain how managers can control dysfunctional politics.

Andrew J. DuBrin, "Power, Politics, and Influence," *Fundamentals of Organizational Behavior*, pp. 249-270. Copyright © 2016 by Academic Media Solutions. Reprinted with permission.

michaeljung/Shutterstock.com

David Novak is the Chairman and CEO of Yum! Brands, a company that consists of 40,000 KFC, Pizza Hut, and Taco Bell locations in 120 countries around the world, making it the largest restaurant chain in terms of units. The company's restaurants are now the leader in the chicken, pizza, and Mexican-style food categories. (KFC was previously called "Kentucky Fried Chicken.") In the United States, Yum! has 60 restaurants per million people.

Novak has become a powerful executive by creating an organizational culture that emphasizes employee recognition and the empowerment of his team members and restaurant managers. The affable executive sees himself as the chief teaching officer of Yum! Brands and believes ardently that recognition is the foundation of motivation. His attitude toward empowerment is expressed in these words: "When you think about what you need to get done in your company, you know you can't get it done by yourself. There is no way you can get it done without taking people with you." Taking People With You has become the name of the company leadership development program.

Novak's first approach to employee recognition became legendary. Each time he was informed that an employee deserved recognition, Novak would give that worker a signed, numbered, rubber chicken, along with a $100 on-the-spot bonus. The Yum! Award now takes the form of a set of smiling plastic teeth with legs that denotes "walking the talk" of leadership. The wall and ceiling in Novak's office is crammed with hundreds of photos depicting him with restaurant managers, office workers, and other employees recognized for noteworthy achievement.

Novak has been referred to as the business world's ultimate team builder. His top-level management team has been exceptionally stable, with an average tenure of 10 years. Among the team members are a "chief people officer," the CEO of Yum Brands–China, the president of Yum Brands–India, and a general counsel and chief franchise policy officer. Novak explains that part of the company's growth can be attributed to the trust team members had in each other, and the belief that they could work together to create something that was bigger than their own individual capabilities. All team members are empowered to manage their vast spheres of influence without micromanagement by Novak. Restaurant general managers are regarded by Novak as the company's No. 1 leaders because they build empowered teams closest to the customers.

Novak believes that the recognition culture he has created, along with the Taking People With You program, is a fulfillment of his life's purpose. "Why am I on earth?" he asks. "I'm on earth to encourage others, lift lives, help create leaders, inspire people, recognize others." Novak graduated from the University of Missouri with a journalism degree with an advertising major.[1]

This story about the CEO of a giant chain of quick-service restaurants illustrates the importance of employee recognition, and also how empowerment of team members can influence them to perform well. Power, politics, and influence are such major parts of the workplace that they have become standard topics of organizational behavior.[1]

In this chapter, we approach power, politics, and influence from multiple perspectives. We describe the meaning of these concepts, how power is obtained, and how it is shared (empowerment). We examine why organizational politics is so prevalent, and then describe the tactics of politics and influence. In addition, we describe the control of dysfunctional politics, and ethical considerations about the use of power, politics, and influence. As you read the chapter, you will learn that some tactics of power, politics, and influence violate ethical codes and therefore should be avoided.

---

1   Original story based on facts and observations in the following sources: Barney Wolf, "David Novak's Global Vision," *QSR* (www.qsrmagazine.com), May 2012, pp. 1–3; Kevin Kruse, "Leadership Secrets from Yum! Brands' CEO David Novak" (www.forbes.com), June 25, 2014, pp. 1–4; Geoff Colvin, "Great Job! Or How Yum Brands Uses Recognition to Build Teams and Get Results," *Fortune*, August 12, 2013, pp. 62–66; J. P. Donlin, "CEO of the Year David Novak: The Recognition Leader," *Chief Executive* (http://chiefexecutive.net), June 27, 2012, pp. 1–3.

power The potential or ability to influence decisions and control resources.

organizational politics Informal approaches to gaining power through means other than merit or luck.

political skill A combination of social astuteness with the capacity to adjust and adapt behavior to different situational demands.

LEARNING OBJECTIVE 1

Identify sources of power for individuals and subunits within organizations.

The Meaning of Power, Politics, and Influence

A challenge in understanding power, politics, and influence in organizations is that the terms appear close in meaning. Here we present meanings of these terms aimed at providing useful distinctions. **Power** is the potential or ability to influence decisions and control resources. The predominant view of power is that it is the influence over others' actions, thoughts, and outcomes.[2] Realize that, like gravity, power cannot be observed directly. Yet you can observe its effects, such as when the corporate name is used as a verb.[3] For example, "Have you 'googled' that job applicant yet?" Or, "Have you 'Scotch Taped' the envelope?"

Many definitions of *power* center on the ability of a person to overcome resistance in achieving a result. Some researchers suggest that power lies in the potential, while others focus on use.[4] As a hedge, our definition includes both potential and use. If you have a powerful battery in your car, isn't it still powerful whether or not it is in use?

Politics is a way of achieving power. As used here, **organizational politics** refers to informal approaches to gaining power through means other than merit or luck. In recent years, scholars have recognized that being skilled in organizational politics is a positive force for individuals and can help the organization. **Political skill** is a combination of social astuteness with the capacity to adjust and adapt behavior to different situational demands. As a result, the person with political skill inspires trust and support, controls and influences the responses of others, and appears genuine and sincere.[5]

Influence is close in meaning to *power*. *Influence* is also the ability to change behavior, but it tends to be more subtle and indirect than *power*. *Power* indicates the ability to affect outcomes with greater facility and ease than *influence*.[6] A person who has political skill is able to use influence behaviors in organizations, such as building strong relationships with key people.

---

2   Book review in *Personnel Psychology*, Summer 2002, p. 502.

3   Jerry Useem, "Power," *Fortune*, August 11, 2003, p. 58.

4   Daniel J. Brass and Marlene E. Burkhardt, "Potential Power and Power Use: An Integration of Structure and Behavior," *Academy of Management Journal*, June 1993, pp. 441–442.

5   Christian Ewen et al., ""Further Specification of the Leader Political Skill-Leadership Effectiveness Relationships: Transformational and Transactional Leader Behaviors as Moderators," *The Leadership Quarterly*, August 2013, p. 317.

6   Robert P. Vecchio, *Organizational Behavior: Core Concepts*, 4th ed. (Mason, OH: South-Western/Thomson Learning, 2000), p. 126.

Managers and professionals often need to use political tactics to achieve the power and influence they need to accomplish their work. An example would be a human resources manager cultivating the support of a top executive so he or she can proceed with a program of employee wellness. Cultivating support is a political tactic.

Sources of Individual and Subunit Power

An encouraging note about the study of power is that the basic ideas behind power have remained stable over time, no matter how much technological change takes place. Part of the reason, explains Jeffrey Pfeffer, is that the use of power can be linked to survival advantages. For example, most people have a self-enhancement motive, and they have a desire to be identified and associated with success and winners.[7]

The sources or bases of power in organizations can be classified in different ways. A useful starting point is to recognize that power can be used to forward either the interests of the organization or personal interests. **Socialized power** is the use of power to achieve constructive ends. An example would be the manager who attempted to gain power to spearhead a program of employee wellness. **Personalized power** is the use of power primarily for the sake of personal aggrandizement and gain.[8] An example would be a new CEO using his power to insist that company headquarters be moved to a location near his home or that his family members be allowed to use a company jet.

Here we classify the sources (and also the bases and origins) of power that stem from the organization, from the individual, and from providing resources.[9]

Power Granted by the Organization (Position Power)

Managers and professionals often have power because of the authority, or right, granted by their positions. The power of a manager's position stems from three sources: legitimate power, coercive power, and reward power. **Legitimate power** is based on the manager's formal position within the

socialized power The use of power to achieve constructive ends.

personalized power The use of power primarily for the sake of personal aggrandizement and gain.

legitimate power Power based on one's formal position within the hierarchy of the organization.

---

7   Jeffrey Pfeffer, "You're Still the Same: Why Theories of Power Hold over Time and across Countries," *Academy of Management Perspectives*, November 2013, pp. 269–280.

8   Leonard H. Chusmir, "Personalized vs. Socialized Power Needs among Working Men and Women," *Human Relations*, February 1986, p. 149.

9   John R. P. French and Bertram Raven, "The Basis of Social Power," in Dorwin Cartwright and Alvin Zander, eds., *Group Dynamics: Research and Theory* (Evanston, IL: Row, Peterson and Company, 1962), pp. 607–623.

coercive power Controlling others through fear or threat of punishment.

hierarchy. A government agency head, for example, has much more position power than a unit supervisor in the same agency. Managers can enhance their position power by formulating policies and procedures. For example, a manager might establish a requirement that he or she must approve all new hires, thus exercising authority over hiring.

Your appearance can contribute to your personal power.

Expert power is a key source of power.

Coercive power comes from controlling others through fear or threat of punishment. Typical organizational punishments include bypassing an employee for promotion, terminating employment, and giving damaging performance evaluations to people who do not support initiatives, even if the initiatives are unethical or illegal. The threat of a lawsuit by an employee who is treated unjustly serves as a constraint on legitimate power and is referred to as *subordinate power*. Another source of power for employees stems from being a shareholder, such as an employee who owns company stock criticizing the CEO during a shareholder meeting, and being listened to.[10] **Reward power** involves controlling others through rewards or the promise of rewards. Examples of this include promotions, challenging assignments, and recognition given to employees.

The effectiveness of coercive power and reward power depends on the perceptions and needs of group members. For coercive power to be effective, the employee must fear punishment and care about being a member of the firm. Conversely, an employee who does not care much for recognition or power would not be strongly influenced by the prospect of a promotion.

Power Stemming from the Individual (Personal Power)

Managers and other categories of workers also derive power from two separate personal characteristics: knowledge and personality. **Expert power** is the ability to influence others because of one's specialized knowledge, skills, or abilities. For expertise to be an effective source of power, group members must respect that expertise.

Exercising expert power is the logical starting point for building one's power base. Powerful people in business, government, and education almost invariably launched their careers by developing expertise in a specialty of value to their employers. Furthermore, expert power keeps a person in demand for executive positions. A representative example is Hugo Barra, who was the vice president of Android product management at Google Inc. when he left the company for a Chinese smartphone maker, Xiaomi. Barra began at Google after the company bought the voice-recognition company Nuance Communications Inc. Barra launched his career as a software engineer and has been an in-demand manager since early in his career.[11]

Referent power is the ability to influence others that stems from one's desirable traits and characteristics. It is based on the desire of others to

reward power Controlling others through rewards or the promise of rewards.

expert power The ability to influence others because of one's specialized knowledge, skills, or abilities.

referent power The ability to influence others that stems from one's desirable traits and characteristics; it is the basis for charisma.

---

10   Lydia Depillis, "Rank-and-File Workers Have a Lot More Power over Corporations Than They Think," (www.washingtonpost.com), June 13, 2014, pp. 1–5.
11   Paul Mozur and Evelyn M. Rusli, "Google Executive Leaves for Startup," *The Wall Street Journal*, August 30, 2013, p. B3.

resource dependence perspective The need of the organization for a continuing flow of human resources, money, customers, technological inputs, and material to continue to function.

implicit leadership theory An explanation of leadership contending that group members develop prototypes specifying the traits and abilities that characterize an ideal business leader.

be led by or to identify with an inspiring person. Having referent power contributes to a perception of being charismatic, but expert power also makes a contribution. For example, being perceived as highly creative contributes to a person's charisma.

Power from Providing Resources

Another way of understanding the sources of power is through the **resource dependence perspective**. According to this perspective, the organization requires a continuing flow of human resources, money, customers, technological inputs, and material to continue to function. Subunits or individuals within the organization who can provide these resources derive power from this ability.[12]

A variation on power from providing resources is the derivation of power from gossip, which is an important resource in many organizations. Most people know that an influential member of the grapevine can accrue a small degree of power, and a scientific analysis supports this idea. The authors of the analysis define *gossip* as "informal and evaluative talk in an organization, usually among no more than a few individuals, about another member of that organization who is not present."[13] According to the model developed, a supplier of gossip will develop the sources of power already described, such as reward, expert, and coercive power. However, if the person provides mostly negative gossip, his or her referent power will decrease.

Power from Meeting the Expectations of Group Members: Implicit Leadership Theory

Another perspective on leadership power is that a leader can accrue power by behaving and acting in the way group members expect. For example, a team leader who is intelligent and dedicated when team members want an intelligent and dedicated leader will have some power based on meeting these expectations. According to **implicit leadership theory**, group members develop prototypes specifying the traits and abilities that characterize an ideal business leader. People are characterized as true leaders on the basis of the perceived match between their behavior and character and the leader category they have in their minds. Implicit leadership theories (or expectations) are the benchmarks group members use to form an

---

12 Jeffrey Pfeffer, *Managing with Power* (Boston: Harvard Business Review Publications, 1990), pp. 100–101.

13 Nancy B. Kurland and Lisa Hope Pelled, "Passing the Word: Toward a Model of Gossip and Power in the Workplace," *Academy of Management Review*, April 2000, p. 429.

impression of their leader/manager. Group members have both prototypes and antiprototypes (what they want the leader not to be).

In organizational settings, the leadership prototypes (desirable characteristics and traits) are as follows: sensitivity, intelligence, dedication, charisma, strength, and attractiveness. The antiprototypes are tyranny and masculinity (a sexist term for being cold and nonrelationship oriented). A study of 439 employees indicated that the closer the employees perceived their manager's profile to fit the implicit leadership theory they endorsed, the better the quality of the leader–member exchange.[14] It can be inferred that, as a result of these high-quality exchanges, the leader has a little more power.

The Organizational Behavior in Action box describes an executive who has made intelligent use of a variety of types of power.

LEARNING OBJECTIVE 2

Describe the essence of empowerment.

empowerment The process of sharing power with group members, thereby enhancing their feelings of self-efficacy.

Empowerment of Group Members

Distributing power throughout the organization has become a major strategy for improving productivity, quality, satisfaction, and motivation. Employees experience a greater sense of self-efficacy (self-confidence for a particular task) and ownership in their jobs when they share power. **Empowerment** is the process of sharing power with group members, thereby enhancing their feelings of self-efficacy.[15] A few basic points about empowerment are shown in Figure 13.1.

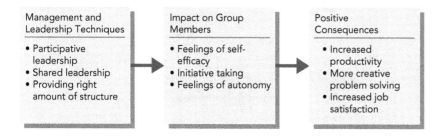

Figure 13.1   The Basics of Empowerment

---

14   Olga Epitropaki and Robin Martin, "Implicit Leadership Theories in Applied Settings: Factor Structure, Generalizability, and Stability Over Time," *Journal of Applied Psychology*, April 2004, pp. 293–310; Epitropaki and Martin, "From Ideal to Real: A Longitudinal Study of the Role of Implicit Leadership Theories on Leader-Member Exchanges and Employee Outcomes," *Journal of Applied Psychology*, July 2005, pp. 659–676.
15   Jay A. Conger and Rabindra N. Kanungo, "The Empowerment Process: Integrating Theory and Practice," *Academy of Management Review*, July 1988, pp. 473–474.

Organizational Behavior in Action

Marillyn Hewson Climbs to Power at Lockheed Martin

In early 2013, Marillyn Hewson, a longtime Lockheed Martin Corp. executive, became the company's chairman and CEO after a 31-year steady climb to the top. Lockheed Martin is the biggest defense company in the history of the world. Hewson became the most powerful person at Lockheed Martin and has been named by both *Forbes* and *Fortune* as one of the 100 most powerful women in business. Hewson's previous position was president, chief operating officer, and executive vice president of the Electronic Systems division. She had held 18 leadership roles since joining Lockheed Martin in 1983 as an engineer, although she was a business administration major. Among these positions were vice president of Global Supply Chain Management and vice president of Corporate Internal Audit.

Hewson combines her knowledge of technology and strategic leadership skills with strong interpersonal skills. When she took over for Robert J. Stevens, the outgoing CEO, he joked with investors, "People seem to like Marillyn more than they like me. She is a genuinely likeable person who understands people and connects with people in this company at an individual level." Another time Stevens said, "Marillyn is an exceptional leader with impeccable credentials She knows our business, our customers, our shareholders, our commitments, and our employees."

A consultant to Lockheed Martin said, "Marillyn will be exactly what Lockheed Martin needed in terms of patching up its relationship with its Pentagon customer. Marillyn manages to combine toughness and knowledge with graciousness and an ability to listen." A Lockheed Martin employee posted, "Great female leader in Marillyn Hewson. She genuinely cares about employees and is very real."

Lockheed Martin has long been led by self-made individuals, with Hewson fitting the pattern. She has gradually risen though the ranks over the years, having succeeded mostly through her self-discipline and determination. Although Hewson has a reputation for being gracious and gregarious, she is an executive ready to make tough choices, such as finding ways to boost earnings per share. Hewson says her management approach is "opportunistic," meaning that her strategy does not change, but her tactics and timing are dictated by market conditions. She is also known to have a deep and unwavering commitment to Lockheed Martin, considered by some analysts to be one of the greatest centers of technological innovation in the world.

Hewson said during an interview with a journalist that she wants to continue to be a role model for women in business. "But I don't think it's necessarily about being a female in our business. I think it's about my track record, my results."

Born in Junction City, Kansas, Hewson received a Bachelor of Science degree in business administration and a Master of Arts degree from the University of Alabama. She also attended executive development programs at Columbia Business School and Harvard Business School.

Questions

1   Which types of power does Hewson display?

2   What career advice might a student of organizational behavior glean from this story?

Source: Original story created from facts and observations in the following sources: Loren Thompson, "Lockheed Martin Chairman & CEO Marillyn Hewson's Vision: Continuous Innovation, Sustained Profitability," *Forbes* (www.forbes.com), August 6, 2014, pp. 1–5; Marjorie Censer, "After Nearly 30 Years with Lockheed, Hewson Is Named Chief Executive," (www. washingtonpost.com), November 13, 2012, pp. 1–6; Doug Cameron and Joann S. Lublin, "Vaulted to Top at Lockheed, and Ready to Navigate 'Cliff," *The Wall Street Journal*, November 12, 2012, pp. B1, B2; "Marillyn A. Hewson: Chairman, President, and Chief Executive Officer Lockheed Martin Corporation" (www.lockheedmartin.com), September 26, 2014; "Lockheed Martin" (www.glassdoor.com), September 5, 2013, p. 1; Andrea Shalai-Esa, "Hewson's Long Lockheed Journey Ends at the Top" (www.reuters.com), November 9, 2012, pp. 1–2.

Participative management or leadership is the general strategy for empowering workers. The techniques of participative management, such as goal setting, modeling, and job enrichment, have been described in previous chapters. The information about empowering teams presented in Chapter 10 is also relevant here. To link empowerment directly to leadership, empowerment can be regarded as shared leadership as opposed to vertical leadership. Such shared leadership is particularly necessary when the work within the group is interdependent, creative, and complex. The typical work of cross-functional teams and virtual teams calls for shared leadership or empowerment.[16]

A study of 35 sales and service virtual teams showed that team empowerment was related to two measures of team performance—process improvement and customer satisfaction. Empowerment was measured by a questionnaire with statements such as, "My team makes its

---

16   Craig L. Pearce, "The Future of Leadership: Combining Vertical and Shared Leadership to Transform Knowledge Work," *Academy of Management Executive*, February 2004, pp. 47–57.

own choices without being told by management." Empowerment was even more effective for the virtual teams with fewer face-to-face meetings, suggesting that the less virtual team members meet with a manager, the more empowerment they need.[17]

g-stockstudio/Shutterstock.com

An empowered group is often productive and satisfied.

To bring about empowerment, managers must remove conditions that keep employees powerless, such as authoritarian supervision or a job over which they have little control. An example of a person in a low-control job would be a manager who cannot shut off interruptions even to prepare budgets or to plan. Employees must also receive information that increases their feelings of self-efficacy. When employees are empowered, they will take the initiative to solve problems and strive hard to reach objectives.

Empowerment may not proceed smoothly unless certain conditions are met. A major consideration is that the potentially empowered workers must be competent and interested in assuming more responsibility. Otherwise the work will not get accomplished. W. Alan Randolph observed 10 companies that made the transition to empowerment.[18] The first key to effective empowerment is *information sharing*. Lacking information, it is difficult for workers to act with responsibility.

Another critical factor for successful empowerment is for management to *provide more structure* as teams move into self-management. To initiate empowerment, managers must teach people new skills and make the parameters clear. Workers need to know, for example, "What are the limits to my empowerment?" The third critical factor is that *teams must gradually replace the traditional organizational hierarchy*. Empowered teams not only make recommendations, they also make and implement decisions and are held accountable. A major contributing factor to

17. Bradley L. Kirkman, Benson Rosen, Paul E. Tesluk, and Cristina B. Gibson, "The Impact of Team Empowerment on Virtual Team Performance: The Moderating Role of Face to Face Interaction, *Academy of Management Journal*, April 2004, pp. 175–192.
18. W. Alan Randolph, "Navigating the Journey to Empowerment," *Organizational Dynamics*, Spring 1995, pp. 19–31.

successful empowerment, found in a study of a large food company, was that teams acted as managers. They hired and fired people, appraised performance, scheduled work, and managed a budget.

Empowerment is also more effective when the empowered individuals and teams are told what needs to be done but are *free to determine how to achieve the objectives*. Allowing people to determine the most efficient and effective work techniques is the essence of empowerment. A final consideration for successful empowerment is implied in the other conditions. *Unless managers trust employees*, empowerment will not be effective or even take place. For example, when employees are trusted, they are more likely to be given the information they need and be granted the freedom to choose an appropriate method.

Meg Whitman, the former eBay CEO who now holds the same position at Hewlett- Packard, is an example of a prominent business leader who believes that sharing power improves organizational effectiveness. She claims, "I don't actually think of myself as powerful" and endorses the statement, "To have power, you must be willing to not have any of it."[19] In practice, this means that Whitman relies on consensus leadership, and believes that the Hewlett-Packard community is the true source of the company's greatness.

Another way of looking at the contribution of empowerment is that, when the leader has too much power, team performance might decline. This conclusion was reached on the basis of a series of three studies conducted with students participating in simulation exercises, including solving a homicide investigation. Team performance was linked to finding the correct solution to the problems. Among the findings was that leaders who felt they had a high degree of power spent more time talking (or verbally dominating) during the team meetings than did leaders who felt they had less power. High-power leadership also was associated with lower levels of open communication in teams, and consequently led to diminished team performance.[20] The take-away from this study for the workplace is that group leaders who feel they have a lot of power might tend to dominate the discussion during meetings and therefore not make good use of talent within the team.

Now that we have described the sources of power and empowerment, we shift focus to more details about political behavior and influence tactics.

Organizational Politics

Our study of organizational politics includes the reasons behind political behavior in the workplace, ethical and unethical tactics, and gender differences in the use of politics. We emphasize again that the effective use of organizational politics can enhance leader effectiveness and the well-being of subordinates. A relatively new concept, **leader political support** points to the

19.   Patricia Sellers, "eBay's Secret," *Fortune*, October 18, 2004, p. 161.
20.   Leigh Plunkett Tost, Francesca Gino, and Richard P. Larrick, "When Power Makes Others Speechless: The Negative Impact of Leader Power on Team Performance," *Academy of Management Journal*, October 2013, pp. 1465–1486.

LEARNING OBJECTIVE 3

Pinpoint factors contributing to, and examples of, organizational politics.

leader political support The concept refers to tactics of organizational politics and influence engaged in by leaders to provide followers with necessary resources to advance individual, group, or organizational objectives.

positive effects just mentioned. The concept refers to tactics of organizational politics and influence engaged in by leaders to provide followers with necessary resources to advance individual, group, or organizational objectives.[21] An information technology manager might build into his or her network a good relationship with the vice president of finance. The goal would be to make the vice president more amenable to funding a project that would develop mobile apps for a wide range of the company's services.

Factors Contributing to Political Behavior

The most fundamental reason for organizational politics is the political nature of organizations. Coalitions of interests and demands arise both within and outside organizations. Similarly, organizations can be viewed as loose structures of interests and demands in competition with one another for attention and resources. The interaction among different coalitions results in an undercurrent of political tactics, such as when one group tries to promote itself and discredit another.

Another contributor to political activity is the pyramid structure of organizations—a reality despite all the emphasis on shared leadership and empowerment. The people at the top of the organization hold most of the power, while people at each successive level down the hierarchy hold less power. The amount of power that can be distributed in a hierarchy is limited. Power-oriented managers sometimes cope with the limited amount of power available by expanding their sphere of influence sideways. For example, the director of the food-stamp program in a government agency might attempt to gain control over the housing assistance program, which is at the same level.

Executive coach Marshall Goldsmith observes what is a major reason for "kissing up" (a form of organizational politics) to people in power. Without meaning to, many managers create an environment in which people learn to reward others with accolades that are not really warranted. People who are kind, courteous, and complimentary toward their managers are most likely to receive the most recognition—assuming their job performance is at least in the acceptable range.[22]

---

21. B. Parker Ellen III, Gerald R. Ferris, and M. Ronald Buckley, "Leader Political Support: Reconsidering Leader Political Behavior," *The Leadership Quarterly*, December 2013, pp. 842–857.
22. Marshall Goldsmith, "All of Us Are Stuck on Suck-Ups," *Fast Company*, December 2003, p. 117.

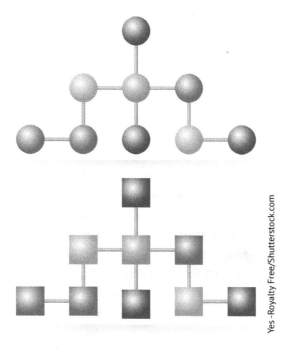

Yes - Royalty Free/Shutterstock.com

A pyramid-shaped organization is a source of organizational politics.

Political behavior by senior management helps establish a climate for such behavior. When C-level executives are highly political, it contributes to a climate of acceptance for organizational politics. One of the most visible aspects of political behavior is favoritism in its many forms. When lower-ranking managers perceive that the practice exists among senior management of placing poorly qualified friends into high-paying positions, the lower-ranking managers are likely to follow suit.

Downsizing and team structures create even less opportunity for climbing the hierarchy, thus intensifying political behavior for the few remaining powerful positions. Worried about layoffs themselves, many workers attempt to discredit others so that the latter would be the first to go. Internal politics generally increase as good jobs, promotions, and bonuses become scarcer. A business columnist made an observation a few years back that continues to be true during economic downturns: "The art of fawning over a boss may be more important now because of the stagnant economy and shortage of well-paying, full-time jobs."[23]

Organizational politics is also fostered by the need for power. Executives have much stronger power needs than others, and thus propel themselves toward frequent episodes of political behavior. Because executives are responsible for controlling resources, their inner desire to do

---

23. Chad Graham and Dawn Sagario, "'Good Fawning' Over Boss Can Help in Tough Times," *The Des Moines Register* syndicated story, April 20, 2003.

Machiavellianism A tendency to manipulate others for personal gain.

LEARNING OBJECTIVE 4

Differentiate between the ethical and unethical use of power, politics, and influence.

so helps them in their jobs. A personalized power need is more likely to trigger political behavior than a socialized power need.

Finally, a devious reason for the existence of politicking is **Machiavellianism**, a tendency to manipulate others for personal gain. (Niccolo Machiavelli was a 15th-century political philosopher whose book, *The Prince*, describes how leaders may acquire and maintain power by placing expediency above morality.) One analysis suggests that many ambitious and successful corporate executives have strong Machiavellian tendencies, such as acquiring other companies just to give the appearance of true corporate growth.[24]

To make effective use of organizational politics, managerial workers must be aware of specific political strategies and tactics. To identify and explain the majority of political behaviors would require years of study and observation. Managers so frequently need support for their programs that they search for innovative political maneuvers. Furthermore, new tactics continue to emerge as the workplace becomes increasingly competitive.

Self-Assessment 13-1 gives you an opportunity to think through your tendencies to engage in organizational politics. In the two following sections we describe mostly ethical, followed by unethical, political tactics.

Mostly Ethical and Positive Political Tactics

Here we describe political tactics that many people would consider to be ethical and positive. Nevertheless, some managers and management scholars regard all political tactics as being ethically tainted. The relevance of being able to use political tactics effectively was demonstrated in a study of 408 leaders (headmasters) and 1,429 subordinates (teachers) of state schools in Germany. Political skill was measured by a standard measure somewhat similar to Self-Assessment 13-1, and effectiveness was measured by teachers' evaluations of the headmasters. The study showed that politically skilled leaders were able to attain effectiveness through both transformational and transactional behaviors.[25]

1 *Develop power contacts through networking.* A fundamental principle of success is to identify powerful people and then establish alliances with them. Cultivating friendly, cooperative relationships with powerful organizational members and outsiders can make the managerial worker's cause much easier to advance.

---

24. Stanley Bing, *What Would Machiavelli Do?* (New York: HarperCollins, 2000).

25. Ewen et al., "Further Specification of the Leader Political Skill-Leadership Effectiveness Relationships: Transformational and Transactional Leader Behaviors as Moderators," pp. 516–533.

Self-Assessment 13-1

The Positive Organizational Politics Questionnaire

Answer each question "mostly agree" or "mostly disagree," even if it is difficult for you to decide which alternative best describes your opinion.

	MOSTLY AGREE	MOSTLY DISAGREE
1. Pleasing my boss is a major goal of mine.	___	___
2. I go out of my way to flatter important people.	___	___
3. I am most likely to do favors for people who can help me in return.	___	___
4. Given the opportunity, I would cultivate friendships with powerful people.	___	___
5. I will compliment a coworker even if I have to think hard about what might be praiseworthy.	___	___
6. If I thought my boss needed the help, and I had the expertise, I would show him or her how to use an electronic gadget for personal life.	___	___
7. I laugh heartily at my boss's humor, so long as I think he or she is at least a little funny.	___	___
8. I would not be too concerned about following a company dress code, so long as I looked neat.	___	___
9. If a customer sent me a compliment through e-mail, I would forward a copy to my boss and another influential person.	___	___
10. I smile only at people in the workplace whom I genuinely like.	___	___
11. An effective way to impress people is to tell them what they want to hear.	___	___
12. I would never publicly correct mistakes made by the boss.	___	___
13. I would be willing to use my personal contacts to gain a promotion or desirable transfer.	___	___
14. I think it is a good idea to send a congratulatory note to someone in the company who receives a promotion to an executive position.	___	___
15. I think "office politics" is only for losers.	___	___

Scoring and Interpretation: Give yourself a plus 1 for each answer that agrees with the keyed answer. Each question that receives a score of plus 1 shows a tendency toward playing positive organizational politics. The scoring key is as follows:

1	Mostly agree	9	Mostly agree
2	Mostly agree	10	Mostly disagree
3	Mostly agree	11	Mostly agree
4	Mostly agree	12	Mostly agree
5	Mostly agree	13	Mostly agree
6	Mostly agree	14	Mostly agree
7	Mostly agree	15	Mostly disagree
8	Mostly disagree		

1–6, Below-average tendency to play office politics

7–11, Average tendency to play office politics

12 and above, Above-average tendency to play office politics; strong need for power

Thinking about your political tendencies in the workplace is important for your career because most successful leaders are moderately political. The ability to use politics effectively and ethically increases with importance in the executive suite. Most top players are effective office politicians. Yet being overly and blatantly political can lead to distrust, thereby damaging your career.

These contacts can support a person's ideas and recommend him or her for promotions and visible temporary assignments. A challenge in the era of electronic communications is that face time, or in-person contact, is helpful for building contacts. It is important to converse with powerful people in person in addition to sending them electronic messages. Although still electronic, an occasional telephone call is a useful supplement to e-mail or text messages for purposes of building a network.

2   *Manage your impression.* You will recall that charismatic leaders rely heavily on impression management, and the same technique is important for other success-oriented people. An example of an ethical impression-management tactic would be to contribute outstanding performance and then make sure key people know of your accomplishments. Making others aware of what you accomplish is often referred to as *achieving visibility.* When tactics of impression management appear insincere, they are likely to create a negative impression and thus be self-defeating. A key person to impress is your immediate superior. Many firms send professionals to etiquette training because

displaying proper etiquette makes a positive impression on customers and clients.[26]

3   *Make your boss look good.* A bedrock principle of organizational politics is to help your boss perform well, which is one of the reasons you probably were hired. Positioning yourself as a supporting player for your boss will help your performance evaluation and therefore your career. Consultant Karl Bimshas suggests that a good starting point is to ask questions of this nature: "What do you think should be my highest priority right now?" Then turn in a good performance with respect to the priority.[27]

Managing your impression is a necessary political tactic.

4   *Keep informed.* In addition to controlling vital information, it is politically important to keep informed. Successful managers and professionals develop a pipeline to help them keep abreast, or even ahead, of developments within the firm. For example, a politically astute individual might befriend a major executive's assistant.

5   *Be courteous, pleasant, and positive.* Courteous, pleasant, and positive people are the first to be hired and the last to be fired (assuming they are also technically qualified).[28] A key part of being courteous, pleasant, and positive is to socialize with coworkers, including having meals and drinks with them. Executive coach Leslie Williams observes: "Socialization has everything to do with influence. It's not enough to just be good at your job." In addition to doing a good job, you have to be somebody that people know and know well enough to trust.[29]

6   *Ask satisfied customers to contact your manager.* A favorable comment by a customer receives considerable weight because customer satisfaction is a top corporate priority. If a customer says something nice, the comment will carry more weight than one from a coworker or subordinate. The reason is that insiders might praise you for political reasons, whereas a customer's motivation is thought to be pure.

26. Susan Ricker, "Manners Make for Good Business," CareerBuilder.com, April 13, 2014, p. 1; "Etiquette for the Young—with Bite," *The Associated Press*, June 8, 2002.

27. Cited in Susan Ricker, "Make Your Boss, Yourself Look Good," CareerBuilder.com, October 26, 2014, p. 1.

28. "'Career Insurance' Protects DP Professionals from Setbacks, Encourages Growth," *Data Management*, June 1986, p. 33. The same principle is equally valid today.

29. Quoted in Amy Joyce, "Schmoozing on the Job Pays Dividends," *The Washington Post*, November 13, 2005.

Organizational Behavior Checklist

A Sampling of Political Blunders and Gaffes to Avoid in the Workplace

Insert a checkmark for each of the following blunders and gaffes you have committed in the past, or are likely to commit in the future.

1. I have criticized my manager or a colleague in an in-person meeting.

2. I have posted a negative comment about company management or the company on social media.

3. I make racist, sexist, or ethnically offensive jokes on the job.

4. When I do not agree with an idea or policy, I will say or write, "It sucks."

5. During a major election, I place campaign banners for my favorite candidate outside my cubicle, office, or table workspace.

6. I have done unfavorable imitations of my boss to humor coworkers.

7. If we have a visitor from another country, I do imitations of that person's speech once he or she leaves.

8. I brag about using a competitor's products or services.

9. I openly claim in talk or on social media about how much my organization overpays the top executive.

10. I am quick to criticize a person's clothing, grooming, or hairstyle if I think it is awful.

Scoring and Interpretation: The closer you are to having checked none or 1 of the 10 blunders, the more skilled you are at organizational politics. If you checked all 10, it is time to study the classic book by Dale Carnegie, *How to Win Friends and Influence People*.

7 *Avoid political blunders.* A strategy for retaining power is to refrain from making power-eroding blunders. Committing these politically insensitive acts can also prevent you from attaining power. Leading blunders include: strong criticism of a superior in a public forum; going around your manager with a complaint; and making a negative social media post about your employer. Another blunder is burning your bridges by creating ill will with former employees. The Organizational Behavior Checklist will serve as a reminder of the types of political blunders (gaffes) to avoid in order to preserve a positive image.

8 *Sincere flattery.* A powerful tactic for ingratiating yourself to others is to flatter them honestly and sincerely. Although one meaning of the term *flattery* is insincere praise, another meaning refers to a legitimate compliment. Charismatic people use flattery regularly. Skill-Development Exercise 13-1 will help you develop flattery skills.

Political skill can be developed through careful observation and experience, coupled with improving one's emotional intelligence. Research with 260 business graduate students showed that mentoring can be an effective way of developing political skill. Ninety percent of the students were employed, and those who had a mentor or mentors responded to a questionnaire about the quality of their mentoring. Results indicated that participants who had a mentor showed significantly better political skill than participants who did not have a mentor.[30]

Mostly Unethical and Negative Political Tactics

In this section we describe tactics of organizational politics that most people would consider to be unethical and negative. The majority of people who use these tactics would not admit to their use.

1 *Backstabbing.* The ubiquitous backstab requires that you pretend to be nice but all the while plan someone's demise. A frequent form of backstabbing is to inform your rival's immediate superior that he or she is faltering under the pressure of job responsibilities. The recommended approach to dealing with a backstabber is to confront the person directly, ask for an explanation of his or her behavior, and demand that he or she stop. Threaten to complain to the person's superior.[31]

2 *Embrace-or-demolish.* The ancient strategy of embrace-or-demolish suggests that you remove from the premises rivals who suffered past hurts through your efforts. (The same tactic is called "take no prisoners.") Otherwise the wounded rivals might retaliate at a vulnerable moment. An illustration of embrace-or-demolish is when, after a hostile takeover, many executives lose their jobs because they opposed the takeover.

---

30 Suzzette M. Chopin, Steven J. Danish, Anson Seers, and Joshua N. Hook, "Effects of Mentoring on the Development of Leadership Self-Efficacy and Political Skill," *Journal of Leadership Studies*, Issue 3, 2013, pp. 17–32.

31. "Face Cowardly Backstabbers in the Workplace," *Knight Ridder* story, February 13, 2000.

territorial games Also known as *turf wars*, territorial games refer to behaviors involving the hoarding of information and other resources.

3   *Stealing credit.* For many workers, the most detestable form of office politics is for their boss, or other worker, to take credit for their ideas without acknowledging the source of the idea. Paul Lapides estimates that up to 80 percent of workers suffer this indignity at some time in their careers. The credit stealing breeds distrust, damages motivation, and is sometimes misperceived as a perk of power.[32] A good starting point in stopping idea thieves is to hold a one-on-one session with the thief, and confront the issue. If the issue is not resolved, tell key decision makers about the idea theft.[33]

4   *Territorial games.* Also referred to as *turf wars*, **territorial games** involve protecting and hoarding resources that give a person power, such as information, relationships, and decision-making authority. The purpose of territorial games is to compete for three kinds of territory in the modern corporate survival game: information, relationships, and authority. A relationship is "hoarded" in such ways as not encouraging others to visit a key customer, or blocking a higher performer from getting a promotion or transfer by informing other managers that he or she is mediocre.[34] Other examples of territorial games include monopolizing time with clients, scheduling meetings so someone cannot attend, and shutting out coworkers on an important assignment.

5   *Good-mouthing an incompetent to make him or her transferable.* A long-entrenched devious political maneuver in large firms is for a manager to give outstanding performance evaluations to an incompetent worker or troublemaker within the group. By good-mouthing the undesired worker, he or she becomes more marketable within the company. Although this technique can sometimes work, most experienced human resource professionals are aware of this tactic. An HR director noted, "We look for a certain pattern when a manager is puffing up a worker for transfer. Typically the problem worker received low evaluations for a long time, then starts getting outstanding evaluations. When

32.   Jared Sandberg, "Some Bosses Never Meet a Success That Isn't Theirs," *The Wall Street Journal*, April 23, 2003, p. B1.

33.   "Stopping Idea Thieves: Strike Back When Rivals Steal Credit," *Executive LeadershipExtra!*, April 2003, p. 3.

34.   Annette Simmons, *Territorial Games: Understanding & Ending Turf Wars at Work* (New York: AMACOM, 1998).

Skill-Development Exercise 13-1

A Short Course in Effective Flattery

Flattering others is an effective way of building personal relationships (or engaging in organizational politics), if done properly. Suggestions for effective flattery are presented here. *Flattery* here refers to pleasing others through complimentary remarks or attention; we are not referring to *flattery* in the sense of giving insincere or excessive compliments. To build your skills in flattering others, practice these suggestions as the opportunity presents itself. Rehearse your flattery approaches until they feel natural. If your first attempt at flattery does not work well, analyze what went wrong the best you can.

- *Use sensible flattery.* Effective flattery has at least a spoonful of credibility, implying that you say something positive about the target person that is quite plausible. Credibility is also increased when you point to a person's tangible accomplishment. Technical people in particular expect flattery to be specific and aimed at genuine accomplishment.

- *Compliment what is of major importance to the flattery target.* You might find out what is important to the person by observing what he or she talks about with the most enthusiasm.

- *Flatter others by listening intently.* Listening intently to another person is a powerful form of flattery. Use active listening (see Chapter 8) for best results.

- *Flatter by referring to or quoting the other person.* By referring to or quoting (including paraphrasing) another person, you are paying that person a substantial compliment.

- *Use confirmation behaviors.* Use behaviors that have a positive or therapeutic effect on other people, such as praise and courtesy. Because confirmation behaviors have such a positive effect on others, they are likely to be perceived as a form of flattery.

- *Give positive feedback.* A mild form of flattering others is to give them positive feedback about their statements, actions, and results. The type of feedback referred to here is a straightforward and specific declaration of what the person did right.

- *Remember names.* Remembering the names of people with whom you have infrequent contact makes them feel important. To help remember the person's name, study the name carefully when you first hear it and repeat it immediately.

- *Explain the impact on you.* Tell the person how his or her actions or behavior positively affect you. An example: "I tried your suggestion about avoiding multitasking on important tasks, and my error rate has gone down dramatically."

- *Avoid flattery that has a built-in insult or barb.* The positive effect of flattery is eradicated when it is accompanied by a hurtful comment, such as "You have good people skills for an engineer" or "You look good. I bet you were really beautiful when you were younger."

To build your skills in flattering others, you must try some of the previous techniques. For starters, within the next few days flatter a classmate, coworker, boss, or friend for something laudable the person accomplished. Or, flatter a customer-contact worker for a service well delivered. Observe carefully the results of your flattery.

Sources: Andrew J. DuBrin, *Political Behavior in Organizations* (Thousand Oaks, CA: Sage, 2009), p. 105; Karen Judson, "The Fine Art of Flattery," *Kiwanis*, March 1998, pp. 34–36, 43; Elizabeth Bernstein, "Why Do Compliments Cause So Much Grief?" *The Wall Street Journal*, May 4, 2010, pp. D, D6; DuBrin, "Self-Perceived Technical Orientation and Attitudes toward Being Flattered," *Psychological Reports, 96* (2005), pp. 852–854.

this happens, we really grill the manager about the worker who has been offered for transfer."

6 *Placing a weak manager under you to help secure your position.* A negative political tactic practiced mostly in the executive suite is for a high-level manager to recruit a lame person to a managerial position reporting to him or her. The lame person is valued because he or she is unlikely to become a candidate as a successor to the first executive—who would not have pulled this stunt if he or she were highly competent and secure. As a financial executive describes the situation, "Normally a boob has a boob for a boss."[35]

E-mail, including instant messaging and text messaging, has become a major vehicle for conducting both ethical and unethical organizational politics. To help manage their impressions, many people distribute e-mails regarding their positive contribution to a project to many key people. E-networking is a convenient way to maintain minimum contact with many people, until the in-person meeting can be arranged. People flatter their target person via e-mail, and send copies to key people. On the downside, some people reprimand others by e-mail and let others know of the target's mistakes. Sometimes managers who are haggling with each other

35. Quoted in Jared Sandberg, "When Affixing Blame for Inept Managers, Go Over Their Heads," *The Wall Street Journal*, April 20, 2005, p. B1.

will send a copy to a common boss, hoping that the boss will intervene in the dispute.[36] A productivity problem with so many people being copied for political purposes is that in-boxes can become overloaded.

Gender Differences in Political Skill

A major message from this section of the chapter is that positive political skills are necessary to succeed in the workplace. Pamela L. Perrewé and Debra L. Nelson argue that, because of barriers hampering their success such as job discrimination, women need to develop even greater political astuteness than men. (Less job discrimination against women appears to exist today, as indicated by so many women holding key positions in major organizations in business, government, and the nonprofit sector.) Political skills will not only enhance the performance of women but will also decrease stress and increase well-being. For example, if a woman fails to network with men in power, she will experience job stress and lower well-being as a result of being excluded from consideration for a promotion or important work assignment.

Perrewé and Nelson contend that women are more reluctant than men to use politics because they are less politically skilled than men, may not see the relevance of politics, and often find politics distasteful. Instead, women are more likely to rely on merit and traditional values to advance their careers. Women tend to be excluded from the inside power group in organizations, so they do not know the informal rules for getting ahead. The authors propose that women in organizations obtain the right coaching and mentoring to obtain the political skills they need to level the playing field in competing with men.[37]

The argument that there are great gender differences in political skill can be challenged. Women leaders are often cited as being more effective at relationship building than are men, and relationship building is a primary political skill. Furthermore, the number of businesswomen playing golf has surged, and golf is important because of its networking potential. Women also tend to score as high as men on the traits within the implicit leadership theory described previously. An example of support for this argument comes from a study conducted by the research firm Caliper. The researchers administered personality tests and conducted interviews with 59 women leaders in 19 different business sectors from major companies in the United Kingdom and the United States. Among the findings were that (a) women leaders are more persuasive than their male counterparts, and (b) women leaders have an inclusive, team-building style of problem solving and decision making. These results suggest strongly that women leaders have good political skills.[38] (Of course, these highly placed women may not be a representative sample of women in organizations.)

---

36. Jeffrey Zaslow, "The Politics of the 'CC' Line," *The Wall Street Journal*, May 28, 2003, p. D2.

37. Pamela L. Perrewé and Debra L. Nelson, "Gender and Career Success: The Facilitative Role of Political Skill," *Organizational Dynamics, 4* (2004), p. 366.

38. "Women Leaders Study: The Qualities That Distinguish Women Leaders" (www.calipercorp.com/womenstudy/index. shtml).

LEARNING OBJECTIVE 5

Identify and describe a variety of influence tactics.

Fresh insights into gender differences in political skill come from a study of participants in a leadership seminar who rated themselves on political skills. They were also rated by managers, direct reports, peers, and clients or customers on 13 skillsets related to organizational politics, such as "knows the corporate buzz," "enhances power image," "essential networking," and "ethical lobbying." With respect to "savvy attitudes," females were rated higher by all four rater groups than they rated themselves. Women tended to be rated slightly higher than men in "essential networking." However, two conclusions drawn by the study were that (a) there were no gender differences in self-perceptions of political skill, and (b) few gender differences exist in the level of organizational political skill as perceived by others.[39]

Organizational Influence Tactics

In addition to using power and political tactics to win people over to their way of thinking, managerial workers use a variety of influence tactics. Extensive research has been conducted on social influence tactics aimed at upward, horizontal, and downward relations.[40] The person doing the influencing chooses which tactic seems most appropriate for a given situation. Nine of the most frequently used influence tactics are described here.

1   *Leading by example* means that the manager influences group members by serving as a positive model of desirable behavior. A manager who leads by example shows consistency between actions and words. For example, suppose a firm has a strict policy on punctuality. The manager explains the policy and is always punctual. The manager's words and actions provide a consistent model. Leading by example is also considered quite useful as a way of encouraging ethical behavior.

2   *Assertiveness* refers to being forthright in making demands without violating the rights of others. It involves a person expressing what he or she wants done and how he or she feels about it. A

39. Thomas S. Westbrook, James R. Veale, and Roger E. Karnes, "Multirater and Gender Differences in the Measurement of Political Skill In Organizations," *Journal of Leadership Studies*, Number 1, 2013, pp. 6–17.

40. Several of the tactics are from Gary Yukl and Cecilia M. Falbe, "Influence Tactics and Objectives in Upward, Downward, and Lateral Influence Attempts," *Journal of Applied Psychology*, April 1990, pp. 132–140. Part of the definitions of assertiveness and ingratiation stem from Perrewé and Nelson, "Gender and Career Success," pp. 372–373.

manager might say, for example, "Your report is late, and that makes me angry. I want you to get it done by noon tomorrow." Assertiveness, as this example shows, also refers to making orders clear.

3 *Rationality* means appealing to reason and logic. Strong managers and leaders frequently use this influence tactic. Pointing out the facts of a situation to group members to get them to do something exemplifies rationality. Intelligent people respond the best to rational appeals.

4 *Ingratiation* refers to getting someone else to like you, often through the use of flattery and doing favors. A typical ingratiating tactic would be to act in a friendly manner just before making a demand. Effective managerial workers treat people well consistently to get cooperation when it is needed. Ingratiation, or simply being likable, is an effective way of gaining the cooperation of others. A study of 133 managers found that, if an auditor is likable and gives a well-organized argument, managers tend to comply with his or her suggestions even when they disagree and the auditor has insufficient supporting evidence.[41]

A theoretical analysis of the subject concluded that humor is an effective type of ingratiatory behavior. One reason humor leads to ingratiation is because it makes the person with the sense of humor more attractive to the target. Humor may also be seen as more acceptable than an ingratiation tactic such as doing a favor for another person.[42]

5 *Projecting warmth before emphasizing competence* is a major workplace influence tactic. Considerable research about human behavior indicates that, by first focusing on displaying warmth and then blending in shows of competence, leaders will be more influential. For example, before presenting facts about the value of using cloud technology, the leader might smile and wave gently. Two specific ways of being perceived as warm are (a) to speak with lower pitch and volume, as if comforting a friend, and (b) to express agreement with something the influence target says.[43] (Projecting warmth might be classified as an ingratiating tactic.)

6 *Exchange* is a method of influencing others by offering to reciprocate if they meet your demands. When asking favors in a busy workplace, it is best to specify the amount of time the task will take, such as by saying "I will need 10 minutes of your time sometime between now and next Wednesday." Be aware of what skills or capabilities you have that you can barter with others. Perhaps you are good at removing a computer virus

41. Research reported in Sue Shellenbarger, "Why Likability Matters More Than Ever at Work," *The Wall Street Journal*, March 26, 2014, p. D3.

42. Cecily D. Cooper, "Just Joking Around? Employee Humor Expression as Ingratiatory Behavior," *Academy of Management Review*, October 2005, pp. 765–776.

43. Amy J. C. Cuddy, Matthew Kohut, and John Neffinger, "Connect, Then Lead: To Exert Influence, You Must Balance Competence with Warmth," *Harvard Business Review*, July–August 2013, pp. 54–61.

Skill-Development Exercise 13-2

High-Quality Exchanges with Coworkers

Groups of about six people get together to simulate an ongoing work team.

A suggestion would be to visualize the group as a product-development team at General Motors (GM) to develop a product (that is not a vehicle). Imagine that top-level management is applying heavy pressure on the product-development team to arrive at an innovative idea today. (If you dislike the GM scenario, invent another group problem.) At the same time, your group believes strongly that high-quality exchanges will help you accomplish your task. As you discuss your potential innovative ideas, engage in high-quality exchanges (including flattery) without going to the extreme of being a sickening office politician.

After you have completed the group role-playing, hold a debriefing session in which you analyze what were some of the best high-quality exchanges among group members. Also, make any observations you can about how the high-quality exchanges affected group creativity.

or explaining the tax code. You can then offer to perform these tasks in exchange for favors granted to you. Skill-Development Exercise 13-2 will help you personalize the use of exchange as an influence tactic.

7   *Inspirational appeal and emotional display* is an influence method centering on the affective (as opposed to the cognitive) domain. Given that leaders are supposed to inspire others, such an influence tactic is important. As Jeffrey Pfeffer observes, "Executives and others seeking to exercise influence in organizations often develop skill in displaying, or not displaying, their feelings in a strategic fashion."[44] An inspirational appeal usually involves an emotional display by the person seeking to influence. It also involves appealing to group members' emotions.

8   *Joking and kidding*, according to one survey, are widely used to influence others on the job.[45] Good-natured ribbing is especially effective when a straightforward statement might be interpreted as harsh criticism. A manager concerned about the number of errors in a group member's report might say, "Now I know what you are up to. You planted all those errors just to see if I really read your reports."

44. Pfeffer, *Managing with Power*, p. 224.

45. Andrew J. DuBrin, "Sex Differences in the Use and Effectiveness of Tactics of Impression Management," *Psychological Reports*, 74 (1994), pp. 531–544.

9   *Strategic sexual performance* has recently been recognized by a group of scholars as a positive influence tactic if used properly. The authors of the research refer to sexuality outside the realm of disruptive behavior such as an office romance or sexual harassment. They define *strategic sexual performance* as "behavior that is imbued with sexual intent, content, or meaning by its performers, observers, or both, and that is intended to influence a target person or persons in some way." Such a behavior would include lightly touching an influence target to capture his or her attention about a work-related suggestion, or simply winking. Other examples include smiling, giving long gazes or intense eye contact, and compliments about the target's physical features. An everyday example would be for a restaurant server to wear provocative clothing in order to receive higher tips.[46] (The strategic use of sexual performance can also be framed as ingratiation.)

vgstudio/Shutterstock.com

Warmth and friendliness are important sources of influence.

Which influence tactic should you choose? Managers are unlikely to use all the influence tactics in a given situation. Instead, they tend to choose an influence tactic that fits the demands of the circumstance. The outcome of a specific influence attempt is also determined by factors such as the target's motivation and organizational culture. For example, strategic sexual performance is likely to be more acceptable in a restaurant or manufacturing plant than in a research laboratory. Also, any influence tactic can trigger target resistance if it is inappropriate for the situation or is applied unskillfully. Tact, diplomacy, and insight are required for effective application of influence (and political) tactics.

---

46. Marla Baskerville Watkins, Alexis Nicole Smith, and Karl Aquino, "The Use and Consequences of Strategic Sexual Performances," *Academy of Management Perspective*, August 2013, pp. 173–186.

LEARNING OBJECTIVE 6

Explain how managers can control dysfunctional politics.

The Control of Dysfunctional Politics and Ethical Considerations

Carried to excess, organizational politics and influence tactics can hurt an organization and its members. One consequence is that when political factors far outweigh merit, competent employees may become unhappy and quit. Another problem is that politicking takes time away from tasks that could contribute directly to achieving the firm's goals. Many managers spend more time developing political allies (including "kissing up") than coaching group members or doing analytical work.

The most comprehensive antidote to improper, excessive, and unethical organizational politics is to rely on objective measures of performance. This is true because people have less need to behave politically when their contributions can be measured directly. With a formal system of goal setting and review, the results a person attains should be much more important than the impression the person creates. However, even a goal-setting program is not immune to politics. Sometimes the goals are designed to impress key people in the organization. As such, they may not be the most important goals for getting work accomplished. Another political problem with goal setting is that some people will set relatively easy goals so they can look good by attaining all their goals.

Meshing individual and organizational objectives would be the ideal method of controlling excessive, negative political behavior. If their objectives, needs, and interests can be met through their jobs, employees will tend to engage in behavior that fosters the growth, longevity, and productivity of the firm. L. A. Witt investigated how goal congruence between the individual and the organization affected political behavior. When employees perceived considerable politics in the workplace, their commitment to the organization and job performance both suffered. However, when employees and their superiors shared the same goals, commitment and performance were less negatively affected by politics. Witt concluded that one way to reduce the negative impact of organizational politics is for the manager to ensure that his or her subordinates hold the appropriate goal priorities. In this way, group members will have a greater sense of control over, and understanding of, the workplace and thus be less affected by the presence of organizational politics.[47]

---

47. L. A. Witt, "Enhancing Organizational Goal Congruence: A Solution to Organizational Politics," *Journal of Applied Psychology*, August 1998, pp. 666–674.

Finally, open communication can also constrain the impact of political behavior. For instance, open communication can let everyone know the basis for allocating resources, thus reducing the amount of politicking. Organizational politics can also be curtailed by threatening to discuss questionable information in a public forum. If one employee engages in backstabbing of another, the manager might ask her or him to repeat the anecdote in a staff meeting. It has been said that sunlight is the best disinfectant to deviousness.

Our discussion of sources of power, political tactics, and influence tactics should not imply an endorsement of all of these methods to gain an advantage in the workplace. Each strategy and tactic must be evaluated on its merit by an ethical test, such as those described in Chapter 4. One guiding principle is to turn the strategy or tactic inward. Assume that you believe that a particular tactic (e.g., ingratiation) would be ethical in working against you. It would then be fair and ethical for you to use this tactic in attempting to influence others.

Another guiding principle is that it is generally ethical to use power and influence to help attain organizational goals. In contrast, it is generally unethical to use the same tactics to achieve a personal agenda and goals not sanctioned by the organization. Yet even this guideline involves enough "grayness" to be open for interpretation. Skill-Development Exercise 13-3 provides an opportunity to evaluate the ethics of behavior.

Recognize also that both the means and the ends of political behavior must be considered. A study of the subject cautioned, "Instead of determining whether human rights or standards of justice are violated, we are often content to judge political behavior according to its outcomes."[48] The authors of the study suggest that when it comes to the ethics of organizational politics, respect for justice and human rights should prevail for its own sake.

Implications for Managerial Practice

1   Recognize that a significant portion of the efforts of organizational members will be directed toward gaining power for themselves or their group. At times, some of this behavior will be directed more toward self-interest than organizational interest. It is therefore often necessary to ask, "Is this action being taken to help this person or is it being done to help the organization?" Your answer to this question should influence your willingness to submit to that person's demands.

2   If you want to establish a power base for yourself, a good starting point is to develop expert power. Most powerful people began their climb to power by demonstrating their expertise in a particular area, such as being outstanding in sales or a niche within information technology. (This tactic is referred to as becoming a subject-matter expert.)

---

48. Gerald F. Cavanagh, Dennis J. Moberg, and Manuel Velasquez, "The Ethics of Organizational Politics," *Academy of Management Review*, July 1981, p. 372.

Skill-Development Exercise 13-3

The Ethics of Influence Tactics

You decide if the following manager made ethical use of influence tactics.

Sara is a marketing manager for a finance company that lends money to companies as well as individuals. She comes up with the idea of forming a division in the company that would collect delinquent student loans, strictly on commission. Her company would retain about one-third of the money collected. The clients would be banks having difficulty collecting loans after students graduate. Sara brings her idea to the CEO, and he grants her the opportunity to make a presentation about the new idea to top management within 1 month. The CEO states that he sees some merit in the idea, but that the opinion of the rest of the committee will be given considerable weight.

With 29 days to go before the meeting, Sara invites all five members of the executive committee to join her for lunch or breakfast individually. All five finally agree on a date for the lunch or breakfast meeting. During the meals, Sara makes a strong pitch for her idea, and explains that she will need the person's support to sell the idea to the rest of the committee. She also promises, "If you can help me get this collection division launched, you will have one big IOU to cash." Sara stays in touch with the CEO about the upcoming meeting, but does not mention her "preselling" lunches.

During the new-initiative review meeting, the five members of the committee support Sara's idea, and the CEO says that he is encouraged and will now warmly consider the idea of a student loan collection division.

Questions

1   Was Sara behaving ethically?

2   Which influence tactic did she use in attempting to achieve her goals?

3   In determining if a particular behavior is motivated by political or merit considerations, evaluate the intent of the actor. The same action might be based on self-interest or concern for others. For instance, a team member might praise you because he believed that you accomplished something of merit. On the other hand, that same individual might praise you to attain a favorable work assignment or salary increase.

Summary of Key Points

1   *Identify sources of power for individuals and subunits within organizations.* Power, politics, and influence are needed by managers to accomplish their work. In the model presented here, managers and professionals use organizational politics to achieve power and influence, thus attaining desired outcomes.

Socialized power is used to forward organizational interests, whereas personalized power is used to forward personal interests. Power granted by the organization consists of legitimate power, coercive power, and reward power. Power stemming from the individual consists of expert power and referent power (the basis for charisma). According to the resource dependence perspective, subunits or individuals who can provide key resources to the organization accrue power. At times, gossip can be a power-giving source. Power can also be derived from meeting the group members' expectations of how a leader should behave (implicit leadership theory).

2   *Describe the essence of empowerment.* Managers must act in specific ways to empower employees, including removing conditions that keep employees powerless and giving information that enhances employee feelings of self-efficacy. Five critical conditions for empowerment are for an organization to share information with employees, provide them with structure, use teams to replace the traditional hierarchy, grant employees the freedom to determine how to achieve objectives, and trust employees. When the leader has too much power, team performance might decline.

3   *Pinpoint factors contributing to, and examples of, organizational politics.* Contributors to organizational politics include the political nature of organizations, the pyramid structure of organizations, encouragement of unwarranted accolades from subordinates, political behavior by senior management, less opportunity for vertical advancement, the need for power, and Machiavellianism.

Among the ethical tactics of organizational politics are: developing power contacts; managing your impression; making your boss look good; keeping informed; being courteous, pleasant, and positive; asking satisfied customers to contact your manager; avoiding political blunders; and using sincere flattery. Among the unethical tactics are: backstabbing, embracing-or-demolishing, stealing credit, playing territorial games, good-mouthing incompetents, and choosing a weak manager as an underling.

According to one analysis, women need to develop greater political skills because of barriers hampering their success. However, it can be argued that many women have exceptional political skills, such as relationship building. Recent research suggests that few gender differences exist in the area of political skill.

4   *Differentiate between the ethical and unethical use of power, politics, and influence.* Political behaviors chosen by an individual or organizational unit must rest on ethical

considerations. A guiding principle is to use only those tactics you would consider fair and ethical if used against you. Also recognize that both the means and the ends of political behavior must be considered.

5   *Identify and describe a variety of influence tactics.* Influence tactics frequently used by managerial workers include: leadership by example; assertiveness; rationality; ingratiation; projecting warmth; exchange; inspirational appeal and emotional display; the use of joking and kidding; and strategic sexual performance.

6   *Explain how managers can control dysfunctional politics.* Approaches to controlling dysfunctional politics include relying on objective performance measures, meshing individual and organizational objectives, minimizing political behavior by top management, and implementing open communication, including threatening to discuss politicking publicly.

Key Terms and Phrases

power, p. 230
organizational politics, p. 230
political skill, p. 230
socialized power, p. 231
personalized power, p. 231
legitimate power, p. 231
coercive power, p. 232
reward power, p. 233

expert power, p. 233
referent power, p. 233
resource dependence perspective, p. 234
implicit leadership theory, p. 234
empowerment, p. 235
leader political support, p. 240
Machiavellianism, p. 242
territorial games, p. 248

Discussion Questions and Activities

1   What differences do you see between being skilled at organizational politics and simply being nice to people?

2   A CEO was observed as dropping the "g" in present participles, such as saying "thinkin'" for "thinking" when visiting different employee groups around the country. Why might such behavior be considered an act of organizational politics?

3   What might be the negative consequences to a manager if he or she ignored power, politics, and influence tactics?

4 How might having a lot of power help a person achieve ethical ends within an organization?

5 What type of power might a worker acquire to help prevent his or her job being outsourced?

6 Why does empowering workers often motivate them to work harder?

7 Job hunters are advised to "size up the political climate" before accepting a job at a company. How might the candidate go about sizing up the political climate?

8 Provide an example of a political blunder or gaffe made by a person in any type of high-level position. Explain why you classify the statement as a blunder or gaffe.

9 What do you think of the ethics of using "strategic sexual performance" to influence others on the job?

10 What can you do today to start increasing your power? Compare your observations with those of your classmates.

Case Problem: Kyle Wants to Gain an Edge

Kyle is an operations manager at Mercury Printers, a manufacturer of commercial printers for both traditional and digital printing. Customers include direct-marketing companies, packaging companies, label manufacturers, newspapers, and magazines. The company has remained profitable partly because so many manufacturers of printing equipment have gone out of business. As Kyle confided to a racquet ball partner, "I often worry about being laid off due to declining demand for our products, so I do what I can to survive." After this brief comment to his buddy, Kyle thought that maybe it was time to begin a more proactive approach to enhance his chances of becoming more important to the company.

The next Monday, Kyle had the chance to chat in person with Aaron, the company CEO. Kyle said to Aaron, "Some of our equipment is almost obsolete, and would be quite expensive to repair. But not to worry. I am going to work with Ginny, one of our sharpest mechanical engineers, to see what we can do to fix the problem. We want to save the company a bundle of cash." Aaron responded, "Go ahead and do what needs to be done."

The following day Kyle sent an e-mail to Katherine, the head of human resources, that read in part, "I wanted to update you on the progress I am making in my career.

I have attended two trade shows recently. I picked up advanced knowledge about commercial print manufacturing, including the hot new idea of additive manufacturing. I have also taken preliminary steps to certify as a project manager professional (PMP)."

On Friday, Kyle had lunch with Tyler, another operations manager at Mercury. He said to Tyler, "Please take this comment with good intent, Tyler, but you do not look well. I know that you have been struggling with high blood pressure, but I am wondering if the job pressures we all face are getting to you. I mean, do you think you might take a short leave of absence from work? Of course, first talk it over with your wife and family doctor."

The next step Kyle took was to make a Facebook post on his own page about Greg, the vice president of engineering. The post read, "Here at Mercury Printers, we are privileged to have one of the finest engineering minds in the business. We all love working with Greg."

Case Questions

1   Which political tactics does Kyle appear to be using to enhance his status at Mercury Printers?

2   What is your evaluation of the most likely effectiveness of Kyle's political tactics?

3   Please advise Kyle about what else he might do to enhance his job security at Mercury.

Discussion Questions

1   Why is having personal power important? What problems are associated with a lack of personal power?

2   Distinguish between ethical and unethical uses of power and influence.

3   How can you better your political skills? What can you gain by behaving more politically at work?

CHAPTER 9

Influencing Others– Best Practices

READING 14

How to Have Influence

Joseph Grenny, David Maxfield, and Andrew Shimberg

> The difference between effective and ineffective change makers
> is that the effective ones don't rely on a single source of influence.
> They marshal several sources at once to get superior results.
>
> Joseph Grenny,
> David Maxfield and Andrew Shimberg

We live in a quick-fix world where people look for easy solutions to solve complex problems. This goes for both business and personal problems. We want one trick to get employees to adopt behavior that improves quality and causes customers to gush with appreciation, or one trick to help us shed 30 unwanted pounds. Unfortunately, most quick fixes don't work because the problem is rarely fed by a single cause. Usually, there is a conspiracy of causes.

If you want to confront persistent problem behavior, you need to combine multiple influences into an overwhelming strategy. In management and in their personal lives, influencers succeed where others fail because they "overdetermine" success.[1] Instead of looking for the minimum it will take to accomplish a change, they combine a critical mass of different kinds of influence strategies.

We have documented the success of this multipronged approach across organizational levels (from C-level managers to first-line supervisors) and across different

---

[1] Freud popularized the term "overdetermine" by arguing that a single symbol in a dream, poem or painting can have multiple valid meanings—that symbols are often the product of several diverse influences. He borrowed the term from geometry, where it is said that "two points determine a line" and "three points overdetermine it."

problem domains (from entrenched cultural issues in companies to leader-led change initiatives to stubborn personal challenges like stopping smoking and getting fit). And while the results are impressive, they do not rely on an obscure calculus—if anything, they are built on simple arithmetic. Effective influencers drive change by relying on several different sources of influence strategies at the same time. Those who succeed predictably and repeatedly don't differ from others by degrees. By combining multiple sources of influence, they are up to 10 times more successful at producing substantial and sustainable change.

This claim is based on three studies. (See "About the Research," p. 48.) We began by looking at nagging organizational problems, such as bureaucratic infighting, lack of collaboration and low compliance with quality or safety standards. Although more than 90% of the executives we interviewed described their problems as powerfully "destructive," even "cancerous," few had done much to confront them. We got similar results when we surveyed executives and senior managers. About 40% of these executives had made some attempt to influence change in these destructive behaviors. In doing so, however, the vast majority had employed only one influence strategy—for example, they offered training, redesigned the organization or held a high-visibility retreat. A handful—fewer than 5%—had used four or more sources of influence in combination. The differences in outcomes were astounding.

Study participants who used four or more sources of influence in combination were 10 times more likely to succeed than those who relied on a single source of influence.[2]

We continued our exploration into how executives exert influence in a subsequent survey about corporate change initiatives such as restructurings, quality or productivity programs and new-product launches—all of which demand new behaviors from employees to be successful. Again, we asked senior leaders to describe the influence strategies they relied on. Nearly 40% reported using only one strategy; only 20% combined more than four strategies. As in the previous study, the few leaders who combined four or more influence strategies were dramatically more successful than those who used one strategy.[3]

In our third study, we shifted the focus from organizational to personal challenges: how people change personal habits such as overeating, smoking, overspending or drinking too much alcohol. We randomly surveyed more than 1,000 individuals, asking them to describe the strategies they had tried. Many had attempted to alter their own behavior by using a single approach (for example, join a gym, follow prescriptions in a book or attend AA meetings)—and nearly all had failed. Only 14% had tackled their problem using four or more strategies; for them, the success rate was 40% compared with 10% for those using one strategy.

---

2   Their success rate jumped from 4% to 40%.

3   In this case, leaders who used four or more sources of influence were four times more successful than leaders who used a single source. The success rate improved from 14% to 63%.

About the Research

This article is based on three separate studies. Our first study was built around interviews with 25 C-level leaders about their leading challenges. Among the challenges we wanted to explore were bureaucratic infighting, silo thinking and lack of accountability. We constructed a survey to measure the scope of these issues and, more importantly, to see what organizations did to deal with them. We administered this survey to 900 managers and supervisors. Fully 90% of the managers surveyed said their organizations struggled with at least one entrenched habit; most said the problem negatively impacted employee satisfaction, productivity, quality and customer satisfaction. Although a high percentage of managers said they did little or nothing to confront these challenges, those who applied multiple sources of influence strategies (more than four sources) were 10 times more likely to see results than those using just one. In our second study, we studied a larger sample of C-level leaders to explore how they approached change initiatives. We focused on 100 mission-critical initiatives—efforts such as internal restructurings, quality and productivity improvement initiatives and new-product launches. We wanted to see which sources of influence the companies used to support their initiatives—and how many. Here, too, we found that a high percentage of executives used only one approach; those who used four or more had the greatest likelihood of success.

Finally, we surveyed more than 1,000 individuals about personal habits they were struggling to change, such as unhealthy eating, insufficient exercise, smoking and overdrinking. More than half reported that they had struggled with their habit for five years or more, many for longer. We asked what they did to overcome their habits, which approaches were most effective and how many different strategies they used. Here again, single solutions proved ineffective. Those who combined different sources of influence (more than four) had the best results by far.

Sources of Influence

Our model organizes influence strategies into six sources. Motivation and ability make up the backbone of this model. We then subdivide these domains into three distinct categories: personal, social and structural, which in turn reflect separate and highly developed bodies of literature (psychology, sociology and organizational theory). (See "The Six Sources of Influence.") The first two domains, personal motivation and ability, relate to sources of influence within individuals (motives and abilities) that determine their behavioral choices. The next two, social motivation and ability, relate to how other people affect an individual's choices. And the final two, structural motivation and ability, encompass the role of nonhuman factors, such as compensation systems, the role of physical proximity on behavior and technology. Effective leaders need to learn how the different sources operate and how to identify implementation obstacles. (See "Understanding the Sources of Influence," p. 50.)

Source 1: Link to Mission and Values Leaders frequently have a hard time getting people to adopt a new behavior. Many healthful behaviors are boring, uncomfortable or even painful. And many unhealthful behaviors can be pleasurable—at least in the short term. When a leader asks employees to undertake dramatic quality improvement efforts, there is an enormous amount of discomfort, conflict and uncertainty. People are pushed to rethink processes, uncover problems and reapportion power in the organization. Reasonable people resist things that are uncomfortable or stressful, which is why most of these efforts fail.[4]

Ineffective influencers assume there is no way to change someone's attitude toward a behavior so they compensate for people's lack of personal motivation by putting pressure on them (social motivation) or bribe/threaten them (structural motivation). Skilled influencers help people transform their attitudes toward a behavior. They are effective at helping people become personally motivated to enact new behaviors.

Influencers understand that human beings are capable of fundamentally transforming their experience of almost any activity. Behaviors that are uncomfortable can be framed as meaningful; behaviors that are boring can become compelling; and behaviors that are painful can become rewarding. The key is to help people see the broad implications of their actions and choices.

We saw this with Matt VanVranken, president of Spectrum Health Systems, in Grand Rapids, Michigan. His challenge was to influence 10,000 weary, overworked and overstressed health care professionals to go beyond their basic job descriptions to create exceptional patient experiences. How does VanVranken persuade people to make the right decision every time? He makes it personal and connects what they do to individual patients.

For example, VanVranken periodically brings together several hundred managers and directors. At the start of a recent meeting, a man in his early 60s began to talk about his accident several months earlier when his motorcycle was hit by a car that ran a red light. He then described his experience with the staff of Spectrum Hospital. He introduced the physicians and nurses who attended him and also singled out countless others—the employees who provided warm blankets before his surgeries and the people who ordered Popsicles he could eat when he wasn't allowed solid foods. Employees were poignantly reminded of how their actions affected the health and well-being of individual patients.

When leaders want to influence people to make significant changes, they need to help them connect the changes to their deeply held values. This establishes a moral framework that shifts

---

4   J.S. Black, H.B. Gregersen, "It Starts with One: Changing Individuals Changes Organizations," 2nd ed. (Upper Saddle River, New Jersey: Wharton School Publishing, 2008).

people's experience of the new behaviors. If leaders fail to engage people's values, they must compensate for a lack of personal motivation with less profound and sustainable sources of motivation, such as carrots and sticks.

Although personal motivation can be powerful, it's rarely enough. Successful influencers find ways to engage personal motivation, but then combine it with several additional sources of influence.

Source 2: Overinvest in Skill Building Far too many leaders equate influence with motivation. Most aren't aware of this tacit assumption. We have an iconic image of the leader at the podium revving up his or her troops, and then sending them off to conquer. To these types of leaders, the name of the game is motivation. But true influencers don't make that mistake. They understand that new behaviors can be far more intellectually, physically or emotionally challenging than they appear on the surface. So they invest heavily in increasing personal ability. If anything, they *overinvest* in ability to avoid making this mistake.

In fact, our study showed that a robust training initiative is at the heart of almost all successful influence strategies.[5] Mike Miller, vice president of business customer billing at AT&T Inc., succeeded in turning around a 3,000-person IT function by creating a culture where everyone spoke up early and honestly about the risks they saw affecting project goals. Early in the change initiative, Miller saw that people needed more than the *motivation* to speak up. He realized people also needed the *ability* to step up to crucial conversations. In the heat of the moment, speaking up about emotionally risky issues requires as much skill as motivation. So Miller made sure people got the right kind of training.

	Motivation	Ability
Personal	**1** Link to Mission and Values	**2** Overinvest in Skill Building
Social	**3** Harness Peer Pressure	**4** Create Social Support
Structural	**5** Align Rewards and Assure Accountability	**6** Change the Environment

The Six Sources of Influence

Leaders who combine four or more sources of influence are up to 10 times more likely to succeed than those relying on just one.

---

5   Seventy-seven percent of the successful initiatives in our sample included training as one of their influence strategies.

Research shows that training is far less effective when it's given in one large dose—people retain less than 10% of what they learn in concentrated classes.[6] Learning that is scheduled over time is markedly more successful. So Miller decided to train slowly, in one-to two-hour segments over several months. His goal was not to "finish" the training, but to keep people focused on it long enough to absorb it—and to adopt new behaviors. He also trained realistically, focusing on real business problems. For example, participants role-played on such issues as how to challenge unrealistic deadlines, how to report project risks and how to hold peers accountable when tasks fall behind schedule. Within six months, internal surveys showed that behavior was changing markedly, and within nine months virtually every software release in Miller's group was coming in on time, on budget and with no serious errors.

Source 3: Harness Peer Pressure It is tempting to conclude that a strong dose of personal motivation and a substantial investment in personal ability is enough to tip us into new behavior. But effective influencers understand that no matter how motivated and able individuals are, they'll still encounter enormous social influences that can block change efforts.

Whether people acknowledge it or not, they often do things to earn praise from friends and coworkers. When a senior engineer tells a junior engineer that "production work is for dropouts," something very important happens. The junior engineer begins to form impressions about the choices that bring honor and prestige, and conversely about choices that lead to a less respected career path. When a new hire challenges an idea in a meeting only to be ostracized by her colleagues, another message is delivered. The sense of isolation is likely to influence how freely that person will speak in future meetings. When senior physicians don't wash their hands before treating patients, the likelihood that their residents will wash up is less than 10%.[7] Social influence is powerful.

Effective influencers understand that what shapes and sustains the behavioral norms of an organization are lots of small interactions. They realize that unless and until they get the social actions positively aligned, their chance of influencing change is slim.

When Ralph Heath was assigned the job of getting the F-22 Raptor off the drawing boards and into production in 18 months, he knew it was a formidable challenge. It was compounded by the fact that he needed the active support of 5,000 Lockheed Martin Corp. employees, many of whom saw the move to production as a threat to the stability of the jobs they knew and loved. Leaders in the organization placed a high value on engineering, ideas, tinkering and design. Production technicians were more practical. Heath knew he couldn't gain the trust and support of everyone. So he decided to invest in the most influential people—both the formal leaders and the opinion leaders.

---

6 R.G. Crowder, "Principles of Learning and Memory" (Oxford, England: Lawrence Erlbaum, 1976).

7 M.G. Lankford, T.R. Zembower, W.E. Trick, D.M. Hacek, G.A. Noskin and L.R. Peterson, "Influence of Role Models and Hospital Design on Hand Hygiene of Health Care Workers," Emerging Infectious Diseases 9, no. 2 (February 2003): 217–223.

Understanding the Sources of Influence

Effective influencers diagnose before they influence. The chart below shows the types of questions savvy leaders use to identify obstacles and strategies for creating positive leverage.

SOURCES OF INFLUENCE	STRATEGIES SUCCESSFUL LEADERS EMPLOYED
Source 1 Personal Motivation: The questions savvy leaders ask themselves • In a room by themselves would people *want* to engage in the behavior? • Do they hate it or enjoy it? • Do they find meaning in it? • Does it fit into their sense of who they are or want to be?	• Identified the aspects of the change that were boring, uncomfortable or painful and found ways to either eliminate them or make them more pleasant. • Found ways to connect the need for change with people's core values—for example, had people meet with the individuals who would benefit from the change or who were experiencing problems due to a lack of change. • Created a strong sense of mission and purpose about the need for change that touched people and motivated them to engage in the process. • Took great pains to get people's personal buy-in to the changes rather than issuing them as mandates.
Source 2 Personal Ability: The questions savvy leaders ask themselves • Do they have the knowledge, skills and strength to be able to do the right thing? • Can they handle the toughest challenges they will face?	• Gave guided practice and immediate feedback until people were sure they could engage in the new behaviors in the toughest of circumstances. • Designed learning experiences that helped people successfully manage any communication, emotional and interpersonal hurdles they would face in changing their behavior. • Had everyone involved in the change participate in real-time drills or simulations that tested whether they could perform as required under challenging circumstances.
Source 3 Social Motivation: The questions savvy leaders ask themselves • Are other people encouraging the right behavior or discouraging the wrong behavior? • Do people whom others respect model the right behaviors at the right time? • Do people have good relationships with those who are trying to influence them positively?	• Gained substantial support and involvement of enough opinion leaders from throughout the organization that the credibility of the effort was unquestioned. Enlisted these opinion leaders as role models, teachers and supporters of change. • Had all members of management from frontline supervisors to the most senior managers go to great lengths to teach, model and coach people toward new behavior. • Identified people who would be most concerned about the changes, and made sure they were involved early. • Made it clear to everyone that these behavioral changes were something top management strongly supported and modeled.

SOURCES OF INFLUENCE	STRATEGIES SUCCESSFUL LEADERS EMPLOYED
Source 4 Social Ability: The questions savvy leaders ask themselves • Do others provide the help, information and resources required—particularly at critical times?	• Used mentors or coaches to provide just-in-time assistance when people stumbled with the new behaviors. • Identified the toughest obstacles to change and made sure people had others to support them whenever they faced these obstacles. • Created "safe" ways for people to get help without feeling embarrassed or being put on the spot. • Provided everyone with the authority, information and resources they would need to step up to new behaviors as easily as possible.
Source 5 Structural Motivation: The questions savvy leaders ask themselves • Are there rewards — pay, promotions, performance reviews or perks? • Are there costs? • Do rewards encourage the right behaviors and costs discourage the wrong ones?	• Adjusted the formal rewards system to make sure people had incentives to adopt the new behaviors. • Made sure people had "skin in the game" by tracking their use of the new behaviors and linking it to rewards and punishments they cared about. • Used a "carrot and stick" approach to make sure people knew the organization was serious about demanding change. • Made sure everyone understood that even the most senior managers would be held accountable if they failed to support these changes—there were no exceptions.
Source 6 Structural Ability: The questions savvy leaders ask themselves • Does the environment (tools, facilities, information, reports, proximity to others, policies, work processes) enable good behavior or bad? • Are there enough cues and reminders to help people stay on course?	• Reorganized people's workplaces to remove obstacles and to make the change convenient and easy. • Provided new software or hardware or other new resources to make the change simpler and more automatic. • Changed existing systems to make it difficult to avoid making the changes needed. • Used cues, regular communications and metrics to keep the need for change "top of mind" for everyone in the organization. • Created potent ways of giving all levels of management feedback about how successfully or unsuccessfully they were leading change.

Heath met monthly with 350 supervisors, managers and directors. He brought in customers from the various military agencies and encouraged them to explain their frustrations and concerns with the program. In these sessions, Heath described the kinds of behaviors that were slowing the transition and which ones needed to change. He spoke candidly about the problems he saw and demonstrated a willingness to be challenged when his own actions conflicted with the behavior he asked of people. As Heath won the trust of supervisors, they began to influence others. Heath also worked closely with opinion leaders, making time available to visit informally with them every week. After only four months of working with opinion leaders, marked changes began to occur.

In the end, the performance of Heath's group exceeded expectations. The group met production deadlines, and the resulting product was a success. The F-22's reliability is better than that of the F-15, which has been in use for decades; its operating costs are lower; its repair times are shorter; and its mission capabilities are far superior.

Source 4: Create Social Support It's tempting to think that social influence is mostly about motivation. Clearly, the things groups praise and punish do a lot to shape future behavior. However, if you focus only on the motivating power of the people around you, you limit your own influence. The reality is that people around you don't just motivate; they can undermine behavior as well.

At AT&T, for example, Mike Miller was the information technology executive charged with improving his group's track record in meeting quality, schedule and cost targets. He found that one behavior essential for employees was the ability to discuss mission-critical issues rapidly and honestly with coworkers. Even when leaders spoke about this behavior, they didn't always enable it. For it to have real meaning, Miller felt that leaders had to be accessible. They had to get out of their offices and be available when people needed their help.

Miller concluded that leaders had to become teachers. So every week or two, he tried to introduce a new skill. He gave his direct reports lesson materials and tasked them with teaching the skill to people who reported to them. Over the next six weeks, the process cascaded down through the ranks until the lesson was implanted throughout the organization. As the process took hold, two powerful things happened.

First, the process of teaching influenced the *teachers*. Leaders identified more closely with the concepts and began to feel more responsible for embracing them and encouraging others to do likewise. The real teaching moments were rarely during the training itself. They occurred more often when someone had to decide how to approach a problem. When leaders were the teachers, they tended to spot these moments more predictably and seize them. They became enablers of change. Second, the process also influenced the *learners*. In addition to getting real-time coaching, employees got real-time encouragement. A respected person (often their boss) was urging them to try something new exactly when they needed the encouragement. The combination of social motivation and social ability became a powerful force for change in Miller's organization. Soon other divisions within AT&T were soliciting Miller's help in influencing change in their areas.

Source 5: Align Rewards and Ensure Accountability If you want to understand people's priorities and why they put their effort into some areas as opposed to others, it usually helps to "follow the money." If a leader talks about quality but rewards productivity, employees will notice. Chronic problems such as lack of accountability, poor productivity and slipshod quality can often be traced to poorly designed incentives that reward the wrong behaviors.

It is difficult to change behavior without changing the incentives. In fact, creating incentives is often the only real way senior leaders can separate serious priorities from pipe dreams. The CEO might stick his neck out and say, "Starting now, at least 25% of our incentive pay should be contingent on achieving these new measures." This statement will instantly redirect the focus of senior managers. At Spectrum Health Systems, AT&T and Lockheed Martin, management made a point of tracking both results and behaviors. Progress was reviewed three to four times a year, sometimes more frequently. Moreover, leaders elected to put their own skin in the game: The top two levels of management had at least 25% of their pay at risk.

But it's not just the top people who need to have a stake in changing entrenched behaviors. Employees at all levels need to see incentives for changing. The external rewards need to be both real and valuable, and they need to send a supportive message. People won't support change if the behavior management wants to encourage doesn't make their lives better (in the form of opportunities, money, promotions and so on). However, our advice is to use incentives third, not first. Otherwise, you might actually undermine people's intrinsic motivation.[8] Begin with personal and social sources of motivation, and then reinforce them with well-designed incentive systems.

Source 6: Change the Environment Three times more people die from lung cancer than from road accidents. Twice as many people die from tuberculosis as from fires. However, this is contrary to the popular view. The reason: The daily information people see—the data stream—is at odds with reality. For example, a typical newspaper has 42 articles about road accidents for every article about lung cancer.[9]

If you want to change an organization's mental agenda, you need to change the data that routinely crosses people's desks. Unlike training or coaching, this involves giving people a different diet of information to help them track problems and solutions. Pat Ryan, vice chairman of OGE Energy Corp., which owns an Oklahoma City-based electric utility, was concerned about the utility's reputation for being insufficiently customer driven. When streetlights were out, people always blamed the company and said it was unresponsive to the problem. In an effort to turn things around, Ryan established a companywide target of having streetlights repaired within five days and created a new weekly reporting mechanism to help managers monitor the problem. The report listed by area streetlights that had been dark for more than five days. Within a short time, all but two areas had fixed the problem. What's more, these improvements led to further quality improvements. Citizens and police officers began to see that when they reported dark streetlights, the problems got fixed. So they improved their reporting, and the entire system became more responsive.

---

8   E.L. Deci, "Intrinsic Motivation" (New York: Plenum Press, 1975).
9   These "observations" come from A. Tversky and D. Kahneman's classic article, "Judgment Under Uncertainty: Heuristics and Biases," Science, New Series 185, no. 4157 (Sept. 27, 1974): 1124–1131.

At OGE, the data stream about streetlights didn't exist, so management had to create it. In other settings, data streams may already exist—they are just waiting for someone to take control of them and put them to effective use. Consider the case of an international logistics company that serves the electronics industry. Although the company was meeting all of its internal customer metrics, an alarming number of customers (more than 12% per year) were defecting to competitors. The vice president of quality was puzzled, so he decided to explore how the customer metrics were calculated. Here's what he found: A salesperson would ask a customer, "How quickly do you need your deliveries?" The customer would reply, "Within two days." The salesperson would analyze the request, and often he or she would say, "Sorry, we can't do it in two days—how about four?" Frequently, the customer would say that was OK.

When it came to tracking the data, this company measured how well it kept its word to the customer—in this case, whether it delivered packages within four days—and the record was nearly perfect. So why was it losing customers? Well, despite what customers agreed to, some of them really *wanted* two-day delivery. Rather than measuring the actual delivery time against the *promised* delivery time, the VP began keeping track of a new number: the delivery time against the customers' *preferred* delivery times. Using this metric, performance fell to below 50%, which helped to explain the increasing number of customer defections. While this performance metric was discouraging to many of the company's employees, it had a positive effect. It reset their mental agendas and motivated the whole organization to revamp the fulfillment system.

Sometimes changing the data stream to influence behavior isn't enough. Then companies need to make structural changes. Spectrum Health recently went so far as to create a separate new physical space where people can work on new ideas without the normal distractions and receive the back-end support they need. In the first year, says Kris White, vice president of patient affairs, company employees identified 35 ideas to pursue commercially and received provisional patents on three of them.

NOVICE INVESTORS FREQUENTLY make the mistake of betting on a single stock rather than creating a diversified portfolio of investments. Leaders of organizations frequently make similar miscalculations in trying to influence change. Too often they bet on a single source of influence rather than tapping a diverse arsenal of strategies. We have learned that the main variable in success or failure is not which sources of influence leaders choose. By far the more important factor is how many.

Culture of Influence

How You Create and Sustain One.

B. Kim Barnes

*A*s leaders, we don't know everything and can't do everything by ourselves. We hire people with the knowledge and talent to accomplish great things—but sometimes we don't see the desired results. Change is slow; resistance is high to anything new. People keep on doing what is within their comfort zone. Innovation is rare. There is a murmur of complaints; morale is low. Results are disappointing. You wonder whether you're dealing with people who have no good ideas or who are focused on their lives outside of work—or looking for their next job, rather than contributing value to the organization.

If you face this situation, your organization may not be seen as influence-friendly. Many good ideas walk out the door between the ears of employees, perhaps because people think that their ideas are not welcome or that they are not in a position to be heard. Or they may be fearful of the career or political consequences. Maybe they have tried to influence others on their team or across boundaries to no avail. And maybe they think that you and other leaders ate not open to influence. So, how can you as a leader create and sustain a climate in which ideas flow freely; where people communicate directly; where disagreement leads to better ideas rather than interpersonal conflict; where common wisdom is challenged and innovation encouraged.

Seven simple leadership practices encourage influencing in all directions:

1. ***Be clear with your team about ends; invite them to develop means.*** Leaders who are clear with people about the goals and leave it to them to figure out how to do it ate likely to gain the team's engagement and ownership in the project. When working with knowledge workers, you won't be the only one with the knowledge and experience to achieve the goal. Professionals

don't like to waste their time as a pair of hands doing work that the boss has ordered. Anyone who takes pride in his or her ability to figure things out and apply brain power to the task at hand will appreciate the respect and trust implied by your leaving the approach up to them. Of course, your team members should know that you'll be available to discuss or even critique their thinking and that you'll expect to be informed about progress. The opposite of micromanaging is not absence—it's offering trust and support but staying out of the way.

2 **State plainly when you can and cannot be influenced about a decision.** Many years ago, the idea of involving team members in decision-making became popular—consultants touted the value of participatory leadership, and many organizations ran their leaders through workshops reminding them that employee involvement led to commitment and results. Unfortunately, many leaders and managers misunderstood the principles and invited team members to contribute ideas only to shoot them down—with the intention of getting them to see that the leader's plan or decision was the best approach. Often the decisions had already been made by the leader or manager (no chance to influence it). This approach leads to cynicism, reluctance to share ideas, and, sadly, reinforcement of the idea that team members don't have anything worthwhile to contribute. Leaders who state clearly where they can and cannot be influenced gain real trust and involvement.

3 **Use receptive influence—questioning and listening—when you want involvement, commitment, and/or new ideas.** Maybe the great idea you're looking for exists in the mind of someone who doesn't know you're interested. You might assume that if your team members have an idea, they'll say so. But there may be differences in level, in cultural attitudes coward hierarchy, or the ideas might relate to other areas where the team member has no connection. Creating opportunities for two-way influence is vital under conditions of change. When large-scale change or major technology or process shifts occur, fear-based resistance is common. People drag their feet, productivity drops. Part of resistance is the sense of helplessness that people feel about influencing the change in any way. When leaders communicate their interest in hearing from people by asking thoughtful questions and then listening to the responses and implementing some ideas discussed, passive resistance can become active engagement. Suddenly people have something to gain by change that succeeds because of their active involvement.

4 **Challenge your assumptions and invite and support others in challenging yours and one another's.** We say the eye cannot see itself and the fish doesn't know it's in water to remind ourselves that we live, without awareness, inside assumptions that we rarely question or move beyond. Assumptions make our lives easier, but also blind us to possibilities that lie outside of these structures. As long as there is a politically correct or seemingly obvious way of understanding a problem or opportunity, we tend to operate under confirmation bias and focus on information and solutions that fit our definition

of the problem. When we limit ourselves in this way, we inevitably miss interesting, creative, out-of-the-box ideas. As a leader, you're in position to model the practice of identifying and questioning assumptions, especially if you begin with your own.

5 *Invite and encourage disagreement and ask for a broad range of options before making important decisions.* Rather than going with the first decent idea that comes up, ask the team to develop several alternative solutions or approaches. Withhold judgment until many ideas are on the table; then apply criteria to all of them and narrow to a few interesting options. Avoid positive as well as negative evaluation of ideas early in the process—your approval can unduly influence the direction of the conversation, even though you don't intend to do so. Ask what would have to be true in order to make each of the options the best choice. Consider what unintended consequences might arise from each. Adding even one more option to your range of choices increases the quality of decisions. Broadening options also allows many people to say something about decisions and gives them a chance to influence one another and you.

6 *Level the playing field in a conscious way when you want to encourage two-way influence.* There are times when it pays to step out of your formal role as leader. In some organizations, this will require repetition and consistency. In flatter, more innovative organizations it may simply require a statement as to which hat you're wearing at the moment. You might have explicit norms in meetings where everyone is supposed to be on the same level—for example, "Speak up if you sense any direct or indirect power plays."

7 *Let your team members know how best to influence you and encourage them to do the same with one another.* Influence is a two-way process. Within a team, effective influence behavior enhances collaboration and efficiency. Unlike manipulation, influence is done in the open, and all parties are aware that it's going on. Everyone has preferences about how he or she prefers to be influenced. As a leader, you can begin a discussion about team influence by saying what works best for you; what makes it more likely that others can gain your support. Perhaps you like to read and think about ideas and suggestions before you meet with a team member. Or you like a free-wheeling conversation with solid pro and con arguments. Or you prefer a more formal meeting with two or three summary slides. Maybe you want to hear about the vision of success before you will consider the means for getting there. Some leaders are best influenced by hearing good questions; then having a chance to consider and respond to them. Some just want to hear a proposal or suggestion and the data that supports it. Whatever your preference, it's fair both to others and to yourself to share it. This makes it easier for influence conversations to take place and it can make them more productive.

> "Leaders who state clearly where they can and cannot be influenced gain real trust and involvement."

Leaders who make it easier for people to influence one another across levels and boundaries stimulate and enhance their organization's ability to innovate successfully. They take advantage of the knowledge and talent throughout the organization and create a culture of active engagement, energy, and commitment.

READING 16

Influence Tactics of Leaders

Andrew J. DuBrin

Learning Objectives

After studying this chapter and doing the exercises, you should be able to:

- Describe the relationship between power and influence.

- Identify a set of honest and ethical influence tactics.

- Identify a set of influence tactics relatively neutral with respect to ethics and honesty.

- Identify a set of dishonest and unethical influence tactics.

- Summarize some empirical research about the effectiveness and sequencing of influence tactics.

- Describe how implicit leadership theories are related to a leader's ability to Influence group members.

Chapter Outline

A Model of Power and Influence

Description and Explanation of Influence Tactics

Essentially Ethical and Honest Tactics

Essentially Neutral Influence Tactics

Essentially Dishonest and Unethical Tactics

In July 2012, Marissa Mayer was hired away from Google to become the fifth CEO In six years at Yahoo! Inc. The well-known search, news, and entertainment website had been struggling versus the competition, and the board was looking for a leader who could revitalize the company's financial results as well as boost morale. Mayer broke ground at the time as the first pregnant CEO of a major company. Some people wondered if the mother of a newborn could handle major business leadership responsibilities at the same time. (Mayer quickly had a nursery built adjacent to her office.)

Born in 1975, Mayer held a variety of technology leadership positions at Google Inc., with her last role at the company being the vice president of consumer products. Mayer had been personally involved with every product and service offered by Google. As the new CEO at Yahoo!, Mayer moved swiftly to strengthen the company. She orchestrated seventeen acquisitions of mostly technology startup companies, including a $1.1 billion purchase of Internet blogging and picture display service Tumblr. In addition, Yahoo! purchased a news summation website, Summly, from its founder, a British teenager. Mayer also spearheaded an upgrade of the Yahoo! website, making it more streamlined, visually attractive, and less cluttered.

Mayer's strategic thrust was to reimagine Yahoo!'s direction as a company. To attract more site visitors and advertisers, she said that she wanted to build beautiful products and execute them well. Mayer said, "This is really the fun part. This is where we get to really think about how we can inspire and delight our end users and how we can provide them with amazing features."

Mayer moved swiftly on making changes in human resource policies. She severely restricted company employees from working at home because she believes that face-to-face interaction enhances creativity and speed. Mayer also initiated the extension of maternity and paternity leave, giving $500 grants to employees who became new parents, and providing free food to employees. Later she encouraged managers to evaluate employees on a bell (normal) curve, and fire the poorest performers.

Mayer's magnetism and vision were credited for boosting morale, and turning around a beleaguered company. (Yet many employees disliked the restrictions on working from home, as well as being rated on a bell curve.) Mayer noted that the Yahoo! culture had improved, as evidenced by a doubling of people applying for jobs at Yahoo! in one quarter. Furthermore, the attrition rate for top talent had been reduced by one-half. Meanwhile, one in seven hires during that quarter were "boomerangs," or former staffers returning to Yahoo!. Mayer said, "Companies with the best talent win, and it's clear we're now back in the game."

Mayer is perceived by many as a visionary leader with a strong focus on product improvement and company operations. She is a self-described geek. Mayer graduated from Stanford University a BS degree in symbolic systems, and then an MS in computer science, majoring in artificial intelligence for both degrees.[1]

In her leadership role, Marissa Mayer is working hard to influence employees to collaborate in her quest to revitalize Yahoo!. She appeals to financial logic, brings considerable expertise to the table, and is personally magnetic. Without effective influence tactics, a leader is similar to a soccer player who has not learned to kick a soccer ball, or a newscaster who is unable to speak. Leadership, as oft repeated, is an influence process.

To become an effective leader, a person must be aware of the specific tactics leaders use to influence others. Here, we discuss a number of specific influence tactics, but other aspects of leadership also concern influence. Being charismatic, as described in Chapter 3, influences many people. Leaders influence others through power and politics, as described in Chapter 7. Furthermore, motivating and coaching skills, as described in Chapter 10, involve influencing others toward worthwhile ends.

The terms *influence* and *power* are sometimes used interchangeably, whereas at other times power is said to create influence and vice versa. In this book, we distinguish between power and influence as follows: **Influence** is the ability to affect the behavior of others in a particular direction, whereas **power** is the potential or capacity to influence. Leaders are influential only when they exercise power. A leader, therefore, must acquire power in order to influence others.

Influence tactics have grown in importance because so often a leader or corporate professional has to influence others without having formal authority over them. An example is that a vice president at Google needed to lobby Gmail engineers who did not work for him to modify software for potential corporate customers. He likens his efforts to a Peace Corps mission: all heart but with little power to enforce his will.[2]

This chapter presents a model of power and influence, a description and explanation of influence tactics (both ethical and less ethical), a description of how leaders influence large-scale

---

1   Original story created from facts and observations in the following sources: Michael Liedtke, "Yahoo! Revived by CEO, Alibaba," *Associated Press,* July 16, 2013; Jenna McGregor, "Marissa Mayer's Performance Review," *The Washington Post* (www.washingtonpost.com), July 11, 2013, pp. 1–2; "Yahoo! Continues Its Search for a New Identity," *Knowledge@Wharton* (http://knowledge.wharton.upenn.edu/), June 19, 2013, pp. 1–4; David Olive, "Yahoo! CEO Marissa Mayer Is Fighting the Odds, Even Without Motherhood," *www.thestar.com,* July 22, 2012, pp. 1–2; Ken Myers, "Leadership Development: 5 Lessons Marissa Mayer Can Teach You About Business Leadership," *Women in Leadership* (www.womeninleadership.com), December 2013, pp. 1–5; Amir Efrati, Ann Rachel, and Emma Silverman, "Yahoo!'s Marissa Mayer, One Year Later," *The Wall Street Journal,* July 16, 2013, pp. B1, B2; Greg Bensinger, "Yahoo!: Profit Stuck, for Now," *The Wall Street Journal,* October 16, 2013, p. B3; Cited in Adam Lashinsky, "Where Does Google Go Next?" *Fortune,* May 26, 2008, p. 108.
2   Gary Yukl, *Leadership in Organizations,* Fifth Edition (Upper Saddle River, N.J.: Prentice Hall, 2002), p. 143.

change, and a summary of the research about the relative effectiveness and sequencing of influence tactics. We also present a theory about the characteristics group members expect in a leader in order to be influenced by him or her.

A Model of Power and Influence

The model shown in Figure 16.1 illustrates that the end results of a leader's influence (the outcomes) are a function of the tactics he or she uses. The influence tactics are in turn moderated, or affected, by the leader's traits, the leader's behaviors, and the situation.

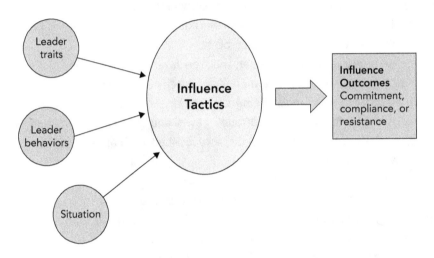

FIGURE 16-1   A Model of Power and Influence.

Looking at the right side of the model, the three possible outcomes are commitment, compliance, and resistance. **Commitment** is the most successful outcome: The target of the influence attempt is enthusiastic about carrying out the request and makes a full effort. Commitment is particularly important for complex, difficult tasks because these require full concentration and effort. If you were influencing a technician to upgrade your operating system software, you would need his or her commitment. **Compliance** means that the influence attempt is partially successful: The target person is apathetic (not overjoyed) about carrying out the request and makes only a modest effort. The influence agent has changed the person's behavior but not his or her attitude. A long-distance truck driver might comply with demands that he sleep certain hours between hauls, but he is not enthusiastic about losing road time. Compliance for routine tasks—such as wearing a hard hat on a construction site—is usually good enough. Resistance is an unsuccessful influence attempt: The target is opposed to carrying out the request and finds ways to either not comply or do a poor job. **Resistance** includes making excuses for why the task cannot be carried out, procrastinating, and outright refusing to do the task.[3]

Going to the left side of the model, the leader's personality traits affect the outcome of influence tactics. An extroverted and warm leader who has charisma can more readily use some influence tactics than a leader who is introverted and cold. For example, he or she can make an inspirational appeal. A highly intelligent leader would be able to influence others because he or she has built a reputation as a subject matter expert. Whichever influence tactics leaders choose, the goal is to get group members on their side.

The leader's behaviors also affect the outcome of influence tactics in a variety of ways. For example, setting high standards facilitates making an inspirational appeal. Additionally, leaders who perform well consistently are better able to lead by example because they are good role models. Finally, the situation partly determines which influence tactic will be effective. The organizational culture or subculture is one such key situational factor. For example, in a high-technology environment, inspirational appeal and emotional display are less likely to be effective than rational persuasion and being a subject matter expert, because high-tech workers are more likely to be impressed by facts than by feelings.

The rest of this chapter identifies and describes influence tactics, including some mention of situational variables. Leader traits and power have been described in previous chapters. Leadership Self-Assessment Quiz 16-1 will give you an opportunity to think about which influence tactics you tend to use.

Description and Explanation of Influence Tactics

Influence tactics are often viewed from an ethical perspective. Following this perspective, the influence tactics described here are classified into three categories: (a) those that are essentially ethical and honest, (b) those that are essentially neutral with respect to ethics and honesty, and (c) those that are essentially manipulative and dishonest. The categorization presented here is far from absolute. Except for the extremes, most of the tactics could conceivably be placed in any of the three categories, depending on how they are used. For example, one can use the tactic "joking and kidding" in either a well-meaning or mean-spirited way. Joking and kidding could therefore be classified as "essentially ethical," "essentially neutral," or "essentially dishonest and unethical."

Essentially Ethical and Honest Tactics

This section describes essentially ethical and honest tactics and strategies for influencing others, as outlined in Table 16.1. Used with tact, diplomacy, and good intent, these strategies can help you get others to join you in accomplishing a worthwhile objective. Because these influence tactics vary in complexity, they also vary with respect to how much time is required to develop them.

---

3 Tal Yaffe and Ronit Kark, "Leading by Example: The Case of Leader OCB," *Journal of Applied Psychology,* July 2011, pp. 806–826.

Leading by Example, Respect, and Trust A simple but effective way of influencing group members is by **leading by example**, or acting as a positive role model. The ideal approach is to be a "do as I say and do" manager—that is, one whose actions and words are consistent. Actions and words confirm, support, and often clarify each other. Being respected facilitates leading by example because group members are more likely to follow the example of leaders they respect. A major way in which a leader obtains respect is by being trusted. Part of the respect Marissa Mayer has received is that she can be trusted to follow through on her plans such as acquiring companies to help Yahoo! grow, and granting more leave time for new parents.

Leading by example is often interpreted to mean that the leader works long and hard, and expects others to do the same, with this type of behavior being prevalent among entrepreneurs who hire a staff. During the startup phase of a company, the entrepreneur will often work over 60 hours per week and expect the new hires to follow a similar work schedule.

Research conducted with 683 workers and managers in a large communication organization indicated that a leader who demonstrates organizational citizenship behavior (OCB) is likely to influence subordinates to behavior in a similar manner. Leader OCB was measured by area managers rating their subordinate managers. One dimension of citizenship behavior measured was performance above and beyond the call of duty and high attention to quality. Group managers rated the OCB of their groups as a whole. The result showed that managers who received high ratings on OCB tended to have subordinate groups that exhibited strong organizational citizenship behavior. Leading by example may therefore promote group-level behaviors that enhance organization effectiveness.[4]

Table 16.1   Essentially Ethical and Honest Influence Tactics

1. Leading by example and respect
2. Using rational persuasion
3. Explaining the benefits to the target
4. Making a personal appeal
5. Developing a reputation as a subject matter expert
6. Exchanging favors and bargaining
7. Legitimating a request
8. Making an inspirational appeal, being charming, and emotional display
9. Consultation with others
10. Forming coalitions
11. Being a team player
12. Practicing hands-on leadership

---

4   Mitchell S. Nesler, Herman Aguinis, Brian M. Quigley, and James T. Tedeschi, "The Effect of Credibility on Perceived Power," *Journal of Applied Social Psychology,* 1993, vol. 23, no. 17, pp. 1407–1425.

Using Rational Persuasion Rational persuasion is an important tactic for influencing people. It involves using logical arguments and factual evidence to convince another person that a proposal or request is workable and likely to achieve the goal. Assertiveness combined with careful research is necessary to make rational persuasion an effective tactic. It is likely to be most effective with people who are intelligent and rational. Chief executive officers typically use rational persuasion to convince their boards that an undertaking, such as product diversification, is mandatory. A major moderating variable in rational persuasion is the credibility of the influence agent. Credibility helps an individual be more persuasive in two ways. First, it makes a person more convincing. Second, it contributes to a person's perceived power, and the more power one is perceived to have, the more targets will be influenced."[5]

The following two statements are samples of how rational persuasion is measured as perceived by subordinates in research about influence processes.

- Explains clearly why a request or proposed change is necessary to attain a task objective.

- Provides information or evidence to show that a proposed activity or change is likely to be successful?[6]

Leaders who emphasize the rational decision-making model favor rational persuasion. For example, a leader favoring this model might say, "Don't tell me what you feel, give me the facts," in response to a subordinate who said, "I have the feeling that morale is down." Leaders at Google heavily emphasize such data-based decision making. A Google professional in a meeting would be rejected if he or she said, "I think there are too many random photos appearing in Google Images." In contrast, he or she would be accepted if the statement were, "I sampled 100 Google Images, and found that eight of them had random images."

Explaining Benefits to the Target A strongly effective way of influencing another person is to explain what's in it for him or her if that individual honors your request. **Apprising** means that the influence agent explains how carrying out a request or supporting a proposal will benefit the target personally, including advancing the target's career.[7] An example of apprising would be for the manager to tell a subordinate, "Perhaps two weeks helping out for one month or the company's oil rig in the Arctic Circle may seem like a tough assignment But you will seem like a hero to top management, and you will make great contacts." Two apprising behaviors on the pail of the leader are as follows:

- Describes benefits you could gain from doing a task or activity (e.g., learn new skills, meet important people, enhance your reputation).

- Explains how the task he or she wants you to do could help your career

---

5   The sample statements indicating the influence tactic in question here and at the other places in the chapter where they are presented are from Gary Yukl, Charles F. Seifert, and Carolyn Chavez, "Validation of the Extended Influence Behavior Questionnaire," *The Leadership Quarterly*, October 2008, pp. 618–620 (© Gary Yukl).
6   Yukl, Seifert, and Chavez, "*Validation of the Extended Influence Behavior Questionnaire*," p. 610.
7   Yukl, Seifert, and Chavez, "*Validation of the Extended Influence Behavior Questionnaire*," p. 610. (For both endnotes 9 and 10 the definitions are credited as Copyright © 2001 by Gary Yukl.)

Making a Personal Appeal A personal appeal in the context of influence theory is the same as it is in everyday life. The agent asks the target to implement a request or support a proposal out of friendship.[8] Another form of personal appeal is to ask for a personal favor before specifying the nature of the favor, as in "How would you like to do something important for me?" Asking for a favor without specifying its nature would likely be interpreted as unprofessional in a work environment. Two behaviors reflecting a personal appeal by a leader are as follows:

- Appeals to your friendship when asking you to do something.

- Asks for your help as a personal favor.

Developing a Reputation as a Subject Matter Expert Becoming a subject matter expert (SME) on a topic of importance to the organization is an effective strategy for gaining influence. Being an SME can be considered a subset of rational persuasion. Managers who possess expert knowledge in a relevant field and who continually build on that knowledge can get others to help them get work accomplished. Many of the leaders described throughout this text use expert knowledge to influence others. The leaders of Internet and social media companies such as Google and Foursquare are usually subject matter experts.

In recent years, General Electric Co. has emphasized the importance of industry expertise for business unit managers. GE is now keeping its senior leaders in place longer with the expectation that deeper understanding of the products and customers will enhance sales. In the past, business unit leaders relocated every few years to give them a broader understanding of the company. David Joyce, the president of commercial engines operation, represents the subject matter expertise approach. He has spent his entire 32 years with GE working his way up the aviation unit.[9]

Small business owners, in particular, rely on being subject matter experts because they founded the business on the basis of their product or technical knowledge. (Also, the major high-tech companies usually began small.) For example, the leader of a software company is usually an expert in software development.

Exchanging Favors and Bargaining Offering to exchange favors if another person will help you achieve a work goal is another standard influence tactic. By making an exchange, you strike a bargain with the other party. The exchange often translates into being willing to reciprocate at a later date. It might also be promising a share of the benefits if the other person helps you accomplish a task. For example, you might promise to place a person's name on a report to top management if that person will help you analyze the data and prepare the tables.

A recommended approach to asking for a favor is to give the other person as much time as feasible to accomplish the task, such as by saying, "Could you find ten minutes between now and

---

8   Kate Linebaugh, "The New GE Way: Go Deep, Not Wide," *The Wall Street Journal,* March 7, 2012, p. B1.
9   "You Scratch My Back ... Tips on Winning Your Colleague's Cooperation," *Working Smart,* October 1999, p. 1.

the end of the month to help me?" Not pressing for immediate assistance will tend to lower resistance to the request. Giving a menu of options for different levels of assistance also helps lower resistance. For example, you might ask another manager if you can borrow a technician for a one-month assignment; then, as a second option, you might ask if the technician could work ten hours per week on the project.[10] To ensure that the request is perceived as an exchange, you might explain what reciprocity you have in mind: That you will mention your coworker's helpfulness to his or her manager.

Two behavior specifics for exchanging favors and bargaining are as follows:

- Offers to do a specific task for you in return for your help and support.

- Offers to do something for you in the future for your help now.

Legitimating a Request To legitimate is to verify that an influence attempt is within your scope of authority. Another aspect of legitimating is showing that your request is consistent with the organizational policies, practices, and expectations of professional people. Making legitimate requests is an effective influence tactic because most workers are willing to comply with regulations. A team leader can thus exert influence with a statement such as this one: "Top management wants a 25 percent reduction in customer complaints by next year. I'm therefore urging everybody to patch up any customer problems he or she can find."

Legitimating sometimes takes the form of subtle organizational politics. A worker might push for the acceptance of his or her initiative because it conforms to the philosophy or strategy of higher management. At Amazon.com, for example, it is well known that CEO Jeff Bezos likes to keep costs to a minimum. A distribution center manager might then encourage workers to be careful about wasting energy because "It's something Jeff would want us to do."

Two leadership behaviors that reflect legitimating are as follows:

- Says that his or her request is consistent with official rules and policies.

- Verifies that a request is legitimate by referring to a document such as a work order, policy manual, charter, bylaws, or formal contract.

Making an Inspirational Appeal, Being Charming, and Emotional Display A leader is supposed to inspire others, so it follows that making an inspirational appeal is an important influence tactic. As Jeffrey Pfeffer notes, "Executives and others seeking to exercise influence in organizations often develop skill in displaying, or not displaying, their feelings in a strategic fashion."[11] An inspirational appeal usually involves displaying emotion and appealing to group members' emotions. A moderating variable in the effectiveness of an inspirational appeal or emotional display

---

10 Jeffrey Pfeffer, *Managing with Power: Power and Influence in Organizations* (Boston: Harvard Business School Press, 1992), p. 224.

11 John H. (Jack) Zenger, "Leadership's Silver Bullet: The Magic of Inspiration," in Marshall Goldsmith, John Baldoni, and Sarah McArthur, eds., *The AMA Handbook of Leadership* (New York: AMACOM, 2010), pp. 103–109.

is the influence of agent's **personal magnetism**, or the quality of being captivating, charming, and charismatic. Possessing personal magnetism makes it easier for the leader to inspire people.

The relevance of inspiration to influence is emphasized by the research of John H. Zenger and his associates. Based on results from 150,000 360-degree feedback assessments of 11,000 leaders, it was found that the key leadership behavior was, "Inspires and motivates to high performance." A key component of inspiring and motivation was found to be understanding the role of emotion in the workplace, as well as being able to use his or her emotions comfortably.[12]

A useful component of inspirational appeal for leaders is to provide meaning to the work, showing that it has significance to the entire organization or the outside world. Most people like to be involved with projects that matter, and sometimes the leader might have to explain why the work matters.[13] For example, the leader of a company that specializes in subprime mortgages might have to explain, "Without our type of work, loads of people with modest incomes would not be able to become homeowners."

Another approach to inspiring workers is to create a vision that surpasses the wants and needs of most people.[14] One of the ways in which leaders at both Apple and Google have inspired workers is to involve them in a vision of "changing the world" with their products and services.

Two recorded behaviors of leaders who make an inspirational appeal are as follows:

- Says a proposed activity or change is an opportunity to do something really exciting and worthwhile.

- Makes an inspiring speech or presentation to arouse enthusiasm for a proposed activity or change.

Consultation with Others Consultation with others before making a decision is both a leadership style and an influence technique. The influence target becomes more motivated to follow the agent's request because the target is involved in the decision-making process. Consultation is most effective as an influence tactic when the objectives of the person being influenced are consistent with those of the leader.[15] An example of such goal congruity took place in a major corporation. The company had decided to shrink its pool of suppliers to form closer partnerships with a smaller number of high-quality vendors. As a way of influencing others to follow this direction, a manufacturing vice president told his staff, "Our strategy is to reduce dealing with so many suppliers to improve quality and reduce costs. Let me know how we should implement this strategy." The vice president's influence attempt met with excellent reception, partially because

---

12   Alan Murray, *The Wall Street Journal Essential Guide to Management* (New York: Harper Business, 2010), p. 90.

13   Carlin Flora, "The Art of Influence," *Psychology Today,* September/October 2011, pp. 68–69.

14   Gary Yukl, *Skills for Managers and Leaders: Text, Cases, and Exercises* (Upper Saddle River, NJ., Prentice Hall, 1990), p. 65.

15   Some of the contacts are listed in Laurie Bennett, "Mellody Hobson: From Chicago to the White House to the Jet Set," *Forbes* (www.forbes.com), January 2, 2012, pp. 1–4.

the staff members also wanted a more streamlined set of vendor relationships. Two specific leadership behaviors reflecting consultation are as follows:

- Asks you to suggest things you could do to help him or her achieve a task objective or resolve a problem.
- Invites you to suggest ways to improve a preliminary plan or proposal that he or she wants you to support or help implement.

Forming Coalitions At times, it is difficult to influence an individual or group by acting alone. A leader will then have to form coalitions, or alliances, with others to create the necessary clout. A **coalition** is a specific arrangement of parties working together to combine their power. Coalition formation works as an influence tactic because, to quote an old adage, "there is power in numbers." Coalitions in business are a numbers game—the more people you can get on your side, the better. However, the more powerful leaders are, the less they need to create a coalition.

Having a network of powerful people facilitates forming a coalition. If you need something done, you can get these other influential people to agree that it is a good idea. An example of getting something done might be getting permission to erect an office building close to a park.

One of the best connected and therefore one of the most powerful people in business is Mellody Hobson, president of Ariel Capital Management, LLC, a large mutual fund company based in Chicago. Hobson has become a nationally recognized authority on financial literacy and financial education. Among the well-known people in her network are John Rogers, Jr., the founder of Ariel; Diane Sawyer of *Good Morning America*; William Lauder, CEO of Estee Lauder; Barack Obama, U.S. president; first lady, Michelle Obama; George Lucas, her husband and billionaire filmmaker; and Paul Allen, cofounder of Microsoft.[16]

Two specific leadership behaviors that reflect coalition formation are as follows:

- Mentions the names of other people who endorse a proposal when asking you to support it.
- Brings someone along for support when meeting with you to make a request or proposal.

Being a Team Player Influencing others by being a good team player is an important strategy for getting work accomplished. A leader might be a team player by doing such things as pitching in during peak workloads. An example would be an information technology team leader working through the night with team members to combat a virus attack on the company's computer network.

Being a team player is a more effective influence tactic in an organizational culture that emphasizes collaboration than one in which being tough-minded and decisive is more in vogue. A study of CEO leadership profiles among buyout firms found that teamwork was less associated with success than traits such as persistence and efficiency. Leaders in buyout firms are

---

16   George Anders, "Tough CEOs Often Most Successful, a Study Finds," *The Wall Street Journal,* November 19, 2007, p. B3.

strongly financially oriented and are much more concerned with making deals than building relationships.[17]

Practicing Hands-On Leadership A **hands-on leader** is one who gets directly involved in the details and processes of operations. Such a leader has expertise, is task oriented, and leads by example. By getting directly involved in the group's work activities, the leader influences subordinates to hold certain beliefs and to follow certain procedures and processes. For example, managers who get directly involved in fixing customer problems demonstrate to other workers how they think such problems should be resolved.

Hands-on leadership is usually expected at levels below the executive suite, yet many high-level executives are also hands-on leaders. A strong example is Sergio Marchionne, the Chrysler and Fiat CEO, who intervenes in such matters as a leaking car door handle. The downside of being a hands-on leader is that if you do it to excess, you become a micromanager.

The accompanying Leader in Action insert describes an automotive company executive who has been successful in influencing others.

Essentially Neutral Influence Tactics

The four influence tactics described in this section and listed in Table 16.2 might best be regarded as neutral with respect to ethics and honesty. If implemented with good intent, they tend to be positive, but if implemented with the intent of duping another person, they tend to be negative.

Table 16.2   Essentially Neutral Influence Tactics

1. Ingratiation
2. Joking and kidding
3. Upward appeal
4. Co-opting antagonists

Ingratiation When ingratiation takes the form of well-deserved flattery or compliments, it is a positive tactic. Yet, getting somebody else to like you can be considered a mildly manipulative influence tactic if you do not like the other person.

Ingratiation is often directed upward, in the sense of a subordinate attempting to get the superior to like him or her, as in organizational politics. Ingratiation also works in a downward direction, when leaders attempt to get their subordinates to like them. Typical ingratiating techniques directed toward subordinates include luncheon invitations, compliments, giving a plum work assignment, and feeding a subordinate's hobby, such as contributing a rare stamp to an employee's collection.

---

17   Gary Yukl and Cecilia M. Falbe, "Influence Tactics and Objectives in Upward, Downward, and Lateral Influence Attempts," *Journal of Applied Psychology,* April 1990, p. 133.

Leader in Action

Doug Scott, Truck Group Marketing Manager at Ford Motor Company

Doug Scott holds the formal job title of truck group manager at Ford Motor Company. Yet, he is so influential in his field that he has been referred to as the Sovereign of Truck Mountain. Scott is the leader of a truck business that generates $22 billion annually and outsells all its rivals. Despite heavy competition from GM, Dodge, and Toyota, the Ford Series pickup trucks have been the best-selling model in the United States for over thirty years.

A University of Michigan graduate, Scott climbed the corporate ladder through the sales route. He was in charge of the of the Ford Explorer SUV marketing before being promoted to head of the truck division in 2002. His present responsibilities include pickup trucks, large SUVs, and commercial vehicles.

Scott is well respected for the marketing insights he brings to his position. One of his most influential decisions was to segment the market for the F-150 pickup truck series. During the 2009 recession, Scott championed a low-cost F-150 for contractors and landscapers. In addition, there are models in the intermediate price range, as well as the high-end luxury range. One truck, labeled the Raptor SVT, is an off-the-road vehicle that climbs boulders and supposedly jump small canyons. The recently introduced Tremor is a two-seater sports truck that can accelerate to 60 miles per hour in 6.4 seconds.

Scott does not consider himself to be a "gearhead" in the traditional sense, but he has long been fascinated by the relationship between the automobile industry and the public's passion for cars and trucks. Scott's love for trucks and his devotion to Ford have helped him be well liked as a leader. He has developed close bonds among designers, marketers, and customers that have brought him substantial clout within the company. Mark Williams, the editor of website pickuptrucks.com, says about Scott, "The depth of his knowledge seems real and genuine. No matter what the situation, he has an answer."

As a leader, Scott has been successful in building a tight-knit team, many of who have been with Ford for decades. The team knows its customers quite well. Scott said that the team attends events such as the Professional Bull Riders Association and the Future Farmers of America. Such activities give the team an opportunity for face-to-face contact with customers.

Questions

1　Which influence tactics can you infer that Doug Scott uses in his leadership role?

2　What career lessons might be taken away from this story about Scott?

Sources: Original story created from facts and observations in the following sources: Mike Ramsey, "Ford Truck Czar Divides to Conquer," *The Wall Street Journal,* November 7, 2013, p. B10; Cameron Miquelon, "The Legend of Ford's Truck Czar's Rule Over Truck Mountain," *The Truth about Cars* (www.thetruthaboutcars.com), November 12, 2013, pp. 1–2; "Doug Scott: Marketing Manager Enjoys Consumer Connection," http://corporate.ford.com, September 24, 2009, p. 1.

Leaders who ordinarily are quite the opposite of ingratiating will sometimes go out of their way to be humble and agreeable to fit an important purpose. An example is the CEO of a large fast-food franchise operation. She might be cutting and sarcastic when at company headquarters. Yet when on a goodwill tour to visit franchisees, she is ingratiating. For example, she compliments the quality of the food of one of the chain restaurants, and asks to be photographed with the franchisee.

Ingratiating tactics identified in a study about influence tactics included the following:

- Says you have the special skills or knowledge needed to carry out a request.

- Praises your skill or knowledge when asking you to do something.

Leadership Self-Assessment Quiz 16-2 provides you an opportunity to measure your own ingratiating tendencies and to think through further what ingratiating yourself to your boss means in practice. Remember that being liked helps you get promoted, receive more compensation, and avoid being downsized, yet you should avoid being dishonest.

Joking and Kidding Good-natured kidding is especially effective when a straightforward statement might be interpreted as harsh criticism. Joking or kidding can thus get the message across and lower the risk that the influence target will be angry with the influence agent. Joking and kidding might be interpreted either as dishonest or as extraordinarily tactful because the criticizer softens the full blow of the criticism. A small business owner successfully used joking and kidding to help the receptionist wear clothing more appropriate for the position. As the owner entered the office, he noticed that the receptionist was wearing a tank top and very large hoop earrings. The owner said, "Melissa, you look great, but I think you have your dates confused. You are dressed for the company picnic, and it takes place tomorrow." Melissa smiled, and then dressed more professionally in the future.

Upward Appeal In **upward appeal**, the leader exerts influence on a team member by getting a person with more formal authority to do the influencing. Some managers and researchers regard upward appeal as an ethical and standard practice, yet it does contain an element of manipulation and heavy-handedness. An example: "I sent the guy to my boss when he wouldn't listen to me. That fixed him." More than occasional use of upward appeal weakens the leader's stature in the eyes of group members and superiors, eroding effectiveness. Leaders can apply upward appeal in other ways. A leader might attempt to persuade another staff member that higher management approved his or her request. The target of the influence event is thus supposed to grant acceptance automatically. Or, the leader can request higher management's assistance in gaining another person's compliance with the request. The influence target thus feels pressured.[18]

Co-Opting Antagonists A potentially effective influence tactic, as well as a method of conflict resolution, is to find a clever way to get the other person or group of persons to join forces with you. In this sense, to **co-opt** is to win over opponents by making them part of your team or giving them a stake in the system.[19] Assume that the director of human resources is receiving considerable opposition to some of her initiatives from the chief financial officer. For example, the CFO is opposed to her proposed program of cross-cultural training. To soften the opposition, and perhaps even make him an ally, the director of human resources invites the CFO to become a member of the "human resources advisory board" composed of company executives and distinguished citizens from the community.

Essentially Dishonest and Unethical Tactics

The tactics described in this section are less than forthright and ethical, yet they vary in intensity with respect to dishonesty. Most people would consider the first two strategies presented here as unethical and devious, yet they might regard the second two tactics as still within the bounds of acceptable ethics, even though less than fully candid. The tactics in question are outlined in Table 16.3.

Deliberate Machiavellianism Niccolo Machiavelli advised that princes must be strong, ruthless, and cynical leaders because people are self-centered and self-serving. As implied in Chapter 7, people in the workplace who ruthlessly manipulate others have therefore come to be called **Machiavellians**. They tend to initiate actions with others and control the interactions. Machiavellians regularly practice deception, bluffing, and other manipulative tactics.[20] A modem example of deliberate Machiavellianism is the practice of forcing managerial and professional employees into working many extra hours of uncompensated overtime. The employees are

---

18   Jeffrey Pfeffer, "Power Play," *Harvard Business Review,* July–August 2010, p. 90.
19   Bernhard M. Bass (with Ruth Bass), *The Bass Handbook of Leadership: Theory, Research, & Managerial Applications,* Fourth Edition (New York: The Free Press, 2008), p. 160.
20   Cited in Heidi Grant Halvorson, "How to Be a Better Boss," *The Wall Street Journal,* January 2, 2013, p. B6.

told that if they refuse to work extra hours, they will not be considered worthy of promotion or as good team players. Even when positions in other companies are readily available, most career-minded people will stay because they want to preserve a good reputation.

Table 16.3   Essentially Dishonest and Unethical Influence Tactics

1. Deliberate Machiavellianism
2. Gentle manipulation of people and situations
3. Undue pressure
4. Debasement

Gentle Manipulation of People and Situations Some people who attempt to influence others are manipulative, but to a lesser extent than an outright Machiavellian. They gain the compliance of another person by making untrue statements or faking certain behaviors. For example, a leader might imply that if a colleague supports his position in an intergroup conflict, the person might be recommended for promotion. Another manipulative approach is to imply dire consequences to innocent people if the influence target does not comply with demands of the influence agent, such as, "Even if you don't want to put in extra effort for me, think of the people with families who will be laid off if we don't make our targets."

A widely used manipulative approach is to tap into social norms in order to gain consensus. According to Steve Martin, behavior specialist at the consulting firm Influence at Work, this technique can move people to model their behavior after others. He gives the example of working with the U.K. tax collecting service. Martin witnessed an increase in the return rate after enclosing messages such as "nine out of ten people pay their tax on time." The rate of returns increased even more when the tax collection service presented messages referring to the number of people who held returns with the individual's own town or postal code.[21] A workplace example is a manager who informs the vice president that she wants an enlarged budget for attendance at the latest social networking seminars because "all other companies are doing it."

The technique of tapping into social norms can be combined with peer pressure to influence a group member. If one person is not stepping forward to work well as a team member, the manager will say, "Bob, everyone in the department is committed to developing a team atmosphere, and we'd like you to be a part of it."[22]

Undue Pressure Effective leaders regularly use motivational techniques such as rewards and mild punishments. Yet, when rewards become bribes for compliance and threats of punishment become severe, the target person is subjected to undue pressure or coercion. An example of a bribe by a manager might be, "If you can work eighty hours on this project this week, I'll recommend you for the highest pay grade." Another approach to pressure is for the manager to

---

21   "Create an Arsenal of Influence Strategies," *Manager's Edge*, March 2003, p. 1.
22   Anthony Bianco and Tom Lowry, "Can Dick Parsons Rescue AOL Time Warner?" *BusinessWeek*, May 19, 2003, p. 089.

scream and swear at the subordinate as a form of intimidation. As one manager under pressure of his own, shouted to a subordinate:

"Get some of these _____ receivables paid by the end of the week or find another job."
Two specific behaviors labeled pressure in a research study were as follows:

- Uses threats or warnings when trying to get you to do something.

- Tries to pressure you to carry out a request.

Debasement A subtle manipulative tactic is **debasement**, demeaning or insulting oneself to control the behavior of another person. Richard Parsons, the former chair of Citigroup, uses debasement to disarm people. A long-time friend said of Parsons, "Richard's ability to get people to underestimate him is a great skill. If you are obvious, they know where to hit you. Who wins between the bull and matador?"[23] Specific debasing tactics revealed by research include the following: "I lower myself so she'll do it," and "I act humble so she'll do it."[24]

In studying the most severe unethical influence (and political) tactics, it is important to recognize that the use of these influence approaches can bring about human suffering. For example, bullying and intimidating tactics may not be illegal, but they are unethical. Cruelty in the organization creates many problems. As one observer notes, "Cruelty is blatantly unethical and erodes the organizational character through intellectual, emotional, moral, and social vices that reduce the readiness of groups to act ethically."[25] Examples of cruelty include insulting a group member's physical appearance or belittling him or her.

Discussion Questions

1   Effective change makers don't rely on a single source of influence. What sources of influence do you currently use as a leader? What sources do you not currently use but would consider using? What can you gain by using these sources of influence?

2   Describe different sources of influence used at different levels: personal, social, and structural.

3   Can you link sources of influence with strategies used by successful leaders?

4   Can you describe best practices associated with the creation of an organizational culture of influence?

---

23   David M. Buss, Mary Gomes, Dolly S. Higgins, and Karen Lauterbach, "Tactics of Manipulation," *Journal of Personality and Social Psychology,* December 1987, p. 1222.

24   Comment contributed anonymously to author by a professor of organizational behavior.

25   Efrati and Silverman, "Yahoo!'s Marissa Mayer, One Year Later," *The Wall Street Journal,* p. B2.

CHAPTER 10

The Important Case of Women

Women's Careers and Power

What You Need to Know

Jeffrey Pfeffer

Introduction

Women confront some unique and difficult issues in finding and navigating their path to power. Organized by a set of questions and some data relevant to answering them, this note is intended to provide background information on some of the important social science research relevant to understanding women, power, and career outcomes and processes. It also discusses some of the implications of the data and research for women who seek a road to the top of work organizations.

Do Women Experience Worse Career Outcomes?

The answer to this question, in a word, is "yes." Statistical analyses using samples of the total labor force,[1] samples of people who have graduated from elite colleges,[2] and analyses of salary within specific occupations[3] consistently find a negative effect of being a woman on salary, changes in salary, and other measures of career success.

---

1   See Yitzhak Haberfeld, "Employment Discrimination: An Organizational Model," *Academy of Management Journal, 25* (1992): 161–180, for a review of some of the evidence.
2   See, for instance, Claudia Goldin and Lawrence F. Katz, "Transitions: Career and Family Life Cycles of the Educational Elite," *American Economic Review: Papers and Proceedings 2008, 98* (2008): 363–369.
3   See, for instance, Marianne A. Ferber, "Professors, Performance, and Rewards," *Industrial Relations, 13* (1974): 69–77.

Professor Jeffrey Pfeffer prepared this case as the basis for class discussion rather than to illustrate either effective or ineffective handling of an administrative situation.

Women tend to be concentrated within lower-paying occupations and job titles.[4] Although occupational sex segregation diminished in the 1970s and 1980s, since the 1990s, change has stalled or even reverted. For instance, "in 1980, 75 percent of primary school teachers and 64 percent of social workers were women. Today, women make up 80 and 81 percent of those fields," while women comprise just 10 percent of electrical engineers.[5] Within occupations such as doctors, lawyers, and professors, the subspecialties with the highest proportions of women tend to pay less well,[6] in part because of the devaluation of work done primarily by women.[7] Job titles filled with higher proportions of women (and minorities) also pay more poorly.[8]

Does Gender Discrimination Affect Professional Women Also?

Absolutely. According to a 2011 report from the Center for Women in Law of the University of Texas, women represented just 15 percent of the equity partners in the largest 200 American law firms and held just 5 percent of the managing partner jobs in these firms; and nearly 50 percent of the largest 200 law firms had either just one or no women on their highest governing committee. Only 20 percent of the general counsel positions in Fortune 500 companies were held by women, and women comprised 16 percent of the board members and 14 percent of the executive officers in these companies.[9] Only 4 percent of the CEOs of Fortune 1,000 companies were women.[10]

Many of the largest financial institutions and investment banks recently faced gender discrimination lawsuits.[11] The underrepresentation of women in the high technology world of the Silicon Valley has been well documented, in addition to the absence of women in large numbers

---

4   William T. Bielby and James N. Baron, "A Woman's Place Is with Other Women: Sex Segregation Within Organizations," in Barbara Reskin (ed.), *Sex Segregation in the Workplace: Trends, Explorations, Remedies,* (Washington, DC: National Academy Press, 1984) pp. 27–55.

5   Stephanie Coontz, "The Myth of Male Decline," *The New York Times,* September 29, 2012.

6   Kathleen E. Hull and Robert L. Nelson, "Assimilation, Choice, or Constraint? Testing Theories of Gender Differences in the Careers of Lawyers," *Social Forces, 79* (2000): 229–264; Marcia L. Bellas, "Comparable Worth in Academia: The Effects on Faculty Salaries of the Sex Composition and Labor-Market Conditions of Academic Disciplines," *American Sociological Review, 59* (1994): 807–821.

7   Paula England, "The Gender Revolution: Uneven and Stalled," *Gender and Society, 24* (2010): 149–166.

8   Jeffrey Pfeffer and Alison Davis-Blake, "The Effect of the Proportion of Women on Salaries: The Case of College Administrators," *Administrative Science Quarterly, 32* (1987), 1–24; James N. Baron and Andrew E. Newman, "For What It's Worth: Organizations, Occupations, and the Value of Work Done by Women and Nonwhites," *American Sociological Review, 55* (1990): 155–175.

9   Linda Bray Chanow and Lauren Stiller Rikleen, "Power in Law: Lessons from the 2011 Women's Power Summit on Law and Leadership," Austin, TX: University of Texas, Center for Women In Law, University of Texas School of Law.

10   Coontz, op. cit.

11   See, for instance, Pater Lattman, "Women Sue Goldman, Claiming Pay and Job Bias," *The New York Times,* September 15, 2010; Thomas Kaplan, "Women Accuse Citigroup of Gender Bias," *The New York Times,* October 13, 2010.

in the venture capital community.[12] Gender discrimination—a negative coefficient for being a woman in affecting salary, the odds of being hired, and the likelihood of being promoted—has been found in studies of careers in medicine and in academia.

There is no evidence that professional women with higher levels of educational attainment and accomplishment are buffered from the effects of gender on careers.

Are These Findings Still Relevant—Hasn't the World Changed?

Although there are people who claim that the world has changed, in part because of differences in the legal environment from past times and also the evolution of social norms about women and organizational leadership—with such changes making the job environment fairer for women—there is no evidence that anything approaching gender equity in careers or salaries has been achieved. Yes, there is evidence that discrimination is less overt and pervasive, with smaller effects than observed in the past. But such changes do not equate to parity in either the processes or outcomes women confront.

To take one relevant and timely example, the research and advocacy organization, Catalyst, noted that women's progress in attaining senior positions in business had seemingly reached a plateau. To investigate this, the organization surveyed more than 4,000 women and men in 2007 and 2008. The study examined people who had graduated from full-time MBA programs at 26 leading schools between 1996 and 2007. To be included in the study, individuals had to be working full-time. The Catalyst results showed:

- Even after statistically controlling for years of experience, industry, and global location, women were more likely to start their first job after the MBA at a lower organizational level than men.[13]

- Men had higher starting salaries.[14]

- Regardless of starting salary, men had more rapid salary growth than did women.[15]

- Men were more likely to be at a higher managerial level than were women, even after controlling for years of experience, time since receiving the MBA, industry norms, and other explanatory factors.[16]

- Women, earning less and residing at lower managerial levels than similarly credentialed men, reported less career satisfaction than did men.[17]

---

12   David Streitfeld, "Lawsuit Shakes Foundation of a Man's World of Tech," *The New York Times,* June 2, 2012.
13   Nancy M. Carter and Christine Silva, *Pipeline's Broken Promise* (New York: Catalyst, 2010) p. 3.
14   Ibid.
15   Ibid., p. 5.
16   Ibid., p. 4.
17   Ibid., p. 8.

Are Women Disadvantaged in Their Careers in Countries Other Than the United States?

Of course. A 2002 survey of 500 Australian MBA graduates found that the median starting salary for women was just *half* that of their male counterparts.[18] In India, just 11 percent of chief executives were women.[19] In Britain, between 1974 and 1994, there was a 2.8 million decrease in the number of men in the labor force while the number of women increased 2 million, but between 1975 and 1984, the percent of women in senior management declined by some 3.5 percent even as the proportion of women in the total labor force increased.[20]

Women generally do fare better in countries in Northern Europe where there are laws promoting flexibility in working hours and mandating paid family leave that provide more support to working parents. Some European countries have passed laws requiring a certain proportion of women on boards or in senior executive ranks. For instance, "Norway enacted a law in 2003 requiring firms to have 40 percent female directors by 2008.... In 2010, the French National Assembly proposed a law that will impose 20 percent gender quotas on boards of listed French firms within three years of the law's adoption and 40 percent quotas after six years."[21] Nonetheless, there is little evidence that women have achieved complete salary and career parity anywhere.

What Accounts for These Differences in Women's Careers?

There are many explanations for women's career disadvantages. They are not mutually exclusive and many of the processes are self-reinforcing. For instance, if women experience less career progress and less career satisfaction and therefore drop out of the workforce in larger numbers, organizations will be less likely to hire and promote women because the employers will expect women to be more likely to drop out. If women, seeing that in general women earn less, enter salary negotiations with lower expectations, they will be satisfied with less and, other things being equal, be offered lower salaries, thus perpetuating the disadvantage.

As briefly reviewed below, there are numerous accounts, all of them supported by empirical evidence, as to why women suffer career disadvantages. These explanations include: 1) women are more likely to drop out of the labor force, at least temporarily, and dropping out creates

---

18   Mara Olekalns and Carol T. Kulik, "Sugar 'n' Spice and All Things Nice: Gender and Strategy Choices in Negotiation," forthcoming in P. Murry, R. Kramar, and P. McGraw (Eds.), *Women at Work in Australia.*

19   Nilanjana S. Roy, "Ambitions Meet Reality in India," *The New York Times,* December 14, 2010, www.nytimes.com/2010/world/asia/15iht letter15.html.

20   Heli K, Lahtinen, and Fiona M. Wilson, "Women and Power in Organizations," *Executive Development, 7* (1994): 16–25.

21   Renee B. Adams and Patricia Funk, "Beyond the Glass Ceiling: Does Gender Matter?" *Management Science, 58,* (February, 2012): 219–235; quote is from p. 219.

permanent career setbacks; 2) women work, on average, fewer hours, and work hours are related to salary; 3) women suffer greater penalties from being married and from having children than do men; 4) women, on average, are less competitive than men; 5) women are less forceful negotiators and frequently expect and demand less in salary negotiations than do men; 6) women are less oriented to social dominance and power than men; and 7) women face conflicting messages and expectations about how to simultaneously conform to the roles of "leader" and "woman."

These (and other) gender-based differences in preferences and behavior could be the result of evolution and natural selection, biology (nature), or social expectations and learning, or some combination of these causes. Remediation would require deep understanding of where such differences come from, and research is still attempting to accomplish this. However, for purposes of exploring differences between men and women in career outcomes and behaviors, understanding the source of such differences is less important.

Are Women More Likely to Drop Out of the Labor Force?

Research shows that even temporarily dropping out of the labor force causes careers to advance more slowly, even when years of experience are included as an explanatory variable in statistical analyses. This means that any career interruptions tend to be harmful for someone's subsequent career.[22] One analysis of Harvard student cohorts from 1970, 1980, and 1990 found that people who had earned an MBA suffered the greatest earnings penalty for taking time off from employment.[23]

Because of differences in shouldering child care responsibilities and in part because of the wage and career disadvantages that women confront, women are more likely than men to at least temporarily drop out of the work force, a fact that provides one partial explanation for lower wages and poorer career progress. For instance:

- Women in India were more likely than men to temporarily leave the work force to care for elderly parents or children—54.5 percent versus 15 percent.[24]

- Goldin and Katz's study of Harvard student cohorts found that women had about 15 months of being non-employed while the comparable figure for men was four months.[25]

---

22   See, for instance, James W. Albrecht, Per-Anders Edin, Marianne Sundstrom, and Susan B. Vroman, "Career Interruptions and Subsequent Earnings: A Reexamination Using Swedish Data," *The Journal of Human Resources, 34* (1999): 294–311; Shelley Phipps, Peter Burton, and Lynn Lethbridge, "In and Out of the Labour Market: Long-Term Income Consequences of Child-Related Interruptions to Women's Paid Work," *Canadian Journal of Economics, 34* (2001): 411–429.

23   Goldin and Katz, op. cit.

24   Roy, op. cit.

25   Goldin and Katz, op. cit.

- "Of white men with M.B.A.'s, 95 percent are working full time, but for white women...that number drops to 67 percent."[26]

- A survey of women from the Harvard Business School classes of 1981, 1985, and 1991 found that only 38 percent were working full-time.[27]

- In other professions, between one-third and one-fourth of the women trained in the profession were out of the work force.[28]

- A study of almost 2,500 highly qualified women reported that 37 percent had voluntarily left the workforce at some point in their careers, and for women with children, 43 percent had left.[29]

Do Women Work Fewer Hours?

Women tend to work fewer hours than men, and hours worked affects wages. Goldin and Katz's study of Harvard student cohorts found that including the number of hours worked in earnings regressions reduced, but did not completely eliminate, the effect of gender on earnings.[30] Olivia O'Neill and Charles O'Reilly studied University of California, Berkeley, MBA graduates in the eight years following graduation. They reported a positive correlation between being male and number of hours worked and a positive effect of hours worked on income. In their study, the difference in hours worked between men and women completely mediated the effect of gender on earnings.[31]

Do Women Suffer A Larger Marriage and Childhood Penalty Than Men?

Data show that being married and having children have quite different effects on men's and women's careers. For example, Martha Hill found that married men earned *more* than single men, whereas married women earned *less* than their single counterparts.[32] A study using Swedish panel data found that men were more likely to be in positions of authority if they were married

26   Lisa Belkin, "The Opt-Out Revolution," *The New York Times Magazine*, October 26, 2003, http://www.nytimes.com/2003/10/26/magazine/26WOMEN.html.

27   Ibid.

28   Ibid.

29   Sylvia Ann Hewlett and Carolyn Buck Luce, "Off-Ramps and On-Ramps: Keeping Talented Women on the Road to Success," *Harvard Business Review, 83* (March, 2005): 43–54.

30   Goldin and Katz, op. cit.

31   Olivia A. O'Neill and Charles A. O'Reilly, "Careers as Tournaments: The Impact of Sex and Gendered Organizational Cultural Preferences on MBA's Income Attainment," *Journal of Organizational Behavior, 31* (2010): 856–876.

32   Martha S. Hill, "The Wage Effect of Marital Status and Children," *The Journal of Human Resources, 14* (1979): 579–594.

and when they became fathers, men were more likely to attain positions of supervisory author-ity, something not true for women who became mothers.[33] The study of some 6,500 Harvard University graduates reported that "male earnings are strongly and positively related to the number of children in the family whereas female earnings are negatively related."[34]

A review of the literature on the effects of being a mother found that women with children earn about 5 percent less per child, over and above any effects of gender and with other variables that might affect wages statistically controlled. That review noted that the motherhood penalty has been found in other industrialized countries and has *not* declined over time.[35]

The negative effect of motherhood on salaries appears to come from the fact that being a mother seemingly conveys a signal that the woman is warm; but the problem is that warmth and competence are often perceived by observers as being negatively related.[36] Social psychologists Amy Cuddy and Susan Fiske asked 122 Princeton University undergraduates to rate fictitious consultants on traits reflecting warmth and competence and also on how likely they would be, if they were clients, to a) request the person on an engagement, b) recommend the individual for continuing training and education, and c) recommend the person described in the profile for promotion. Cuddy and Fiske found that "when working women become mothers, they trade perceived competence for perceived warmth," while men do not face a similar tradeoff. It was the competence ratings that predicted the study participants' interest in hiring, training, and promoting people.[37]

Another, complementary perspective maintains that "motherhood" is a status characteristic, cognitively linked to a set of perceptions such as being more nurturing, but less available for work, organizationally committed, and capable.[38] Both lines of research are consistent with the oft-observed empirical fact that motherhood has a negative effect on wages above and beyond the negative effect of gender on earnings.

---

33   Magnus Bygren and Michael Gahler, "Family Formation and Men's and Women's Attainment of Workplace Authority," *Social Forces, 90* (2012): 795–816.

34   Goldin and Katz, op. cit., p. 367.

35   Stephen Benard, In Paik, and Shelley J. Correll, "Cognitive Bias and the Motherhood Penalty," *Hastings Law Journal, 59* (2008): 1359–1387.

36   There are numerous studies consistent with this statement. See, for instance, Nicolas Kervyn, Vincent Yzerbyt, and Charles M. Judd, "Compensation Between Warmth and Competence: Antecedents and Consequences of a Negative Relation Between the Two Fundamental Dimensions of Social Perception," *European Review of Social Psychology, 21* (2010): 155–187.

37   Amy J. C. Cuddy and Susan T. Fiske, "When Professionals Become Mothers, Warmth Doesn't Cut the Ice," *Journal of Social Issues, 60* (2004): 701–718; quote is from p. 707.

38   Cecelia L. Ridgeway and Shelley J. Correll, "Motherhood as a Status Characteristic," *Journal of Social Issues, 60* (2004): 683–700.

Are Women Less Competitive?

There is a proliferation of research addressing the question as to whether or not women are as competitive as men and if differences in competitiveness can help explain differences in women's and men's careers. Many studies, but not all, find that men are more competitive than women, as well as some moderating conditions.

In one experiment, when men and women were paid by a piece rate (payment based on individual performance), there was no difference in their performance. But when the payoff structure was a tournament in which payoffs depended on relative (not absolute) productivity (a more competitive payoff structure), women did less well than men, an effect that was even larger when women had to compete against men.[39] A study of Israeli school children reported that when boys and girls ran a 40-meter race alone, they ran at about the same speed. But when the children competed in pairs, performance of the boys, but not the girls, increased significantly.[40] Yet another study used the natural experimental setting afforded by a game show where competitors answered questions reflecting general knowledge. After each round, one person was eliminated or could quit voluntarily. The authors found that women earned 40 percent less than men and exited the game prematurely at a faster rate.[41]

Subsequent research has begun to outline boundary conditions for this general effect of gender on competitiveness. One study of 15-year-old students found that girls who attended single-sex schools behaved more like boys even in mixed-gender experimental groups.[42] Another study argued that women's and men's competitive behavior depended on the specific task. In presumably "male" tasks, men responded more to competition than did women, while in "female" tasks, women reacted to competition more strongly than did men.[43] In neutral tasks, there were no differences between men's and women's responses. Still other studies, such as one conducted in Sweden, have found no differences in the competitive behavior of girls and boys.[44]

Overall, there does seem to be evidence for differences in competitive behavior by gender.[45] And one analysis demonstrated that such differences and the resulting consequences for

39   Uri Gneezy, Muriel Niederle, and Aldo Rustichini, "Performance in Competitive Environments: Gender Differences," *Quarterly Journal of Economics, 118* (2003): 1049–1074.

40   Uri Gneezy and Aldo Rustichini, "Gender and Competition at a Young Age," *American Economic Review Papers and Proceedings, 94* (2004): 377–381.

41   Robin M. Hogarth, Natalia Karelaia, and Carlos Andres Trujillo, "When Should I Quit? Gender Differences in Exiting Competitions," *Journal of Economic Behavior and Organization, 83* (2012): 136–150.

42   Alison Booth and Patrick Nolen, "Choosing to Compete: How Different Are Girls and Boys?" *Journal of Economic Behavior and Organization, 81* (2012): 542–555.

43   Christina Gunther, Neslihan Arsland Edinci, Christiane Schwieren, and Martin Strobel, "Women Can't Jump?—An Experiment on Competitive Attitudes and Stereotype Threat," *Journal of Economic Behavior and Organization, 75* (2010): 395–401.

44   Anna Dreber, Emma von Essen, and Eva Ranehill, "Outrunning the Gender Gap—Boys and Girls Compete Equally," *Experimental Economics, 14* (2011): 567–582.

45   Rachel Croson and Uri Gneezy, "Gender Differences in Preferences," *Journal of Economic Literature, 47* (2009): 448–474.

occupational choice could partly explain gender segregation in the fields of law, business and management, health, and education.[46]

Do Women Have a Different Orientation Toward Power and Negotiation?

Because of different expectations for appropriate behavior and different socialization experiences, it is scarcely surprising to find that women and men exhibit differences in their attitudes toward power and negotiations as well as differences in achieved outcomes.

One study of almost 500 college students and the same number of voters found that men were more social dominance-oriented than women.[47] An experimental study asking participants to rate the likelihood of their taking various actions in the case of an organizational dispute reported that men were more likely to use coercion and women were more likely to use personal/dependent and negotiation strategies. That same study noted that women "reported more negative attitudes toward having power than men."[48] A study of people serving on boards of directors found that even in that context, where presumably women were more competitive and power oriented than average in order to have reached such a senior level, women were less power oriented than men.[49]

Women have lower salary expectations than do men,[50] are less likely under some conditions to initiate negotiations,[51] and are less likely to negotiate over their careers. This is the case even though a study in an investment bank found that employees who were willing to negotiate received promotions on average 17 months earlier than others.[52]

Although the observed differences were small, a review of the literature found that men obtained significantly better outcomes in negotiations than did women.[53] This result occurred in part because women are expected to be, and were, more cooperative than men. A survey

---

46   Kristin J. Kleinjans, "Do Gender Differences in Preferences for Competition Matter for Occupational Expectations?" *Journal of Economic Psychology, 30* (2009): 701–710.

47   F. Pratto, L. M. Stallworth, and J. Sidanius, "The Gender Gap: Differences in Political Attitudes and Social Dominance Orientation," *British Journal of Social Psychology, 36* (1997): 49–68.

48   Lynn R. Offermann and Pamela E. Schrier, "Social Influence Strategies: The Impact of Sex, Role, and Attitudes Toward Power," *Personality and Social Psychology Bulletin, 11* (1985): 286-300.; quote is on p. 295.

49   Adams and Funk, op. cit.

50   This literature is nicely reviewed in Teresa M. Heckert, Heather E. Droste, Patrick J. Adams, Christopher M. Griffin, Lisa L. Roberts, Michael A. Mueller, and Hope A. Wallis, "Gender Differences in Anticipated Salary: Role of Salary Estimates for Others, Job Characteristics, Career Paths, and Job Inputs," *Sex Roles, 47* (2002): 139–151.

51   Deborah A. Small, Michele Gelfand, Linda Babcock, and Hilary Gettman, "Who Goes to the Bargaining Table? The Influence of Gender and Framing on the Initiation of Negotiation," *Journal of Personality and Social Psychology, 93* (2007): 600–613.

52   Fiona Greig, "Propensity to Negotiate and Career Advancement: Evidence from an Investment Bank That Women Are on a 'Slow Elevator'," *Negotiation Journal, 24* (2008): 495–508.

53   Alice F. Stuhlmacher and Amy E. Walters, "Gender Differences in Negotiation Outcome: A Meta-Analysis," *Personnel Psychology, 52* (1999): 653–677.

of research using the dictator and the ultimatum two-person games found that women were generally more egalitarian than men, were more likely to reach an agreement, and expected to receive and asked for less.[54]

Do Women Face Incompatible Expectations in Leadership Roles?

As implied in much of the forgoing, to reduce their career disadvantages women apparently should be tougher negotiators, more power and dominance oriented, more competitive, display competence rather than warmth, and figure out ways to spend more hours (and years) at work. There is one obvious problem with these recommendations—they contradict the stereotypes of how women should be as women. When women behave differently than gender roles prescribe, they face resentment and backlash. Thus, women face a double bind—if they conform to social expectations for how women should behave, they fail to conform to expectations for leader behavior; and if they fit typical definitions of leaders, they depart from how women are expected to act.[55]

Women also face a problem of "proving their worth" against skepticism, because the traits typically ascribed to women are not traits strongly associated with leadership. Catalyst research found that both women and men held similar beliefs about male and female traits and also held reasonably similar views concerning the traits possessed by leaders.[56] Other research shows that characterizations of men and women managers have been remarkably stable over time, with men generally described as more similar to successful managers than women.[57]

Research shows that when women in leadership roles engaged in more "male" behaviors (autocratic and directive), women were devalued compared to male counterparts who exhibited similar behaviors.[58] A review article noted the discrepancy between the expectations for fulfilling the "female" role and the "leadership" role, and that this divergence led to seeing women as less appropriate for leadership positions and to evaluating tough or directive behaviors less favorably when they were done by a woman.[59]

---

54 Catherine Eckel, Angela C. M. De Oliveira, and Philip J. Grossman, "Gender and Negotiation in the Small: Are Women (Perceived to Be) More Cooperative Than Men?" *Negotiation Journal, 24* (2008): 429–445.

55 Catalyst, "The Double-Bind Dilemma for Women in Leadership: Damned If You Do, Damned If You Don't," Research Report, July 2007.

56 Catalyst, "Women 'Take Care,' Men 'Take Charge': Stereotyping of U.S. Business Leaders Exposed," Research Report, October 2005.

57 Madeline E. Heilman, Caryn J. Block, Richard F. Martell and Michael C. Simon, "Has Anything Changed? Current Characterizations of Men, Women, and Managers," *Journal of Applied Psychology, 74* (1989): 935–942.

58 Alice H. Eagly, Mona G. Makhijani, and Bruce G. Klonsky, "Gender and the Evaluation of Leaders: A Meta-Analysis," *Psychological Bulletin, 111* (1992): 3–22.

59 Alice H. Eagly and Steven J. Karau, "Role Congruity Theory of Prejudice Toward Female Leaders," *Psychological Review, 169* (2002): 573–598.

Because the traits associated with leadership and masculinity overlap much more than the traits associated with femininity, women face a difficult, almost impossible dilemma. As Catalyst argued in their 2007 report, "Women are often perceived as going against the norms of leadership or those of femininity."[60] While some people argue that organizations have changed in ways that make traditional views of leadership obsolete, with more feminine, relationship-oriented, collaborative qualities now more valued and valuable, there is precious little evidence to support what is probably more of a hope than a reality.[61]

So What Should Women Do?

Acknowledging or even bemoaning the inherent unfairness of the social science literature briefly overviewed in this note will not change anything. People need to see circumstances as they are and navigate the organizational world as it exists.

Both women and men face career trade-offs, particularly between work and family obligations. The fact that public policy in the U.S. lags other industrialized countries in mandating workplace flexibility and more family-friendly policies has a particular consequence for women: "U.S. labor force participation for prime working age women...is now lower than it is in 14 of the 20 high-income countries...." and "labor force participation for college educated women in the United States is lower than in *any* of the other 20 countries."[62]

In a report on the career obstacles facing Asians in the U.S., Sylvia Ann Hewlett provided some important insights and recommendations that apply, as she pointed out, to all disadvantaged groups, and that would include women. The report noted the importance of "executive presence" for advancement in the most senior ranks, with appearance, self-confidence, and poise being factors that contribute to executive presence. "Corporate culture in the U.S. places a high premium on assertiveness and individualistic thinking," while "self-effacement and modesty... is at direct odds with the realities of the contemporary workplace where assertiveness and directness are central."[63] Self-advocacy and self-assurance were seen as "essential leadership qualities in the American corporate environment,"[64] and this in a report published in 2011.

Therefore it is not surprising that women who have succeeded have, for the most part, done so by being willing to break gender stereotypes and play the same game as men. Former Hewlett-Packard CEO Carly Fiorina noted, "I think women feel a special pressure to be pleasant and accommodating.... That day [when, as a new sales manager, she was called "our token bimbo"

---

60   Catalyst, "The Double-Bind Dilemma for Women in Leadership," op. cit.

61   Jeffrey Pfeffer, "You're Still the Same: Old Theories for a New World—With a Specific Application to the Subject of Power," Keynote Address to the British Academy of Management, Cardiff, Wales, September 11, 2012.

62   Ariane Hegewisch and Janet C. Gornick, *Statutory Routes to Workplace Flexibility in Cross-National Perspective* (Washington, DC: Institute for Women's Policy Research, 2008), p. 2.

63   Sylvia Ann Hewlett and Ripa Rashid, with Diana Forster and Claire Ho, *Asians in America: Unleashing the Potential of the "Model Minority"* (New York: Center for Work-Life Policy, 2011), pp. 21–22.

64   Ibid., p. 23.

during a meeting] I decided that sometimes it's more important to be respected than liked."[65] Of course, women—and men—can learn to exhibit multiple emotions and display a variety of behaviors, both sequentially and simultaneously. Leaders often need to convey empathy with the people they lead and simultaneously display strength and set high expectations. Women can be firm and tough while also signaling that they place value on the relationship and are sensitive to how others perceive them. Women—and men—can use humor as well as facial expressions and body language to mitigate what might be an otherwise harsh message. Nuria Chinchilla, an IESE professor who has done research and advocacy for policies promoting work-family conciliation, often talks quite bluntly to corporate CEOs about their inaccurate ideas and how they are causing social pollution, but does so with a smile and a friendly demeanor. Placing behavior in context can also help—noting that taking a tough position reflects the importance of the issue. So Laura Esserman, director of the Carol Franc Buck Breast Care Center at the University of California, San Francisco, noted that people do not react quite as negatively to her impatience and anger when she reminds them of the 45,000 women who die each year from breast cancer and the urgency of taking action to reduce this enormous toll.

Women—and men—also need to understand and then develop the personal qualities and behaviors that provide power.[66] Everyone is capable of developing themselves in areas where they are not as strong, and if they seek power, should do so. None of the behavioral subtlety or personal development essential to building power is necessarily easy to master or assured by following some readily-implemented formula. But if prevailing in the competition for power and status were easy, everyone could, and would, do it. Climbing organizational hierarchies or, for that matter, surviving in a start-up (even if you started it) is tough work and the competition gets more intense the closer to the top and the bigger the stakes are. We should learn from those who have been successful, and certainly not discount their tactics by telling ourselves their lessons are no longer relevant.

Discussion Questions

1   Are there gender differences in leadership effectiveness?

2   One of the questions presented in this chapter is, "Do women suffer a larger marriage and childhood penalty than men?" What is your opinion about this topic? How and why should organizations help close this gender gap?

3   Are gender differences in leadership a matter of geography?

---

65   Judy Lin, "Fiorina Learned Conservative Philosophy Early," *UT San Diego*, October 6, 2010, http://www.utsandiego.com/news/2010/oct/06/fiorina-learned-conservative-philosophy-early/ [http://www.mercurynews.com/fdcp?1286477621723. *I couldn't find this under Mercury News but did find it under the link above*].

66   Jeffrey Pfeffer, *Power: Why Some People Have It—and Others Don't*, (New York: Harper Business, 2010).

CONCLUSION

This anthology presented a wide variety of literature on leadership, power, and politics. You were introduced to classical as well as more updated leadership theories and studies that hopefully helped you learn about the many facets of this phenomenon. I also hope that this anthology has helped you find your unique voice within all these perspectives and ideas. As I stated in the introduction, my main goal as a scholar and an educator is to help you gain knowledge and understanding that you can put to practical use as you develop your personal leadership practice. I would like to encourage you to continue your education in this field as you develop your leadership and political skills. New studies and books on these topics are published every day, and there are wonderful mentoring and coaching opportunities out there for people who are willing to invest time and energy for their self-development. I hope that you enjoyed learning about leadership, power, and politics using this this collection of articles, but, more important, I hope that this experience increased your appetite for more knowledge and experience.